SCHOLARS IN EXILE

The Ukrainian Intellectual World in Interwar Czechoslovakia

Scholars in Exile

The Ukrainian Intellectual World in Interwar Czechoslovakia

NADIA ZAVOROTNA

UNIVERSITY OF TORONTO PRESS
Toronto Buffalo London

Toronto Buffalo London
utorontopress.com

ISBN 978-1-4875-0445-8 (cloth)
ISBN 978-1-4875-3021-1 (EPUB)
ISBN 978-1-4875-3020-4 (PDF)

Library and Archives Canada Cataloguing in Publication

Title: Scholars in exile : the Ukrainian intellectual world in interwar Czechoslovakia / Nadia Zavorotna.
Names: Zavorotna, Nadia, 1969– author.
Description: Includes bibliographical references and index.
Identifiers: Canadiana 20190181818 | ISBN 9781487504458 (hardcover)
Subjects: LCSH: Ukrainians – Czechoslovakia – Intellectual life. | LCSH: Ukrainians – Czechoslovakia – Social conditions. | LCSH: Ukrainians – Czechoslovakia – Social life and customs. | LCSH: Czechoslovakia – Intellectual life. | LCSH: Czechoslovakia – History – 1918–1938. | LCSH: Czechoslovakia – Emigration and immigration.
Classification: LCC DB2198 .Z38 2019 | DDC 943.7/00491791009042 – dc23

The research and writing of this book was supported by a Professor Wasyl Janischewskyj Scholarship Fund from the Ukrainian Canadian Research and Documentation Centre, Toronto, Canada.

This book has been published with the help of a grant from the Federation for the Humanities and Social Sciences, through the Awards to Scholarly Publications Program, using funds provided by the Social Sciences and Humanities Research Council of Canada.

University of Toronto Press acknowledges the financial assistance to its publishing program of the Canada Council for the Arts and the Ontario Arts Council, an agency of the Government of Ontario.

Canada Council for the Arts
Conseil des Arts du Canada

Funded by the Government of Canada
Financé par le gouvernement du Canada

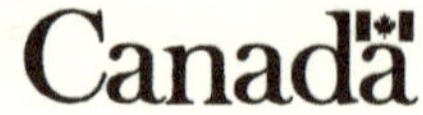

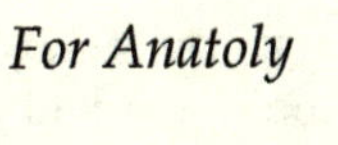

For Anatoly

"... I am glad that you have found here, though not home, of course you cannot find it – but, at least, good neighbours amongst a brotherly people, and with that you can be content. You yourself say that you are satisfied and happy ..."

Tomáš Garrigue Masaryk
Poděbrady, Czechoslovakia
9 May 1923

"... Těším se z toho, že jste u nás našli ne otčinu – tu ovšem nemůžete najíti – ale u bratrského národa dobré sousedství, s nímž můžete býti spokojeni. A sami pravíte, že spokojeni a šťastni jste ..."

Tomáš Garrigue Masaryk
Poděbrady, Československo
9. květen 1923

Contents

Tables

Preface

This study grew out of my interest in Czech and Ukrainian history and culture in general, and in Ukrainian institutional and intellectual history specifically. Having been born during Soviet times in the easternmost part of the former Austro-Hungarian Empire in the capital of Bukovyna – then Czernowitz, now Chernivtsi – I spent a great deal of my childhood in a beautiful UNESCO-designated building, the Residence of Bukovinian and Dalmatian Metropolitans, which is now a seat of the university. This building was designed by the renowned Czech architect and philanthropist Josef Hlávka. Of course, as a child, I was not allowed to know why Hlávka's building happened to be in my city, on the very western edge of the Soviet Union. But even then, I was well acquainted with his name and felt very much at home within the walls of this beautiful building, where I spent many Saturdays with my father, who worked there. Only later, after the Soviet Union dissolved, did I learn why the Czech architect's masterpiece had come to be built in my city, and I discovered this along with many other things that had previously been blocked from me.

My interest in the life and works of Tomáš Garrigue Masaryk, another famous figure, developed during the *perestroika* years. Certainly, any knowledge of him, his works, and his ideas was prohibited back then. Yet some of his books, along with numerous others, somehow made their way across the militarized border, with all its barbed wire and security zones. By the time I was preparing my bachelor's thesis, my supervisor Volodymyr Fisanov had introduced me to some of Masaryk's works, even though they were still officially banned in the soon-to-fall Soviet Union. This, my first reading in the Czech language – slow, challenging, and requiring the use of a dictionary – opened a new world to me. Overall, the experience of reading and discovering new things every day was incomparably intense during the *perestroika*. Besides gaining access to plenty of new books and journals, sometimes borrowed overnight, we were able to read for the first time literature written by exiles. My favourites were Russian poets (knowledge about Ukrainians had not yet reached us), and some of those poems (i.e., Marina Tsvetaeva's poems written in Czechoslovakia) I can still recite by heart.

My interest in Czechoslovakia – its people, history, and culture – blossomed during my graduate studies at the Centre for European, Russian, and Eurasian Studies at the Munk School of Global Affairs and Public Policy at the University of Toronto, with its strong tradition in Czech and Slovak studies. At that time, I also discovered the history, literature, and culture of Ukraine, all of which I had long been shielded from. Reading hundreds of book, attending numerous conferences, and meeting countless fascinating people was an eye-opening experience that had a deep and lasting effect on my intellectual development.

My interest in these countries was further nurtured by my stint at the Robarts Library at the University of Toronto, where I worked for more than a decade. Working on another degree did not distract me from the constant discoveries that library has to offer, about all aspects of Ukraine as well as Czechoslovakia. I remember vividly how as a graduate student I discovered at Robarts a volume of documents concerning Russian and Ukrainian émigrés. I vividly recall sitting on the floor in the stacks for hours reading one document after another. It was a revelation. And that was the beginning of the decade I would spend reading and researching the topic of this study. To write this book, I also visited other libraries and archives in Canada, the Czech Republic, and Ukraine. So this work is the result of many years of research.

This is a synthetic study intended for an English-speaking audience. While over the past twenty-five years considerable scholarship on different aspects of the topic has appeared in Ukrainian, Czech, and Slovak, the literature in English is slim. This book is an attempt to fill in the gaps and provide a general overview of the scholarly life of Ukrainian immigrants in Czechoslovakia during the interwar years. The work has benefited greatly from in-depth studies of personalities and institutions that have appeared in Ukrainian and some in Czech. I am deeply beholden to these scholars for their works, which are included in the bibliography.

I am grateful to Luba Frastacky, a librarian – now retired – at the Thomas Fisher Rare Book Library, who greatly enhanced my knowledge of Czechoslovakia. Whether it involved preparing an exhibition on the Prague Spring of 1968 or working on Czech-Canadian writer Josef Škvorecký's documents, she taught her graduate student a great deal about Czechoslovakia in 1968, Škvorecký's books, the publishing house '68 Publishers, *samizdat*, and much more. It was insightful and fun; she further endeared me to the country, and I am extremely thankful for this.

My subsequent research and educational journeys to the Czech Republic, particularly Prague, only deepened my interest. Over the years, I have travelled to the Czech Republic for research and language study. But it was actually for more than that. As Paul Wilson, Canadian translator of Škvorecký and other Czech writers, neatly put it: "Prague is a city where visitors can still experience something of the ancient magnetism that charmed both commoners and kings over the centuries ... a place like no other on earth." I feel exactly the same way! In this country, I have met people who not only helped me with my research but also shared with me their inspirations, their kindness, and their wit.

I am deeply beholden to Lukáš Babka of the Slavonic Library in Prague for his extensive help with the research, for reading and commenting on the parts of this study, for helping with access to materials, and, last but not least, for patiently answering my numerous questions. Special thanks goes to Dagmar Petišková of the Pedagogical Museum and Library of J.A. Comenius in Prague, for reading the manuscript, commenting on it, and scrutinizing its Czech diacritics. I would like to thank Michaela Kuthanová of the Museum of Czech Literature in Prague for helping me access the archival collections of Ukrainian émigrés. I am also grateful to Eva Sokolová of the Slavonic Library and Klára Kolinská of Charles University in Prague for their generous help while I was researching the book. Also, I am grateful to my friend Nasťa Avdějeva, who, for more than a decade of our friendship, always made sure that I read, saw, and tried as many Czech things as possible. All my Czech colleagues and friends gave me a renewed sense of collegiality and friendship for which I am extremely grateful.

As mentioned, the decade I spent discovering and reading materials at Robarts considerably broadened my knowledge of the complicated history of Ukraine, particularly of the history of emigration. Attending events devoted to various aspects of Ukraine at the University of Toronto, as well as meeting and listening to experts on the subject from around the world, was of vital importance to my education, but meeting interesting and insightful people was the true gift.

I owe a special debt of gratitude to Paul Robert Magocsi for his valuable suggestions about handling this project and for his interest in it. I am also grateful for his help improving the outline of this study at its earliest stages, as well as for reading and commenting on parts of the manuscript. His astute remarks were very beneficial for deepening my understanding of the theme. Additionally, his course on Ukrainian history helped me immensely to gain a deeper knowledge of the subject.

I would also like to thank Thomas Prymak, to whom I am deeply indebted for reading the entire book and for his generous comments on it. His insights were very beneficial. Our decade-plus friendship and our cooperation on various research projects helped me enormously to understand the historian's craft. Years ago, our first collaborative project was on a Ukrainian émigré historian, who will feature in this study, and this work heightened my interest in the subject even more. I am also thankful to Myron Momryk, the now-retired archivist who years ago introduced me to valuable archival collections at Library and Archives Canada, in Ottawa, and then over the years very kindly assisted me with my many questions.

I am very grateful to the interlibrary loan staff members at Robarts Library at the University of Toronto for their enormous help in finding requested materials for me. Special thanks go to all of the staff at the Slavonic library at the National Library of the Czech Republic in Prague for their kind-hearted assistance. I appreciate two anonymous readers. Their comments, suggestions, and constructive critiques have enriched this study. I would like to thank my editor Stephen Shapiro for his professionalism and advice. My special gratitude also goes to the Ukrainian Canadian Research and Documentation Centre in Toronto for providing me with a Professor Wasyl Janischewskyj Scholarship Fund to support my research and writing.

My gratitude also goes to my friend Lee Haviland for reading parts of the manuscript and for her helpful suggestions. Deepest thanks to my sister, Maryna Chernyavska, who read and commented on the first draft of the manuscript. Her comments and insights were most helpful. Last but not least, my greatest thanks go to my husband, Anatoly, without whose support, understanding, and tolerance neither this book nor other projects would have come into being. I owe him more than I can express.

While this study was enriched with the help of all the people mentioned above, all shortcomings and mistakes are mine alone.

SCHOLARS IN EXILE

The Ukrainian Intellectual World
in Interwar Czechoslovakia

Introduction

At the beginning of 2014, Charles University in Prague announced a special Václav Havel Scholarship. It was intended for students who could not study in their home countries because they lived under a totalitarian or authoritarian regime or suffered persecution of some sort. Ukrainians were invited to apply. Most of the students who were accepted were from the Crimea and Donbas; several had been wounded in 2014 on the Maidan, in Kyiv, during the popular revolution that overthrew the corrupt and authoritarian Ukrainian president who was in power at the time. Other universities and institutions followed the example of Charles University. Among those who offered the scholarships were Palacký University in Olomouc, the Czech Technical University in Prague, and the Czech University of Life Sciences Prague. The students began studying the Czech language in Prague, Poděbrady, and other cities and towns in the country.

This was not the first time that the Czech government and the university helped Ukrainians by offering support through education. The Havel Scholarship initiative was an echo of events that had taken place in Czechoslovakia in the 1920s and 1930s, when the Czechoslovak government financially supported educational and employment initiatives for different groups of émigrés. The newborn democracy was then generously assisting various émigré educational institutions and providing scholarships for émigré students. The largest groups among the émigrés in 1920s and 1930s in Czechoslovakia were Russians and Ukrainians, but there were also Belarusians, Lithuanians, Georgians, Armenians, and others.

During 1920s, Prague became one of the most important destinations for Ukrainian émigrés in Europe and one of the centres of Ukrainian scholarly, cultural, political, and civic life. Assistance from the Czechoslovak government enabled established émigré scholars to do their work and to develop their fields as well as to educate and nurture a new generation. After flourishing in the 1920s, the assistance program gradually wound down over the following decade. The world economic crisis, the improvement in Czechoslovak–Soviet relations, and tensions in political life in the Transcarpathian region (*Podkarpatská Rus*) all played important roles in reducing the support given to the émigrés.

This book focuses on Ukrainian émigré scholarly life in Czechoslovakia between the world wars, particularly in Prague and Poděbrady (a town in what is now the Czech Republic). The scholarly life of Ukrainian émigré intellectuals in Czechoslovakia between the wars deserves special consideration as a vital part of twentieth-century Ukrainian intellectual and institutional history. This is because that scholarship forged an inextricable link between academic work prior to the First World War and its development after the Second World War, particularly in North America. It ensured a much-needed continuity of Ukrainian scholarship, especially considering the repeated purge of Ukrainian intellectuals in Soviet Ukraine.

The interwar period of Ukrainian academic life is investigated in the context of the Czechoslovak government's general policies toward the émigrés it welcomed to the country and those who came of their own accord. This is a history of those individuals who had just lost their chance of building their own state during the events from 1917 to 1921 in Ukraine. For them, the experience of living, studying, and working in democratic Czechoslovakia was a positive lesson, and an impactful one. In their host country, they carried out scholarly and educational activities that were often remarkable.

At the time, the very word "Ukrainian" was little-known in the West among scholars as well as the general public. Thus, it is important to specify what the terms "Ukrainian scholar" and "Ukrainian intellectual" meant in the 1920s and 1930s. In the context of this study, these terms are applied to scholars who belonged to the Ukrainian émigré intellectual environment through their work and who considered it their mission to promote knowledge about Ukraine. These scholars taught at institutions of higher learning, belonged to scholarly societies, wrote monographs and textbooks, and delivered public lectures. They also educated a new and younger generation of students, who became professionals while retaining a sense of national identity. Within a relatively short period, they built an impressive intellectual and educational infrastructure in their host country.[1]

The creation of this academic infrastructure would not have been possible without the generous help of the Czechoslovak government and particularly President Tomáš Garrigue Masaryk (1850–1937). The humanistic values of the Czech and Slovak enlighteners of the nineteenth century greatly influenced Masaryk's ethics and informed his interest in the Slavonic peoples. He believed it was necessary for Slavonic peoples to study one another and wanted to make Prague the Slavonic academic and cultural centre of Europe. This was official policy, and émigré groups in Czechoslovakia – including the Ukrainians – benefited from it, particularly in the 1920s. It was, in fact, instrumental in Czechoslovakia becoming the centre of Ukrainian scholarly life between the world wars.

The Ukrainians were appreciative of both the Czechoslovak government and Masaryk himself. Many members of the Ukrainian émigré community, from professors and political leaders to students, wrote letters of gratitude to Masaryk.[2] As early as 1923, the scholar–philologist Stepan Smal'-Stots'kyi (1859–1938) wrote a letter to the political and cultural figure Kyrylo Studyns'kyi (1868–1941) with regard to accepting Masaryk as a member of the Shevchenko Scientific Society, based in L'viv in the Ukrainian-populated part of interwar Poland, in which he noted "the great good that Masaryk has bestowed upon us ... [He] has the eternal gratitude of the Ukrainian people."[3]

The Ukrainians developed a vibrant scholarly, cultural, and political life in Prague. More than 210 Ukrainian societies, groups, unions, and communities were active in Czechoslovakia between the wars.[4] At the time, Ukrainian life had been largely suppressed in the Ukrainian lands: Soviet Ukraine, Polish-ruled Galicia, and Romanian-ruled Bukovyna. After the failed attempt to found an independent state, many émigrés in Czechoslovakia devoted themselves entirely to scholarly work and to educating the younger generation. Professors – many of whom were former state-builders – succeeded in educating a generation of students, most of whom, at least initially, were former soldiers. The Canadian historian Orest Subtelny (1941–2016) wrote of these personalities that "given the many well-educated, talented, and committed individuals in their ranks," in spite of great economic difficulties, they created numerous institutions, published much, and "introduced West Europeans to Ukrainian national aspirations."[5]

For Ukrainian scholars, living in Czechoslovakia had both advantages and disadvantages. The former included academic freedom – they were free to study what they wanted and to choose research methods they deemed suitable, and they were close to European research institutions and European scholars. As to the latter, these people were "abroad": historians, archaeologists, linguists, and ethnologists in particular needed research materials that could only be found in the Ukrainian lands. Lack of access to libraries and archives with primary materials and, on a more general level, feelings of isolation from and nostalgia for their native land had an obvious impact on their lives and scholarship.[6]

Non-Ukrainians contributed to their cause – for example, the pedagogue Sofiia Rusova (née Lindfors) (1856–1940), who had French and Swedish roots and grew up in pro-Russian surroundings; the sociologist and political figure Ol'gerd Ipolyt Bochkovs'kyi (1885–1939), who was of Lithuanian and Polish descent; and the statistician and economist Fedir Shcherbyna (1849–1936), from Kuban, corresponding member of St Petersburg Academy of Sciences, who started writing in the Ukrainian language in his sixties, all made significant contributions.[7] Some prominent figures in Ukrainian scholarly life in Prague belonged to distinguished families in the Ukrainian intellectual community. For instance, Dmytro Antonovych (1877–1945) was the son of renowned historian Volodymyr Antonovych (1834–1908); Oleksander Kolessa (1867–1945) was the brother of distinguished folklorist Filaret Kolessa (1871–1947); and Ivan Horbachevs'kyi (1854–1942) was the brother of the lawyer and political figure Antin Horbachevs'kyi (1856–1944). Some of these scholars had received their education in Europe before the First World War: Dmytro Antonovych, as well as his wife – painter and art historian Kateryna Antonovych (1887–1975) – studied in Italy; Bochkovs'kyi received his education in Prague; and some Ukrainians from Galicia and Bukovyna were educated in Vienna.

The initial goal of the institutions founded by Ukrainian scholars in Czechoslovakia was to prepare their students for productive work in their hoped-for future – that is, in a democratic Ukraine. For a long time, however, this dream did not come to pass, and many students left Czechoslovakia in search of work. After the Second World War, many of the émigrés fled to other European countries, such as Germany, and eventually immigrated to the United States, Canada, Australia, Brazil, Argentina, and elsewhere. But not all managed to flee to the West. The fates of some of those who stayed in Czechoslovakia in 1945, when the Soviet Army came, were tragic: some of them died in Soviet prisons or in the Gulag, and some committed suicide. Others, however, remained in Czechoslovakia, and some continued to work, but after 1945 Prague ceased to be a centre of Ukrainian scholarly life in Europe.

This study is limited to Ukrainian émigré scholarly life in two places: Prague and Poděbrady, with the bulk of the discussion focused on Prague. The capital of Czechoslovakia became the heart of Ukrainian émigré scholarship between the wars due to the concentration of scholars who lived and worked there. Poděbrady was home to a Ukrainian technical institution that played an important role in educating a new generation of Ukrainian professionals in an array of technical fields. Ukrainian intellectual life existed in other cities and towns in Czechoslovakia as well – for example, in Brno, Bratislava, and

Uzhhorod – but this is beyond the scope of this book. The story starts in the early 1920s, when the Czechoslovak government launched an impressive assistance program for émigrés and the country became a centre of Ukrainian émigré life. The period covered in this study ends in 1938. Since the years 1938 to 1945 constitute a distinct historical era, they will not be discussed in this work; however, occasional references will be made to this period, particularly to the year 1945, when the life of the Ukrainian émigré community abruptly ended.

Between the wars, Prague also became an important centre of Ukrainian poetry. It was home to the "Prague Poetic School," a group of émigré Ukrainian poets and writers, including Ievhen Malaniuk (1897–1968), Leonid Mosendz (1897–1948), Oleksandr Oles' (1878–1944), Iurii Darahan (1894–1926), Olena Teliha (1906–1942), Oksana Liaturyns'ka (1902–1970), and Halyna Mazurenko (1901–2000). This phenomenon too, however, lies beyond the scope of our work. Scholarship and learned societies are the focus here.

Prague was also a centre of Ukrainian political life, given that many former Ukrainian politicians and officials had found refuge in the city. Having failed to create an independent state, the émigrés in Czechoslovakia tended to blame one another, so the environment in which they found themselves was often acid. Ukrainian political life in Czechoslovakia between the world wars is not the subject of this work; although many of the scholars discussed here had taken part in political life before the Czechoslovakia period, during the emigration most of them restricted themselves to scholarly life, and their engagement in politics before their arrival in Czechoslovakia is not covered in this book.

Prague was also a vibrant Russian émigré scholarly centre, with pre-eminent figures from the Russian academic world, such as renowned linguists Roman Jakobson (1896–1982) and Nikolai Trubetskoi (1890–1938), as well as distinguished Russian Slavist Vladimir Andreevich Frantsev (1867–1942), living and working there. The city was home to famous Russian academic institutions, including the Economic Institute of Professor Prokopovich (Ekonomicheskii kabinet professora Prokopovicha) and the Kondakov Institute of Byzantine Studies (Institut imeni N.P. Kondakova). This study, however, focuses solely on Ukrainian developments.

While writing this monograph I consulted an array of sources. The papers of many émigrés and the archives of major institutions had tragic histories. In 1945, when the Soviet Army entered Prague, vast quantities of material on the activities of the Ukrainian émigrés were confiscated and removed to the Soviet Union. In subsequent years, more émigré archives were transferred to the Soviet Union, the bulk of which ended up in Kyiv in repositories such as the Central State Archive of Higher Organs of Government and Administration of Ukraine (Tsentral'nyi derzhavnyi arkhiv vyshchykh orhaniv vlady ta upravlinnia Ukrainy). During the Soviet period, researchers were barred from these collections. The materials that stayed in Czechoslovakia can still be found in archives in Prague and in other cities and towns in the Czech Republic; most of them are in the special collections of the Slavonic Library (Slovanská knihovna), the Museum of Czech Literature Archive (Literární archiv Památníku národního písemnictví), and the National Archives in Prague (Národní archiv), the Archive of the Ministry of Foreign Affairs of the Czech Republic (Archiv Ministerstva zahraničních věcí), and the State District Archives Nymburk based in Lysá nad Labem (Státní okresní archiv Nymburk se sídlem v Lysé nad Labem), with some materials in the Institute of the History of Charles University and the Archive of Charles University (Ústav dějin Univerzity Karlovy a archiv Univerzity Karlovy).[8] A few personal papers made their way to Canada and today are held in Ottawa by Library and Archives Canada, as well as in the Archives of Carleton University. Many documents from the above-mentioned collections were examined for this study. In addition to these, printed materials published by Ukrainian émigré scholars were very useful.

In the 1990s, previously inaccessible archival materials were made available, and scholars in Ukraine made great use of these collections, writing dissertations, books, and articles on various aspects of the lives and activities of Ukrainian émigrés in Czechoslovakia. At the same time, Czech scholars produced important articles, edited volumes, and published conference proceedings and bibliographies that have been valuable sources for this study. Several volumes of printed archival material, especially correspondence, were also utilized, and printed archival guides and bibliographies proved helpful for locating materials in the archives. Encyclopaedias published in Czechoslovakia were searched for articles written by or about Ukrainian émigré scholars. Relevant memoirs written during this period were also examined. Finally, a few interviews were conducted with individuals who had some memory of the events under discussion. All of those who were directly involved in the events have since died, but conversations with people who knew them and knew about their activities were invaluable and helped humanize the subject.

This monograph has nine chapters. Chapter 1 analyses the politics of the Czechoslovak government toward Ukrainians, focusing on the assistance program provided by the government. Also, a brief quantitative analysis of the Ukrainian émigré community in Czechoslovakia is provided, with an emphasis on the earlier years of the emigration. The major reasons for, and developments of, the assistance are analysed. Politics involving Ukraine, particularly the Ukrainian People's Republic, the Western Ukrainian People's Republic, and Soviet Ukraine, are briefly discussed.

Chapter 2 focuses on the Ukrainian Free University (Ukrains'kyi vil'nyi universytet). Highlighted are its founding in Vienna, the politics surrounding its early development, and its subsequent transfer to Prague with the help of the Czechoslovak government. The university's structure, objectives, and financing are examined, as well as the scholarly activities of its faculty members and its student life. Chapter 3 investigates the Ukrainian technical institution known as the Ukrainian Economic Academy in Czechoslovakia (Ukrains'ka hospodars'ka akademiia v Ch.S.R.). It was founded in Poděbrady and was the first technical institution that aimed to prepare a future generation of engineers and other specialists in the technical professions. Its goals, structure, and financing are all explored. Its students and faculty – both Ukrainian and Czech – are described, and the subsequent transformation of the academy and its affiliated institutions is examined.

The Ukrainian Higher Pedagogical Institute, named after Mykhailo Drahomanov (Ukrains'kyi vysokyi pedagogichnyi instytut im. M. Drahomanova) is the subject of chapter 4. It was established in Prague to prepare secondary school teachers for Ukrainian schools in a future independent Ukraine. The institute's goals, structure, and finances are discussed, as well as the studies of its students and the activities of its faculty. Chapter 5 covers the Ukrainian School of Plastic Arts (Ukrains'ka studiia plastychnoho mystetstva), which was known as the "Ukrainian Academy." It had a modest status but played a crucial role in the education and lives of many Ukrainian and other artists. The chapter also highlights the school's participation in various exhibitions in Prague between the wars.

Chapter 6 focuses on the most important scholarly and professional societies and organizations created by Ukrainian émigrés in Czechoslovakia. The role of the umbrella organization known as the Ukrainian Academic Committee (Ukrains'kyi akademichnyi komitet) is discussed, and important activities of the Ukrainian Historical–Philological Society (Ukrains'ke istorychno-filologichne tovarystvo) are highlighted. In this chapter, the renowned Prague Linguistic Circle (Pražský linguistický kroužek) is also considered, as several Ukrainian émigré scholars took part in its activities. Other societies created by Ukrainian émigré scholars and professionals, including the Ukrainian Law Society (Ukrains'ke pravnyche tovarystvo) and the Union of Ukrainian Doctors in Czechoslovakia (Spilka ukrains'kykh likariv v Chekhoslovachchyni), are also examined. Chapter 7 looks at the archives, libraries, and museums founded by the Ukrainian émigrés as well as the famous Slavonic Library in Prague, an important institution with a large Ukrainian collection. Also discussed are the libraries of the Ukrainian institutions of higher education and, finally, the heritage institutions. The Museum of the Struggle for the Liberation of Ukraine (Muzei vyzvol'noi borot'by Ukrainy), a heritage institution that played an important role in the scholarly life of the Ukrainian community, both in Czechoslovakia and abroad, is discussed. The role of the Ukrainian National Museum and Archive (Ukrains'kyi natsional'nyi muzei-arkhiv) – another museum and archive in Prague – is analysed, as is that of the Ukrainian Historical Institute (Ukrains'kyi istorychnyi kabinet), which came into existence some time later. Chapter 8 is devoted to Ukrainian-language publishing in Czechoslovakia. From the early 1920s to the early 1930s, Prague was a major centre of Ukrainian-language scholarly publishing and was subsidized by the Czechoslovak government. In the 1930s, most privately owned Ukrainian-language publishing houses continued to produce books, but they published primarily historical fiction, children books, and political writings; these developments are also briefly discussed in this chapter.

The ninth and final chapter of this work examines many little-known intellectual connections and relations between the Ukrainian émigré scholars in Czechoslovakia and their colleagues in various other European countries. Cooperation with the International Committee on Intellectual Cooperation at the League of Nations (La Société des Nations et la coopération intellectuelle) in Paris is discussed. Examined are the scholars' contributions to promoting Ukrainian scholarship in Europe as a whole and the cooperation between the Ukrainians and their colleagues in various countries. Participation in various conferences, works in European scholarly journals in various languages, contributions to encyclopaedias, and books published to promote an understanding of Ukrainian history, literature, and culture in Europe are all considered.

Certain important figures will be described. In this book, their lives and accomplishments are examined in the context of their times. Although some of these people have been studied extensively in the Ukrainian and (to a lesser degree) Czech languages, their names are little-known in English-language scholarship. In general, the world of the Ukrainian émigré intellectuals in Czechoslovakia between the wars is a bright spot in the history of Ukrainian scholarship and culture. This book is an attempt to examine that world for the purpose of fostering a better understanding of the general intellectual and institutional history of Ukraine.

Chapter One

Czechoslovak Émigré Policy and Characteristics of the Ukrainian Emigration

After the First World War and the fall of the Russian and Austro-Hungarian empires, Czechoslovakia became home to many refugees. In the early 1920s, people from the recently collapsed empires came to the newly born country; some were invited to do so. Russians and Ukrainians in particular, but also Belarusians, Georgians, Armenians, Lithuanians, and Latvians, immigrated to Czechoslovakia. Later, in the 1930s, refugees from Germany and Austria also came. For some, Czechoslovakia was a transit point along the way to some other destination, but for others it became their second home. The latter was particularly true for émigrés from the former Russian and Austro-Hungarian empires. Czechoslovakia's liberal refugee policies attracted individuals who had been displaced for many reasons, but usually for political ones. The Czechoslovak government at the time perceived the problem of émigrés entirely differently from the way in which other countries did, and it implemented its internal and foreign policies accordingly, making it a unique case in history.[1]

The Russian Assistance Program (Ruská pomocná akce), as it was known, was launched in July 1921 under the sponsorship of the Ministry of Foreign Affairs of the Czechoslovak Republic and with the personal backing of Masaryk. At first, this program was intended to evolve in two directions: to help people affected by the 1921–22 famine in Russia and Ukraine, and to assist refugees in Czechoslovakia. Wars, revolutions, and famine had had a strong impact on the Czech settlements in Volhynia and other territories, and the Czechoslovak government considered itself obligated to assist these settlers. The country initiated an international program to help famine victims. It also took an active part in the Nansen Mission, a non-governmental humanitarian organization led by the Norwegian explorer, scientist, and humanitarian Fridtjof Nansen (1861–1930), which did much to help refugees in postwar

Europe. At first, most of that assistance was directed towards the Czech settlers, who numbered approximately 15,000. The government provided 10 million crowns in 1921 and hoped to provide 15 million in 1922. This was more than a humanitarian mission: the government undertook it in the context of developing economic relations with Russia and Ukraine, and it even exchanged trade missions with both countries in 1921. All of this ended suddenly, however, when in late 1922 the Soviet government banned all activities by charitable organizations. In Ukraine alone, fifteen international charitable organizations, which helped around 300,000 people – including the Czechoslovak mission – were "liquidated." From then on, the assistance program could only help refugees in Czechoslovakia.[2]

In Czechoslovakia's handling of the emigrants, Masaryk saw the moral duty of the young democracy to save a treasured cultural element. Thus, émigrés received considerable financial and moral support in the spheres of scholarship, education, and culture. In Czechoslovakia, primary schools and gymnasiums were created, as well as institutions of higher learning, scholarly organizations, and professional schools. The assistance program aimed to help exiles from all lands of the former Russian empire, regardless of nationality. Many refugees from the former Austrian provinces of Galicia and Bukovyna also received assistance. The immigrants to Czechoslovakia settled in Prague, Brno, Bratislava, and elsewhere in the country.[3]

Causes of Emigration of Ukrainians

A strong driver of the immigration of Ukrainians to Czechoslovakia at the beginning of the 1920s was the failure of their struggle to achieve state independence in 1917–21 and the repression that followed. The Soviet regime in central and eastern Ukraine arrested, executed, or exiled many thousands of former Ukrainian political and national figures, members of the former Ukrainian governments, and officers and enlisted men who had fought in the armies of the Ukrainian People's Republic (which was a radical socialist but democratic regime) and the Ukrainian State (governed by a "Hetman" or monarch with much German military support). In western Ukraine too, a Ukrainian national government had briefly existed before it was crushed militarily by the new Polish Republic to its west. At the end of that Polish–Ukrainian war, that region, the eastern parts of the former Austrian Galicia, was annexed to Poland. Exiles from that Western Ukrainian People's Republic also made their way to Czechoslovakia.

Various of these Ukrainian state formations – the Ukrainian People's Republic, the Hetmanate, and the Directory of the Ukrainian People's

Republic (a continuation of the People's Republic), as well as the Western Ukrainian People's Republic – were very active in diplomacy, and at times some were recognized by a number of states. During the Hetmanate, there were considerable developments in education and culture, and important Ukrainian institutions such as two universities, a Ukrainian Academy of Sciences, a State Theatre, a National Library, and State Archives were founded. Some of the staff of these institutions eventually were compelled to emigrate.

Politically, Ukrainians were deeply divided. Some supported and had fought for complete independence, while others were willing to accept some sort of affiliation with Russia. They belonged to several parties with different orientations, such as the Ukrainian Social Democratic Labour Party (Ukrains'ka sotsial-demokratychna robitnycha partiia), the Ukrainian Party of Socialist Revolutionaries (Ukrains'ka partiia sotsialistiv-revoliutsioneriv), and the much smaller, liberally inclined Ukrainian Socialist Federalist Party (Ukrains'ka partiia sotsialistiv-federalistiv). After the various attempts at independence failed, many members of these parties emigrated, and very many of them ended up in Czechoslovakia. They brought their disagreements to their new countries, and this would colour the entire culture of the Ukrainian émigré community in Prague and elsewhere.

The Assistance Program

Émigrés in Czechoslovakia were generally perceived as an important factor in maintaining good relations with a future democratic Russia and Ukraine. The main goal of the assistance program was to rescue existing intellectuals and professionals and prepare them for future work. The assistance was intended to be for a short time. This program and the manner in which it was implemented lent great credibility to the Czechoslovak government in the eyes of all Europeans. However, the composition of this émigré community was not uniform. Many scholars, doctors, journalists, and pedagogues, as well as students, military personnel, and farmers, settled in the country. Many of them were political émigrés who could not return home; others had been prisoners of war. These immigrants belonged to different social strata, and there were many former government officials, intellectuals, military personnel, and peasants among them. The émigrés varied widely in political orientation – they ranged from apoliticals to representatives of almost every political group. Fragmented and disillusioned, those who immigrated to Czechoslovakia were also very diverse in their needs, so it was a challenge for the new government to help them effectively while building a new country at the same time.[4]

The focus of the assistance program soon turned to helping refugees within the country. In this regard, it had three main objectives. First, to help the impoverished and homeless by establishing dormitories and cafeterias, supplying clothing, and offering cash assistance. This included starting employment agencies. Second, to provide medical services to the sick, the injured, the disabled, and the elderly. Third, to offer young people an opportunity to finish their education, as well as to create conditions under which scholars, artists, and writers could complete their work, including publishing. Regarding this third point, the government declared several principles. First, applicants' needs were to be the weightiest factor when considering their applications; second, the aim was not simply to feed applicants, but also to train them to perform work – work of an intellectual nature, in particular; third, applicants were not to be discriminated against on any national, religious, or political basis; and fourth and finally, the assistance was not to be used for "counter-revolution" (here meaning interference in Czechoslovak internal affairs).[5]

To better organize its assistance, the ministry divided the émigrés into three groups. The first included intellectuals; the second, individuals who performed physical work; and the third, the elderly, the wounded, and the ill, as well as school-age children and other people who could not perform either intellectual or physical work. To assist the first and second groups, the ministry set up émigré organizations; the Czechoslovak Red Cross assisted the third group. The government's stated reasons for helping the émigrés were based on notions of humanism, Slavic unity, and gratitude toward the thousands of soldiers who had given their lives in the First World War. There were certainly other reasons why Czechoslovakia generously accepted and helped refugees. While the main reasons were related to the humanistic vision of the Czechoslovak political elite, there were other important ones, which included the internal politics of the government, the desire to offer a positive image of the young democracy on the world stage, moral obligations toward specific groups of refugees, and the objective of making Prague the centre of Slavic scholarship. In addition, the personal connections of certain political leaders played a crucial role in the launching of the assistance program. Also important here were, for instance, the contact between the first prime minister of Czechoslovakia, Karel Kramář (1860–1937), and the Russians, and Masaryk's relations with the Russians and Ukrainians.[6]

The above-mentioned motives evolved considerably over the course of the program. While one of the initial objectives was to provide education for refugees to enable them to return home and develop their countries, as time passed this evolved into the preservation of those institutions that brought prestige to the young democracy. The assistance program was heavily influenced by the conflict between Masaryk and Kramář. The Russophile Kramář appealed for intervention against the Bolsheviks and saw this as a great chance for the new country to prove itself on the world stage. At the same time, Masaryk was confident that the assistance program would create a positive international image of Czechoslovakia as a liberal and democratic country – and in this he was correct. After resigning the prime ministership in 1919, Kramář could no longer affect the assistance program directly, so he influenced it indirectly as the leader of his National Democratic Party. At the same time, Masaryk's opinions were of crucial importance to the assistance program. The president believed that the new democratic Czechoslovakia had a duty to support intellectuals and cultural figures from of the former Russian empire. But he was also a practical man. In the early 1920s, there was a strong belief that the Bolshevik regime would be short-lived. The desire to preserve the cultural and intellectual elements that had found themselves in Czechoslovakia was a crucial factor in launching the assistance program. Masaryk believed that individuals who were able to work and study in democratic Czechoslovakia would later play an active role in the political development of their own democratic countries; it followed that Czechoslovakia's acceptance of these individuals would have only positive effects on relations between free countries. In addition, the Czechoslovak government saw friendly relations with the East as a counterbalance to German influence.[7]

The importance of newly born Czechoslovakia's standing in world politics was another reason behind the government assistance program. The Czechoslovak government's approach toward émigrés was different from that of other European countries, and its handling of the émigré question was a great credit to the country. The primary instigators of this approach were Masaryk, foreign minister Edvard Beneš (1884–1948), and his deputy Václav Girsa (1875–1954), the head of the political department of the foreign ministry. Interestingly, some Czechoslovak officials tried to make the assistance program an international effort, but upon learning that the League of Nations had limited means, little Czechoslovakia proceeded alone.[8]

As mentioned above, the idea of Slavic brotherhood was also of great importance to this undertaking. Masaryk's prewar personal connections with intellectuals from the former Russian and Austro-Hungarian empires played a prominent role in the development of the program. By offering a nurturing place for intellectuals, Masaryk hoped to turn Prague into a major centre of Slavic studies in Europe. In the 1920s, through its academic institutions, Prague indeed became the centre of Slavic scholarship. Under the auspices of the Czechoslovak foreign ministry, the Institute of Slavic Studies (Slovanský ústav) was founded in 1928 (having been approved in 1922). This institute included not only Czech and Slovak Slavists but also scholars from other Slavic countries. Also created around this time was the Slavonic Library, where considerable Slavic collections were gradually assembled. With the encouragement of its philosopher-president, Czechoslovakia actively promoted Slavic studies, not only at home but also throughout Europe, particularly in England and France. For example, in 1919 the government supported the founding of the Institute of Slavic Studies (L'Institut d'études slaves) by the French historian Ernest Denis (1849–1921) at the University of Paris. This cooperation between French Slavists and those from Slavic countries was intended to create in Paris the centre of Slavic studies in the West, which would replace the prewar international centres in Vienna, Berlin, and Leipzig. In 1921, on the death of Denis, the Ernest Denis Foundation was established in Paris with the goal of helping support the institute. This public gesture by the Czechoslovak government was intended to show the significance of promoting Slavic studies as an academic discipline. The Czechoslovak government also provided assistance for Slavic studies in England, where the Chair of Central European History at King's College London established the *lektorat* of Czechoslovak language and literature. In addition, it supported the activities of London's School of Slavonic Studies (now the UCL School of Slavonic and East European Studies), founded by Masaryk during the First World War. This assistance to Slavic studies in the West reflected the tenets of Czechoslovak foreign policy as well as a desire to showcase Czechoslovakia's role in the Slavic world and to popularize Czech and Slovak culture worldwide. Thus, promoting Slavic studies was not only in accord with domestic policy but also an important part of Czechoslovak foreign policy. Masaryk, a scholar as well as a politician, undoubtedly heavily influenced these developments.[9]

The Czechoslovak government, when it could, regulated emigration from the former Russian empire as much as possible, with a focus on supporting the democratic forces among émigrés. The Soviet and Polish governments often protested against the assistance program. These protests, which grew stronger after Czechoslovakia established diplomatic relations with the Soviet Union, helped bring about the program's eventual closure. Yet even after it officially ended, some institutions continued to receive financial support; for instance, the personal funds of President Masaryk, his daughter Alice, and Beneš supported some émigrés and their institutions.[10]

Many documents issued by the Czechoslovak government declared that the refugee assistance program was apolitical. These same documents advised that émigrés should not interfere in the country's internal affairs. In fact, the program *was* political in the sense that some parties, such as the Social Democrats, were favoured, as were democratic forces among the émigrés. It is also of note that Czechoslovak society knew very little about the program and lacked knowledge about developments in the Soviet Union and especially about Ukrainians.

Financing

The commercial attaché at the American embassies in Petrograd (now St Petersburg) and Paris, William Chapin Huntington (1884–1958) stated on the assistance program in 1933, "this expenditure was according to a plan based on humanity compounded with far-sighted policy."[11] Table 1 indicates how much the Czechoslovak government spent on the assistance program: more than half a billion crowns, amounting to 5 per cent of the country's average annual budget.[12]

The Ukrainian community also received financial support from Ukrainians in Canada and the United States and, to a lesser degree, from

Table 1. Czechoslovak government expenditure on the Assistance Program (crowns)[13]

Year	Ministry of Foreign Affairs	Ministry of Education	Ministry of Agriculture
1921	10,367,479	–	–
1922	49,704,491	–	–
1923	65,871,212	–	–
1924	99,775,427	–	–
1925	72,934,702	–	–
1926	71,010,894	–	–
1927	52,137,154	–	–
1928	26,315,643	7,982,052	4,000,000
1929	18,068,104	8,022,903	4,000,000
1930	14,615,716	7,293,312	3,600,000
1931	7,215,515	6,536,205	1,999,600
1932	3,799,622	4,626,365	1,250,770
1933	3,000,000	3,713,400	1,400,000
1934	2,950,000	–	–
1935	3,000,000	–	–
1936	3,100,000	–	–
1937	2,800,000	–	–
Total: 561,090,566			

Table 2. Financial assistance given to Ukrainian institutions in Czechoslovakia in 1926 and 1927 (crowns)[14]

Institutions	Czechoslovak crowns
The Ukrainian Free University	720,000
The Ukrainian Economic Academy	2,777,000
The Ukrainian Higher Pedagogical Institute	805,000
Total	4,302,000

Ukrainian lands. These additional funds were modest and often only occasional, but they were important to Ukrainian academic and cultural life in Czechoslovakia. In particular, the Museum of the Struggle for the Liberation of Ukraine – a significant Ukrainian centre of scholarship and culture – was entirely independent of the Czechoslovak government. This "outside" support was especially important in the late 1920s and 1930s when the Czechoslovak government's assistance came to an end. Table 2 shows the financial support provided to the major Ukrainian institutions of higher learning in Czechoslovakia in 1926 and 1927.

According to the same source, financial assistance for the Ukrainians in 1926 and 1927 totalled roughly 5.5 million crowns. That amount includes financial support provided to the institutions as well as assistance provided to Ukrainian students studying at Czechoslovak institutions of higher education. Note that this figure is approximate and that the support started to decline from this period on.[15] In 1922–23, the foreign ministry reported that financial support had been provided for a total of 6,341 students, 4,663 of them at universities and 1,678 at various vocational secondary schools in the country; 2,328 of these students were Ukrainian. Ukrainian students also studied in Czechoslovak institutions. Between 1921 and 1931, 1,062 Ukrainians graduated and received degrees from Czechoslovak universities and other institutions.[16]

Policies Concerning Ukraine and Ukrainians

The Ukrainian question occupied an important place in the politics of the republic until 1922. The Czechoslovakian government approached that question in the context of its attitude toward its Ukrainian émigrés, its policy towards the Transcarpathian region, which became part of Czechoslovakia in 1919, and its relations with the Ukrainian People's Republic and the Western Ukrainian People's Republic, and later with Soviet Ukraine. This perspective resulted in policies toward Ukraine that were largely realistic and constructive and that at the same time reflected the national interests of the young republic. The Czechoslovak political establishment declared its neutrality regarding events in the Soviet Union, including in Ukraine, while closely following developments there. This stance changed, however, as circumstances evolved and as events played out in the Ukrainian lands and in Russia, and also as the Entente adjusted its attitude toward Ukraine. (The Entente did not favour Ukraine's independence.) Czechoslovakian government policy was also heavily influenced by developments within the country's political establishment.[17]

After 1922, Czechoslovakian policy toward Ukraine and the Ukrainians became essentially a domestic one, focusing entirely on the Ukrainian émigrés in Czechoslovakia. This change was generally supported by intellectual and cultural workers as well as by some political parties and social groups in the newly established democracy. The new stance drew the cream of the Ukrainian intelligentsia to Czechoslovakia and made that country – especially Prague, its capital – the most vibrant centre of Ukrainian emigration. The government's initiatives regarding the émigrés focused mainly on supporting scholarship, education, and culture. Consequently, various scholarly, educational, and cultural institutions and societies were created. As a result of this assistance and the creation of these institutions, many Ukrainian émigré scholars were "saved," as the Ukrainian émigré historian Dmytro Doroshenko (1882–1951) recalled – and he likely included himself in that group. This support also raised their spirits and encouraged them to organize scholarly work, which later spread beyond the borders of Czechoslovakia.[18]

The new Czechoslovak state, which saw itself as a defender of the Slavic nations, at first welcomed most of the Ukrainian exiles, as well as exiles from other nationalities, including Russians, both monarchist and democratic. However, these policies toward various émigré groups, including Ukrainians, started to change in tandem with changes in international politics in general and Czechoslovak–Soviet relations in particular. These latter relations were rather difficult, because democratic Czechoslovakia was hosting and supporting thousands of émigrés who opposed the regime in their home country, and also because for many years the country refused to officially recognize the Soviet Union. In the early 1920s, both Masaryk and Beneš had hoped to see Russia evolve toward democracy and felt that Russia and Europe needed each other. After 1924, these hopes faded. Eventually, Czechoslovak–Soviet relations turned frosty, as the Czechoslovak government remained democratic and opposed to the totalitarian Bolshevik regime. By 1924 the Soviet Union had been officially recognized by Germany, France, Great Britain, Italy, and various other countries, but not by Czechoslovakia.

A dramatic change came after the United States recognized the Soviet Union in 1933 and Hitler came to power in Germany. These two diplomatic earthquakes caused the Czechoslovak government to reconsider its international position. With a newly aggressive Germany to its west, it moved closer to the Soviet Union. In 1934, Czechoslovakia recognized the Soviet Union, and in 1935 the two countries signed a treaty of mutual assistance. These developments profoundly affected anti-Soviet émigrés in Czechoslovakia, and it is against this background that one must interpret the Czechoslovaks' change in attitude toward the various anti-Soviet émigré groups, specifically the Ukrainians.[19]

Another reason was internal politics: forces that supported a pro-Russian tilt in foreign policy had started to prevail. The world economic crisis was affecting the republic's budget, and internal politics in the Transcarpathian region was generating additional pressure. The Ukrainian orientation became stronger in that region in the 1930s, often due to the Ukrainian émigrés, for many graduates of Ukrainian institutions moved to Transcarpathia after finishing their schooling; obviously, they were strongly pro-Ukrainian. The government came to see this as a threat to the country's territorial integrity. As a result, in the early 1930s some Ukrainian institutions were closed and others lost much of their funding.[20]

Nevertheless, some assistance was still provided, and not just in the form of financial aid. Noteworthy here is that the Czechoslovak government eventually backed efforts by Ukrainians to have their Ukrainian nationality stated on their Nansen passports. These identity certificates were intended for émigrés from the former Russian empire, regardless of their nationality. In the early 1930s, the Czechoslovak government began issuing these passports for its refugees. Since the form, adopted by the League of Nations in 1922, stated that these passports were intended for individuals of "Russian origins, who are not citizens of an [*sic*] other country," Ukrainians had begun receiving Nansen passports that identified them as Russians. They immediately protested by organizing a committee that sent memoranda to Masaryk, to the Secretary-General of the League of Nations, and to Nansen and his advisory commission. In the letter to Nansen, Ol'gerd Bochkovs'kyi emphasized that it was unacceptable to call Ukrainian émigrés Russians, given that the Ukrainians had founded their own state after the demise of the empires. Some countries recognized Ukraine as a state, he argued, and had diplomatic missions and Ukrainian embassies that provided Ukrainian passports that other states recognized as valid. It is with these passports that the Ukrainians lived as émigrés, and in the 1930s it was unacceptable for them to have their nationality changed to "Russian." Bochkovs'kyi also pointed out that Nansen's own home country, Norway, had struggled to gain its own independence from Sweden, and asked him to understand why Ukrainian émigrés were demanding that they be referred to in the manner of their own choosing on their passports. The issue was eventually resolved in the Ukrainians' favour.[21]

Personalities

There was another reason for the friendly attitude toward, and substantial financial support of, Ukrainian émigrés in Czechoslovakia. Historian of Ukrainian emigration Volodymyr Maruniak (1913–1997) noted:

> the ideological affinity of the Czech and Ukrainian socialist parties during World War I. Crucial to the Czech politics in the interwar period, were not only ... Masaryk and ... Beneš ... František Soukup, [František] Němec and others, but also Czechoslovak parties of people's socialist and social-democrats, leaders of those parties not only had personal connections with then-Ukrainian socialist circles ... but they all were members of international socialist organizations. That is why it is no accident the leadership of the Ukrainian Civic Committee, which ... played a crucial role in the first period of the history of Ukrainian emigration in Czechoslovakia ... were ... Shapoval ... Hryhoriiv-Nash ... Mytsiuk ... Martos [and others]. Played a role [also] the Czech colonies in Volhynia and about this friendly neighborly coexistence between two peoples was well known to the Czechoslovak government and cultural circles of the capital Prague.[22]

Several individuals were instrumental in the development of the assistance program and in fostering a positive attitude toward the Ukrainians. Václav Girsa, the Czechoslovak deputy foreign minister from 1921 to 1926 and head of the assistance program, was very important in this sphere. Girsa was born to a family of Czech settlers in Ukraine. After studying in Prague, he returned to Kyiv, where he worked in a hospital as a doctor, and after 1911 for many years as the hospital's head surgeon. During the revolutionary years, he occupied several key positions, one of them with the Czechoslovak National Council in Russia, and was important in the negotiations concerning the Czechoslovak Legions. Girsa's personal experience, deep knowledge of the region, and devotion to the political platform of Masaryk and Beneš made him important throughout the years of the Czechoslovak government assistance program. Girsa was also supportive of Ukrainian culture. During his stay in Kyiv, he established contacts among the Ukrainian intelligentsia. Borys Martos (1879–1977) recalled that Girsa often asked "the Ukrainians in Prague to speak with him in the Ukrainian language, and often replied in Ukrainian even though not in a pure one." Girsa also had a stellar reputation among the Russian émigré community in Czechoslovakia.[23]

Another supporter of the Ukrainians was a Czechoslovak politician of social-democratic orientation, the economist Jaromír Nečas (1888–1945). Besides being social affairs minister from 1935 to 1938, between 1920 and 1924 he advised Masaryk's office on Transcarpathian affairs. Nečas was very knowledgeable about Ukrainians and deeply committed to the Ukrainian cause. As personal secretary to the president, he often presented information about the Ukrainians to him in a positive light. Nečas apparently knew the Ukrainian language well and even translated some of Shevchenko's poems into Czech. In 1918, he published two works on Ukrainians titled *Prosím za jeden slovanský národ (Našim delegátům na mírovém kongresu)* (Asking for One Slavic Nation: To Our Delegates at the Peace Conference) and *Ukrajinská otázka* (The Ukrainian Question). His fate was ultimately a tragic one. After the Munich agreement, he spoke out against Nazism and went into exile in Paris and then London, where he occupied several positions in the Czechoslovak government-in-exile. His wife and daughter perished in Auschwitz; Nečas died in 1945 in Wales.[24]

František Soukup (1871–1940), another social democratic politician, was also sympathetic to Ukrainians. A lawyer, he had been a member of the Austrian Parliament from 1907 to 1918; he also held various positions within his party. For a brief period after the war, Soukup was justice minister; after this, he became the Senate's deputy chairman (1920–29) and later chairman (1929–39). One member of the émigré community recounted a visit by Soukup to the Ukrainian gymnasium in the summer of 1938. He recalled how the chairman arrived, shared meal with the students, and then delivered a short and positive speech. Later, while walking and talking with the director of the gymnasium, he discreetly passed him a thick bundle of banknotes. He also recalled that after his visit, life in the gymnasium became less poor and generally improved for some time.[25]

Another politician of social democratic persuasion who was important in Czechoslovak politics at the time was František Němec (1898–1963). Němec was a union official and Member of Czechoslovak Parliament between 1935 and 1939 and was presumably sympathetic to Ukrainians. In the 1940s, like Nečas, he escaped to France and then England, where he held several ministerial posts in the Czechoslovak government-in-exile. In 1944, he returned to Czechoslovakia and journeyed to the Transcarpathian region, where he argued with the Soviets about their plans to annex the region. While he was in exile, his family too was killed in Auschwitz.[26]

In the mid-1920s, the Czechoslovak government created favourable conditions for émigrés in the hope that they would return to their homes, where they would apply the education, knowledge, and skills that they acquired in democratic Czechoslovakia. This notion was widespread in the 1920s, not only within Czechoslovak government circles but also among the émigrés themselves. Indeed, they truly believed they would soon return home. In October 1921, Mykyta Shapoval (1882–1932), an influential political and civic figure in the Ukrainian émigré community, concluded a letter to Masaryk with these words:

> Mr. President, who was personally in Ukraine in the period of the battle for Czechoslovak independence, [you] saw firsthand that the hard-working and kind Ukrainian people will be able to give back generously to the Czechoslovak people the help [now being given to them], as soon as the situation in Ukraine normalizes. Ukrainian refugees, after encountering the spirit and character of the Czechoslovak people, are grateful for support and will be pioneers of Czechoslovak-Ukrainian rapprochement and fraternal understanding.[27]

Characteristics of the Ukrainian Émigré Community

As discussed above, the Ukrainian émigré population in Czechoslovakia was very diverse. It included members of the former Ukrainian armies, military professionals, and members of the former Ukrainian governments. Also, many professors, doctors, engineers, musicians, literary men and women, and others members of the intelligentsia were among the Ukrainian émigré community.[28] It is almost impossible to estimate the precise number of émigrés in any European country after the First World War. The émigrés did not register in any particular country in a controlled manner. Often people who had escaped dire conditions entered Czechoslovakia illegally, or they simply did not register for one reason or another, or they spent some time in one country and then moved on to another. All of this made it hard to calculate the exact numbers of refugees in any country, and this was certainly the case with the Ukrainian émigrés in Czechoslovakia. Scholars generally agree, however, that between 20,000 and 25,000 Ukrainians found themselves in Czechoslovakia in the early 1920s.[29]

The principal causes of Ukrainian immigration to Czechoslovakia and to other European countries between the wars was defeat in the Ukrainian independence war of 1917–21. A smaller number of Ukrainians had emigrated earlier during the 1905 Revolution in the Russian empire. Members of the former governments of the Ukrainian People's Republic and the Western Ukrainian People's Republic were among the émigrés. Also, some Ukrainians were fleeing the famine of 1921–2 and other calamities. Many Ukrainians had been forced to join various non-Ukrainian or anti-Bolshevik organizations, and after these armies were defeated they fled abroad. A significant percentage of Ukrainian émigrés were former POWs who could not or would not return home. In Czechoslovakia, former military personnel were relocated to the towns of Německé Jablonné (now Jablonné v Podještědí), Liberec, and Josefov. For them to return home often would have meant danger or even death; for many, to return would have been to betray their people and their ideals. So many émigrés were former military men that at one point the Czechoslovak government was concerned about what to do with them. It worried that if these people were simply released without any assistance, they might provoke undesirable events on the territory of the young republic, given that in those post-war years it would have been hard for them to find jobs and survive on their own in a foreign country. Gradually, the government started to dissolve the camps that housed them and formed worker groups out of them. By 1921, there were around seventy such groups in Czechoslovakia.[30]

For these early years, to help illustrate the composition of the Ukrainian émigré community at the time, some statistical data are available from the Ukrainian Civic Committee (Ukrains'kyi hromads'kyi komitet). The figures below include not all émigrés, but only those who registered with the committee to receive assistance between 1921 and 1924. As a sample, it is quite representative for these earlier years and presents a picture of the social, educational, and other characteristics of the Ukrainian émigré community in Czechoslovakia.[31]

By mid-1924, 5,209 individuals were registered with the committee. Most of those who registered were Ukrainians, but people of other nationalities did so too. Whether they chose to register because they felt they belonged to the Ukrainian national or cultural sphere or whether they did so out of necessity is unknown. Table 3 shows the national composition of this group. As shown in the Table 3, Ukrainians comprised more than 94 per cent of the total, which is unsurprising as the committee was a Ukrainian organization. People of other nationalities were present as well, although the number of registrants from other nationalities was relatively small. All registrants were entitled

Table 3. Individuals by nationality[32]

Nationality	Number of people	Percentage
Ukrainians	4,925	94.6
Jews	126	2.4
Belarusians	34	0.7
Czechs	49	0.9
Germans	27	0.6
Russians	16	0.4
Bulgarians	10	0.1
Moldovans	8	0.1
Poles	5	0.1
Others (Greeks, French, Hungarians, Armenians)	9	0.1
Total	5,209	100

to receive assistance from the committee regardless their nationality. All subsequent Ukrainian institutions always included a certain number of students of different nationalities. Also of note is that at the time under discussion the notion of Ukrainian nationality itself was not consistent; while many individuals were nationally conscious, others were not, and it is possible they used some committee services opportunistically.

The favourable treatment of émigrés by the Czechoslovak government was widely publicized among Ukrainians. They came to the country from Dnieper Ukraine, Kuban, Galicia, and Bukovyna and even from the Green Wedge (Zelenyi Klyn) in the Far East. Table 4 shows a breakdown of the community by country of origin and overall is quite representative of the composition of the Ukrainians in Czechoslovakia.

The Ukrainians who found themselves in Czechoslovakia had a variety of social backgrounds. As shown in the next table (Table 5), more than half of them were of peasant origin; it is possible that many former soldiers were included in this category, and they formed a large part of the emigration in the early years. Almost one third of them, however, belonged to the intelligentsia – quite a high proportion compared to the equivalent Ukrainian émigré communities in other countries. This high concentration of educated Ukrainians was one of the main reasons why a vibrant Ukrainian scholarly and cultural life was later established in Czechoslovakia. The émigré community also included workers and, in smaller numbers, tradespeople and landowners.

Table 4. Individuals by place of origin[33]

Territory	Number of people	Percentage
Right Bank	1,561	29.9
Left Bank	1,004	19.3
Bessarabia	40	0.8
Kuban	35	0.7
Green Wedge	7	0.1
Galicia	2,134	40.9
Bukovyna	151	2.9
Other	277	5.4
Total	5,209	100

Table 5. Individuals by social background[34]

Social background	Number of people	Percentage
Peasants	2,724	52.4
Workers	651	12.4
Intelligentsia	1,682	32.4
Tradespeople	79	1.4
Landowners	73	1.4
Total	5,209	100

With regard to the age, Table 6 shows that the largest group of émigrés was aged 25 to 34, followed by those aged 15 to 24. Overall, 82.6 per cent of the Ukrainian émigrés were between 15 to 34; this is because there were many former soldiers among them.

Education was very important for the Ukrainian émigré community in Czechoslovakia. This was partly due to the high concentration of members of the Ukrainian intelligentsia, but also due to the large number of young people. Those who could educate and those who desired to receive education were now in the country, and this created opportunities for both. Table 7 shows the level of education of the community members.

To conclude, the Czechoslovak government helped the émigrés during their difficult times. It felt it had a moral duty to support the émigrés and to prepare the future young generation of Ukrainians, Russians, Belarusians, and others for dynamic and productive work in their future democratic countries. It focused on assistance in the areas of scholarship, education, and culture. The government's treatment of the refugees strongly boosted the global reputation of this young

Table 6. Individuals by age[35]

Age	Number of people	Percentage
1–7	144	2.8
8–14	77	1.3
15–24	1,533	29.5
25–34	2,768	53.1
35–54	628	12.1
55 and older	59	1.2
Total	5,209	100

Table 7. Individuals by level of education[36]

Level of education	Number of people	Percentage
Illiterate (including young children)	440	8.5
Low-level literacy	646	12.4
Elementary school	1,152	22.2
Some secondary school	590	11.2
Secondary school	1,917	36.7
Professional (lower level)	104	2
Professional (middle level)	189	3.6
Higher education	171	3.4
Total	5,209	100

democracy. As time passed and the émigrés lost hope of returning home, the Czechoslovak government shifted its goals for the program but continued to help. In later years, because of the world economic crisis and for other reasons discussed above, the assistance was considerably reduced although some support was still provided.

The concentration of large numbers of intellectuals and young people created favourable conditions for their education. The Czechoslovak government used this situation wisely; the scholars were provided with jobs and with opportunities to develop their fields, and the students – who in the early 1920s were mostly former soldiers – received an opportunity to study. Their disillusionments and disappointments with their failed fight for independence were sublimated into education. Since the government, including especially Masaryk, was keen on education, its plans came together and produced positive results.

Numerically, the Ukrainian émigré community in Czechoslovakia was much smaller than in other countries like France or Germany.

However, the impact of this community on scholarly and cultural developments far outpaced that of émigrés in other countries. This happened thanks to auspicious conditions created by the Czechoslovak state in the form of its assistance program, as well as the concentration and activities of the educated class of Ukrainian émigrés, who created and developed a vibrant scholarly life in Czechoslovakia, to which the following chapters are devoted.

Chapter Two

The Ukrainian Free University in Prague

The Ukrainian Free University was one of the major educational and research institutions founded by Ukrainian émigré scholars in exile.[1] It became the principal centre of Ukrainian intellectual life in Czechoslovakia and abroad, playing a vital role in increasing awareness about Ukraine among various scholarly communities in Europe as well as across the Atlantic. After almost a century, the university continues to function in Munich – the capital of Bavaria – where it attracts students and scholars in Ukrainian studies from around the globe.

Establishment of the University in Vienna

For centuries, Vienna was an important centre of Ukrainian scholarship and culture. From the end of the eighteenth century to the collapse of the Austro-Hungarian empire, Vienna was the political, intellectual, and cultural epicentre for Ukrainians from Galicia and Bukovyna. Ukrainian students studied at the University of Vienna, and some Ukrainian scholars lived in Vienna.[2]

After losing its struggle for independence in 1917–21, many Ukrainians found themselves in Vienna. Some of them were scholars, who began to organize lectures in various disciplines. Their topics varied greatly, as did the backgrounds of the teachers and attendees. Some of the participants in the lectures were university-educated; some wished to expand their education. Lectures took place in the building of the workers' society Unity (Iednist') in Vienna. Jurist Stanislav Dnistrians'kyi (1870–1935) lectured on the self-determination of the Ukrainian people and the "theory of constitutions"; Mykola Sabat (1867–1930) delivered lectures on Greek and Roman architecture; distinguished Ukrainian historian Mykhailo Hrushevs'kyi (1866–1934) taught about primitive forms of social life and their impact on Ukrainian tradition;

Kolessa expounded on the major directions and methods in folklore; Stepan Rudnyts'kyi (1877–1937) educated his audience on Ukrainian geography; Volodymyr Starosol's'kyi (1878–1942) lectured on the Russian constitution; Antonovych talked about wooden churches in Ukraine; and Ivan Hanyts'kyi (1879–1921) lectured on energy sources and their use in different countries.[3] Thus, the lectures reflected the knowledge and specializations of the scholars in Vienna but otherwise lacked systematic organization. These lectures had been successful, however, and this provided an incentive to organize courses more systematically. It was a time, as Rusova put it, when Ukrainians "gathered in Vienna and waited for 'the miracle' that it would be possible to return home."[4]

In Vienna after the First World War, there were several Ukrainian organizations, four of which were very active in Ukrainian life: the Union of Ukrainian Journalists and Writers Abroad (Soiuz ukrains'kych zhurnalistiv i pys'mennykiv na chuzhyni), the Sich Student Society of Vienna (Ukrains'ke students'ke tovarystvo "Sich" u Vidni), the Ukrainian Society of Supporters of Education (Ukrains'ke tovarystvo prykhyl'nykiv osvity), and the Ukrainian Women's Union (Ukrains'kyi zhinochyi soiuz). The first of these, the writers' and journalists' union, was among the earliest Ukrainian associations in Austria to attract Ukrainian professors, writers, and journalists. In its first three months it amassed almost seventy members, not only in Austria but also in other countries. The union was led by journalist and writer Volodymyr Kushnir (1881–1933), a co-founder and editor of the Ukrainian periodical *Ruthenische Rundschau* (The Ruthenian Review, 1903–5), published in German in Vienna, which was later renamed *Ukrainische Rundschau* (The Ukrainian Press, 1906–[15]). Members of the union included the scholars Kolessa, Antonovych, Dnistrians'kyi, and Rudnyts'kyi, public and political figures Kyrylo Tryl'ovs'kyi (1864–1941) and Ievhen Levyts'kyi (1870–1925), and writers Bohdan Lepkyi (1872–1941) and Antin Krushel'nyts'kyi (1878–1937). The union tasked itself with informing the Western public and press about developments in Ukraine, defending the professional interests of its members, establishing a relief fund for Ukrainian writers, artists, composers, and scientists, organizing exhibitions, work on a Ukrainian encyclopaedia, and establishing a library and a primary school. The union's principal mission, however, was to found the Ukrainian Free University, which it accomplished.[5]

Initially, the aim was to establish a Ukrainian university in Prague with the support of the president of newly born Czechoslovakia, Tomáš Masaryk. To that end, in late 1919, a delegation of professors that included Horbachevs'kyi, Kolessa, and Dnistrians'kyi travelled to the Czechoslovakian capital. There, negotiations with the embassy of the Ukrainian People's Republic's did not succeed, so the decision was made to postpone the founding of a university. It is worth noting that the professors who went to Prague for the negotiations had for years been the principal advocates for the founding of a Ukrainian university in L'viv. Meanwhile, more and more Ukrainian students kept arriving in response to the closure of the universities in Kyiv and Kam'ianets'-Podil's'kyi by the Soviet authorities and of the Ukrainian departments at the universities in L'viv by the Polish authorities and in Chernivtsi by the Romanian ones.[6]

In the fall of 1920, several meetings were held in Vienna at which the founding of a university – or, more precisely, the subject of university courses – was discussed. Hrushevs'kyi was to become the rector of the future university. Very soon, however, disagreements regarding the character of the future university started to arise among the organizers. While Hrushevs'kyi insisted on the creation of a people's university (*narodnyi universytet*), other professors insisted on a university with a structure like that of Western higher education institutions. Hryshevs'kyi and his supporters were proposing a university without required courses and without requirements for qualifications for its professors and students. They also wanted the Ukrainian Sociological Institute (Ukrains'kyi sotsiolohichnyi instytut), founded by Hrushevs'kyi in Vienna in 1919, to have the right to appoint professors without consulting with the university committee. Perhaps this was because Hrushevs'kyi wanted to preserve the structure of the institute without changes within the Ukrainian Free University. In addition, he wanted the right to appoint lecturers without academic degrees, given that some of his fellow Ukrainian Socialist-Revolutionary Party members, such as Mykola Chechel (1891–1937) and Shapoval, did not have any academic degrees or teaching experience. The other group of professors, led by Kolessa, insisted on a university with a Western structure, with requirements for professors, students, and courses. This group won, and Hrushevs'kyi refused to work at the university. As a result of his strong disagreements with his colleagues on the nature of this university, he rejected the post of president. It was not their first disagreement: Hrushevs'kyi, Kolessa, Dnistrians'kyi, and Horbachevs'kyi were familiar with one another; some of them worked together and had long history of disagreements dating back to the late nineteenth and early twentieth centuries, when they worked at the Shevchenko Scientific Society in L'viv. Hrushevs'kyi's temperament and leadership style did not mix well with some scholars, who considered him authoritarian.[7]

During the first semester in Vienna, financing was the most difficult issue. Most of the funding was obtained thanks to the union's deputy leader, Ukrainian writer and poet Oleksander Oles'. The union obtained a bank loan and Oles' pledged the royalties from his works to achive this. At the time, inflation in Austria was soaring, so the university also sought sources of income outside the country.[8] The university's first academic senate was chosen by ballot in January 1921, and Kolessa was elected its first rector. The vice-rector and the dean of the Department of Law and Social and Economic Sciences was Dnistrians'kyi, with Starosol's'kyi as vice-dean of that department and secretary of the senate. The dean of the Department of the Philosophy was Stepan Rudnyts'kyi, and its vice-dean was Hanyts'kyi. The gala opening of the university was held on 17 January 1921 in the hall of the Society of Engineers and Architects, at Eschenbachgasse 9 in Vienna; one of the finest examples of Secession architecture, this hall still exists close to the city's Museum Quarter. The event's program included a speech by Kolessa, welcoming remarks by the union, the Sich Society, and other organizations, and lectures by Serhii Shelukhin (1864–1938) ("Law, Ethics, Religion, and Justice") and Rudnyts'kyi ("Ukraine, as a Geographic Unit").[9]

The new university consisted of a Department of Philosophy and a Department of Law and Social and Economic Sciences. The language of instruction was Ukrainian, with teaching in other languages allowed only in special circumstances. The university's aim was to develop scholarship by means of lectures and writings. The administration was to be supervised by a board of professors, and academic matters were to be the responsibility of faculty councils. The rector oversaw the administration and representative functions; the secretary was responsible for finances. There were fifteen professors and associate professors (*docents*): six professors and two associate professors in the Department of Philosophy, and six professors and one associate professor in the Department of Law and Social and Economic Sciences. Among them were Antonovych, the classical philologist Agenor Artymovych (1879–1935), Dmytro Doroshenko, Dnistrians'kyi, and the legal scholar Mykhailo Lozyns'kyi (1880–1937).[10] In the Department of Philosophy the courses focused primarily on various fields in Ukrainian studies, such as history, geography, literature, language, art, and political thought, whereas in the Department of Law and Social and Economic Sciences the courses were more theoretical and focused on law. The courses reflected the areas of expertise of the university's professors and associate professors. Table 8 shows the courses taught at the university in this period.

There were ninety students enrolled in the first semester: sixty-five in the Department of Philosophy and twenty-five in the Department of Law and Social and Economic Sciences. The lectures took place in two schools in Vienna, which the city provided for the university free of charge. Since it was the university's very first semester, the only thesis

Table 8. Courses taught at the Ukrainian Free University in Vienna in 1921[11]

Department of Philosophy	
Lecturer name	*Course Title*
Antonovych, Dmytro	History of Ukrainian Art; Modern Art
Artymovych, Agenor	History of Roman Poetry
Doroshenko, Dmytro	A Course of Ukrainian Historiography
Hanyts'kyi, Ivan	Industry Development in Ukraine
Kolessa, Oleksander	Ukrainian Paleography; History of Ukrainian Language; History of Ukrainian Literature
Lozyns'kyi, Mykhailo	History of Ukrainian Political Thought
Lypyns'kyi, Viacheslav	Governance of Bohdan Khmelnytsky
Rudnyts'kyi, Stepan	Geography of Ukraine
Sabat, Mykola	Greek Theatre and Drama; Greek Carving
Turians'kyi, Osyp	Issues of Comparative Indo-European Linguistics with Special Emphasis on the Ukrainian language
Zalozets'kyi-Sas, Volodymyr	History of Middle Ages and Renaissance Art
Department of Law and Social and Economic Sciences	
Dnistrians'kyi, Stanislav	Law Theory; Constitutional Law; International Law
Hanyts'kyi, Ivan	The Ukrainian Cooperative Movement and its Economic Basis
Iekh, Lev	Administrative Law
Koropatnyts'kyi, Dmytro	Theory of Criminal Law
Lozyns'kyi, Mykhailo	Monarchy and Republic; Federated and Confederated States; Parliamentary and Soviet Forms of Government
Lysiak, Pavlo	A Critical Overview of Economic Theories
Shelukhin, Serhii	Law, Ethics, Religion, and Justice; A Historical Survey of Ukrainian Law
Starosol's'kyi, Volodymyr	Foundations of Law; State Law

submitted to it was by Ivan Mirchuk (1891–1961), titled *Metageometriia i gnoseolohiia* (Meta Geometry and Gnoseology), prepared at the University of Vienna. The university's first publication appeared in Vienna as well: a monograph by Kost' Los'kyi (1864–1933) on Roman law, which was an abridged version of the first volume of another of his works issued in the same year titled *Istoriia i systema ryms'koho pryvatnoho prava. Istoriia dzherel ryms'koho prava*, vol. 1 (History and System of Roman Private Law: History of the Sources on Roman law).[12]

Transfer to Prague

In the process of transferring the university from Vienna to Prague, Kolessa's scholarly reputation, organizational skills, and dedication were instrumental. For a long time he had been the driving force behind the idea of a Ukrainian university. He had proposed it in the Austrian Parliament in Vienna, and he strived to ensure that the Austrian authorities met Ukrainian demands for a Ukrainian university by 1916. The First World War and subsequent events, however, brought this project to an end.[13]

In February 1921, in Prague, the Council of the Academic Community (Rada akademichnoi hromady) wrote a letter to the university asking that it be transferred to Prague. The reason for this request was that many Ukrainian students were now gathered in Prague and wanted to start or continue their education in their native language. As noted earlier, only a small number of Ukrainians had arrived in Prague after the 1905 Revolution, but more had arrived from Galicia and Bukovyna after the Russian army occupied those lands early in the First World War. After May 1919, former soldiers of the Ukrainian Galician Army began to arrive and were interned in camps in Czechoslovakia. Also, some Ukrainians who had been forcibly conscripted into Wrangel's and Denikin's White Armies stayed in the country. These groups contained many young people, who were potential students.[14]

In March 1921, Dnistrians'kyi, Hanyts'kyi, and Stepan Rudnyts'kyi wrote a letter to Masaryk on behalf of the university council in which they informed him about the founding of the university and its importance. They asked his permission to move it to Prague and for financial and logistical support. In May, Kolessa and Dnistrians'kyi passed to Masaryk a memorandum on the university. The Ukrainian scholars were received by Nečas, Beneš, the education minister Vavro Šrobár (1867–1950), and the Senate of Charles University. They were granted permission to make the move. As Kolessa later stated in his letter to the priest and cultural and political figure Avhustyn Voloshyn (1874–1945), the transfer of the Ukrainian university from Vienna to Prague was possible because of far-sightedness of Masaryk and Beneš.[15]

The university was soon transferred to Prague. It began operations in accordance with the decree of the Ministry of Foreign Affairs of Czechoslovakia of 16 September 1921 (291045/21), the decree of the Department of Policies of the Ministry of Schools and Education of Czechoslovakia of 30 September 1921 (35319/21), and the decree of the President of the Republic of 5 October 1921 (92477/21), as well as decrees from the academic senate and several departments of Charles University. Overall, the Czechoslovak government accepted émigrés, including those from the Ukrainian lands, quite openly. In the beginning, however, the university encountered a great deal of resistance from some government and university circles, in particular from influential Russophile circles. But with help of old acquaintances in the Austrian Parliament and through numerous talks and conferences, Kolessa managed to soften opinions.[16]

Goals and Structure

According to the statute of the university, the goal of that institution was to spread education through lectures and various forms of learning, and academic freedom must be preserved. The basis of all activities at the newly created university was the law of 27 April 1873, adopted in the former Austro-Hungarian empire, regarding the structuring of universities and the qualifications of professors. After the university moved to Prague, it adopted the statute of Charles University, which became the foundation for its scholarly and administrative development. As in Vienna, the university in Prague had two departments. Its scholarly affairs were supervised by the professorial board of each department, while its administrative matters were under the authority of the senate, which included the rector, the vice-rector, and the deans and vice-deans. The first senate consisted of the same professors who had served on it in Vienna, except for Hanyts'kyi. In his place, Smal'-Stots'kyi and Antonovych joined the senate. Rectors and deans were elected every year, and former rectors and deans often became vice-rectors and vice-deans, although sometimes they were elected. All documentation regarding the rector's election was sent to the ministry; since the university was entirely dependent on the Czechoslovak government for funding, it had to provide reports on all elections it held. The language of teaching was Ukrainian, but several languages were also taught: Czech, German, French, English, and the classical languages. Students could and did study simultaneously at other universities and institutions while pursuing studies at the Ukrainian Free University. The lectures took place on the Charles University campus, including in the historic buildings of the Clementinum (Klementinum) and the Carolinum (Karolinum). The university was a private institution, and most universities in Czechoslovakia did not recognize its diplomas. However, according to Kolessa, some universities in other countries recognized them, as did some departments of Czechoslovakian universities. Czechoslovak officials did not formally recognize the university's diplomas, but neither did they reject them.[17]

Finance

The university had acquired a subvention approved by the Czechoslovak Parliament; even so, as it is evident from its annual reports, it often encountered fiscal difficulties. The institution received the most funding during the 1923–24 period. After that, funding gradually declined, in particular after 1932. The government still helped the university considerably, and as mentioned above, Masaryk and Beneš supplemented the government funding with their personal funds.[18]

Initially, the university requested financial support from the government for the following purposes: to increase the number of departments and hire more professors; to provide scholarships; to publish textbooks and series; to organize lectures; and to found a library and a bibliographic institute. It also intended to help Ukrainian scholars in dire circumstances outside Czechoslovakia, especially in the Academy of Sciences in Kyiv in Soviet Ukraine. In 1922, the initial monthly assistance of 100,000 crowns was reduced to 65,000 crowns. In 1925 and 1926, the university officially received 60,000 crowns per month, but because it had to pay some amounts to a publishing house for its publications, it received less overall. By the end of 1926, the ministry had reduced its assistance to all émigré institutions, including the university, which from then on received only 45,000 crowns each month. The deficit in that academic year was covered only because some professors, including Stepan Rudnyts'kyi, had left the country, and because Dmytro Doroshenko, economist Volodymyr Tymoshenko (1885–1965), and art historian Volodymyr Zalozets'kyi-Sas (1896–1959) were on unpaid leave. In 1928, responsibility for the university was transferred to the education ministry, which oversaw all Czechoslovak universities. This move was significant because it formally extended the university equal status with the other Czechoslovak universities; the administration hoped this would bring increased funding. In fact, the monthly subsidy was reduced, to 41,600 crowns, which prompted the university to reorganize its budget. Professors' salaries were not reduced that year, but the university did not pay for the work of assistant professors (*privat*). During this academic year, the ministry provided five more postdoctoral stipends, as well as a one-time 1,000-crown support for one student. The university continued to receive an extra subsidy of 12,000 crowns per month from Masaryk Fund, which continued until 1938 and was crucial to the existence of the university.[19]

The Czechoslovak government provided 500,000 crowns per month to 1,247 students starting in November 1921. In addition to this financial support, Ukrainian students received funding from the YMCA, the Methodist Mission, and the Student Relief Fund. The Ukrainian students also organized themselves to raise funds from Ukrainians in the United States. This organization, the Ukrainian Students' Help Union (Tsentralia dopomohy ukrains'komu studenstvu, TsEDUS), was highly active in this regard. It made contact with Ukrainian Americans and with international bodies, including the League of Nations and the European Help Fund, as well as with Fridtjof Nansen's organization. Yet another organization, the Czech–Ukrainian Committee for Ukrainian and Belarusian Students Support (Ches'ko-ukrains'kyi komitet dopomohy ukrains'kym ta bilorus'kym studentam), did much to distribute financial assistance from the government to Ukrainian students. The Czechoslovak foreign ministry had created this organization in November 1921 and worked closely with it. Jaroslav Bidlo (1868–1937), the Czech historian and a professor at Charles University, became its head, with Kolessa as his deputy. The committee included Czech and Ukrainian professors and students as well as members of the Ukrainian Civic Committee. Through this committee, the government paid monthly stipends to students and provided other assistance. The committee also helped students who studied at other institutions of higher learning. In November 1921, the committee began receiving 500,000 crowns a month from the foreign ministry; this figure later rose to a high as 1.5 million crowns a month. In the ten years of its existence, the committee helped 1,992 Ukrainian students. In addition, in 1923–24, from the Masaryk Fund, Ukrainian young scholars obtained ten scholarships. Those who received financial support from this fund studied topics in subject areas such as Roman law, sociology, geography, and mathematics; they were required to submit their scholarly papers within a year. This was a remarkable example of the philosopher-president's support of young scholars.[20]

In 1929, the ministry began distributing money for different uses separately: salaries for faculty and administration used the original channels; for other needs, such as office supplies, rent, and heating, the university had to apply separately. In 1929–30, the ministry supported, for example, several postdoctoral students and covered the costs of conference travel to Lund, Sweden, for several scholars. As a consequence of the economic depression, the ministry intended to stop funding the university altogether as of 1932, but negotiations and personal contacts led it to reconsider, and the university received 376,000 crowns for the academic year 1932–33. In 1932, to somehow tackle fiscal problems, the senate founded the Society of Friends of the Ukrainian Free University in Prague (Tovarystvo pryiateliv Ukrains'koho vil'noho universytetu v Prazi), which was tasked with finding funds for the university.[21]

In 1933, according to Jan Rypka (1886–1968), an Orientalist and a professor at Charles University, the Czechoslovak government had a positive attitude toward the university, but because of the financial crisis it could no longer finance the institution. In the 1930s, in the aftermath of a change in government policies toward Poland and the Soviet Union, funds were drastically reduced. It was still possible, however, for the university to function with the money it had, although not to the extent desired by the émigré scholars.[22]

Faculty

The central members of the faculty of the university were former professors at universities in the Austro-Hungarian and Russian empires. In Czechoslovakia, these individuals became key movers of Ukrainian émigré scholarly life. Among the most prominent were the above-mentioned linguist and literary scholar Oleksander Kolessa, art historian Dmytro Antonovych, historian Dmytro Doroshenko, philologist Stepan Smal'-Stots'kyi, the renowned biochemist Ivan Horbachevs'kyi, jurist Stanislav Dnistrians'kyi, sociologist Volodymyr Starosol's'kyi, statistician Fedir Shcherbyna, archaeologist Vadym Shcherbakivs'kyi (1876–1957), and legal scholar Otto Eikhel'man (1854–1943). As discussed above, some of these faculty members were instrumental in the founding of the university and its transfer to Prague. They not only taught at the university but also worked at other institutions and participated in scholarly societies and organizations in Prague, as will be discussed in detail in later chapters.[23]

Table 9 lists the rectors of the university in the period under discussion. Some of these figures merit closer examination. The life of the renowned biochemist, epidemiologist, and hygienist Ivan Horbachevs'kyi (1854–1942) was closely connected with Prague and the

Table 9. Rectors of the Ukrainian Free University, 1921–38[24]

	Academic Year																
Names of Rectors	1921–1922	1922–1923	1923–1924	1924–1925	1925–1926	1926–1927	1927–1928	1928–1929	1929–1930	1930–1931	1931–1932	1932–1933	1933–1934	1934–1935	1935–1936	1936–1937	1937–1938
Kolessa, Oleksander	■				■	■	■								■	■	
Dnistrians'kyi, Stanislav		■															
Horbachevs'kyi, Ivan			■								■	■	■	■			
Shcherbyna, Fedir				■													
Antonovych, Dmytro								■	■								■
Iakovliv, Andrii										■							

Czech people. He played an important role in the founding of Czech biochemistry. Born in a small village in what is currently Ternopil' *oblast* in Ukraine, he studied medicine at the University of Vienna, and as a student he worked in the department of chemistry and physiology. He later became an assistant at this department, which was headed by renowned chemist Ernst Ludwig (1842–1915). During this period, Horbachevs'kyi made an important discovery regarding the synthesis of uric acid, which had implications for the study of pathological processes. This breakthrough received high recognition in professional circles, especially the fact that a relatively young and unknown assistant had made a discovery of this scale. In 1883, Horbachevs'kyi became an associate professor, and in 1884 he attained the rank of full professor of medical chemistry at the Czech University in Prague, where he worked until 1917.[25] Horbachevs'kyi founded the Institute of Biochemistry at Charles University at the age of twenty-nine, and from that point on he contributed extensively to the development of the Czech university. In 1902–3, he was the rector of the university, and he was elected dean of the medical faculty several times. The scientist mentored and educated several generations of Czech doctors, as well as three great Czech chemists: Emanuel Formánek (1869–1929), Karel Černý (1871–1922), and Antonín Hamsík (1878–1963). Producing the first Czech textbook in medical chemistry (1904–1908) in four parts, Horbachevs'kyi published extensively in German-language scientific journals, as well as in Czech medical journals such as *Chemické listy* (Chemistry Papers) and *Časopis lékařů českých* (Journal of Czech Physicians). Horbachevs'kyi also contributed to organizing a sanitarian council in Prague devoted to the environment and a reduction of the negative effects of industry on human health. He became the first health minister in the Austro-Hungarian empire before its dissolution. Notwithstanding his professional accomplishments in the Austro-Hungarian empire and then in Czechoslovakia, Horbachevs'kyi devoted his long life to the Ukrainian cause. The years during which he devoted himself to Ukrainian life and scholarship the most were the 1920s and 1930s. Teaching at Ukrainian institutions, participating in Ukrainian conferences, and publishing in Ukrainian scholarly periodicals, he made a significant contribution to Ukrainian émigré scholarship. Horbachevs'kyi taught courses at various institutions: at the Ukrainian Free University and the Ukrainian Higher Pedagogical Institute, and at the Ukrainian Economic Academy. He was one of the organizers of two Ukrainian scholarly conferences in Prague, conducted his research, published in Ukrainian and Czech scholarly journals, published his textbook *Orhanichna khemiia* (Organic Chemistry) in Ukrainian in 1924, and prepared his *Neorhanichna khimiia*

(Inorganic Chemistry) for publication in Ukrainian. Horbachevs'kyi was also involved in many other scholarly activities within the Ukrainian community.[26]

As mentioned above, Kolessa was very important in the life of the university. He had been a professor at the University of L'viv (then Universitas Franciscea) from 1898 until 1918 and a full member of the Shevchenko Scientific Society. During the state-building period, in 1921, Kolessa headed the Western Ukrainian People's Republic's diplomatic mission to Rome. He was also the author of many academic works on Ukrainian literature and language as well as on folklore. As a politician, Kolessa lobbied hard for a Ukrainian university while he was a long-time member of the Austrian Parliament, and the Ukrainian Free University was his lifelong cause.[27]

Another individual who devoted himself to the development of the university was Dmytro Antonovych. An art and theatre historian before the war, he researched and studied art in Paris, London, Munich, and Florence, as well as in other cities in Italy. Before the emigration, Antonovych had been a political leader and a founder of the Revolutionary Ukrainian Party (Revoliutsiina ukrains'ka partiia). During the revolutionary years, Antonovych served on the Central Council (Tsentral'na Rada) and, for a very brief period, as Minister of Naval Affairs and Minister of Arts. In addition, during this period, he was the president of the Ukrainian diplomatic mission of the Ukrainian People's Republic in Rome. In Czechoslovakia, however, Antonovych devoted himself entirely to scholarship. Besides teaching at the university, he was a founder and director of the Ukrainian School of Plastic Arts and chair of the Ukrainian Historical–Philological Society. His lectures were remarkable in their erudition, liveliness, and wide scope of material. His main devotion, though, was to the Museum of the Struggle for the Liberation of Ukraine, which he founded in Prague.[28]

Stanislav Dnistrians'kyi, a long-time dean of the Department of Law at the university, also made a significant contribution. A renowned jurist and professor of Austrian civil law at the University of L'viv. He was also a full member of the Shevchenko Scientific Society and editor of the first Ukrainian law journal, *Chasopys' pravnycha i ekonomichna* (The Law and Economics Journal, 1900–6; 1912). Dnistrians'kyi was also a member of the Austrian Parliament and author of the constitution of the Western Ukrainian People's Republic. He wrote more than fifty scholarly works on constitutional, family, and civil law, as well as on theory of the state and law in Ukrainian, German, Czech, Polish, and French.[29]

The renowned linguist and literary scholar Stepan Smal'-Stots'kyi taught Ukrainian philology at the university. Born in Galicia, he studied in Chernivtsi in Bukovyna, at the university (then Franz-Josephs-Universität). Throughout his life he was closely associated with Ukrainian life in this easternmost Austrian province. As a politician, he was a deputy representing the National Democratic Party in the Bukovynian Diet between 1892 and 1911 and the diet's deputy marshal between 1904 and 1910. He was also a member of the Austrian Parliament from 1911 to its dissolution. As a scholar, Smal'-Stots'kyi headed the department of Ukrainian (Ruthenian) language and literature at Chernivtsi University for thirty-three years, from 1885 to 1918. He taught courses in Ukrainian (Ruthenian) literature and phonetics, along with courses in philosophy, palaeography, and stylistics. He joined the Shevchenko Scientific Society in 1899 and published extensively. Along with Theodor Fedir Gartner (1843–1925), a professor of Romance philology, he published the famous *Rus'ka hramatyka* (Ruthenian Grammar) which underwent several editions in Chernivtsi and L'viv, as well as in Canada under the title *Ukrains'ka hramatyka* (Ukrainian Grammar). One of Smal'-Stots'kyi's students was the future writer, scholar, political leader Ivan Franko (1856–1916), who recalled his European scholarly methods. Two other scholars, with whom Smal'-Stots'kyi would collaborate later in Prague, were also his students: Kolessa, and the linguist Vasyl' Simovych (1880–1944). There is a little-known story of Smal'-Stots'kyi helping Shcherbakivs'kyi, a future archaeologist from Dnieper Ukraine, when he was arrested in 1905 in Chernivtsi for allegedly spying for the Russians, while Shcherbakivs'kyi was in fact on a research trip to Europe. They would all meet again in Prague.[30]

The most prominent Ukrainian émigré historian, Dmytro Doroshenko, was also a professor at the university. Popularizing knowledge about Ukraine, he wrote on its history in Ukrainian, Czech, German, English, French, Swedish, Polish, Russian, Serbian, Croatian, and Italian. He contributed scholarly works on the history of Ukraine to several encyclopaedias and many Western scholarly periodicals. Contemporary historian of Ukrainian and Ukrainian Canadian history Thomas Prymak wrote about Doroshenko that he "made significant, indeed, sometimes irreplaceable contributions in the fields of biography, historiography, contemporary history, historical synthesis, bibliography, and memoir writing." Born in Vilnius in 1882, Doroshenko was a descendant of prominent Cossack hetmans of the seventeenth century. He studied at the universities in Warsaw, St Petersburg, and Kyiv and participated in Ukrainian social and cultural life. After the revolution of 1905, he began publishing in periodicals. At this time, he was also the editor of the Ukrainian-language journal *Zapysky Ukrains'koho naukovoho tovarystva* (Annals of the Ukrainian Scholarly Society), published in Kyiv;

he contributed extensively to the periodicals *Rada* (Council), also issued in Kyiv; *Literaturno-naukovyi vistnyk* (Literary Scholarly Herald), published in L'viv; and *Ukrainskaia zhizn'* (Ukrainian Life), which came out in Moscow. After his graduation in 1909 Doroshenko moved to Katerynoslav (now Dnipro), where he was active in the Katerynoslav Provincial Learned Archival Commission (Katerynoslavs'ka huberns'ka vchena arkhivna komisiia), a society of historians, ethnologists, and civic leaders. He was also active in the Prosvita Society. During the First World War, Doroshenko worked for several charitable and social organizations, notably the Union of Cities (Soiuz Mist), a relief organization. During the revolutionary years, he occupied several administrative posts, and in 1918 he became the Minister of Foreign Affairs in the Hetmanate government of Pavlo Skoropadsky, whom Doroshenko supported. After that, he taught briefly in the newly created Kam'ianets'-Podil's'kyi Ukrainian State University (Kam'ianets'-Podil's'kyi ukrains'kyi derzhavnyi universytet) before going into exile in 1919. As an émigré, Doroshenko was a professor of Ukrainian history at the Ukrainian Free University and Charles University in Prague. After 1923, he was a full member of the Shevchenko Scientific Society and belonged to other scholarly societies as well. He also taught and worked as a historian in Berlin, Warsaw, and Winnipeg. Doroshenko died in Munich in 1951, shortly after returning from Canada. His many activities in emigration are highlighted throughout this study.[31]

Stepan Rudnyts'kyi, another notable figure at the university, was a prominent geographer. He founded the geography of Ukraine as a scholarly discipline. Born in 1877 in Przemyśl, he studied at the universities in L'viv and Vienna. He received his doctorate in 1901, the year he became a full member of the Shevchenko Scientific Society. After several years teaching in gymnasiums, Rudnyts'kyi acquired a professorship at the Department of Geography at the University of L'viv. His contribution to the field of Ukrainian geography is significant. Rudnyts'kyi penned scholarly works, including comprehensive geographic surveys of Ukraine and works of political geography. He also wrote a textbook in geography as well as other works to popularize the subject. In Vienna in 1918, Rudnyts'kyi created the first wall maps of Ukraine. In emigration, he helped organize the university and became a professor of geography. Rudnyts'kyi was among those who returned to the Soviet Union in the mid-1920s. In Kharkiv he founded the Ukrainian Scientific Research Institute of Geography and Cartography (Ukrains'kyi naukovo-doslidnyi instytut heohrafii i kartohrafii), of which he was the director, in addition to being a professor of geography at the Kharkiv Institute of People's Education (Kharkivs'kyi instytut narodnoi osvity im. O. Potebni). In 1933, during the purges of the Ukrainian elite, Rudnyts'kyi was arrested and later executed in the Solovets Islands.[32]

In addition to the aforementioned scholars, there were other individuals among the university teaching staff who played significant roles in the life of the university. Shcherbakivs'kyi, an archaeologist, was another notable figure who taught at the university and contributed considerably to its development. Shcherbakivs'kyi studied under the famous Czech archaeologists Lubor Niederle (1865–1944) and he had good standing and connections with Czech academies. He published extensively and participated in seventeen conferences between the wars.[33] Other notable scholars were literary historian Leonid Bilets'kyi (1882–1955), archaeologist Ivan Borkovs'kyi (1897–1976), church historian Vasyl' Bidnov (1874–1935), and legal scholar Andrii Iakovliv (1872–1955).

As noted above, in addition to teaching at the university, some of the professorial staff taught at other institutions of higher education, both Ukrainian and others. Some of them taught at the Ukrainian Economic Academy, the Ukrainian Higher Pedagogical Institute, and the Ukrainian School of Plastic Arts. Dmytro Doroshenko and Kolessa also taught at Charles University; Simovych and Smal'-Stots'kyi lectured at the Higher Trade School in Prague (Vyšší obchodní škola v Praze); Bidnov, Dmytro Doroshenko, and Oleksander Lotots'kyi (1870–1939) taught at Warsaw University. In the second half of the 1920s, some members of the technical and scholarly intelligentsia returned to Soviet Ukraine, among them university faculty members Lozyns'kyi and Rudnyts'kyi. In the 1930s, almost all of them became victims of purges.[34]

The work of the university teaching staff included delivering lectures, organizing workshops, and supervising exams, as well as reviewing dissertations and habilitation works and providing advanced training. The most important part of their mission was to develop courses at the university level; this was especially important for courses in Ukrainian studies, because the majority of disciplines had never before been taught at the university level in that language. The professors created and, in part, published course books on Ukrainian history and historiography, Ukrainian language, Ukrainian geography, history of Ukrainian art, Ukrainian philosophy, Ukrainian theatre, Ukrainian law, Ukrainian religion, and Ukrainian ethnography, ethnology, and archaeology. Some of these works retain their scholarly value today.[35]

Initially, the university had sixteen teaching staff: twelve professors and four associate professors. Over the course of the university's existence in the interwar period, that number fluctuated. The highest number of staff members was in 1930–31, when there were forty-six: twenty-four full professors, one associate professor, two assistant professors (*suplents*), one adjunct professor, seven associate professors *privat*, four lecturers, and seven assistants. Over time, the university created its own young teaching force; around ten young scholars – all graduates of the university – became assistant professors there and in other institutions of higher education. Between 1921 and 1931, fifty-seven doctors of law and thirty-one doctors of philosophy graduated from the university. Some of the university faculty also worked at other universities and institutions in Prague, L'viv, and Warsaw, and, in some cases, in the United States and Germany; thus, they did not stay in Prague permanently and periodically took unpaid leave. In 1926, for example, Dmytro Doroshenko took a year's leave from the university to establish the Ukrainian Scholarly Institute in Berlin (Ukrains'kyi naukovyi instytut u Berlini), where he was a director until 1931; later he held a chair in church history in the Department of Orthodox Theology at Warsaw University.[36]

As in any institution, relations among professors were not always smooth, and politics, good and bad, were present. In émigré scholarly circles, these scholars held positions at different ranks, so there was definitely some manoeuvring. There were likely some tensions between Ukrainians from the former Austrian Galicia and Bukovyna and those from Dnieper Ukraine. Presumably, though, the key figures in this scholarly community respected one another, thus preserving one another's dignity. In a letter, Antonovych asked Kolessa's advice on whether to participate in a congress organized by the Prosvita Society as a representative of the university and the Ukrainian Academic Committee. The tone of this letter was warm and respectful; it did not read like a formal correspondence. Similarly, the young Iaroslav Rudnyts'kyi (1910–1995), who would later become a leading Ukrainian Canadian scholar of the Cold War era, showed respect for Kolessa when this seventy-eight-year-old scholar, who had devoted his whole life to building the Ukrainian university, agreed with a heavy heart to serve as its rector during the Second World War (for the seventh time). Because he thought of the university as his "child" and wanted to save it from being closed, he accepted the position – but with the proviso that he must be democratically elected. Rudnyts'kyi recalled that "Kolessa projected power and greatness of the academic leader ... I left with [a feeling of] reverence, admiration, and respect."[37]

The fates of the faculty members differed greatly. Stepan Rudnyts'kyi returned to the Soviet Union and perished during the purges in the 1930s. His sister's husband, Dnistrians'kyi, left Prague in 1933 after two heart attacks and moved to Uzhhorod, where he died suddenly from another heart attack in 1935. Some, like Smal'-Stots'kyi and Horbachevs'kyi, succumbed to old age before or during the war; others survived the war, like the elderly Kolessa, who died in May 1945, and Antonovych, who died in November of the same year in a hospital in Prague, where he had engaged in ideological arguments with NKVD officers who had come to the hospital intending to spirit him back to the Soviet Union. Dmytro Doroshenko immigrated to Canada and then returned to Europe, where he died in 1951, in Munich. Those who managed to evade the Soviet Army gathered in Munich, reopened the university, and continued to teach and conduct research. With the loss of the old faculty and the relocation of the university, an era had ended. The contributions of the faculty members deserve recognition in the intellectual history of Ukraine.[38]

Students at the Ukrainian Free University and Charles University

Between the wars, Czechoslovakia had the highest number of Ukrainian students. As of September 1923, 1,360 studied there, and by March of the following year the number had increased to 1,896. Most of them (1,255) studied in Prague, 382 in Poděbrady, 170 in Brno, 83 in Příbram, and 6 in Bratislava.[39] Ukrainian students showed a strong desire for higher learning. Many of them combined their studies at Charles University and other institutions with their studies at the Ukrainian university. Many of them were mature and wanted to study because higher education would open more possibilities for them. Another reason was a desire to obtain professional knowledge so that they could contribute to their native land after returning from emigration. There was no requirement for Ukrainian students to sign up at the Ukrainian university, but many of them did. In the summer semester of 1922, 615 out of 844 students who received funding signed up for courses at the university, and in the winter semester of the same year, 874 out of 1,071 did so. Overall, during the first ten years, 7,702 students enrolled in courses at the university. In the 1921–22 winter semester, there were already 438 Ukrainian students studying at Charles University (171 in law, 161 in medicine, 69 in philosophy, 35 in the natural sciences, and 2 in theology). The students received financial assistance of 400–500 crowns per month during their studies.[40]

Students who applied were from a variety of places, not just Prague. There were also collective applications submitted to study at the university – for example, from members of the Sich Society of Ukrainian Students in Chernivtsi, from members of the Union of Ukrainian

Students at an internee camp in Oradea-Mare (now Oradea) in Romania, and from elsewhere. Over the entire Prague period, most of the students at the Ukrainian Free University were Ukrainians, but there were also Czechs, Belarusians, Lithuanians, Jews, Armenians, Georgians, Slovaks, Russians, Germans, Bulgarians, Serbs, Tatars, and others.[41]

The above-mentioned Czech–Ukrainian Committee was responsible for all issues related to Ukrainian students in Czechoslovakia. It helped not only students in Prague but also those in other cities and towns. In addition to undergraduates, it supported graduate and high school students, as well as other groups; it also helped with clothing, medicines, textbooks, and other necessities. The same committee was responsible for helping Belarusian students in Czechoslovakia. Twenty-three Belarusian students received help from it in 1923, a number that later grew to 150. Students even received financial assistance from the committee for travel abroad. In 1923 alone, students travelled to Denmark, England, Italy, Germany, Yugoslavia, Egypt, Switzerland, Bulgaria, France, and Romania.[42]

In the early 1920s, many international students studied in Prague. The authoritative authors of a history of the most important Czech university write:

> In the winter semester 1922–1923, 1,487 foreign students were registered, including 454 Russians, 453 Ukrainians, 341 Yugoslavs, and 130 from Romania. A year later, 1,100 students claimed Russian, Ukrainian, or Ruthenian nationality, while the number of Yugoslavs and Romanians fell to 145 and 170 respectively. There were also students from Bulgaria, whose numbers approached a hundred during the 1920s. The largest number of foreign students came from Poland: in 1923–1924, there were 523 of them, although only 37 claimed Polish nationality, while the rest were Ukrainians.[43]

According to the same source, in 1921, students who had fled the Bolshevik regime constituted over 15 per cent of all students at Charles University. They were especially well represented in the Medical Department, where, in the 1920s, international students constituted up to 40 per cent of the total. Most of them were Russian and Ukrainian émigrés. There were also students from Yugoslavia, followed in the late 1920s by students of Jewish background from Romania, Poland, and Hungary. Between 1920 and 1939, in the Natural Sciences Department, of the students who defended their dissertations, 19 per cent were international (199 dissertations out of 1,060 in total). That number included 52 Ukrainian students. Of the 64 international students who defended their dissertations between 1920 and 1927, 20 were Ukrainians; this number rose to 28 out of 78 between 1927 and 1932 before falling to 4 out of 57 by 1939. Overall, one quarter of the international students in the Natural Sciences Department who submitted dissertations in the interwar period were Ukrainians. The dissertations submitted were in various fields: chemistry, botany, geography, anthropology, mathematics, physics, zoology, geology, mineralogy, philosophy of science, meteorology, photochemistry, palaeontology, astronomy, history of science, and demography.[44]

Many of the Ukrainian students studied at two universities simultaneously. In general, they were hard-working and devoted considerable time to their studies. Presumably, they earned good reputations among the Czech professors at Charles University and in other Czechoslovak institutions where they studied. One Czech professor, František Pastrnek (1853–1940), wrote in a letter to Studyns'kyi: "We have here, as you know, many Ukrainian students and I have to admit that we all love them. The majority of them are hard-working and diligent, modest, and decent. It is surprising how their spiritual traits are consistent with ours."[45]

When the Ukrainian Free University first opened, the faculty sought out students with talent. A financial support system was created for this purpose, but it was apparently effective only during the early years. In 1921–22 there were nine recipients, in 1922–23 there were seventeen, in 1923–24 there were twelve, and in 1924–25 four out of twelve were already without support, prefiguring the decline and halt of this system in subsequent years. Some of these recipients joined the teaching staff of the university and other Ukrainian institutions as associate professors, associate professors *privat*, or *suplents*. Overall, between 1921 and 1931 the university granted 82 doctorates.[46]

After finishing their studies, most graduates worked in various places and fields. Many of them went to the Transcarpathian region and to Polish-ruled Galicia; some went to Croatia or even Canada. After the Second World War, some graduates became active in Ukrainian communities in Germany, the United States, and Canada. Some stayed and contributed to Ukrainian studies in Czechoslovakia, including Orest Zilynskyj (1923–1976) in Prague and Mikuláš Nevrlý (1916–) in Bratislava. All of them had been profoundly influenced by their experience at the university.

Women and the University

Between the wars, several highly educated Ukrainian women served as lecturers at the university. Lidiia Shul'hyna (1888–?) taught the French language there. She had a medical degree, had studied in France, and knew the French language well. In 1927, the Shul'hyn family moved to Paris, and after that the French language was taught by Oksana Kosach-Shymanovs'ka (1882–1975), the youngest sister of the Ukrainian poet and playwright Lesia Ukrainka (1871–1913). Kosach-Shymanovs'ka had studied in Lausanne and knew four other languages besides French. Mariia Slavins'ka (1879–1958) was another woman who taught at the university, from 1924 to 1941. She was the wife of Maksym Slavins'kyi (1868–1945), who was ambassador of the Directory of the Ukrainian People's Republic in Prague. At the university, Slavins'ka taught the English language; she was also fluent in Russian, Czech, German, and French. Besides teaching, she helped her husband with his translation work. Finally, Mariia-Asia Horbachevs'ka (1885–1979), daughter of Ivan Horbachevs'kyi, worked in the university offices. As evident from this very brief outline, women who taught at the university were very knowledgeable and well-qualified to teach their subjects. They were mostly family members of the university professors, and most of them taught languages. Almost all of the women who worked at the university were active members of the Ukrainian Women's Union in Prague (Ukrains'kyi zhinochyi soiuz v Prazi). That organization included Ukrainian women of different religions and political views, but all were supporters of independence for Ukraine. The union had ties with the World Women's Union, the Czechoslovak Women's Council, and the World Women's League for Peace and Freedom, and sent delegates to various congresses. Some Czech women's organizations helped the union, particularly in fundraising and through participation in important women's international organizations. The Ukrainian Women's Union in Prague founded a Ukrainian library, organized lectures, and invited speakers from other countries, including the United States and Canada. It also opened a dining room to help poor students, which was so popular that over time it became a Ukrainian club. The union's first leader was the pedagogue Rusova; her successor was the civic and political leader Zinaida Mirna (1875[8]–1950).[47]

The Ukrainian Scholarly Congresses in Prague

The Ukrainian academic community organized two scholarly congresses in Prague. The first took place on 3–7 October 1926, and its goal was to summarize the scholarly accomplishments of the Ukrainian scholarly community and develop ties with Ukrainian and other scholarly institutions and academic circles. The Ukrainian Academic Committee initiated the congress. The members of the organizing committee were university professors; they included Horbachevs'kyi, Dnistrians'kyi, Volodymyr Tymoshenko, Simovych, the dendrologist Borys Ivanyts'kyi (1878–1953), Lotots'kyi, and Mirchuk (later replaced by Iakovliv). The participants at the congress were predominantly émigré scholars, joined by a small number of scholars from outside Czechoslovakia.[48]

The congress was held on the premises of Charles University. At the opening, the rector of Charles University, Josef Vančura (1870–1930), and the president of the Czechoslovak Academy of Sciences (Československá akademie věd), Josef Zubatý (1855–1931), were present at the head table. Vančura spoke of the accomplishments of Ukrainian scholarship and wished it well in its further developments. The dean of the Department of Law, Karel Kadlec (1865–1928), the dean of the Department of Medicine, Rudolf Kimla (1866–1950), and the dean of the Philosophy Department, Bedřich Hrozný (1879–1952), were also present at the opening. The congress was attended by Charles University professors Bidlo and Pastrnek and the Slovene scholar Matyáš Murko (1861–1952), among others. Presumably, this attendance at the congress by the Czech professors was an indication that they supported their Ukrainian colleagues, wanted Prague to become the centre of Slavic scholarship, and saw Ukrainians as part of that project.[49]

The congress consisted of the following four sections: historical–philological, law and social sciences, natural sciences, and technical–mathematical. The historical–philological section included the following subsections: history, philology, philosophy and pedagogy, and archaeology and art history. The law and social sciences section had two subsections: law and sociology, and economy and cooperation. The natural sciences section had subsections in natural history, agronomy and forestry, and medicine. The technical–mathematical section had no subsections. The participants included Kolessa, Smal'-Stots'kyi, Dni-strians'kyi, Slavins'kyi, Shelukhin, Iakovliv, and Artymovych, among others. Topics ranged from the theory of history of Rikkert and Ksenopol, delivered by Oleksander Shul'hyn (1889–1960), to the monasteries of Left Bank Ukraine in the seventeenth and eighteenth centuries, delivered by Bidnov, to culture, civilization, and law, delivered by Dnistrians'kyi.[50] Table 10 details the participation of Ukrainian scholars in the congress.

This was the first gathering of Ukrainian scholars in Czechoslovakia. New research in various areas was presented and discussed. It was organized by the émigré academic community, and the Ukrainians needed as much positive attention as they could get.

The second Ukrainian scholarly congress was held in Prague on 20–24 March 1932. It took place in a very different atmosphere from the previous one. The émigrés' hopes of returning home had disappeared,

Table 10. University staff participation at the First Ukrainian Congress in Prague, by section and subsection[51]

Sections and subsections	Meetings	Presentations	Participation in discussions	Panel participants		
				Members	Guests	Total
1. History	5	18	44	79	253	332
2. Philological	4	18	31	47	91	138
3. Philosophic–Pedagogical	3	6	16	15	47	62
4. Archaeology and Art History	2	7	9	20	43	63
5. Legal–Sociological	6	24	42	55	146	201
6. Economy and Cooperation	4	13	41	34	70	104
7. Natural History	3	11	12	30	25	65
8. Agronomy and Forestry	5	17	39	59	135	194
9. Medicine	5	20	23	33	79	112
10. Technical	4	20	10	49	99	148
Total	41	154	267	421	988	1,419

and horrible news was starting to come from Soviet Ukraine about purges of their colleagues and friends. Moreover, the Czechoslovak government assistance program was winding down, and two major institutions of higher learning created by the scholars, the Ukrainian Economic Academy and the Ukrainian Higher Pedagogical Institute, would eventually have to close.

The purpose of this congress was to summarize the accomplishments of Ukrainian émigré scholarship in various fields over the past ten years. There were 137 participants. Among them were not only scholars from the Ukrainian institutions in Czechoslovakia, but also Ukrainian scholars from Germany, Poland, Romania, France, Belgium, and Austria. The congress took place in the building of the Philosophy Department at Charles University. Opening remarks were presented by the vice-rector of Charles University, the dean of the Department of Philosophy, Oldřich Hujer (1880–1942), and a representative of the Institute of Slavic Studies, Miloš Weingart (1890–1939).[52]

In their papers, the scholars outlined the development of Ukrainian émigré scholarship in their respective disciplines. Simovych offered an overview of achievements in linguistics; Bilets'kyi reviewed work in literary studies; Dmytro Chyzhevs'kyi (1894–1977) talked about developments in philosophy; pedagogue and bibliographer Stepan Siropolko (1872–1959) discussed accomplishments in pedagogy; and Antonovych spoke about arts. Ivanyts'kyi provided an overview of developments in forestry studies; doctor of medicine Borys Matiushenko (1883–1944) made an overview of progress in medical science; economist Borys Martos talked about the cooperative movement; and Iakovliv reviewed the field of law.

The congress was accompanied by a book exhibition at the Central Library in Prague (Ústřední knihovna v Praze). It displayed approximately 1,000 titles published by various Ukrainian publishing houses and produced by Ukrainian scholars over the preceding ten years. In addition to congress participants, non-Ukrainian (predominantly Czech) scholars, bibliographers, and bibliophiles attended the exhibition. Congress participants also visited the Museum of the Struggle for the Liberation of Ukraine, an important cultural and scholarly institution founded in 1925, which will be discussed in a later chapter.[53]

To conclude, the Ukrainian Free University in the interwar period was an important part of the life of this scholarly community. Ukrainian intellectuals saw it as their mission to preserve and develop their disciplines. Of no less importance was their task of educating a new generation of Ukrainians, who would become professionals and (in some cases) scholars in their respective fields. The brief revival of Ukrainian scholarship in Soviet Ukraine came to an abrupt and tragic end in the 1930s, thus rendering the role of this émigré university as a Ukrainian institution in the free world even more important. Also significant was that the university functioned in a democratic country that had a friendly and tolerant attitude toward it. Those who came from the former Austro-Hungarian lands had experienced more freedom than those who had arrived from the former Russian empire. In Czechoslovakia, both groups had to prove themselves through intellectual and cultural work. Politics certainly played a role in their lives, but regardless, the intellectuals were able to produce impressive scholarship and work to the best of their abilities. For the first time, they were able to present topics on Ukrainian history, literature, language, and related fields to a broader scholarly world. Along with the dedicated work of the scholars, the support of the Czechoslovak government – and

Masaryk in particular – was crucial; without this assistance, the development of the university would not have been possible.

The process was far from flawless. The Ukrainian émigré scholars could have published more extensively than they did. Also, when the Czechoslovak government decreased subsidies for the university, it could have reorganized itself so as to operate by correspondence and continue to teach selected subjects in this new way. It is true that the activities of its faculty in the 1930s were on a very modest scale relative to their activities in the 1920s. The university did not function in a vacuum, so developments in Europe, and particularly in Czechoslovakia, had an impact. In the 1930s, the rise of nationalistic movements among students and professors, tensions between Czechs and Germans, and the global financial crisis influenced life at the university. Overall, constant financial pressure, infighting, and the émigré environment in general negatively affected the atmosphere at the university. Iaroslav Rudnyts'kyi wrote in a draft of his autobiography that notwithstanding these challenges, in the interwar years, the university was of vital importance for Ukrainian scholarship and culture, as were the excellent qualities of the Ukrainian émigré professors. He added that, based on his experience in various academic institutions, the "bad" and "good" influences in the university were more or less the same as in academic institutions in Europe or North America. Despite its shortcomings, this university was profoundly important to Ukrainian émigré scholarship.[54]

Chapter Three

The Ukrainian Economic Academy in Poděbrady

Establishment

The founding of the Ukrainian Economic Academy in Czechoslovakia was initiated by the Ukrainian Civic Committee. As noted, the committee played an important role in distributing financial assistance from the Czechoslovak government to Ukrainians. Using its contacts in government circles, the committee – led by Shapoval – was vital in establishing the institution as well as providing financial and logistical support in the initial stages of its development. Overall, this committee was instrumental in the life of the Ukrainian émigré community in Czechoslovakia in the 1920s. Besides founding the academy, the committee established several other important institutions, namely the Ukrainian Higher Pedagogical Institute, the Ukrainian secondary education evaluation courses (*matura*), the secondary education evaluation courses in Josefov, the Ukrainian Sociological Institute (Ukrains'kyi instytut hromadoznavstva, 1925–32), the Ukrainian Civic Publishing Fund (Ukrains'kyi hromads'kyi vydavnychyi fond), and the Ukrainian National Museum and Archive, as well as several other professional courses. An important role in the creation of the academy was also played by the All-Ukrainian Union of Agricultural Technicians (Vseukrains'ka spilka sil's'kohospodars'kykh tekhnikiv), which was based in Poland at the time; members of this group were invited to Czechoslovakia to teach in the future institution and created the curriculum. The Czechoslovak government provided generous – indeed, crucial – support to the academy.[1]

The academy's organizing committee was formed in January 1922 with the goal of helping Ukrainian scholars in the Ukrainian lands and abroad. It also aimed to prepare young Ukrainian intellectuals to enter the technical and economic sectors. The committee members included Shapoval, writer and pedagogue Nykyfir Hryhoryiv (1883–1953), doctor of medicine Borys Matiushenko, economist and sociologist Oleksander Mytsiuk (1883–1943), arboriculturist Mykola Kotsiura, economist Borys Martos, civic and political leader Solomon Gol'del'man (1885–1974), pedagogue Ivan Palyvoda (1885–1985), and Mykola Halahan (1882–1955), who was named secretary. The committee engaged in correspondence with the council of the union in Poland, whose members received with enthusiasm the idea of creating the academy and were eager to take part in it. The union included, for example, the expert hydrotechnologist Ivan Shovheniv (1874–1943) and engineer Oleksander Mykhailovs'kyi (1882–1932).[2] For its part, the Czechoslovak government received the idea of a private Ukrainian economic institution positively, although some Czechs as well as Ukrainians were opposed to it. Their argument was that the Ukrainians did not have enough qualified people to teach at such an institution. Czech professors from the Higher Agronomic and Forestry School (Vyšší agronomická a lesnická škola) in Prague proposed establishing separate Ukrainian departments within the Czech Higher Technical University in Prague (České vysoké učení technické), which would teach in areas relevant to the Ukrainian economy. After various issues were resolved, initial opposition was overcome; the initiative to establish an independent Ukrainian technical school gained the government's support, and on 25 February 1922, Masaryk warmly received the delegation.[3]

Several cities and towns across Czechoslovakia were considered for the location of the future academy: Chrudim in eastern Bohemia, Tábor in southern Bohemia, and Roudnice (now Roudnice nad Labem) in the north, as well as Brno, the capital of Moravia. Brno was especially seriously discussed, as the idea was to establish the academy within the Higher Agronomic School in Brno (Vysoká škola zemědělská v Brně). However, the time was ripe for the opening of the academy, and any delay threatened to void the undertaking altogether. So the committee acted quickly and decided to temporarily open the academy in Poděbrady, a spa town near Prague, and later transfer it to Brno.[4]

The civic committee developed a statute for the institution. In April, it had received confirmation from the Ministry of Agriculture that the submitted statute would be approved, thus enabling the activities to start immediately. The first joint meeting of the professors, who were appointed by the organizing committee, had taken place earlier, on 28 April 1922. The agriculture ministry approved the institution and signed the decree that established the private Ukrainian Economic Academy in Czechoslovakia on 16 May 1922. However, disagreements arose quickly regarding how to interpret certain rights and obligations, and this led to issues between the committee and the academy's faculty council. The institution was granted independent status by the foreign ministry on 28 August 1923; from that point on it dealt with the government directly, without the committee as mediator. On 23 May 1925, a new statute was enacted that transformed the academy into an institution of higher learning with a four-year program, and with Ukrainian and Czech as the languages of instruction.[5]

Goals

The aim of the academy was to prepare students to participate in the future economic development of an independent Ukraine by educating them in various technical fields. It also intended to gather Ukrainian scholars in those fields, thereby creating a centre of Ukrainian scholarship.This technical academy would train agronomists, forestry specialists, statisticians, technologists, economists, and others. Moreover, the academy sought to create not only highly skilled professionals but also well-rounded and competent individuals. The founding of the academy in Czechoslovakia – a country with a developed economic culture – was a sterling opportunity for Ukrainians to learn from the best practices of the Czech economy. This was extremely important for the academy's development and success.[6]

Besides preparing a new generation of professionals in a variety of fields, the academy took on an additional mission – to develop technical and economic fields theoretically and create a new professional literature in Ukrainian. At that time, science textbooks in the Ukrainian language were almost non-existent. Future students would require them, so the production of textbooks in various technical fields was an extremely important task for the professors. For lecturers, creating textbooks in their fields was a prerequisite for promotion, with the result that many textbooks were written in a variety of fields during the school's first year of operation alone. Terminology presented a considerable challenge and would need to be established. To that end, terminological committees were created in every department, after which a single common committee was struck, led by renowned civic leader and philanthropist Ievhen Chykalenko (1861–1929). This committee included Ukrainian-language experts Valeria O'Konnor-Vilins'ka (1866–1930) and Modest Levyts'kyi (1866–1932).[7]

While visiting Poděbrady on 9 May 1923, President Masaryk visited the academy, where he was warmly welcomed by the teaching staff and students. It was an opportunity for the academy to show the president its efforts and achievements and to express profound gratitude to the Czechoslovak government for its support. In his brief speech, Masaryk expressed satisfaction that the government had been able to implement Slavic programs and help support the undertakings of Slavic nations.[8]

Structure and Study Program

From 1922 until 1928, regarding the organization of its programs of study, the academy was subordinate to the Education Department of the Ministry of Agriculture. At the same time, it reported to the foreign ministry on all administrative and organizational matters, and that ministry also provided financial assistance and scholarships to underprivileged students. After 1928, the academy reported only to the agriculture ministry, which also approved decrees regarding the professional development training certification of the teaching staff as well as elections for administrative positions. However, the academy enjoyed a high degree of autonomy in its academic affairs and administration. Its management was built on democratic principles; the highest governing body was the council of professors, with faculty affairs falling under the professorial councils of the academy's three departments. As the executive body, the senate oversaw administrative and economic matters; it consisted of the rector, the vice-rector, three deans, and the secretary of the professorial council. The academy applied the best practices of the Czechoslovak technical schools, while tailoring its curriculum to the needs of Ukrainian lands. This institution, like other Ukrainian institutions of higher learning in Czechoslovakia, always hoped its students would to return home. Thus, the academy's departments were created with an eye to the economic and technical needs of various Ukrainian lands, for which it prepared its graduates.[9]

The academy had three departments: Agriculture and Forestry, Economics and Cooperative (which included a statistics section), and Engineering, composed of the hydro-technical and chemical-technological sections. Overall, there were fifty-nine subdivisions: nineteen in the Department of Agriculture and Forestry, twenty in the Department of Economics and Cooperatives, and twenty in the Department of Engineering. Table 11 provides information about these departments and their offices (*kabinet*) and laboratories.

Supplementary units at the academy included a terminology committee, a forestry nursery, a meteorological station, a tractor garage, a training consumer cooperative, and a training credit cooperative. In addition to seminars in various subjects, the academy offered special classes (*lektury*) in foreign languages, among other additional classes. The duration of the program was four academic years, divided into eight semesters. Students who finished the entire program and who passed their exams received the title of engineer, with their area of expertise specified: economist, forester, agronomist, technologist, or hydraulic engineer. In addition, students had the option of continuing their studies and receiving a

Table 11. Offices and laboratories at the academy[10]

Offices (*kabinety*)	
Botany and Bacteriology	Meteorology
Construction	Mechanical Wood Technology
Application of Hydropower	Local Self-Government
Geodesy	Public-Sector Husbandry
Geology and Mineralogy	Forest Preservation and Hunting
Hydraulic Engineering	Private-Sector Husbandry
Graphostatics	Bookkeeping
Entomology and Zoology	Statistics
Breeding – General and Specialized	Agricultural Economy and Statistics
Draftsmanship	Agricultural Engineering
Cooperation	Science of Commodities
Forestry Estimation	Physics
Forestry Exploitation	Animal Physiology and Anatomy
Forest Disposition	Physical Chemistry
Forestry and Dendrology – General and Specialized	Chemical Technology
Engineering	Husbandry – General and Specialized
Melioration	
Laboratories	
Pedology	Fermentation Chemical Engineering
Agrochemistry	Technical and Chemical Analysis
Analytical Chemistry (Qualitative Analysis)	Leather Processing
Analytical Chemistry (Quantitative Analysis)	Organic Chemistry
Chemical Preparation	Physics and Electrical Engineering
Technical Mycology	Dairy Production
Sugar Production	Geology

doctorate in economics, agronomy, forestry, or technical sciences, after defending their dissertation and passing the exams.[11]

Finance

The Czechoslovak government's subsidies for the academy varied every year, for they were tied to the needs of the academy as well as to the overall Czechoslovak budget earmarked for assisting émigrés. In the first year, the academy received 70,000 crowns of financial support monthly; the subsidies were increased to 250,000 crowns in 1927.[12] In this peak year of the academy's activities, by which time the organizational process had been completed and normal operations had begun, the academy's expenses, including student scholarships, were 2,777,848 crowns (a little over US$84,000). The professors themselves made much of the laboratory equipment, which helped save money. After 1928, the financial assistance started to decrease, and the academy was prohibited from accepting new students and ordered to prepare for a slow closure. By 1931, annual assistance for the academy had decreased to 1.6 million crowns and the estimated cost of all its inventoried property was 1.573 million crowns; the most valuable assets were the library and the geodesy, botany, physics, and chemistry labs. The academy's true wealth, however, was non-monetary, held in various systematically created collections and their utility for the academy's learning process.[13]

Students also received financial support from various organizations that the academy's staff and students had themselves created. Especially noteworthy were the activities of the Charitable Relief Committee (Blahodiino-dopomohovyi komitet), which raised funds from Ukrainians in or outside Czechoslovakia. In reality, however, those funds were raised from individuals close to the academy: professors, staff, and the students themselves. The first two voluntarily imposed deductions from their salaries in order to help poor students. Between 1926 and 1931, 530,000 crowns were collected in this way: 52.3 per cent from professors and staff, 10.6 per cent from students, and 19.9 per cent in the form of subsidies from the academy and affiliated organizations. Only 17.2 per cent was raised from other Ukrainians, with Bukovynians was the most generous in their donations. Another organization that assisted students was the Student Support Committee (Komitet dopomohy studentam), which operated in accordance with the budget approved by the academy's financial committee. This committee – the members of which were professors and students – provided students with clothing, arranged medical assistance for them, helped their families, and provided them with small loans. Also, alumni of the academy established a scholarship to enable students without means to study.[14]

Faculty

The academy's teaching staff consisted of professors, assistant professors, lecturers, assistants, auxiliaries, and technical staff. The professors and assistant professors possessed higher education degrees in their fields. Most of the other teaching personnel had obtained higher education qualifications in Czechoslovakia. Several obstacles to staff expansion were encountered besides financial ones: it was difficult to find appropriate staff for the academy's programs due to the thin ranks of the Ukrainian scientific force. Over time, however, the staff numbers grew. By 1928, the teaching staff consisted of 25 professors, 21 assistant professors, 16 lecturers, and 10 assistants. From 1922 to 1932, the academy had 118 teaching staff, of whom 92 were from the Ukrainian lands and 26 were Czechs. At its height, the academy had 96 teaching staff.[15]

Most of the teaching staff had participated in the events of 1917–21 in Ukraine, and some had been members of the government of the Ukrainian People's Republic. Among the faculty were statistician Fedir Shcherbyna, economist Valentyn Sadovs'kyi (1886–1945), geodesist Leonid Hrabyna (1885–1971), agronomist Viktor Domanyts'kyi (1893–1962), chemist Serhii Komarets'kyi (1881–1952), and cooperative organizer Serhii Borodaievs'kyi (1870–1942). In Czechoslovakia, they were building the academy and providing education to students who, at least initially, consisted largely of former soldiers. These former politicians, having fallen short in their efforts to found an independent country, now tried to educate these former soldiers and thereby create experts for a future independent Ukraine. As Rusova recalls in her memoirs:

> Many professors who taught at the academy often did not have any teaching experience in a higher learning institution; some of them did not even speak Ukrainian. But these people tackled books and became immersed in them with youthful enthusiasm, whole nights they were working on preparing their lectures and working on their latest scientific discoveries, which they enthusiastically presented to their audience. So far from Ukraine, Ukrainian science grew in a small Czech resort. For that we feel eternal gratitude to the organizers of the academy and to the Czechoslovak government that financed its development. In three or four years, very valuable work has been accomplished in the form of textbooks for high schools that interested also other scientists. [Also], collections for zoology, geology, forestry and other fields were created, which surprised even the Americans, who came to Czechoslovakia to examine various cultural institutions.[16]

The teaching staff lived modestly. Each professor received 1,800 crowns a month, assistant professors 1,500 crowns, and lecturers 1,200 crowns, which was quite modest. For professors and associate professors, that was the equivalent of 48 and 41 US dollars, respectively. The ministry transferred funds to the academy each month, and the professors determined their own salaries and other expenses. Assigning themselves minimal salaries allowed them to hire more people.[17]

The rectors throughout the academy's years of operation were the scientist and engineer Ivan Shovheniv, the forester Borys Ivanyts'ky, and professor of construction Serhii Tymoshenko (1881–1950). The first rector, Shovheniv, was born in the Kharkiv region. From 1893 to 1899, he studied at the Institute of Transport (Institut putei soobshcheniia) in St Petersburg. He also studied in Germany and the United States. For eleven years, he worked on or led a variety of hydro projects on various rivers in the Russian empire, and he later became the state inspector of shipping. Shovheniv was more than a good practitioner; he was also a theoretician who produced many works in his field. In 1917 he moved to Kyiv and accepted the post of director of the Water Department in the Ukrainian People's Republic government. Over several years at that post, he organized Ukraine's water management while simultaneously serving as a professor at the Polytechnic School in Kyiv. After the Bolsheviks established their rule, along with other members of the government, he moved to Czechoslovakia, where he served as rector of the Ukrainian Economic Academy between 1922 and 1928. At the same time, he taught as a guest professor at the Czech Higher Technical University. During this period he published extensively, producing technical books and textbooks in Ukrainian, including the following: *Analitychna heometriia na ploshchi* (Analytical Geometry of Two Dimensions, 1923), published in Poděbrady; *Hydravlyka. Ch. 1. Hydrostatyka* (Hydraulics. Part 1. Hydrostatics, 1923), also published in Poděbrady; and *Hidravlika pidzemnykh vod* (Ground-Water Hydraulics, 1929), published in Prague. After the academy closed, he moved to Poland, where he worked as a contract inspector for melioration projects until his death in 1943.[18]

Another rector of the academy, Ivanyts'kyi, was born in 1878 in Sumy, a town founded by Cossacks in the mid-seventeenth century. His father was an agronomist from the gentry, his mother was a Ukrainized Pole. From 1897 to 1902, Ivanyts'kyi studied at the St Petersburg Forestry Institute (Sankt-Peterburgskii lesnoi institut), where he specialized in arboriculture. While there, he joined a number of student organizations, with which he participated in demonstrations until he was arrested. In St Petersburg, he took up the Ukrainian cause and joined the Ukrainian Student Hromada (Ukrains'ka students'ka hromada). In 1901, he was sent to Poltava, where he established close ties with local pro-Ukrainian individuals. Until 1917, he worked as a forester, primarily in the northern part of the Kyiv region. He gained considerable experience in forestry, and in 1907 Prosvita in Kyiv published his work, which became the first work on forestry published in Ukrainian. At that time, he was also a member of a forestry society in Kyiv that held meetings and offered professional lectures on various topics. During the revolutionary years 1917 to 1920, Ivanyts'kyi, along with Shapoval, established the Forestry Department of the Ukrainian People's Republic government. Taking an active part in the reorganization of forestry in the new Ukraine, Ivanyts'kyi planned several congresses for foresters. After the Ukrainian national revolution failed, he fled to Vinnytsia and then to Kam'ianets'-Podil's'kyi in Ukraine before ending up in Tarnów in Poland. There, a union of former ministers was created, of which he became head. Ivanyts'kyi helped develop a plan for a two- or three-year economic school, which later served as the template for the academy in Poděbrady. He contacted Shapoval at the civic committee with this plan and the idea of organizing a technical school, providing a list of union members who might staff the planned institution. Later, along with Shovheniv and others, he was invited to teach in the new establishment. There, he served as rector, vice-rector, and dean of the Forestry Department. He taught dendrology, forestry, and forest policy, besides taking on some teaching in forest protection.[19]

Another rector of the academy was Serhii Tymoshenko, who was born in the Chernihiv region in 1881. He finished his schooling in the Poltava region and studied at the Institute of Civil Engineers in St Petersburg, where he belonged to the Hromada and participated in Ukrainian life. After finishing his studies in 1906, he moved to Kovel, in the Volhynia region, and then to Kyiv. In 1909, he relocated to Kharkiv, where he served as chief architect for the North-Donetsk' Railways. In this most productive period of his life he designed many buildings in and around Kharkiv, and during this time received ten architectural awards. Tymoshenko saw his mission as the restoration of the old Ukrainian style in architecture. In 1917, when the revolution broke out, he became an official in the Kharkiv region and later fought with the army of the Ukrainian People's Republic's. Between 1921 and 1924 he lived in L'viv, where he worked on several projects, including a hotel on Potots'ky Street and the redesign of a church in that city's Levandivka district. With his family, Tymoshenko came to Poděbrady in 1924, where he taught architecture and agricultural construction. His lectures were well structured and informative, and he got along well with his students, dedicating considerable amounts of time to them. In 1930, he returned to Lutsk, a city in the Volhynia region, where he worked on many architectural projects close to his heart. He survived the war and emigrated to the United States in 1946, settling in California. Over the course of his life, he designed more than four hundred buildings and complexes in cities where Ukrainians lived, not only in Ukraine, but also in Canada, in Toronto, Edmonton, Saskatoon, and Vancouver.[20]

These three rectors differed in their backgrounds, personalities, and professional fields, but in some ways they were also similar. All were born in eastern Ukraine, which at the time was part of the Russian empire. All of them studied their professions in St Petersburg and then worked for many years in their respective fields in different parts of the empire. Shovheniv worked in the central region of the Russian empire; Ivanyts'kyi and Tymoshenko spent their professional careers in the Ukrainian lands. In Poděbrady, all three contributed greatly to the academy's development.

It is interesting to note that twenty-six of the professors at the academy were Czechs. They had been invited to teach there because in some fields there were no experts among the Ukrainian émigrés. Their presence was also meant to develop and strengthen professional ties between Czechs and Ukrainians. Among these Czech scholars were the Czech Higher Technical University professor of forestry and dendrology Vilibald Ševčík (1890–1945), the Czech Higher Technical University professor of the history of cooperation and cooperative law Antonín Hůlka (1892–?), and Karel Dusl (1884–1948), a mathematician and professor at the same institution. One of the Czech professors was the renowned chemist, physiologist, and biologist Julius Stoklasa (1857–1936). Well-known in the field of agricultural chemistry and biology, Stoklasa contributed to the organization of higher education in agriculture in Czechoslovakia. He was founder and first dean of the Department of Agronomy at the Czech Higher Technical University and founder of the Czechoslovak Agricultural Academy. At the academy, he taught agrochemistry and a course titled New Ideas in Agronomy.[21]

Almost fifty years later, one of the students of the academy, Valentyn Simiantsiv (1899–1992), recalled in his memoirs the Czech professor Rudolf Kukač (1889–1957), who taught ferroconcrete at the Czech Higher Technical University in Prague and was a very good teacher, although a demanding one. Simiantsiv also remembered another Czech professor, Jan Vladimír Hráský (1857–1939), who came from a Czech family in Galicia. Hrásky was widely recognized in Czechoslovakia as an expert in hydrology as well as an engineer, balneologist, and architect. To his students, Hrásky often recalled the land of his birth and expressed his warm feelings toward Ukrainians. Simiantsiv also mentioned Czech professor Theodor Ježdík (1889–1967), who taught hydrotechnics, and passed on as much of his knowledge as possible to his students.[22]

There were other Czechs teachers at the academy, including soil scientist Vladimír Kosil (pseud. Vladimír Gössl (1898–1977)); one of the republic's leading forestry experts, Vojtěch Kaisler (1870–1943); and doctor and veterinarian Theodor Kašpárek (1864–1930). Over time, as the Czech professors at the academy became familiar with the work of the Ukrainian professors, they established respectful and friendly relations with them. Whether the Czech professors taught at the academy for career, financial, or other reasons, they did their jobs well and left a significant mark on the lives and professional growth of their students. It is noteworthy that professional collaboration took place between the Czech and Ukrainian scientists and engineers.

Students

The composition of academy's students changed over the years. Initially, they were former soldiers of the Ukrainian People's Republic and the Western Ukrainian People's Republic, as well as the children of members of former governments, so the academy was largely an émigré institution. After 1926, more and more Ukrainian students from Galicia and Volhynia came to study because there were no Ukrainian institutions of higher learning in Polish-ruled Galicia, and especially none that provided a technical education. There were also some students from the Kuban region.[23]

Many of the former soldiers had fled the internee camps in Poland in the hope of finding support in liberal Czechoslovakia. These young men had had their educations interrupted by the war, and those who had already graduated often found that their documents had gone missing during the turbulent years. In 1922, to prepare these young people for further studies, secondary education courses were created in order to qualify them for higher institutions. The director of these courses was professor of mathematics Ievhen Ivanenko (1883–1941). A few years later, the courses were terminated, but those who had yet to take those exams could do so at the academy in the presence of a representative of the Czechoslovak education ministry. The Czechoslovak government, besides subsidizing the academy and other institutions, tried to maintain some form of control over the professional and educational level of students entering them. After finishing the courses, students went on to Ukrainian or Czechoslovak schools. Those who wanted to study in schools that were tailored towards the future needs of Ukraine went to Ukrainian schools. Some students chose to study fields that the academy did not offer and sought diplomas from Czechoslovak institutions of higher learning.[24]

A total of 786 students enrolled in the academy, with their numbers divided fairly equally among the three departments. In the years with the highest activities, 1926 and 1927, 613 students studied there. With the agreement and support of the Czechoslovak government, the academy gathered Ukrainian youth not only from Czechoslovakia but also from Poland, Romania, Yugoslavia, Bulgaria, Germany, Austria, Latvia, and Turkey. Most of the students were Ukrainians, but some Belarusians, Czechs, and Jews studied there as well. Of special interest is the case of the Belarusians; they did not have their own school, so they often studied at the Ukrainian one. Overall, 559 students graduated from the academy.[25]

Some statistics are available on Ukrainian, Belarusian, and Georgian students in Czechoslovakia from 1919 to mid-1924. These data tell us the student composition during the earlier stages of the academy's existence. Out of 1,824 surveyed students, 45.6 per cent came from Galicia and 42.6 per cent from Dnieper Ukraine; 91.6 per cent were men and only 8.4 per cent were women. During these years, only 32.3 per cent of students entered the country legally with visas, while 64.3 per cent came without. In these years, 82.5 per cent of the men who enrolled at the academy were single; married men constituted only 12.3 per cent. During that time, 52 per cent of the students had had their higher education interrupted as a result of war mobilization; 15 per cent as a result of the war for independence, and 13 per cent for both reasons. Overall, 80 per cent of students had had to pause their education. In Czechoslovakia, almost two thirds of the surveyed students chose to receive higher technical education. Student health during that period was a great concern, especially for those who had lung catarrh or tuberculosis, who constituted 36.5 per cent of the surveyed students. There were also the war-wounded, who of course required extra care. According to the same survey, 61.6 per cent of the students reported poor health.[26]

The students who received scholarships to the academy were required upon graduation to work in the Ukrainian lands one and a half years for every year they had spent there. Kateryna Antonovych recalled that students studied hard and had to pass all their exams each semester. If they did not pass their tests, scholarships were not paid to them. She also remembered that relations between professors and students were open and sincere.[27] During summers, students worked or took apprenticeships in various industries to obtain hands-on experience. Future hydro-technologists found apprenticeships on construction sites; future technologists practised their craft in factories. In addition, students took occasional part-time jobs in the academy's laboratories and offices. Simiantsiv recalled in his memoir that the Ukrainian students had not expected the warm welcome they received in Czechoslovakia. He recalled that during their apprenticeships the students worked not only for the money but also because they were truly interested in obtaining new skills, and they did their jobs well. They also worked on construction and in other fields to complement their modest incomes.[28]

Naturally, there were many moments in the lives of these young people that were unrelated to study or work. The hopes of Ukrainian students to return home were high in the 1920s but had waned by the 1930s, and this certainly affected them. Rusova in her memoir recalled instances of suicide and alcoholism; Simiantsiv recalled that one student shot himself and that another poisoned himself as a result of unrequited love for a Czech woman. Simiantsiv recalled several get-togethers, which were attended by students from various Slavic nations – Czechs, Serbs, Croats, Bulgarians, Slovaks, and Slovenes – during his early years in Czechoslovakia. As for Czech society in Poděbrady, Ukrainian students did not manage to assimilate. Simiantsiv wrote that this was mainly because the Ukrainians did not try hard enough; another reason was their poverty.[29]

Some students – especially those with considerable talent for their fields – devoted themselves fully to their studies. The academy saw it as one of its tasks to prepare new scientists and teachers for institutions of higher learning in Ukraine. Scholarships were established at the academy to support these young students, who were eager to do scholarly work; twenty-four of these scholarship holders later joined the academy's staff. Some of them continued their research after finishing at the academy, some wrote many scholarly and professional works, and some were esteemed researchers in various research institutes.[30]

Fifty organizations were active at the academy over the years. Nine were of a scholarly and professional nature, ten educational, twelve economic, and nineteen related to culture or sports. Some of these organizations included only professors, some only students, and some both, and alumni of the academy often remained members. These organizations, which arranged discussions, performances, lectures, and concerts, greatly enriched the lives of students and their teachers. Some of these organizations established contacts with other Ukrainian, Czechoslovak, and international organizations. Examples of the latter included the Society for the League of Nations (Tovarystvo dlia Lihy Natsii) in the international Union for the League of Nations, and the Union of Organizations of Ukrainian Émigré Engineers Abroad (Soiuz orhanizatsii inzheneriv ukraintsiv na emihratsii), in which alumni and various organizations took active roles. Likewise, the Ukrainian Sokil Society (Tovarystvo "Ukrains'kyi Sokil") had some contact with the Czechoslovak and other Slavic Sokil societies. These organizations also undertook some publishing activities, though their efforts were not sustained. Examples include *Nasha hromada* (Our Community) – the student organ of the Academic Community (Akademichna hromada), and *Ukrains'kyi ekonomist* (Ukrainian Economics) – the organ the Society of Ukrainian Economists (Tovarystvo ukrains'kykh ekonomistiv).[31]

After graduation, some of the young engineers found employment in Galicia, Volhynia, and the Transcarpathian region. They helped significantly improve regional agriculture, especially in Galicia. Other economists and financiers worked in Czechoslovakia, Poland, and later in the United States and Canada. According to the available data, as of 1931, the engineers were working in sixteen countries: 189 in Czechoslovakia (including the Transcarpathian region), 185 in Poland (including Galicia), 14 in the United States, 11 in France, 6 in Germany, 5 in Soviet Ukraine, 5 in Canada, 4 in Romania, 3 in China, 2 in Brazil, 2 in Argentina, and 1 in each of Bulgaria, Belgium, Luxemburg, Lithuania, and Switzerland. In all of these countries they built reputations for themselves as knowledgeable professionals, which boosted the academy's reputation in the Ukrainian lands and beyond. Notwithstanding the difficulties of émigré life, the academy had allowed them to establish a solid base for their future lives as professionals and as human beings. This school had created a learning environment for them – something that would not have been possible in their homeland.[32]

Scholarly Activities

The academy's professors and lecturers took part in many conferences in Czechoslovakia and abroad. Examples are abundant. In Czechoslovakia, Isaak Mazepa (1884–1952) participated in the Czechoslovak Congress of Natural Scientists and Doctors; Domanyts'kyi presented at the International Agricultural Congress in Prague; the agronomist Volodymyr Cherediiv (1885–1961) participated in the International Congress of Slavic Botanists in Prague; and Hrabyna took part in the International Scholarly Congress of Geodesy and Geographic Union in Prague in 1927. In April 1932, Borodaievs'kyi participated in the International Congress of Middle Class in Prague. Academy professors also took part in the International Economic Conference in 1928 in Prague. Professors tried to participate in conferences in other countries as well. For instance, in 1924, professors Martos and Borodaievs'kyi represented the academy at the Eleventh Congress of the International Cooperative Alliance in Ghent, Belgium. Hrabyna took part in the International Congress of Surveyors in Paris in 1926. In October 1932, Borodaievs'kyi took part in the Conference of Founders of International Scholarly Co-operative Institute in Basel, where he was admitted as a member. In addition, members of the

Society of Ukrainian Engineers (Tovarystvo ukrains'kykh inzheneriv) took part in the Congress of Slavic Engineers.[33]

Many of the academy's scholars participated in the two Ukrainian congresses, which were held in 1926 and 1932. At the first congress, there were five sections and subsections in which they participated: economics and cooperatives, natural sciences, agronomics and forestry, medical sciences, and technical and mathematical sciences. Altogether, there were 21 scholarly meetings in these sections and subsections, with 81 papers presented, discussions in which 125 individuals took part, and an overall turnout of 623 attendees.[34] Table 12 details academy's scholars participation.

While some participants spoke on more general subjects, especially in the medical, technical, and mathematical sections and subsections, the topics of many other presenters were strongly linked to Ukraine and its future development. Hrabyna spoke about geodesic samples in Ukraine, Ivanyts'kyi delivered a paper that focused on the main tasks of foresters in Ukraine based on developments in Central European forestry, Matiushenko focused on the health of Ukrainians and the impact of the war and revolution on it. Clearly, the scholars were still very much concerned with developments in the future Ukraine and tailored their research toward these.

At the second congress, in 1932, when the political situation was very different, the professors focused on summarizing their work in emigration. They delivered nine papers that were reviews of their previous

Table 12. Academy scholars at the First Ukrainian Congress, 3–7 October 1926[35]

Sections and subsections	Meetings	Presentations	Participation in discussions	Panel participants		
				Members	Guests	Total
1. Economics and cooperatives	4	13	41	34	70	104
2. Natural sciences	3	11	12	30	25	65
3. Agronomics and forestry	5	17	39	59	135	194
4. Medical sciences	5	20	23	33	79	112
5. Technical sciences	4	20	10	49	99	148
Total	21	81	125	205	408	623

ten years' work in various disciplines. For instance, Komarets'kyi talked about the work of émigré chemists in theoretical and applied chemistry, Martos reported on work undertaken in the field of cooperative movements, hygienist Vsevolod Harmashiv (1863–1953) described developments in the field of natural sciences, and Cherediiv talked about émigré scholars' work in the field of agronomy. These comprehensive reports highlighted the achievements of the émigré scholars and scientists; they also provided a more general picture of activities in their respective areas in the Ukrainian émigré scholarly community.[36] The scholars participated in these congresses because they believed they were significant for the development of Ukrainian scholarship and their own fields. How important they were for the outside world is a separate matter. The language of these two congresses was Ukrainian (although the participants knew other languages), which indicates that the presentations were geared not for outsiders but for the Ukrainian émigré community.

The academy encouraged its teaching staff to expand their knowledge and made it possible for them to obtain books for the library as well as devices and materials for laboratories and offices. This was mainly possible in the first years, when the academy's funding was at its highest. At that time, several faculty members and lecturers conducted research trips around Czechoslovakia and abroad. Sixty-one research trips were undertaken between 1924 and 1927: 35 from the Department of Agriculture and Forestry, 10 from the Department of Economics and Cooperative, and 16 from the Department of Engineering. Many research trips were undertaken on the scholars' own initiative and were paid for from their personal funds. Many undertook research trips to study forests in Czechoslovakia and in the Transcarpathian region. Petro Andriievs'kyi (1880–1945) went to France to familiarize himself with new soil analysis methods; Cherediiv spent time in Moravia and Slovakia to learn about agricultural machinery; and agronomist Irodion Sheremetyns'kyi (1873–1937) travelled to various Czechoslovakian lands to learn more about stockbreeding. They also conducted research in tree nurseries and in offices of the Agriculture and Forestry Department.[37]

The first four or five years of the academy's existence were the organizational years, during which the teaching staff published 165 textbooks. As noted above, this was of crucial importance for the students, for it enabled them to learn their subjects in Ukrainian. Almost all of the textbooks published at that time were the first textbooks in the Ukrainian language in their respective disciplines. Shovheniv, Borodaievs'kyi, Ivanyts'kyi, Shcherbyna, and many others wrote the textbooks for their courses in their respective fields. In the second decade of the academy (after its reorganization), when the need for textbooks was less demanding, the scientists focused largely on writing monographs or articles.[38] When the works of the academy professors became known to their colleagues outside of the academy, and after they had attended international conferences and published in scholarly and scientific journals, their prestige increased in their professional world. In particular, the professors' presentation of their works at the Chicago World's Fair had a great impact on the academy's image.[39]

Outreach

The academy's teaching staff made efforts to reach out to Czechoslovak society. The opening of the academy in a little spa town was certainly surprising for its inhabitants, for it soon filled the town with students speaking a language they could not understand but that was somehow similar to their own. At some point, the senate of the academy delegated to Martos the task of organizing a series of public lectures in the Czech language to inform the locals about Ukrainian issues. Bochkovs'kyi was very helpful to him; he had lived in Prague for many years, was fluent in Czech, and had developed a broad network of Czech political and literary figures. Of special interest for the audience was a lecture on the influence of the Czech enlighteners on Ukrainians, featuring Karel Havlíček Borovský (1821–1856), and another about Masaryk. Simiantsiv recalled that every year the academy organized parties in Poděbrady, to which they invited the town's most influential people.[40] In addition, a small book in the Czech language was published in Poděbrady titled *Ukrajinská hospodářská akademie v Č.S.R.: soukromý ústav s vysokoškolskou organisací: 16. IV. 1922–1926* (Ukrainian Economic Academy in the Č.S.R.: Private Institute of Higher Education: 16. IV. 1922–1926). This book was aimed at a Czechoslovak audience and highlighted the academy's goals and faculty. The impact of the book was uncertain, but its intent was clearly stated: to explain the academy's work and build connections between the two peoples.

Reorganization of the Academy

In 1931, anticipating the abolition of the academy, the professors founded the Society of Supporters of the Ukrainian Economic Academy (Tovarystvo prykhyl'nykiv Ukrains'koi hospodars'koi akademii). This charitable organization intended to collect funds by means of membership fees and fundraising among Ukrainians who lived both in the Ukrainian lands and in the emigration. However, it soon became evident that the society would be unable to collect the funds needed to save and sustain the academy, largely because of the evolving economic crisis. So the professors decided to organize a school in which all educational processes would be conducted by correspondence. Thus, on 12 November 1932, the Ukrainian Technical-Economic Institute (Ukrains'kyi tekhnichno-hospodars'kyi instytut) was founded, offering correspondence-based learning. Like its predecessor, it provided education to students in all Ukrainian lands and to Ukrainian émigrés. The society promoted the idea of the Ukrainian polytechnic institute by running articles in various publications as well as disseminating brochures and press releases. In the first six years of its existence the society managed to collect 283,800 crowns, of which 223,600 were given to the institute; this served as its financial base and constituted half its budget. In 1936, Bochkovs'kyi, the society's head, travelled to Canada with a mission to raise funds for the institute. He visited Ontario, Manitoba, Saskatchewan, and Alberta and delivered more than one hundred lectures. Bochkovs'kyi encountered many friends of the institute and was able to collect many donations.[41]

The Ukrainian Technical-Economic Institute's objectives were stated thus: to produce highly qualified professionals in economics and the technical fields, to provide individuals with experience to enhance their knowledge in their fields, and to promote the expansion of technical knowledge among Ukrainians. Ivanyts'kyi was the institute's director from 1932 to 1936, Martos from 1936 to 1937, and jurist Luka Bych (1870–1945) from 1937 to 1939. It had the same structure as the academy, comprising departments of Economics and Cooperative Studies, Agronomy and Forestry, and Engineering, with the first of these being the most popular. It eventually restructured itself in response to students' demands, establishing additional courses in accounting, foreign languages, and radio technology, among others. For a very modest fee, the professors sent their students lectures and textbooks, as well as instructions for hands-on exercises. In its first two years, the institute mailed out 4,287 letters and 6,799 parcels, which indicates the intensity of the learning process. It is of note that around 80 per cent of the students were from the western Ukrainian lands, while the institute received around 80 per cent of its funding from Ukrainians in emigration. Between 1932 to 1937, 749 students signed up for the institute's courses.[42]

The closing of the Ukrainian Economic Academy in Poděbrady was a misfortune for its professors, who had devoted themselves so deeply to the academy and had built it from scratch. Its closing was no less painful for the students, who lost their first higher polytechnic institution. Both professors and students were forced to curtail their activities at the zenith of their academic success. The cessation of government funding was partly a consequence of the world economic crisis. Also playing a role was the waning of hope that the Soviet Union would collapse; it seems there was no longer a need to prepare professionals for work in Ukraine that remained part of it. Nevertheless, the professors succeeded quite well at reorganizing the academy and would continue for decades to educate young people in their fields of expertise via correspondence. Despite having to cease operations, the academy's founders did accomplish their goal in creating the first generation of the Ukrainian technical intelligentsia. In emigration, they managed to build the academy based on the long-tested structure of technical institutions in Europe. They created the first Ukrainian scholarly centre in technical disciplines, where scholars wrote monographs, articles, and textbooks. They also transferred their knowledge to future generations of students, many of whom considered their years in Poděbrady the best of their lives. After the war, many of the students were able to develop their knowledge in their countries of settlement, particularly in Canada and the United States. As Rusova stated in her memoir, "the Ukrainian Economic Academy is one of the creations that will always be in the history of Ukrainian culture as a vivid manifestation of creative forces of the Ukrainian intelligentsia."[43]

Chapter Four

The Ukrainian Higher Pedagogical Institute

Establishment

The Ukrainian Higher Pedagogical Institute, named after Mykhailo Drahomanov, was another important institution of higher learning created by Ukrainians. In 1923 in Prague, it was founded by the Ukrainian Civic Committee, and Beneš, Girsa, and the education minister Rudolf Bechyně (1881–1948) reportedly supported it. The government's positive response was likely in accordance with the current policies of the Czechoslovak government and with Masaryk's deep convictions regarding the fundamental role that education served for individuals and societies. In one of his prewar speeches in the Austrian Parliament, Masaryk had directly addressed the Ukrainian deputies, urging them to continue to develop schools and educate their people. As the son of a coachman who became a world-renowned figure and the president of a young democracy, Masaryk greatly valued education. He was convinced that, as he put, "the development of democracy is closely tied to the development of education." Also, the fact that the initiator of the institute was the Ukrainian Civic Committee, which was supported by the government, influenced the government's positive response to the idea of creating the institute.[1]

Goals

The faculty of the institution saw its mission as to provide theoretical and practical knowledge for future teachers in Ukrainian schools in a variety of disciplines. However, over the course of its existence, the institute's aims changed along with its status. Initially de facto a pedagogical institute, it aimed to prepare educators for teaching in the higher grades of primary schools and lower grades of gymnasiums as well as in teachers' colleges. Graduates were also expected to be able to teach general subjects in technical schools. Another of its goals was to prepare qualified administrators for Ukrainian schools and educational institutions. When the institute was transformed into a higher institution, that mission changed, to one of preparing teachers for high school classes in secondary schools; its subjects were now the Ukrainian language, literature, and history as well as the natural sciences and geography. The institute also aimed to enable the most talented students to learn methods for future scholarly work and thus prepare them to be professors and, in turn, create a new generation of teachers. When the institution was established, hopes of returning home were still very high. In émigrés' minds, primary and secondary education would play a paramount role in the new democratic Ukraine, so they saw the preparation of qualified pedagogues as a particularly important task. But over time these hopes faded. In the ten years of its existence the institute prepared more than one hundred qualified teachers in diverse fields, and after graduating the majority of them found employment teaching in cities, towns, and villages in the Transcarpathian region and Galicia.[2]

Structure and Study Program

The idea of establishing an institution was conceived by Mykyta Shapoval, and thus the Ukrainian Civic Committee played a critical role in the institute's early development. Initially, that committee was an administrative organ of the institute, which appointed a director who would be responsible for all administrative, scholarly, and economic matters and who would be accountable to the committee. However, by the end of the 1923–24 academic year, the director was being chosen by the professorial council and merely approved by the committee. All of Shapoval's efforts to secure the government's support were valuable, but to be a truly educational institution the institute would have to be governed by academics and professionals in the field. In the 1924–25 academic year, the professorial council chose a rector and vice-rector for the first time. They took on the same responsibilities that individuals holding these positions had in other institutions of higher learning. Beginning in 1925, after several reorganizations, the professorial council consisted of the heads of the departments and was responsible for academic and pedagogical matters at the institute. The head of the council was a rector of the institute. The council oversaw all departments and other units of the institute, but the foreign ministry, and later the education ministry, held ultimate authority. The senate, created in 1925, consisted of a rector, a vice-rector, deans, vice-deans, and a secretary. Its responsibilities included handling financial, administrative, and organizational matters. The senate admitted and dismissed students (with the approval of the council), approved timetables, organized various events, and built contacts with other scholarly and pedagogical institutions. In addition, individuals within the senate were responsible for various matters, such as the gymnasium (until 1932) and the institute's library.[3]

The institute initially offered a three-year program, with the first year as a preparation year and the other two as specialized years. During this initial stage it was almost fully dependent on the committee regarding its financial and administrative functions, and it could definitely not be considered a higher education institution.[4] In 1925, it separated completely from the committee and was transformed into an institution of higher learning with a four-year program. Its organizational structure followed that of similar European pedagogical institutions. It had three departments: History and Literature, Mathematics and Natural Sciences, and Music and Pedagogy. In turn, the Department of History and Literature was divided into History and Literature subdivisions. The Department of Mathematics and Natural Sciences had Mathematics and Natural Sciences subdivisions. The Department of Music and Pedagogy had two subdivisions: Vocals and Instrumental. At the institute, there were thirty-three sections (*katedra*), six of which taught core courses that were mandatory for all students in all three departments. These six sections were: Pedagogy, Pedagogical Psychology, Philosophy, Hygiene, Economy, and Sociology. Among the mandatory courses taught at the institute were Theory of Pedagogy, History of Pedagogy, Logics, an Introduction to Philosophy, and the Ukrainian, Czech, and German languages. Among the second-year compulsory courses were Didactics, Sociology, and the Foundations of Pedagogical Psychology. In the third year, all students had to take courses in Experimental Pedagogy, Library Sciences, and Developments in Schools in Czechoslovakia and Other Slavic Countries. In the fourth year, the mandatory courses were Pedagogical Psychology, Reflexology, and a Seminar in Pedagogy.[5]

As mentioned, the Department of History and Literature consisted of the History and Literature subdivisions, which were further divided into the History and Social Sciences and Literature and Arts units; these in turn were organized into specialized sections. The History and Social Sciences unit included the following sections: History of Ukraine, History of Slavs, Ancient History, World History of the Middle Ages, and Modern Times. The Literature and Arts unit contained these sections: Ukrainian Language, History of Ukrainian Literature, History of Slavic Literature, History of Western European Literature, Classical Languages and Writing, Linguistics, and Art. Each of these sections offered courses that were required for students in this department but that varied in scope and coverage. Those students who specialized in history studied History of the Ancient East, Greece and Rome, History of Ukraine, World History, and History of Czechoslovakia, Poland, Russia, the Balkans, and the South, as well as the Latin and Old Bulgarian languages. They also took courses in archaeology, paleography, and ethnology, among other subjects. Students in the Literature and Arts unit were required to take History of Greek Literature, History of Roman Literature, History of the Arts, Linguistics, History of Western European Literature, History of Ukrainian, Russian, and Czech literatures, Introduction to the History of the Ukrainian Language, and Comparative Grammar of Slavic Languages and Indo-European Languages. They also studied the Greek and Old Bulgarian languages. There were also elective courses for each subdivision that included the French language, Printing, Geography of Ukraine, and Ancient Mythology.[6]

The Department of Mathematics and Natural Sciences included units for Mathematics and Natural Sciences. The Mathematics unit consisted of Mathematics, Astronomy, Physics and Meteorology, and Theory of Mechanics. The Natural Sciences unit included Biology, Chemistry, Zoology, Botany, Geography, Geology, and Physical Chemistry. Required courses in the Mathematics subdivision included Algebra, Differential Calculus, Theory of Functions, Calculation of Probabilities, Analytical Geometry, Spherical Trigonometry, Physics, and Theoretical Mechanics. In the Natural Sciences unit students had to take courses in Anatomy, Zoology, Physical Geography, Geology, Organic and Non-Organic Chemistry, Biology, and Mineralogy, among others.[7]

The Music and Pedagogy subdivision consisted of the following sections: Theory of Music and Composition, History of Music, Musical Ethnography, Musical Acoustics, and Musical Psychophysiology. In addition, this subdivision had four workshops: Piano, Conductorship, Violin, and Solo Singing. Required courses in this subdivision included Musical Diction and Recitation, Violin Performance, Piano Performance, Conductorship, Accompaniment and Score Reading, Musical Esthetics, History of World Music, History of Czech Music, and History of Ukrainian Music, among others. The Italian language was also a required course in this subdivision. All of these course listings reflected the curriculum of a higher education institution that provided its students with broad range of knowledge. On the whole, it corresponded to the four-year programs in similar institutions, but also offered additional courses related to the study of Ukraine. After completing their education, students were undoubtedly well-qualified to perform their teaching duties when given the opportunity.[8]

Finance

Financially, like most other émigré institutions in Czechoslovakia, the institute depended on the Czechoslovak government. Initially, that assistance was quite substantial and covered the faculty's salaries, scholarships for students, and other expenses related to the institute's functions and development. Over time, however, this aid decreased and the assistance program wound down. To augment the government's support, the institute developed supplementary means of funding; specifically, salaried professors became self-funding and established small foundations to help students. But these were only small sums; while they supported some students, they could not resolve the institute's financial problems.

At the outset, the institute's circumstances looked quite sunny. In April 1923, the foreign ministry allocated 50,000 crowns per month for the institute. Of this sum, 25,000 crowns were earmarked for teachers' salaries, the institute library, and various supplies, and the remaining 25,000 for fifty scholarships for students who had no financial support. Later in the same year, funds were found for a further twenty-two scholarships. The following academic year, 1924–25, 120 scholarships were granted, and in 1925–26, 150. The aid was not as substantial as what the government provided to other institutions, such as the Ukrainian Economic Academy, but it was sufficient to establish the institute and to get it functioning. When the institute was transformed into an institution of higher education in 1925, the foreign ministry began determining the salaries of its professors and lecturers. From this time on, full professors received 1,500 crowns per month, associate professors 1,200 crowns, lecturers 1,000 crowns, and assistants 600 crowns.[9]

In 1926, the institute received its largest government subsidy: 805,905 crowns. After that, the amount steadily declined. In 1932, when the closing of the institute became a certainty, the education ministry provided only personal support to the faculty: 800 crowns for full professors, 700 crowns for associate professors, 600 crowns for lecturers, and 500 crowns for the assistants of the sections. As of April 1933, the government was still providing subversions to twenty-four staff who had no other employment and who did not hold Czechoslovak citizenship. At this stage, except for a small amount from the sale of the institute property, the institute's only source of income was the 2 per cent the remaining staff voluntarily contributed from their modest government assistance. Unfortunately, this sum was not enough even to pay the rent for the office and the library. All scholarly, administrative, and technical work from that time on was unpaid and was provided on a voluntary basis.[10]

Students were supported from a variety of sources, but mainly government scholarships. Initially, these were worth 500 crowns per month, but after 1927 they were reduced to 450 crowns per month, with some extra funding for students with families. A second group of students obtained financial assistance from the fund created from voluntary self-taxing by professors and staff. This support provided 150 to 200 crowns per month. It is noteworthy that prior to May 1925, when a decision about this self-tax was made, the same self-tax was being collected for schools in western Ukraine. The Horbachevs'kyi Fund was another private source of student income; it was established in 1925 from Horbachevs'kyi's donation of 1,542 crowns. Horbachevs'kyi donated his salary for lectures, and the fund was continuously supported by his and Artymovych's salaries and other donations and contributions. This fund existed until 1931 and was then closed. In addition, there were several scholarships for doctoral students who wished to do scholarly work. In all, the government provided twenty-six such one-year stipends.[11]

Since the institute was fully dependent on the government, it had to report to the government on all aspects of its operations. For instance, it had to submit its curriculum for every semester to the education ministry. These reports were highly detailed, including names of all the professors, the courses they taught, and the dates and times of each one. In 1930, the institute also submitted to the ministry a detailed list of staff, including their backgrounds, places of origin, and dates of employment, as well as another document detailing staff members' salaries and information on any other employment they had.[12] Apparently, it was not easy to work, study, and research in an atmosphere of financial restrictions and uncertainty. Signals from the government regarding the future closure of the institute began appearing as early as 1926–27. This constant sense of insecurity formed a cloud over the institute's faculty and students, and it is quite admirable that the professors continued to teach and write and the students to study.

Faculty

Among the institute faculty were several notable Ukrainian scholars, who undertook considerable scholarly work, writing textbooks, monographs, and articles and presenting their research at various conferences, congresses, and other scholarly meetings. Their contributions were important to the development of Ukrainian scholarship; they made an impact not only on pedagogics but also in the fields of Ukrainian linguistics, literary studies, and philosophy. During the institute's existence, ninety-two individuals taught there (eighty Ukrainians, twelve of other nationalities). Their ranks included professor, associate professor, lecturer, and assistant. Some were members of the Shevchenko Scientific Society, and others were members of various academic associations. During the ten years of the institute's existence, they created a whole new generation of young teachers.[13]

The first rector of the institute was Leonid Bilets'kyi, who held this position while the institution was organizing itself. Bilets'kyi was born in the Kyiv region and attended a classical gymnasium in Kyiv, where, in 1907, he entered the university. There, he first studied in the Department of Mathematics and Natural Sciences before completely changing his direction of study. He transferred to the Department of History and Philology, where he studied literature under the mentorship of renowned literary historian and philologist Vladimir Perets (1870–1935). After completing his studies with honours, he remained at the university as a research fellow with teaching responsibilities. In 1918, after his habilitation, he was appointed *privat*-adjunct professor at the newly founded Kam'ianets'-Podil's'kyi University, where he worked until 1920. After that, from 1921 to 1923, he taught Ukrainian literature at the Ukrainian Secret University (Ukrains'kyi taiemnyi universytet) in L'viv. Later, at the institute in Prague, he taught the history of Ukrainian literature, Ukrainian poetry, and theory of poetry. In Czechoslovakia, besides teaching at the institute, Bilets'kyi was a professor at the Ukrainian Free University, where he taught history and philosophy of law. In addition to teaching, he researched and published not only in Prague but also in L'viv, Chernivtsi, Berlin, and Warsaw. Between the wars, he published nearly sixty works, most of them articles. At the very last stage of the institution's existence, he was elected vice-rector, undertaking all the procedures connected to its closure, which was undeniably a very sad undertaking. After fleeing Prague for Munich in 1945, he was very active in establishing a network of educational institutions for Ukrainians there. After immigrating to Canada in 1949, he worked in several areas of Ukrainian literature. His main achievement, the fulfilment of a long-cherished dream, was the publication of a heavily annotated four-volume edition of Shevchenko's *Kobzar*.[14]

During the most vibrant stages of the institute's activities, its rector was the prominent linguist and cultural figure Vasyl' Simovych. Born in Galicia, he studied at Chernivtsi University under the mentorship of Stepan Smal'-Stots'kyi. After finishing his studies, he taught Ukrainian language and literature at that city's Teachers' Seminary. He became interested in the Czech language quite early in his life. While still at the gymnasium, in 1897, he wrote to František Řehoř (1857–1899), a Czech ethnographer and promoter of Ukrainian (Ruthenian) culture in the Bohemian lands, expressing his desire to learn the Czech language and asking him to send some textbooks, which Řehoř gladly did. In 1913, Simovych defended his doctorate at the university in Chernivtsi. During this period, he was a member of the Revolutionary Ukrainian Party and co-edited some of its periodicals. Simovych was associated with Bukovyna throughout his life, and when he died he left his archive to its university, which is still housed there. During the First World War, Simovych conducted cultural work for the Union of the Liberation of Ukraine (Soiuz vyzvolennia Ukrainy), in POW camps for Ukrainian soldiers in the Russian Army in Germany and Austria. There he wrote an important work titled *Praktychna hramatyka ukrains'koi movy* (A Practical Grammar of the Ukrainian Language), published in 1918. It was so popular and sold out so quickly that in 1919 it was reprinted as the 584-page *Hramatyka ukrains'koi movy* (A Grammar of the Ukrainian Language). It was generally considered the best grammar at that time and received very positive reviews. After the war, Simovych moved to Prague, where he became a professor of Ukrainian and Slavic philology at the institute. There he taught Ukrainian Language, Old Bulgarian Language, Introduction to Linguistics, Comparative Grammar of Slavic Languages, and other courses. From 1923 to 1930 he was also a lecturer at the Higher Trade School in Prague. He devoted himself to scholarly research as well as pedagogical work. In 1933, after the institute closed, he moved to L'viv, where he worked as the publications editor for the Prosvita Society and at the Shevchenko Scientific Society. He was also an editor of an influential Ukrainian general encyclopaedia, which will be discussed in the final chapter of this book. During the Second World War, Simovych worked at the University of L'viv. He passed away in 1944 and thus avoided the purges that came later. Simovych penned works in morphology, phonology, and word formation, as well as history of linguistics, literary language, and orthography.[15]

Vsevolod Harmashiv, another rector of the institute, was a professor of biology and hygiene. Prior to the wars, Harmashiv was a surgeon, and worked for almost twenty years in a military hospital in Kyiv. After immigrating to Czechoslovakia, he became an organizer of clinical sanatoriums for émigrés, many of whom required medical care. Harmashiv was the author of the first textbook on hygiene in the Ukrainian language, published in Prague in 1926 and titled *Shkil'na hihiiena. Korotkyi kurs dlia studentiv i uchyteliv* (School Hygiene: A Short Course for Pupils and Teachers).[16]

There were other noteworthy scholars among the staff. Professor of classical philology Agenor Artymovych was born in Bukovyna. His father, who was from Galicia, moved to Bukovyna and became Germanized there, while his German mother raised her children in the national tradition of her husband. The language of the family was still German, and only at seventeen, when he moved to Chernivtsi, did Artymovych begin studying Ukrainian on his own. He later became director of a gymnasium in Kitsman' (then Kotzman), a small town near Chernivtsi, and under his leadership this gymnasium developed a strong Ukrainian character. Before the war, Artymovych habilitated at Chernivtsi University in classical philology. He then worked as director of a Ukrainian gymnasium in Chernivtsi and, during the revolutionary years, became Minister of Education of the Western Ukrainian People's Republic. In emigration, Artymovych taught Indo-European linguistics at the institute besides teaching at the Ukrainian Free University. He presented at many conferences and was a member of many scholarly societies, including the renowned Prague Linguistic Circle.[17]

Renowned Slavist Dmytro Chyzhevs'kyi, a scholar with an international reputation, taught at the institute from 1924 to 1932. He began working there as an associate professor, and after 1926 as a full professor, and was also an associate professor at the Ukrainian Free University. Chyzhevs'kyi was very knowledgeable about the literatures of all Slavic peoples, but Czech, Slovak, Polish, Russian, and Ukrainian literatures were his particular interest and expertise. A prolific scholar, he contributed extensively to his fields and wrote prolifically on philosophy, literature, and philology. The prominent Ukrainian linguist Iurii Shevel'ov (1908–2002) recalled of Chyzhevs'kyi that "he did not shy away from the Ukrainian perspective and Ukrainians, though he was also at home among Russians and Czechs." Chyzhevs'kyi himself acknowledged that his greatest contributions were to Czech culture. He also took a deep interest in Slovak culture and produced the book *Štúrova filozofia života: kapitola z dejín slovenskej filozofie* (Štúr's Philosophy of Life: A Chapter of the History of Philosophy of Slovakia, 1941). He made a major discovery in Halle of a valuable manuscript of the seventeenth century by John Amos Comenius, long thought to be lost. Chyzhevs'kyi also contributed extensively to Russian studies, with works including *Gegel' v Rossii* (Hegel in Russia, 1939) and, later, *History of Russian Literature from the Eleventh Century to the End of the Baroque* (1960). Chyzhevs'kyi also wrote a two-volume comparative history of Slavic literatures titled *Vergleichende Geschichte der slavischen Literaturen* (Comparative History of Slavic Literatures), published in 1968 in Germany. After the war, he taught for a time at Harvard University before returning to Heidelberg, where he taught until his death in 1977.[18]

The head of the pedagogical department was Sofiia Rusova, an influential Ukrainian pedagogue, writer, and civic figure. She was born in the Chernihiv region to a gentry family of Swedish and French backgrounds. Rusova lost her mother at an early age and moved with her father to Kyiv. There she studied at a gymnasium and became exposed to a Ukrainophile art and musical environment. At the moment of choosing her path in life, Rusova was torn between her love for music and her love of pedagogy. She chose the latter and became a devoted lifelong pedagogue who contributed considerably to the field. From a young age, Rusova began studying the theory and methodology of teaching in primary schools. She was heavily influenced by Western European pedagogues such as Friedrich Adolph Wilhelm Diesterweg (1790–1866) and Johann Heinrich Pestalozzi (1746–1827). With her sister, she went to St Petersburg to study primary education; then, after returning to Kyiv, they opened a children's daycare together in 1871. She also travelled extensively in Europe; being fluent in French, she visited France and Belgium as well as Germany, where she deepened her knowledge of pedagogical theory and practice and visited a number of schools and daycares. In the Russian empire, Rusova was imprisoned a number of times for her educational and social activism. During the revolutionary years, she was a member of the Central Council, and in the Ministry of Education during the Hetmanate, she was the head of two departments: Preschool Education and Extracurricular Education. Her deep background in those fields was vital, at the time, Ukrainian educational institutions and general education were both ungoing rapid development. In 1918, Rusova published her fundamental work *Doshkil'ne vykhovannia* (Preschool Education). After Ukraine lost its independence, she moved to Kam'ianets'-Podil's'kyi, where she taught at the university for some time; then, after brief stays in Tarnów and Vienna, she settled in Prague. There, at the age of sixty-seven, Rusova became a professor of pedagogy and the head of the Department of Pedagogy at the institute; she also became very active in the cultural and civic life of the Ukrainian émigré community. She authored numerous works, primarily in the field of pedagogy but also in literature and art. She also penned her memoirs, which remain a valuable source for the history of education at the end of the nineteenth and beginning of the twentieth centuries, of education during the revolutionary times, and, to a lesser extent, of Ukrainian emigration.[19]

Another institute faculty member, Volodymyr Sichyns'kyi (1894–1962), was a well-known scholar, architect, art historian, and graphic artist. Born in Kam'ianets'-Podil's'kyi, he studied engineering in St Petersburg, and in 1918 he helped found the Architecture Institute in Kyiv, while holding a number of other positions. When the Ukrainian revolution failed, after a short stay in L'viv, Sichyns'kyi moved to Prague, where he studied at Charles University and worked on his doctorate. He became a prominent figure in the Ukrainian intellectual world in Prague. Besides teaching at the institute, and later at the Ukrainian Free University, he taught at the Ukrainian School of Plastic Arts (see the next chapter). He also worked in the field of book design, which was influenced by the important Ukrainian graphic artists Heorhii Narbut (1886–1920) and the architect, painter, graphic artist, and art scholar Vasyl' Krychevs'kyi (1873–1952). Sichyns'kyi was a prolific scholar in the field of Ukrainian architecture and art, and his bibliography includes more than five hundred works. Particularly well-known is his work titled *Chuzhyntsi pro Ukrainu* (Ukraine through the Eyes of Foreigners), which has seen many editions. In addition to his scholarly activities, Sichyns'kyi was an architect in his own right, designing schools, churches, and other buildings in many countries, including Slovakia, Ukraine, Canada, and the United States.[20]

It seems that some professors taught at the institute without pay. In 1930, in addition to Horbachevs'kyi, other scholars teaching at the institute *gratis* included Dmytro Doroshenko, Iurii Rusov (1895–1961), Shul'hyn, and Cherediiv. These professors had other sources of income teaching in other institutions; however, it still shows their dedication to the cause of educating a young generation of Ukrainians.[21] Over the years, the institute attracted many scholars who worked hard to develop the institution and contributed considerably to their respective fields.

Students

Over the ten years of the institute's existence many students graduated from it. Like their professors, these students were of diverse backgrounds, ages, and political orientations. They included men and women; émigrés from the Ukrainian lands of the former Russian empire and from those of the former Austro-Hungarian empire; younger and mature students; those in the centre of the political spectrum and those on the right and the left; those who studied only at the institute and those who did so in other educational institutions simultaneously; and those who were émigrés and those who later came to study from Galicia, Volhynia, Bukovyna, Bessarabia, and other lands.[22]

In order to graduate, students were required to complete eight semesters in four years and pass all their exams. Those who passed additional written and oral exams received the title of Secondary School Teacher. Some students remained at the institute after graduation to pursue their doctorates, for which they had to pass the relevant exams and write a dissertation. Between 1923 and 1933, 178 students attended all eight semesters; out of them, 116 graduated, and of the graduates 84 received the title of Pedagogue. Of the individuals who received this title, 48 graduated from the Department of History and Literature, 28 from the Department of Mathematics and Natural Sciences, and 8 from the Department of Music and Pedagogy. In addition, 31 students obtained a doctorate: 17 in History and Literature, 10 in Mathematics and Natural Sciences, and 4 in Music and Pedagogy. One of those who received a doctorate from the institute was the future Czechoslovak archaeologist and numismatist Liudmyla Kraskovs'ka (1904–1999).[23]

Most of the students at the institution were Ukrainians, but there were also a number of Belarusians, Czechs, Jews, Georgians, and Bulgarians, as well as some Romanians, Armenians, and Lithuanians. Many women studied at the institute. In the 1927–28 academic years, for example, 48 out of 206 students were women (around 25 per cent). Most of the students had "regular" status; some were auditors. In the institution's early years many students received scholarships from the government, but that number later decreased and many students became self-funding. The number of students who enrolled was different from the number who graduated, and graduation rates depended on many factors. Poor health and the difficult conditions of émigré life prevented some émigré students from graduating. Another important consideration was the future employment prospects of the graduates. Some students who came from Galicia, Volhynia, and other places experienced difficulties finding employment in schools in interwar Poland with a diploma from a Ukrainian institution. As a result, some of them transferred to other institutions to complete their education.[24]

At the institute, there were two student societies: the Student Community (Students'ka hromada) and the Academic Community (Akademichna hromada). The former was founded in September 1923 soon after the institute, with the aim of uniting, organizing, and supporting all of its students. Initially, it undertook many useful activities, such as publishing a bulletin, organizing literary events, and participating in the work of the institute's publishing house. The society also created a savings bank that helped provide students with clothing and medical care. The Student Community also represented the students in all internal and external matters. It was also very active in the events that led to the transformation of the institute into an institution of higher learning with a four-year program. Disagreements, mainly regarding political orientation, began to arise early on, and as a consequence, in March 1925, approximately one quarter of the students left to organize another group. This was the Academic Community, which gathered together students who leaned more toward the right as well as the left of the political spectrum. The Academic Community, however, did not last long, and in 1926 it ceased its activities because of internal disagreements. The Student Community continued to function until 1932, but its membership and activities steadily declined. In 1927 its membership was 98 students, but a year later only 18, at a time when the total number of students was 142. This decline was due to the change in students' demographics. As time passed, the core of the community was still formed from émigré students who received the government's support, but most of the students were now from Galicia and Volhynia. This cohort was self-funded, and most of them studied in other institutions in Czechoslovakia concurrently with their studies at the institute; as a consequence, they took less interest in the institute's internal affairs. The decrease in the institute's activities overall, and the constant threat of dissolution, went hand in hand with the reduction in student activism as they became more disillusioned with their, and the institute's, prospects and less involved in general.[25]

In addition to classroom studies, students took in various excursions organized by professors, and later by a special committee. Czechoslovakia had much to offer and teach the students, and they and their professors took advantage of it. Excursions varied depending on the students' fields of study. There were also general educational trips organized to enrich students' knowledge and understanding of the country in which they lived. During the institute's existence, 45 geological trips were organized, which varied in length from several days (to the town of Kutná Hora or the Posázaví region in Czechoslovakia) to more than two months (to the Transcarpathian region). There were also geographical excursions; the first of these was guided by prominent Ukrainian geographer Stepan Rudnyts'kyi (discussed above). Also, several botanical field trips were organized for students in the natural sciences, as well as many short excursions for those who studied in the Departments of History and Literature and Music and Pedagogy.[26]

Rusova mentioned some of the institute's students in her memoirs. She recalled one of them, Iakiv Ohorodnyk, who, while battling tuberculosis, wrote beautiful works on Ukrainian history, and who died from that disease after defending his doctoral thesis. Another student, Borys Homzyn (1887–1965), defended his doctorate in literature exceptionally well, and another, Hryhorii Derkach, devoted himself to archaeology. Some of the institute's graduates left their mark on Ukrainian literary life, including the following poets, writers, and translators: Olena Teliha, Halyna Mazurenko, Homzyn, Stepan-Iurii Masliak (1895–1960), and Iurii Shkrumeliak (1895–1965). During the Second World War, some of them became active in the Ukrainian nationalist movement. Some returned – for example, Masliak, who produced an unsurpassed translation into Ukrainian of the famous novel *The Good Soldier Švejk* by the Czech writer and satirist Jaroslav Hašek.[27]

Notwithstanding their financial difficulties and political differences, the students at the institute engaged deeply in new subjects and pursued professions in pedagogy. After graduation, they could not teach Ukrainian subjects in an independent Ukraine, as the institute had intended them to do. They did, however, become the first generation of Ukrainians who attained positions as pedagogues, and that was very important for them.

Scholarly Activities

Scholars at the institute conducted academic activities both within the institute and outside it. Several scholarly societies operated at various times at the institute, such as the Scholarly Pedagogical Society and the Mathematics and Natural Sciences Society, which organized meetings where papers were delivered and discussed. Scholarly work at the institute reportedly intensified toward the end of its existence; this could have been because at the initial stages a great deal of time and energy was spent on organizing the institute itself. In the later stages, there were discussions within the government and among the institute's faculty and staff about converting it into a research institute. Nothing came of these discussions, but the intensified scholarly activities at that time may have been a sign that the scholars were trying to save the institute and their positions in it.

Among the scholars at the institute, the most prolific ones were Rusova, Simovych, Bilets'kyi, and, in particular, Chyzhevs'kyi. During this period, Rusova wrote many works on pedagogy in which she addressed issues related to schooling and upbringing. Of particular importance were *Teoriia i praktyka doshkil'noho vykhovannia* (A Theory and Practice of Preschool Education, 1924) and *Novi metody doshkil'noho vykhovannia* (New Methods of Preschool Education, 1927). Also during this period, in Prague and later in L'viv, Simovych penned and published numerous works on various aspects of linguistics. His main interests were phonetics, historical morphology, Ukrainian onomastics, and orthography. Bilets'kyi was the author of *Osnovy ukrains'koi literaturno-naukovoi krytyky: sproba literaturno-naukovoi metodolohii* (Foundations of Ukrainian Scholarly Literary Critics: An Attempt in Literary Research Methodology), published in 1925 in Prague. Between the wars, Chyzhevs'kyi made valuable contributions to Ukrainian studies by writing *Fil'osofiia na Ukraini: sproba istoriohrafii* (Philosophy in Ukraine: An Attempt in Historiography, 1926, 1931).

The principal topics of the institute's scholarly publications included the pedagogical activities of Ukrainian scholars and writers such as Mykhailo Drahomanov (1841–1895), Omelian Popovych (1856–1930), and Mykhailo Halushchyns'kyi (1878–1931), as well as school reforms, which at the time were taking place in Czechoslovakia, Poland, and other countries. The scholars also explored the pedagogical ideas of internationally renowned educators of that time: John Dewey, Adolphe Ferrière, Maria Montessori, and Helen Parkhurst. This demonstrates that the scholars did not focus only on problems and developments in Ukrainian pedagogy. They also explored the ideas of European pedagogues, hoping to apply their methods in Ukrainian schools in a future democratic Ukraine.[28]

The scholars also took part in conferences and congresses in Czechoslovakia and across Europe. In the 1924–25 academic year, faculty members took part in the Pedagogical Congress of the Society of New School in Heidelberg. The following academic year, they participated in a scholarly–pedagogical congress in Germany and in a pedagogical congress in England. In the 1926–27 academic year, they attended the "By School to Peace" congress in Prague; the year after that, the Congress of Czechoslovak Teachers; and the year after that, a pedagogical congress in Geneva. They were especially active in the two Ukrainian congresses discussed earlier. The scholars took part not only in conferences and congresses related to pedagogy but also in scholarly gatherings in their specific disciplines, including the Congress of Slavic Geographers and Ethnographers in Prague, the Philosophical Congress in Berlin, and, the International Congress of People's Art in Prague, among many others.[29]

The faculty members also delivered lectures at various events organized by the institute. This included lectures at which an outside audience was present, as well as those organized mostly for the institute's community. These lectures augmented various important events dedicated to renowned figures in Ukrainian and Czech and Slovak history and to prominent individuals in general. Among the major presenters at these events were Bilets'kyi and Simovych; but other members delivered lectures as well, among them Rusova, Chyzhevs'kyi, and Fedir Steshko (1877–1944). These events were held in such prominent places in Prague as the Municipal House (Obecní dům) and the Artistic Society (Umělecká beseda) and were sometimes attended by members of the Czechoslovak government and institutions of higher learning, as well as representatives of other Ukrainian institutions and various Belarusian, Georgian, Lithuanian, and Cossack organizations. Annual celebratory events were devoted, for example, to Drahomanov; at these, Bilets'kyi delivered lectures on the role of Drahomanov in Ukrainian literary criticism (1923), and Simovych talked about Drahomanov's orthography (1926). Other gatherings were devoted to Masaryk, the mathematician and astronomer Johannes Kepler, the composer Ludwig van Beethoven, the historian and philologist Mykhailo Maksymovych, the pedagogue Pestalozzi, and others.[30]

The Ukrainian Gymnasium in Czechoslovakia and Other Organizations

Several organizations were affiliated with the institute, and faculty were closely involved in their founding and administration. One of these was the School for Orphans (Internat ditei-syrit). In December 1923, twenty-nine orphans arrived in Prague from an internment camp in Szczypiorno, Poland, with their tutors. There, these children had lived in a separate barracks under the care of the Czechoslovak Red Cross. This School for Orphans was moved to Czechoslovakia; their entry into the country was possible thanks to Girsa and Beneš and the organizational efforts of Shapoval. Along with the School for Orphans, the courses mentioned above and known as the Ukrainian Graduation Course (Ukrains'ki matural'ni kursy) were transferred from Poděbrady to Prague. The aim of the courses was to enable those whose education had been interrupted by the war to brush up their knowledge and pass entrance exams for Ukrainian institutions. As mentioned, the director was Ievhen Ivanenko. There were sixteen teaching staff: ten institute professors and lectors and six special invitees. All students were divided into groups based on their level of knowledge. Under the auspices of the institute, 141 students attended the courses, of whom 104 received scholarships from the government. The first group of graduates passed their exams on 4 September 1924, and the last on 5 March 1925, after which the courses were rolled up.[31] The Ukrainian Control and Exam Committee (Ukrains'ka kontrol'na i ispytova komisiia) was organized in June 1926 at the request of the education ministry. The goal of the committee was to verify the secondary education documents of prospective students of the institute and the Ukrainian Economic Academy. The committee was also responsible for verifying the records of all Ukrainian and Belarusian students, regardless the schools at which they studied. It continued in existence until January 1930.[32]

The most important and long-lasting institution created by Ukrainians for children and youth was the Ukrainian gymnasium, which operated for twenty years, from 1925 to 1945. In 1925, the above-mentioned graduation courses and the School for Orphans were merged, and the Ukrainian gymnasium began operations. From the start, it was under the supervision and directorship of the institute's senate. Its syllabus was based on Czechoslovak gymnasium curricula. Along with the

Ukrainian language, the subjects it offered included history, geography, literature, and Czechoslovakian history, as well as the German language, descriptive geometry, natural sciences, chemistry, physics, and mathematics. Many children of the faculty of Ukrainian institutions studied there, and its pupils attended events and lectures offered by Ukrainian scholars in Prague; the scholars, in turn, visited the gymnasium. All of this had a great influence on life in the gymnasium. The pupils did not feel isolated, but rather felt themselves part of the wider intellectual world of Ukrainians in Czechoslovakia.[33] Hundreds of students studied there, and formed their lifelong world view there. Some of the graduates died fighting the Soviets or the Nazis. Some pupils and teachers survived Nazi prisons and isolation wards. Later in life, many of them became part of the civic, political, cultural, and national fabric of many Ukrainian émigré communities around the world. In Munich, fifty years after the gymnasium's founding, its graduates from around the world published an almanac that included valuable and informative memoirs.

The gymnasium functioned as a boarding school. The classes were initially held at various schools in Prague; later, the gymnasium was transferred to a small town near Prague called Řevnice. There the gymnasium had three buildings for the boarding school and one for auxiliary functions; the classes were held in a local school after-hours. In 1937, the gymnasium secured a three-storey house in Modřany (now a suburb of Prague) and a newly built cafeteria (*idal'nia*) for pupils. The gymnasium received a monthly subsidy of 15,000 crowns from the foreign ministry, and later from the education ministry – an amount that increased as the gymnasium grew. The "self-taxing" of the gymnasium's teaching and administrative personnel provided supplementary funding. They gave, for example, 3 per cent of their salaries to the Help Committee (Dopomohovyi komitet) that had been created in 1930 to assist pupils who did not receive government support. In addition, several Ukrainian institutions and individuals established scholarships to support these students. Overall, the spirit of support for pupils and the gymnasium was strong in the Ukrainian community.

At the end of the 1926–27 academic year, there were 111 pupils at the gymnasium, of whom 98 were supported by the government and 13 were financed by their parents. From its inception, the gymnasium was part of the Ukrainian Higher Pedagogical Institute, whose senate decided on all its educational and economic matters. Until 1932, the gymnasium was controlled by inspectors appointed by the education ministry. In the 1927–28 academic year, the teaching staff included eight members as well as seven "guest" teachers, five of whom were teachers of the Czech language. The education ministry appointed directors based on a competition developed by the institute's senate. The gymnasium's directors between the wars were professor of the institute Iakym Iarema (1884–1964), Artymovych, and Ivan Kobyzs'kyi (1894–1930), as well as the deputy director and acting director Marko Khliur (1889–1942), and Hryhorii Omel'chenko (1884–1945). When the institute was about to be closed, the ministry decided to separate the gymnasium from the institute and founded the Society for Support of Ukrainian Schools in Czechoslovakia in Prague (Spolek pro podporu ukrajinských škol v ČSR v Praze), whose task was to oversee the gymnasium. The society's members represented the Czechoslovak and Ukrainian communities. Even when the institute was threatened with closure, the government continued to support the gymnasium. Despite this support, the gymnasium faced closure a number of times over the course of its existence, particularly in 1931.[34]

The role of the Ukrainian Higher Pedagogical Institute was important and visible on the Ukrainian intellectual scene in interwar Czechoslovakia. For ten years, it prepared hundreds of qualified teachers for primary and secondary schools; thus, the institute created the first generation of Ukrainian pedagogues. They could not teach in schools in an independent Ukraine, as had been envisioned at the institute's inception, but they found employment elsewhere, particularly in the Transcarpathian region. The institute's curriculum arguably duplicated that of the Ukrainian Free University, but with a specific focus on the pedagogical disciplines. It was designed to equip teachers with broad general knowledge in many disciplines outside of their areas of expertise. In this respect, the institute achieved its goal of educating well-rounded professionals. Professors at the institute contributed extensively to Ukrainian scholarly life in Czechoslovakia and abroad by presenting at conferences and by publishing their research. The constant threat of abolition and the generally difficult and uncertain nature of émigré existence undoubtedly diminished the employment prospects of its graduates, and other matters certainly negatively influenced life at the institute. Nevertheless, the education received in the institute was formative for many of its graduates and left a significant mark on their lives.

Chapter Five

The Ukrainian School of Plastic Arts in Prague

By the beginning of the First World War, Prague had become a major centre of modern art on the European continent. The city has always been inspired by the European art tradition, and between the wars it was wide open to artistic influences from further west. Ukrainian artists who found themselves in Czechoslovakia were certainly influenced by Prague art, particularly its graphic tradition. Interwar Prague became the centre of Ukrainian art in Europe after the Ukrainian School of Plastic Arts was established there. This school had a strong impact on the lives of Ukrainian émigré artists and artists of other nationalities who studied there during the almost three decades of its existence.[1]

Establishment and Structure

In 1922, the Ukrainian Circle of Plastic Arts (Ukrains'kyi hurtok plastychnoho mystetstva) was established in Prague, and by 1923 this group had organized an exhibition of its members' works. At the end of that year, the group was renamed the Ukrainian Society of Plastic Arts at the Ukrainian Civic Committee (Ukrains'ke tovarystvo plastychnoho mystetstva pry U.H.K.), and founded the Ukrainian School of Plastic Arts. The school was established on 24 December 1923 and would soon become the centre of the Ukrainian émigré art world between the wars. It was a private institution that offered a broad program of academic studies and had the status of an institution of higher learning. In large part, it was a creation of Dmytro Antonovych, who insisted that "the academy ... cannot limit itself to certain trends in art." During the revolutionary years, he had been deeply involved in the development of arts in Ukraine. At that time, he took an active role in establishing various artistic, cultural, and scholarly societies and organizations; in particular, he helped organize the Ukrainian Academy of Arts. Later, he incorporated the idea of building Ukrainian scholarly, artistic, and cultural institutions into his life in emigration and worked tirelessly to establish and develop abroad what could not be achieved at home. It seems that in building these institutions in Czechoslovakia, Antonovych was attempting to replicate his past efforts in revolutionary Ukraine. Besides playing a crucial role in establishing the university (see chapter 2), he took an active part in building most of the important émigré scholarly societies and organizations (see the following chapters). As an art historian, he played an especially vital role in creating and managing the Ukrainian School of Plastic Arts, which would be modelled along the lines of the Ukrainian Academy of Arts.[2]

The school provided academic training in the visual arts, following the pattern of the Western art academies. Initially it was called the Ukrainian Academy of Plastic Arts (Ukrains'ka akademiia plastychnoho mystetstva); however, the Prague Academy of Fine Arts (Akademie výtvarných umění v Praze) objected to this name, so it was changed. In any event, the school became known as the Ukrainian Academy (Ukrains'ka akademiia). The art historian Myroslava Mudrak wrote that "the program of the Ukrainian Academy – focused on art as practice, as craft, and even as techne in the classical sense – was geared towards understanding art as art."[3] The school's academic program involved four years of study. It included courses in theoretical disciplines usually taught at art academies, as well as classes taught by several artist-practitioners. Antonovych taught art history; Mirchuk lectured on aesthetics; Volodymyr Sichyns'kyi taught perspective and architecture; Fedir Sliusarenko (1886–1958) focused on classical archaeology; anatomy was taught by Stepan Litov (1895–1966) and later by Iurii Rusov. Practical classes were led by the following artists: drawing and painting by Ivan Kulets' (1880–1952) and Serhii Mako (1885–1953); graphics and applied art by Ivan Mozalevs'kyi (1890–1975) and Robert Lisovs'kyi (1893–1982); sculpture by Kost' Stakhovs'kyi (1882–1959); and architecture by Serhii Tymoshenko. The school played a formative role in the careers of many Ukrainians and artists of other backgrounds. It offered traditional grounding, "exposing students to the fundamentals of good drawing, texture as a compositional element, and the theory of color."[4] Mudrak wrote:

> Unlimited in its support of artistic directions and styles, the Academy provided the obligatory nexus for emigration that would allow Ukrainian artists to renew and sustain their national ties while pursuing serious academic training in the visual arts. Its first premise was that all artists develop out of the culture in which they are born; when they are displaced, nationalist sentiments lie dormant until artistic impulses find their expression in the international setting.[5]

Goals

As Dmytro Antonovych stated: "Art of Ukrainian people is wider than fusion of the certain art trends that find their expression and place in wide trend of general Ukrainian art development." The school's goal was to satisfy the artistic needs of students abroad. It set out to provide theoretical and practical training in the visual arts. Its professors considered it their responsibility to provide students with traditional professional training and to teach them "to understand spiritual needs of their surrounding[s], [to] not fear the collision of rational and intuitive in their creation."[6] The need for this school also arose from the circumstances, in that the situation in Prague for those who wanted an education in art was competitive: "Since Czech higher schools of art were filled to capacity, there arose a special need to prepare students for formal careers outside established circles and, even more important, to satisfy the ambitions of displaced artists of various nationalities then living in Prague."[7]

Finance

Between 1923 and 1926, the school received very little financial support from the host country's foreign ministry. In 1927, that funding was cancelled altogether, but in 1928–29, the school began receiving some financial support from the education ministry. In the early 1930s, financial assistance to the school stopped entirely. From that time on, the school operated on small student fees of 100 to 140 crowns per month, as well as on charitable donations. Ivan Kulets', who became the school's director in 1932 and who remained in that position until it closed, saved the school repeatedly. According to poet and painter Halyna Mazurenko, then a student there, the school was often in financial distress, and Kulets' saved it on many occasions by pawning his father's silver watch. Like other drivers of Ukrainian émigré life in Prague, the school was his brainchild.[8]

Faculty

A council oversaw the school under its long-time head, Antonovych. It was composed of all the department heads (classes) and professors who taught theoretical disciplines, as well as some functionaries. The faculty was diverse in its artistic directions and styles, but all members were well-rounded and creative individuals. Antonovych called them "a group of five independent [and] artistic individuals."[9]

Ivan Kulets' was an important figure at the school and dedicated many years of his life to it, developing it into an enclave for Ukrainian and other artists. He had graduated from the Cracow Academy of Fine Arts (Akademia Sztuk Pięknych w Krakowie) under the renowned Polish painters Jan Stanisławski (1860–1907), Wojciech Weiss (1875–1950), and Józef Pankiewicz (1866–1940). Travelling extensively around Europe, he became familiar with the prominent trends in the visual arts. During the First World War, he was a painter in the Austro-Hungarian Army in Moravia. Eventually, after the loss of his parents, he settled in Prague rather than returning to Galicia. At the school, he was a professor of drawing and painting. He directed the school from 1932 to 1952, and it closed after his death that same year.[10] According to Mudrak:

> What Kulec [*sic*] undertook in the Ukrainian Academy was to create for talented Ukrainians an enclave that would serve not to propagate a single style but to provide an atmosphere through which to find solace, inspiration, and kinship within a foreign land. Artists perplexed by emigration and by a changing world steeped in modernist expression of every kind, might find there a venue for the expressive airing of their own particular worldview. Thus, every possible artistic tendency was encouraged within the ateliers of the Ukrainian Academy.[11]

Another professor of drawing and painting was the artist Serhii Mako, who was of Russian origin. A painter and portraitist, he spent most of his life in France, but he devoted many years to the school. He had studied art in the Higher Art School (Imperatorskaia Akademiia khudozhestv) in St Petersburg before training at the renowned Académie Julian in Paris. In 1908, he moved to Nice, where, two years later, he opened an art school that he headed for twelve years. While in Kyiv in 1918, he met Antonovych, who offered him a spot with the diplomatic mission of the Ukrainian People's Republic in Rome, which Mako reportedly accepted. In 1923, Antonovych invited Mako to Prague to teach at the school; he taught there until early 1930s, when he returned to Nice. After 1924, Mako also taught at the Ukrainian Economic Academy. In 1933, he had a solo exhibition in Prague and also exhibited his works in Paris and Nice. He undoubtedly had a great impact on his students' artistic development.[12]

Ivan Mozalevs'kyi was another artist who taught at the school. He had studied art in Kyiv and St Petersburg. During the revolutionary years, he returned to Ukraine and joined Kyiv's union of professional artists. In 1920, he moved to Vienna, where he opened an art studio. Then in Prague, he taught drawing at the graphics and applied arts class until 1926. His time in Prague was an important creative period for him. His works included a logo for the Ukrainian Free University (1923). He also designed the book *Dobirni dumky T.G. Masaryk* (T.G. Masaryk's Selected Thoughts), published by the Ukrainian Civic Committee in 1925, and drew a portrait of Masaryk, which the president autographed. In 1926, he moved to Paris, where he became active in Ukrainian émigré life. Mozalevs'kyi was a frequent contributor to the newspaper *Ukrains'ki visti* (Ukrainian News). Many of his articles were devoted to the connections between Ukrainian art and France, particularly artists who tied their lives to Paris in the 1930s. In 1947, he returned to the Soviet Union, where he lived and worked in Kyiv, Moscow, and Simferopol until 1975. At various times in his life, his works were exhibited in Prague, Berlin, Leipzig, Kyiv, L'viv, and Moscow. He worked in the field of easel and book graphics and created bookplates, publishing signs, and posters.[13]

Another artist who taught graphics at the easel was Robert Lisovs'kyi. He was of mixed background, as his mother was German. First, he studied in Myrhorod in the Poltava region. Then in Kyiv, at the Kyiv Art College (Kyivs'ke khudozhnie uchylyshche) from 1910 until 1914 under renowned artists Oleksander Murashko (1875–1919). After that Lisovs'kyi studied at the Ukrainian State Academy of Arts (Ukrains'ka derzhavna akademiia mystetstv) from 1917 until the early 1920s under the painter and graphic artist Heorhii Narbut and influential painter-monumentalist Mykhailo Boichuk (1882–1937), who perished in the purges in the 1930s. In the early 1920s, he moved to Warsaw for a year, then spent some time in L'viv and Leipzig before moving to Berlin to study at the Academy of Arts (Akademie der Künste). In 1930, Lisovs'kyi was invited to be a professor of graphics and applied art at the school, where he taught until 1946. He also worked in the fields of book graphics and ceramics.[14]

Kost' Stakhovs'kyi, a sculptor and ceramicist, taught sculpture at the school from 1923 until the end of the Second World War. Born in Podolia, he studied in Warsaw, Paris, St Petersburg, Munich, and Berlin. He took part in exhibitions in Paris and London, and many of his works can be found today in art galleries around the world. Stakhovs'kyi was a master of several sculptural materials: he worked with wood, bronze, clay, and gypsum. He excelled at his principal interest, which was creating animals. His students had positive memories of him; one of them, Mariia Leontovych-Loshak, remembered him as a "remarkably kind and noble-minded individual."[15]

Lectures in the philosophy of art were given at the school by Mirchuk. His "lectures formulated a basic philosophy of training for the school."

He wrote the textbook *Zahal'na estetyka* (General Aesthetics) specifically for this class. It was published in 1926 and reprinted by the Ukrainian Free University in Munich in 2003. Other artists and art scholars also taught at the school; they too had a great impact on the development and reputation of the institution as well as on the lives of its students.[16] Over the years, the composition of the school's faculty changed. Mozalevs'kyi, Serhii Tymoshenko, and Mako left the school. After Mako's departure, Kulets's workshop became the school's focal point. Lisovs'kyi led a graphics workshop; Stakhovs'kyi led a sculpture workshop after 1925; an architectural workshop was cancelled.[17] The school gathered artists and scholars of different art directions under one roof, and this fostered an inspiring atmosphere. The teachers' tenures varied: some taught there only briefly, while others did so for decades. In any case, they prepared a cohort of students, leaving a powerful mark on their lives as well as on their creative works.

Students

Prague in the 1920s was important for Ukrainian artists for several reasons. First of all, it allowed them to receive their artistic training in that city's rich cultural environment. Czech influences in art intersected with Western European patterns, and this created a stimulating atmosphere for students. Also, the concentration of Ukrainian émigrés in Prague – particularly the young – created a uniquely favourable environment for artistic learning and development.[18] Mudrak wrote: "The openness of the studio environment in the Ukrainian Academy in Prague created a unique opportunity for artistic training in a time of great uncertainty and kept many aspiring artists abreast of modernist trends in art. Though distanced from Ukraine and working independently, this generation of artists was not disconnected from the autonomous nature of modern art."[19]

Hundreds of students studied at the school over the course of its existence. As mentioned, the duration of studies across all departments was four years. Students were accepted after an examination, and in order to graduate they had to participate in annual exhibitions organized by the school; also, they had to pass all their theoretical exams in order to receive their Master of Arts degree (Magister Artis). Each year, between twenty-five and fifty students studied at the school.[20]

The school was popular in Prague. Initially, most of the students were Ukrainians, but there were also Russian, Bulgarian, Hungarian, and Austrian students and especially Czechs and Slovaks. Among the Czech artists who studied there were František Josef Archalous (1906–?), Jan Krahulík (1908–?), and Jaroslav Paur (1918–1987). Students from outside Czechoslovakia who trained at the school included Jozef Šesták (Yugoslavia) and Blanka Tauber (Hungary). Mako had many Ukrainian and Russian students. He was an outstanding teacher and was very friendly with his students. Kulets' accepted many Czechs, who would remember him long after for his gifts as a teacher.[21]

In Prague, Ukrainian artists viewed themselves as aligned with new directions in European art and did not feel marginalized. They were open to the outside art world and tried to build connections with it. Some artists, during or after their training at the school, also studied at Prague's own art institutions, particularly at the Prague Academy of Fine Arts (Akademie výtvarných umění v Praze) or the School of Arts and Crafts (Uměleckoprůmyslová škola v Praze). Artists whose works made substantial contributions to Ukrainian art, including Oksana Liaturyns'ka, Halyna Mazepa (1910–1995), Viktor Tsymbal (1902–1968), Artemii Korniichuk (1898–1978), Mykola Krychevs'kyi (1898–1961), Sofiia Zaryts'ka (1897–1972), and Stepan Koliadyns'kyi (1893–1926), studied also in Czechoslovak art schools and had good relations with Czech artists.[22] For example, among the Ukrainian students at the Prague Academy of Fine Arts were Petro Omel'chenko (1894–1952), Vasyl' Kasiian (1896–1976), Mykhailo Bryns'kyi (1883–1957), and Iulian Butsmaniuk (1885–1967). Other Ukrainian students attended the School of Arts and Crafts. Their art was influenced by the Czech professors under whom they studied. For example, Prague Academy of Fine Arts professor of figurative drawing Willi Novák (1886–1977) influenced and deepened Mazepa's art. The famous School of Arts and Crafts painter, illustrator, and caricaturist Zdeněk Kratochvíl (1883–1961) also taught Mazepa for six years.[23]

Liaturyns'ka, a talented sculptor, graphic artist, and poet, was a student at the school, at the School of Arts and Crafts, and at the Department of Philosophy at Charles University. She studied sculpture under Stakhovs'kyi and under professor Karel Dvořák (1893–1950) at the School of Arts and Crafts. She became a successful sculptor. Following in Stakhovs'kyi's footsteps, she excelled at creating sculptures of animals. Among her works were portraits of Shevchenko and Masaryk as well as a series of graphic portraits of Ukrainian historical figures, published as postcards. She participated in exhibitions in Prague, Paris, Vienna, L'viv, and New York. Unfortunately, many of her works from the interwar period have been lost.[24]

Mazurenko, another student at the school, was an artist and poet. She attended classes taught by Kulets', Mako, Stakhovs'kyi, Mozalevs'kyi, and Lisovs'kyi. After the war, she taught art in London at the art school (studio) known as the Tuesday Group. In the 1960s, she had solo exhibitions in London and in other cities and countries. Mazurenko was the most prolific among the Ukrainian émigré poets and published many collections of poems. Her introduction to her collection of poetry published in London in 1970 provided a rare and invaluable insight into life at the school.[25]

Another talented Ukrainian artist, Viktor Tsymbal, studied simultaneously at the school and the School of Arts and Crafts and was among its best students. The latter school had a strong reputation and taught practical skills besides providing artistic training. Tsymbal's focus there was on publishing techniques. Prague was an important graphics and publishing centre, so it was the good place to acquire knowledge in that field. At the school, Tsymbal studied under Josef Schusser (1864–1941) and František Kysela (1881–1941), among others. Since it was possible for students to obtain funds for educational travel abroad, Tsymbal received a scholarship to travel to Italy in 1926. He visited Naples, Venice, and Capri, and this journey undoubtedly had an impact on him. When in 1925, in the run-up to the commemoration of the imminent historian and politician František Palacký (1798–1876), the government announced an art contest for the best graphic portrait of Palacký, Tsymbal submitted his work. Czech graphics were in their heyday, so there were an impressive hundred submissions for the contest. The winner, however, was the Ukrainian émigré Tsymbal. Besides building his reputation, his win made a strong impression on Czech artists. His portrait of Palacký was reproduced in many magazines and newspapers, as well as on postcards. To create Palacký's portrait, Tsymbal utilized the knowledge he had gained at the School of Arts and Crafts as well as at the Ukrainian School of Plastic Arts.[26]

Another student at the school, Nina Levyts'ka-Shemans'ka (1902–1974), was born in Luts'k in Volhynia. She moved to Czechoslovakia in 1923 and lived there for the rest of her life. She studied in the Department of Philosophy at Charles University and the Ukrainian Higher Pedagogical Institute. She also studied at the School of Arts and Crafts under Dvořák. At the Ukrainian School of Plastic Arts, she studied sculpture under Stakhovs'kyi and excelled in that field. However, she worked primarily as a portraitist. She painted several portraits of Shevchenko as well as portraits of Dmytro Antonovych and Oleksander Oles', among other works. She also worked as a children's portraitist. After the war, however, Levyts'ka-Shemans'ka lived in Communist Czechoslovakia, where the environment was hardly stimulating. For many years she worked at the Slavonic Library, where she was in charge of periodicals.[27]

Among the prominent students at the school was Kateryna Antonovych. She was born in Kharkiv, where, after finishing gymnasium, she studied at the School of Drawing and Painting. She then studied medicine in St Petersburg, after which she spent two years in Italy, dividing her time between Venice, Florence, Rome, Naples, and Milan. She subsequently studied in Munich at the private school of renowned Hungarian artist Simon Hollósy (1857–1918). After that, she was educated in Kyiv at the Academy of Arts under Vasyl' Krychevs'kyi, Boichuk, and Narbut. In the early 1920s, Antonovych, with her children, joined her husband, Dmytro Antonovych, in Prague. After the war, and the death of her husband in Prague and the loss of one of her sons, Mykhailo Antonovych (1910–1954), who in 1945 had been deported to the Soviet Union and later died in the Gulag, she moved to Canada and lived in Winnipeg. There she opened her own painting and drawing studio; she exhibited her works in Toronto, Montreal, New York, and Philadelphia.[28]

The school's atmosphere was warm and welcoming. Mazurenko recalled that students were even allowed to bring children, which was something of a surprise to the Czech students. Kulets' explained to them that it was the school's policy so that an artistic atmosphere could surround small children from their earliest years.[29]

Exhibitions

For most of its existence, the school organized exhibitions of its students' works. Most of these exhibitions were covered not only in the Ukrainian émigré press but also in the Czechoslovak media. Even in the hardest times, these exhibitions were an important part of the creative lives of the professors and students, and they resonated in Czech art circles. The inaugural exhibition ran from 26 October to 17 November 1924 and presented works by Kulets', Mako, Mozalevs'kyi, Stakhovs'kyi, and Serhii Tymoshenko. The intention was to show the quality of work of the individuals who were going to be leading the school.[30]

For the 1925–26 academic year, the school organized an exhibition that coincided with the International Congress of Art Education. All national committees that attended the congress visited the exhibition, as did President Masaryk. The American delegation bought a work from one of the school's students as an example for their own art school. At another exhibition in Prague, in winter of 1925–26, held at the Pavilion of Exhibition, Mozalevs'kyi's pupils were praised as the most sophisticated at their craft. In 1935, the display consisted of approximately 125 oil paintings and drawings from Kulets's workshop, and included landscapes and portraits. The exhibition also included around fifty coloured pottery and plaster works by Stakhovs'kyi's students, and one hundred or so graphic pictures and engravings were on display from Lisovs'kyi's graphics workshop. This demonstrated the scope of works created by the school's young artists, as well as the various directions of the students' work and the development of their talents. By 1939 the school had organized thirteen exhibitions.[31]

In 1924, the Ukrainian Civic Committee on Ukrainian Books organized an exhibition of Ukrainian graphic works and books. This exhibition was presented in two locations in Prague: in a building near Wenceslas Square, and at a society for the promotion of arts called the Fine Arts Union (Krasoumná jednota). The graphic exhibition showcased more than two hundred works by Ukrainian artists including Narbut, Mykola Butovych (1895–1961), Petro Kholodnyi (1902–1990), Lisovs'kyi, Sichyns'kyi, and Les' Lozovs'kyi (1900–1922). Fifty Ukrainian publishing houses took part in the exhibition, and more than one thousand books were on display. The exhibition comprised Ukrainian books published in Czechoslovakia, Austria, Germany, Poland, Volhynia, Galicia, Bukovyna, and Soviet Ukraine. The exhibition was valuable because it introduced the accomplishments of Ukrainian art and publishing to a Czechoslovak audience.[32]

The artists took part in a variety of other exhibitions in Prague, among them a display of book culture at the International Congress of Bibliophiles in 1926, Ukrainian graphics exhibitions in 1931 and 1933, and an exhibition of Slavic *ex libris* in 1932. All of this underscores the intensity of the creative lives of Ukrainian artists in Prague during this period. Reviews of some of these exhibitions appeared in Prague art journals such as *Hollar – Sborník grafické práce* (Hollar – Collection of Graphic Works).[33] In 1926, works by Korniichuk, Koliadyns'kyi, and Tsymbal were presented at an exhibition at the School of Arts and Crafts in Prague. That same year, the works of several of the school's students – Kasiian, Zaryts'ka, and Petro Omel'chenko – were included at the Prague Academy of Fine Arts exhibition. To some degree, Ukrainian artists were being included in Prague's artistic life.[34]

The participation of Ukrainian artists in exhibitions was not limited to Prague. In early 1927, a Ukrainian graphics exhibition was held in Brussels, where several artists showed their work. There were also exhibitions of Ukrainian graphic art in other European cities, such as Berlin in February 1933, organized by Dmytro Antonovych and Lisovs'kyi, and Rome in 1938. Ukrainian artists also exhibited their works in Polish-ruled Galicia. In September 1935, they participated in an exhibition in L'viv devoted to the past thirty years of Ukrainian art, featuring works by Pavlo Hromnyts'kyi (1889–1977), Butovych, Lisovs'kyi, and Mazepa.[35]

In 1945, when the Soviet army came, the NKVD arrested the talented artist Liaturyns'ka. She later recalled the horrors of prison, where she remembered "blood and brain on the walls, blood and brain on the floor ... because there, [they] shot in that cellar." She was eventually released, but many were not. Another student, Halyna Mazepa, and her husband suffered a tragic loss during the bombing of Prague by the US Air Force in February 1945. Her mother, a doctor, had just left their house for a walk with their two little sons when the bombing started. All three were buried under the ruins of bombed-out building close to their home. There were more tragic destinies to come for those who ended up in the hands of SMERSH, which was Stalin's wartime counter-intelligence organization and was responsible for the arrests and executions of many thousands. Most of the artists, however, left Czechoslovakia before the Soviet Army arrived. Liaturyns'ka, Mazepa, Rusov, Lisovs'kyi, and Petro Omel'chenko all left, as did others. With their departure, the country – particularly Prague – ceased to be the cultural and artistic focal point for Ukrainian émigrés.[36] Mudrak noted:

> Despite the diversity of genres and the ostensible range of artistic directions that were promoted in the Ukrainian Studio of Plastic Arts, the students who emerged from the school were united by clear-sighted and discernible artistic goals and outcomes. In the midst of interwar Prague, they represented an artistic subculture whose legacy awaits to be recorded not only in the history of Ukrainian art, but also in the history of modern Czech culture as well.[37]

For three decades, the Ukrainian School of Plastic Arts was an important part of the Ukrainian émigré art world. The school brought together talented artists such as Kulets', Mako, Mozalevs'kyi, Lisovs'kyi, and Stakhovs'kyi, who provided professional training for their students and permanently marked their lives overall. Among the graduates were the renowned Ukrainian artists Hromnyts'kyi, Kasiian, Liaturyns'ka, Zaryts'ka, Koliadyns'kyi, Mazepa, and Kholodnyi. As with other institutions discussed in this study, the creation of the Ukrainian School of Plastic Arts can be seen as a continuation and realization in Czechoslovakia of projects started but left unfinished in Kyiv in the revolutionary years. The circumstances in which the school functioned certainly cannot compare with those in which an Academy of Arts would have functioned in an independent Ukraine. Nevertheless, the school served as a vital enclave for Ukrainian émigré artists as well as artists of other backgrounds.

Chapter Six

Ukrainian Scholarly and Professional Societies and Organizations

Between the wars, various Ukrainian scholarly and professional societies were founded in Czechoslovakia. These societies assembled scholars in a variety of fields and provided a much-needed platform for them to share and discuss their work with colleagues. Over the years, some of the scholarly groups were very active and some quickly dissolved. At the same time, professional organizations helped unite different groups of experts, and some of these groups helped their members find work both in Czechoslovakia and abroad. This chapter discusses the most important Ukrainian societies and their activities, accomplishments, and failures.

The Ukrainian Academic Committee

Founded by Ukrainian émigré intellectuals in Czechoslovakia, the Ukrainian Academic Committee was an important organization. It was established in late 1924 as a branch of the Ukrainian Historical–Philological Society; two years later, it became an independent organization. The goal of the committee was to bring together Ukrainian scholars and ensure their participation in international scholarly life. It was an umbrella organization representing Ukrainian scholarship in various fields in the broader scholarly world. Oleksander Shul'hyn first proposed this committee; at one of the society's meetings he delivered a paper about an organization of Ukrainian scholars and the League of Nations. Fluent in French and with connections in Paris, Shul'hyn was instrumental in representing Ukrainian scholars at the League of Nations' International Committee on Intellectual Cooperation. As a rule, the Ukrainian Academic Committee's chairperson was the rector of the Ukrainian Free University, so Kolessa led the committee for quite some time. In the 1920s, he devoted himself to the committee's mission and thought highly of its work and its achievements in representing Ukrainian scholarship abroad and forging links with European scholarly circles.[1]

Another of the committee's tasks was to create new Ukrainian émigré scholarly institutions and to assist those already in place. It also aimed to support the work of Ukrainian scholars and to establish cooperation with international scholars and institutions. This included organizing scholarly congresses, supporting the participation of Ukrainian émigré scholars at international congresses and conferences, and conducting some publishing activities. The committee achieved these and other goals with varying levels of success, and its activities significantly affected the Ukrainian intellectual world in Czechoslovakia during the interwar years. Ukrainian institutions and individuals were members of the committee. As shown in Table 13, its institutional membership included all Ukrainian émigré institutions of higher learning, many Ukrainian unions, as well as the Shevchenko Scientific Society and the Ukrainian Scholarly Institute in Berlin; the individual members were all professors at the Ukrainian Free University.[2]

The committee organized the two Ukrainian scholarly congresses in Prague (see chapter 2). Its members also took part in two international congresses organized by the International Committee on Intellectual Cooperation in 1926 and 1929. In particular, the committee helped

Table 13. Institutional and individual members of the Ukrainian Academic Committee, 1938[3]

Institutional members	Individual members
Shevchenko Scientific Society	Horbachevs'kyi, Ivan
Society of Ukrainian Economics in Czechoslovakia	Iakovliv, Andrii
Ukrainian Bibliophile Society	Kolessa, Oleksander
Ukrainian Economic Academy in Poděbrady	Lotots'kyi, leksander
Ukrainian Free University	Shul'hyn, leksander
Ukrainian Higher Pedagogical Institute	Slavins'kyi, Maksym
Ukrainian Historical–Philological Society	Smal'-Stots'kyi, Stepan
Ukrainian Law Society	
Ukrainian Pedagogical Society	
Ukrainian Scholarly Association	
Ukrainian School of Plastic Arts in Prague	
Ukrainian Scholarly Institute in Berlin	
Ukrainian University Group for the League of Nations	
Union of Organizations of Ukrainian Émigré Engineers	
Union of Ukrainian Doctors	
Union of Ukrainian Technicians of Agriculture	
Union of the Professors of the Ukrainian Economic Academy in Poděbrady	

many Ukrainian scholars and bibliographers participate actively in a bibliological conference in 1926 in Prague. It also prepared several festive events in honour of prominent Czechs and Ukrainians – for instance, it commemorated Palacký in 1926, Hrushevs'kyi in 1935, and Smal'-Stots'kyi in 1938. Other events arranged by the committee commemorated Virgil (1931) and Goethe (1932).[4]

Another notable event the committee arranged was an evening with the prominent Bukovynian writer Olha Kobylians'ka (1863–1942). This cultural event took place in June 1928 at the Municipal House in Prague, one of the city's most beautiful Art Nouveau buildings. The event was important for Prague's entire Ukrainian community. Kolessa in particular devoted a great deal of time and energy to preparing for the evening, as is evident from the many drafts of his speech at the celebratory event. That speech was beautifully written and identified Kobylians'ka as a writer and a feminist. Some Czechs were present at the gathering, which was covered by the Czechoslovak media.[5]

Regarding publishing activities, the committee published its bulletin, two volumes of the proceedings of the Ukrainian congresses, a bibliography of scholarly works of the Ukrainian emigration of 1920–31 (*Bibliohrafichnyi pokazhchyk naukovykh prats' ukrains'koi emigratsii 1920–1931*) compiled by Petro Zlenko (1891–1954), and a work by Dmytro Doroshenko about Chykalenko (published in 1934). There were also failures: in December 1929, the Ievhen Chykalenko Foundation was established by the committee with the task of publishing Chykalenko's diaries, memoirs, and other works, but only an excerpt of his 1917 memoirs was published in 1932 as well as Dmytro Doroshenko's above-mentioned work. In addition, the committee organized a special group to prepare a scholarly volume on Ukraine in the English language; this work was completed but never published.[6] By the end of the 1930s, the committee had greatly reduced its activities owing to the general drop-off of activities among the Ukrainian scholarly community in Czechoslovakia.

The Ukrainian Historical–Philological Society

In the 1920s, Prague brought together many scholars from the Ukrainian lands who continued their individual researches in the humanities. This led to the organizing of a scholarly society in which these intellectuals could exchange ideas and share their research. The professors who founded this society included Antonovych, Petro Andriievs'kyi, Bidnov, Dmytro Doroshenko, Kolessa, and Shcherbakivs'kyi. On 30 May 1923, Ukrainian émigré scholars founded the Ukrainian Historical–Philological Society in Prague. Most of the professors in this group were prominent in Ukrainian scholarly life in Prague, and had previous experience working at the universities of the former Austro-Hungarian and Russian empires. Such academic societies were common enough at Russian universities but not at Austrian ones. Given that all of the founding members except Kolessa were from Dnieper Ukraine, the efficient organization and activities of the society were also likely due to the experience these scholars had acquired in prewar scholarly societies. The principal prewar societies had been the Historical Society of Nestor the Chronicler (Istorychne tovarystvo Nestora-litopystsia) in Kyiv; the Historical–Philological Society at Kharkiv University (Istorychno-filolohichne tovarystvo pry Kharkivs'komu universyteti), the Ukrainian Scholarly Society (Ukrains'ke naukove tovarystvo) in Kyiv, and the scholarly societies of Kam'ianets'-Podil's'kyi, Katerynoslav, Odesa, Poltava, and other cities. For those from the Austro-Hungarian empire, the experience they gained as members of the Shevchenko Scientific Society was invaluable. In a 1924 letter to the historian and political figure Viacheslav Lypyns'kyi (1882–1931), Dmytro Doroshenko wrote that he along with Antonovych, Kolessa, Bidnov, and Shcherbakivs'kyi led the society.[7]

The board was elected with Antonovych as the head and Bidnov as the secretary. Support for this society very quickly gained momentum. That it generated interest among Ukrainian intellectuals in Prague is confirmed by the fact that around sixty people from the fields of history and philology attended the second meeting, held on 7 June. Doroshenko and Bidnov delivered two lectures on that day. At the same meeting, the first eleven members were elected; a week later another meeting was held at which eleven more members were elected. In its first year the society had thirty-one members; by 1931 the number had grown to fifty-seven. In subsequent years, the membership remained steady, with a slight decrease owing to the death of some members.[8]

As noted, the goals of the society were to present scholarly research, foster the exchange of opinions, and broaden scholarly discussions among Ukrainian émigré scholars. The scholarly papers focused mainly on research on Ukraine: its history, as well as the history of the Ukrainian language, literature, philosophy, arts, culture, music, theatre, and ethnology. Research findings on the history of law and the history of economic relations relevant to Ukraine were also sometimes delivered and discussed. Between 1923 and 1938, the most active participants were the head of the society, Antonovych, who delivered sixty papers; Bidnov, thirty-seven; Bilets'kyi, forty-one; Chyzhevs'kyi, thirty-five; Dmytro Doroshenko, thirty; the historian Symon Narizhnyi (1898–1983), forty-six; and Shcherbakivs'kyi, fifty. Other scholars, such as Artymovych, Smal'-Stots'kyi, Iakovliv, Oleh Kandyba (1907–1944),

Shelukhin, Sliusarenko, Sichyns'kyi, Siropolko, and Simovych, also contributed to the society with their research.[9]

Between 1923 and 1938, more than six hundred papers were delivered and discussed. As a rule, the scholars debated their research findings at these meetings before delivering them at larger international congresses or publishing them in scholarly periodicals. Attendance at meetings was quite steady. For example, in the 1930–31 academic year, the society held thirty meetings, which were attended by 536 people – 391 members and 145 guests. Average attendance per meeting was around 18. In addition, some Czech scholars supported the society and its members in their work. Several renowned Czech scholars attended the society's jubilee scholarly meetings, demonstrating collegial support that the society members undoubtedly appreciated.[10]

The society's activities were highly valued by émigré scholars. In a letter from Warsaw dated November 1930, Bidnov congratulated Kolessa on the two hundredth meeting of the society. In that letter, he highlighted Kolessa's role as initiator and founder of the society and noted how, even under difficult circumstances, it had continued to develop and provide a platform for research discussion among both established and junior scholars. Bidnov continued by acknowledging that internal and external difficulties had raised obstacles for Ukrainian scholarship. In Prague, however, thanks to the university and the society, scholarship was steadily developing. Bidnov added that the society's activities were especially important now that the Department of the History of Ukraine had been shut down at the Ukrainian Academy of Sciences in Soviet Ukraine. The letter was heartfelt in tone. Interestingly, even though Kolessa was one of the society's founders, he was not an active presenter and delivered only one paper. He was apparently more involved in teaching at two universities, among other scholarly duties.[11]

The official organ of the society was *Pratsi Ukrains'koho istorychno-filolohychnoho tovarystva* (Works of the Ukrainian Historical–Philological Society, 1926–44). The first volume was published on 22 February 1926 and had a circulation of five hundred. The copies were distributed among the members of the society and sent to a variety of scholarly institutions, societies, libraries, and scholars in Czechoslovakia, Poland, and Soviet Ukraine. This volume featured articles based on papers discussed at scholarly meetings by Antonovych, Dmytro Doroshenko, Mirchuk, Smal'-Stots'kyi, and Shcherbakivs'kyi, among others. The publication of this volume placed financial strain on the society, for it had to repay the publishing house a large loan, which it cleared by 1930.[12]

From 1923 to 1941, the society also published annual reports, *Spravozdannia Ukrains'koho istorychno-filologychnoho tovarystva v Prazi* (Reports of the Ukrainian Historical–Philological Society in Prague), in lithographic form. These included descriptions of the society's scholarly and organizational activities, lists of its members and publications, and reports on educational excursions and participation in jubilee events. This publication was distributed among members and sent to various scholarly institutions. Publishing opportunities within the society were limited, so the members published their works in a variety of other scholarly publications wherever possible. Their research appeared most often in émigré publications, but it also found outlets in Galicia and some, in the 1920s, in Soviet Ukraine. It was also published in various European periodicals in different languages. Notable publications by society members included Siropolko's work *Istoriia osvity na Ukraini* (A History of Education in Ukraine, 1937) and Chyzhevs'kyi's research *Filosofiia H.S. Skovorody* (Philosophy of Skovoroda, 1934), as well as Smal'-Stots'kyi's *Rozvytok pohliadiv pro semiu slovians'kykh mov i ikh vzaimne sporidnennia* (Development of Views on the Family of Slavic Languages, 2nd ed., 1927).

For more than two decades, the society provided a forum were scholars could engage in discussions and exchange ideas. The society continued until 1945, albeit with varying levels of intensity. Its activities were an important contribution to the Ukrainian intellectual world in Prague.

The Ukrainian Bibliophile Society

In the 1920s, as Prague became an important centre for Ukrainian publishing, the need for an organization of Ukrainian bibliographers became apparent. The city gathered together several Ukrainian bibliographers between the wars. Bibliographers such as Petro Zlenko, Lev Bykovs'kyi (1895–1992), and Ievhen Vyrovyi (1889–1945) worked as librarians with Ukrainian collections, created bibliographies, and were generally active in all aspects of Ukrainian publications. In addition, some émigré scholars had a keen interest in bibliography, particularly Dmytro Doroshenko, who had published some bibliographies long before his emigration. The idea of creating a bibliophile society was first suggested during the preparations for the 1926 International Congress of Bibliographers, held in Prague. A proposal for one was presented, discussed, and overwhelmingly supported at a special meeting of the Ukrainian delegation to this congress. A committee was elected and tasked with writing a draft for a statute for the future organization. The Ukrainian Bibliophile Society in Prague (Ukrains'ke tovarystvo prykhyl'nykiv knyhy v Prazi) was founded on 5 January 1927, with Siropolko as the head, Vyrovyi as the deputy head, and Ukrainian publisher Iurii Tyshchenko (pseudonym Siryi) (1880–1953) as the secretary. Siropolko and

Vyrovyi led the society from its establishment until 1934; on 8 February 1934, a new council was elected with Sichyns'kyi as the head.[13]

Besides the above-mentioned scholars, Antonovych, Artymovych, Bidnov, Bykovs'kyi, Iakovliv, Kolessa, Ivan Mirnyi (1872–1937), Rusova, Vasyl' Simovych, Izydora Simovych, Shcherbakivs'kyi, Slavins'kyi, Zlenko and others helped found the society. The society was most active when it was led by Siropolko. It was an organization of bibliographers, librarians, and publishers and was open to all bibliophiles. It had several objectives, but its main responsibility was to organize scholarly meetings with professional presentations and discussions on Ukrainian bibliography. It also intended to publish a journal devoted to Ukrainian books and to establish contacts with professional organizations in Czechoslovakia and abroad. In addition, it planned to register Ukrainian publications that had been released outside of Soviet Ukraine as well as works devoted to Ukraine in various other languages and to organize exhibitions dedicated to Ukrainian books and periodicals. The society's other goals included establishing branches in other places where Ukrainians dwelled – for example, in L'viv, Uzhhorod, Chernivtsi, Paris, and Berlin. It achieved its goals with varying levels of success.[14]

The society had two special committees. The publishing and editorial committee was charged with publishing an important organ of the society: *Knyholiub* (A Book Lover). The head of this committee was the scholar and bibliographer Vladimir Tukalevskii (1881–1936) and the secretary was Viktor Sapits'kyi (1889–1942). However, Siropolko was the editor-in-chief of the periodical between 1927 and 1932, and thus their roles in this committee were unclear. The second committee was a library and bibliographic one, with Sichyns'kyi as its head and Zlenko as the secretary. In its first year, the society already had seventy-one members, and by 1934 there were ninety-six. In 1934, along with Ukrainian scholars and institutions, the institutional members of the society included the Slavonic Library in Prague and the Association of Czechoslovak Librarians (Spolek československých knihovníků). Ukrainian bibliographers took a close interest in the practices of their colleagues in Czechoslovakia, and learned from them. In 1928, Bykovs'kyi published a work devoted to library science in Czechoslovakia. He and Siropolko also cooperated with the Czechoslovak journal *Časopis československých knihovníků* (The Journals of Czechoslovak Librarians, 1922–38).[15]

The society was a member of the Ukrainian Academic Committee and cooperated with other societies and institutions. Scholars from all the Ukrainian institutions of higher learning participated in its activities. Among its most important happenings were scholarly meetings at which scholars and bibliographers presented their research. At the first and second meetings, for example, Vyrovyi talked about Ukrainian books in Soviet Ukraine, Bidnov discussed Ukrainian religious publications during the revolutionary years, and Antonovych spoke on the subject of Narbut and the art of new Ukrainian books. In total, between 1927 and 1931, thirty-nine scholarly meetings took place at which more than sixty papers were delivered and discussed before they were published in *Knyholiub*. The journal had several sections, including library science; publishing; "Ukrainica," which featured publications on Ukraine in different languages; new Ukrainian publications in Czechoslovakia; and bibliography. The bibliography section included materials published beyond the borders of Soviet Ukraine. In addition, the society had strong ties with the Ukrainian Bibliophile Society in L'viv, and published its works in the journal *Ukrains'ka knyha* (The Ukrainian Book, 1937–43). Members of the society, primarily Arkadii Zhyvotko (1890–1948), Sichyns'kyi, and Zlenko, but also Antonovych, Bidnov, Vyrovyi, Vasyl' Simovych, Siropolko, and Chyzhevs'kyi, published articles and smaller items in this journal.[16]

Ukrainian bibliographers also took part in the development of bibliographic theory, published several indexes, and incorporated substantial bibliographies into their scholarly works. They also registered Ukrainian publications and publications about Ukraine in various languages in the journal *Slavianskaia kniga* (A Slavic Book, 1925–26) and subsequently in *Knyholiub*. As part of promoting Ukrainian publications, the society developed bibliographies of publications by Ukrainian scholars for indexes published by the League of Nations' Committee on Intellectual Cooperation. All of these activities were valuable for the promotion of Ukrainian books and periodicals.[17]

The scholarly meetings discussed above were sometimes accompanied by exhibitions presenting new Ukrainian publications or devoted to a specific theme. Exhibitions were devoted to Shevchenko's and Kobylians'ka's works, Ukrainian *ex libris*, and Ukrainian publications in the United States and in POW camps for Ukrainian soldiers. These displays were intended for an audience of professionals to create stronger bibliographic awareness. The society also organized larger exhibitions for outside audiences, one of which took place in 1924 and was devoted to the 350th anniversary of the publication of *Apostol* (the Gospels) in L'viv. The newspaper *Československá republika* (The Czechoslovak Republic) published a review of this exhibition of Ukrainian books. It noted that the exhibition included books from all Ukrainian territories, namely Soviet Ukraine, Galicia, Bukovyna, and the Transcarpathian region. The same newspaper acknowledged the existence of the Ukrainian language as the one understood by inhabitants of Dnieper Ukraine, Galicia, and the Transcarpathian region. The review was highly positive. In 1926, the bibliographers organized another exhibition of Ukrainian books in conjunction with the International Congress of Librarians and Bibliophiles in Prague, which was organized by the Association of Czechoslovak Librarians. Kolessa was among the members of the organizing committee, and the university, the academy, and the institute, as well as the Ukrainian publishing house, the Ukrainian Civic Publishing Fund, took part in this congress and presented their books. This exhibition included Ukrainian books published in all Ukrainian territories and abroad, as well as periodicals, materials on Ukraine in other languages, Shevchenko's works, and graphics of various publishing houses and libraries. The society also organized a book exhibition at the second Ukrainian scholarly congress, held in Prague in 1932. In 1933, it arranged (already mentioned) a large exhibition of Ukrainian graphic works from the nineteenth and twentieth centuries; more than one hundred Ukrainian artists took part in this, and more than one thousand works were presented. The exhibition received positive coverage in the press.[18] The society also intended to collect all Ukrainian publications published in Czechoslovakia and to preserve them for the National Library in Kyiv. With the end of Ukrainianzation in Soviet Ukraine, these plans were likely never realized. Overall, the society's activities, like those of all the Ukrainian institutions discussed in this study, tapered off in the 1930s.[19]

The Ukrainian Law Society

Between the wars, there were dozens of Ukrainian legal scholars in Prague. They gathered mainly at the Department of Law and Social Sciences at the Ukrainian Free University, as well as at the Ukrainian Law Society. On 17 March 1923, the Czechoslovak government approved the statute of this society. Credit for the idea of organizing it went to Ukrainian jurists. The organizers intended the society to continue the work of the Ukrainian Law Society (Ukrains'ke pravnyche tovarystvo v Kyievi) that had been founded in Kyiv in 1917, which had been a society of judges, lawyers, and other legal professionals. According to the statute of the newly created society, the goals were to bring together Ukrainian theorists and jurists, to promote research in Ukrainian law, to help Ukrainian jurists in Czechoslovakia, and to develop cooperation between Ukrainian and Czechoslovak jurists.[20]

Dnistrians'kyi was the leading Ukrainian legal scholar in Prague. He was born in the Ternopil region and graduated from a Polish gymnasium in Ternopil. After concluding his university studies in Vienna, he moved to Berlin and Leipzig to deepen his knowledge of law. In 1899, he became a professor of civil law at the University of L'viv. Before the war, he had been the founder and president of the Society of Ukrainian Lawyers in L'viv (Tovarystvo ukrains'kykh pravnykiv u L'vovi), and he was a Member of Parliament in Vienna from 1907 to 1918. Dnistrians'kyi was the editor of the journals *Chasopys' pravnycha i ekonomichna* (Journal of Law and Economics, 1900–6, 1912) and *Pravnychyi visnyk* (Journal of Law, 1910–13), which had appeared in L'viv before the war. As the author of many works on civil law in the German, Ukrainian, and Czech languages, he was noted for his contributions to the development of Ukrainian legal terminology. In Prague, he was a professor at the Ukrainian Free University and taught law in the Czechoslovak Higher School of Political Sciences and civil law at the German University in Prague.[21]

Andrii Iakovliv, a professor of civil procedure at the Ukrainian Free University, was another important figure. He was an expert on the history of Ukrainian law, particularly of the Hetmanate period. He studied law at Derpt (now Tartu) University before returning to Kyiv, where he worked in state administration and advocacy. There, he became a member of the Ukrainian Scholarly Society and, in early 1917, formed the Ukrainian Law Society. During the Ukrainian Revolution, he occupied several posts, the last one being ambassador to Holland and Belgium, after which he settled in Prague. At the university, he passed his habilitation at the Department of Civil Procedure and later taught there. Iakovliv was a very knowledgeable legal scholar, and according to one author it was a blunder that he was not nominated and chosen as a dean of the department when the post became vacant in 1929. Iakovliv would go on to prepare a comprehensive textbook on Ukrainian law.[22]

Rostyslav Lashchenko (1878–1929), another notable member of the community, was the head of the society until his death. Before the war he was a judge in Kyiv, and during the revolutionary years he occupied several important posts. In Prague, he taught history of Ukrainian law at the university. He lectured on the history of sources and on state, civil, and criminal law; his lectures were lively and interesting. Lashchenko managed to publish the first two parts of his planned work: the first part on law in the Kyivan Rus', the second on the sources of law in the Polish–Lithuanian Commonwealth. Lashchenko died suddenly at the age of fifty-one, leaving many of his scholarly plans unrealized.[23]

There were other full and associate professors whose research and activities lay within this developing field: Opanas Andriievs'kyi (1878–1955), who was a justice of the peace and a lawyer and later taught Ukrainian law at the university; Otto Eikhel'man, a professor of administrative law; Lotots'kyi, a professor of church law; Los'kyi, a professor of the history of Roman law; and Shelukhin, a professor of criminal law. Two members of the society who returned suffered tragic ends. The first, Mykhailo Lozyns'kyi, taught international law at the Ukrainian Free University. He perished during the purges. The second, Volodymyr Starosol's'kyi, was a lawyer and sociologist who taught state law at the university and the Ukrainian Economic Academy. In 1902, he helped organize the secession of Ukrainian students from the University of L'viv. He returned to L'viv in 1927 and reopened his law office. In 1939, he was arrested by the Soviets and perished. Both these scholars taught at Ukrainian institutions of higher learning in the 1920s and presumably were also active in the society.

In 1923, the society had twenty-one members; ten years later, that number had almost tripled. Besides Lashchenko, the heads of the society were Iakovliv, Los'kyi, and Dnistrians'kyi. Its main activity was organizing scholarly meetings, which included presentations and discussions by its members. In its first five years, the society hosted fifty-four scholarly presentations; during the first ten years of its activities, it held 120 scholarly meetings. Legal scholars wrote articles and monographs, but these often remained unpublished because of the lack of funding. The society's work was closely linked with the university, as many of its members were on the university faculty. Their research topics included sources and history of Ukrainian law, history of church law, history of state-building in Ukraine, foundations of Ukrainian private law, general legal obligations, criminal law of the Hetmanate, administrative and private law in Soviet Ukraine, the constitution of Soviet Ukraine, and Ukrainian state law.[24]

Members of the society also participated in the first and the second Ukrainian congresses. At the first congress, Lotots'kyi, Iakovliv, Dnistrians'kyi, Opanas Andriievs'kyi, and Shelukhin presented and discussed several papers in various fields of law. At the second congress, Iakovliv summarized the achievements and shortcomings of Ukrainian legal scholarly work in Czechoslovakia. Due to disagreements with the congress's council, a separate congress was planned for jurists and lawyers; this Ukrainian Law Congress took place in Prague on 4–7 October 1933, under the leadership of Dnistrians'kyi. Notwithstanding the congress's title, it was a gathering not only for legal scholars but also for scholars in economics and sociology. Society members participated in this congress, delivering twenty-three papers on various topics in law, economics, and sociology. As for legal scholars, they addressed many themes in their field: Eikhel'man presented on the codification of international law, Dnistrians'kyi on issues in economic law in the modern era, and Shelukhin on the participation of individuals in courts. Several papers were devoted to the history of Ukrainian law. Oleksander Haimanivs'kyi (1886–1963) discussed *Rus'ka Pravda* (Rus' Truth [Law]), the collection of legal norms in Kyivan Rus', and *Lytovs'kyi statut* (The Lithuanian Statute), the medieval law code of the Grand Duchy of Lithuania as applied in Ukrainian territories from the sixteenth to the early nineteenth century, while Iakovkiv spoke on the development of Ukrainian law in the seventeenth and eighteenth centuries. In addition, Eikhel'man, Dnistrians'kyi, and Shelukhiv delivered papers on Ukrainian state law, civil law, and criminal law, respectively.[25]

Ukrainian legal scholars took part in the congresses of Czechoslovak jurists in 1925 and 1930, as well as the International Congress of Criminologists held in Prague in 1930. The society also organized or took part in several events where its members delivered lectures. For instance, in December 1923, the society organized an event dedicated to Dnistrians'kyi's twenty-five years of scholarly activities. It also took part in a celebration of Horbachevs'kyi's seventieth birthday and Shcherbyna's seventy-fifth, among other events.[26]

Publishing was a challenge because of the lack of funds; nonetheless, Ukrainian legal scholars published their research on various branches of law and on the history of law. Specifically, they published works on theory and philosophy of law, customary law, constitutional law, state and administrative law, civil law, family law, trade law, land law, and tax law, among others. Dnistrians'kyi was the most prolific, publishing works on state law, civil law, and the general principles of law. Lashchenko produced works on civil law, Lozyns'kyi and Eikhel'man on international law, Los'kyi on Roman law, Shelukhin on criminal law, and Lotots'kyi on the church law of the Kyivan Rus'. Clearly, these legal scholars' interests were broad.[27]

Society members also published several monographs and collective works. For example, Dnistrians'kyi's *Základy moderního práva soukromého* (Foundations of Modern Private Law) was published in 1928 by the Czechoslovak Academy of Sciences, and Iakovliv wrote *Vplyvy staroches'koho prava na pravo ukrains'ke lytovs'koi doby* (Influences of Old Czech Law on Ukrainian Law in the Polish–Lithuanian Commonwealth, 1929). Articles were published in annals of Ukrainian institutions in Czechoslovakia as well as in publications in L'viv, for example, in the journal *Zhyttia i pravo* (Life and Law, 1928–39), published by the Shevchenko Scientific Society. Much more, however, remained unpublished. By some estimates, Ukrainian legal scholars between the wars published more than one hundred scholarly works in various fields of law.[28]

During the 1930s, the activities of the society, as with other Ukrainian émigré institutions, wound down. In addition to the difficult financial situation, the nature of the profession itself may have been a factor in this. It was difficult but possible for Ukrainians to work, for example, as engineers in their host country; it was impossible for them to work as lawyers or judges. For this reason, the activities of the society's members had to remain purely theoretical and strictly limited to writing books and articles as well as participating in scholarly meetings and conferences. At present, their works are being steadily discovered by legal professionals in Ukraine.[29]

The Union of Ukrainian Doctors in Czechoslovakia

Many doctors from the Ukrainian lands found themselves in Czechoslovakia between the wars. Much like the members of other émigré professional groups, physicians felt a need to create a professional organization that would unite them and, in times of need, act on their behalf. In 1922, therefore, an exploratory group was organized, whose members included Borys Matiushenko, Ivan Rykhlo (1891–1968), and Oleksa Bilous (1868–1929). At a meeting in October 1922, a draft of the statute was accepted and passed to the Czechoslovak government for authorization. With the government's approval secured, the Union of Ukrainian Doctors was founded in December 1922 in Prague. The organization had several objectives: to connect Ukrainian émigré doctors in Czechoslovakia; to improve and broaden the professional development efforts of its members; to arrange lectures for the public on medical topics; to provide financial and legal aid to its members; and, with the government's help, to offer them an opportunity to practise in hospitals and institutions in Czechoslovakia. Throughout its existence (i.e., until 1940), the union was active in these areas. From its inception until 1935, the head of the union was its founder, Matiushenko; Iurii Dorbylovs'kyi (1891–1955) led it from 1935 to 1940, followed by Mykhailo Zaval'niak (1902–1963) for six months in 1940 until it dissolved. The union had 33 members when it was founded; by 1939, it had 119.[30]

In the 1920s, the union received substantial financial help from the Czechoslovak government. Between 1923 and 1928 it received 551,950 crowns in financial assistance for the doctors and 120,000 crowns for their publishing activities. Thanks to this, the union was able to offer stipends to Ukrainian doctors in Czechoslovakia. With this money, they were able to practise in the country's hospitals and clinics. At that time the assistance program was led by Girsa, who, as discussed in chapter 1, had been a doctor in Kyiv before the war and was sympathetic toward the Ukrainians; he likely made this substantial financial assistance possible.[31]

The union also organized several lectures. In February and March 1923, with the assistance of the Ukrainian Student Medical Community, it organized eight public lectures with drug demonstrations, tables, and slides. The lectures were held in the hall of the Physiological Institute at the Department of Medicine of Charles University and were well attended. In 1923, at the union's meetings, eleven scholarly lectures on a variety of medical topics were delivered and discussed.[32]

The union's publishing activities were very important. One of its major accomplishments was the publication of the first dictionary of Ukrainian medical terminology. The author was a surgeon from Bessarabia, Martyrii Halyn (1856[8]–1943), who had studied medicine and worked in St Petersburg as well as in Kyiv before the First World War. When the Ukrainian Scholarly Society was founded in Kyiv in 1907 under the leadership of Hrushevs'kyi, Halyn was among its first members, and in 1908 he became head of the society's Natural Sciences and Medicine section. In 1920, in Kyiv, Halyn published *Rosiis'ko-ukrains'kyi medychnyi slovnyk* (A Russian-Ukrainian Medical Dictionary). He gave the union the manuscript of the dictionary with permission to publish it in early 1924, but it already had a manuscript for a similar dictionary developed by another Ukrainian physician, Vasyl' Nalyvaiko (1887–1938). The two manuscripts followed different principles, so the decision was made to take Halyn's work as the basis and edit and enhance it with terms from Nalyvaiko's manuscript. Nalyvaiko agreed to this. The editorial office, which included Matiushenko, Nalyvaiko, Rykhlo, and later Matiushenko's wife Mariia, worked for two years, consulting with other authoritative bodies. *Medychnyi latyns'ko-ukrains'kyi slovnyk* (The Medical Latin–Ukrainian Dictionary) was published in 1926 in Prague; it consisted of 304 two-columned pages and included approximately 16,400 terms.[33]

Another important undertaking of the union was the publication of the medical scholarly journal *Ukrains'kyi medychnyi vistnyk* (Ukrainian Medical Review), which the union issued from 1923 to 1925 under its editor-in-chief Matiushenko. This journal published scholarly articles on clinical and theoretical medicine. During this period six volumes were published, which received positive reviews in Czech, German, and Russian professional literature, as well as in publications for a more general readership. The periodical provided Ukrainian medical professionals with a much-needed platform. The authors of the journal articles included, among many others, Tyt-Ievhen Burachyns'kyi (1880–1968), and Evhen Lukasevych (1871–1929). The same periodical provided an overview of medical conferences and congresses in Europe, an annotated bibliography of medical literature, and a listing of scholarly and professional events and organizations in the field, including activities of the Ukrainian Red Cross and Czechoslovak Red Cross. During these years, the medical periodical *Likars'kyi vistnyk* (Physician's

Herald, 1920–21, 1925–39), published by the medical section of the Shevchenko Scientific Society in L'viv, temporarily stopped publishing. The fact that *Ukrains'kyi medychnyi vistnyk* was a platform for physicians from all Ukrainian lands was especially evident in the third and fourth volumes, dedicated to Horbachevs'kyi, in which physicians from Galicia, Bukovyna, and Soviet Ukraine as well as émigré doctors published their research. Horbachevs'kyi's former pupil, the Czech doctor and chemist Emanuel Formánek, who was director of the Institute of Medical Chemistry at Charles University, wrote an introduction to these volumes. Other Czech students and colleagues of Horbachevs'kyi wrote papers on various themes, including Gustav Kabrhel (1857–1939), Antonín Hamsík, and Vladislav Růžička (1870–1934). The importance of this periodical lay in its rich content and in the fact that it was published during the years in which no other Ukrainian medical journals were being published in Galicia or Soviet Ukraine. In 1925, with the relaunch of *Ukrains'ki medychni visti* (Ukrainian Medical News) in Kyiv, which was modelled on *Ukrains'kyi medychnyi vistnyk*, and with in the resumption of *Likars'kyi vistnyk* the same year in L'viv, the journal published in Prague ceased its activities. On the pages of this journal, Ukrainian medical terminology was formed, tested, and refined.[34]

The union also arranged educational excursions and took part in several others with Czechoslovak physicians. However, its members' relations with Czechoslovak doctors and their professional organizations were not happy ones. Reportedly, physicians in Czechoslovakia had pro-Russian sentiments and were unsympathetic toward their Ukrainian colleagues.[35] Job availability also have been a factor: before the war, employment prospects for all professions had been much stronger, as professionals were able to work anywhere in the former Austro-Hungarian empire. For example, before the war, many Czech physicians found jobs in Vienna. Now that the job market had contracted, Czech physicians may have looked unfavourably upon competition from foreign doctors.

In the 1920s, the union, together with the Ukrainian Medical Society (Ukrains'ke likars'ke tovarystvo) in L'viv, was a member of the All-Slavic Medical Union. Both participated as a national delegation in the first and second congresses, held in Belgrade and Warsaw respectively. Before the third congress, however, the decision was made to change the membership rules so that stateless delegations had to be included in the delegations of their previous states, but without the right to vote. Both the Ukrainian Medical Society and the union strongly protested this and quit the union completely. *Likars'kyi vistnyk* reported that before the war Ukrainians had been members of the All-Slavic Medical

Union, as were other nations that were stateless at that time, because membership had been on a national basis, not a state one.[36]

The union's activities were important for Ukrainian physicians in Czechoslovakia. In its early years, when it had financial means, it was able to issue several important publications and to support doctors in their practices. It was able to unite a substantial number of the Ukrainian physicians living and practising in the country at that time.

Other Organizations and Groups

Ukrainians in Czechoslovakia created or participated in other scholarly and professional organizations. For various reasons, not all of these organizations were able to fully implement their plans. Disagreements among various groups were a factor; the timing of their creation was another, as in the 1930s – as discussed above – scholarly and professional activities in Czechoslovakia decreased considerably. Nevertheless, these societies were able to leave some mark on the Ukrainian émigré scholarly and professional worlds in Czechoslovakia.

One very important group was by no means Ukrainian; nevertheless, several members of the Ukrainian intellectual community participated in it. This particular group, known as the Prague Linguistic Circle, was international in nature and assembled Czech, Russian, German, and Ukrainian linguists, among others. It was founded in 1926 and became highly visible. It was initiated by the Czech linguist and literary historian Vilém Mathesius (1882–1945). The group's aim was to create a new approach to linguistics, and "they developed methods of structuralist literary analysis." The members of the circle took a phonological approach that amounted to a new direction in linguistics; they "researched linguistic phenomena from the point of view of structural rules of language and from the point of view of its functions, which these phenomena have in language." Along with Mathesius, the circle included Czech linguists Bohumil Trnka (1895–1984), Bohuslav Havránek (1893–1978), and Jan Mukařovský (1892–1974). Among the Russian members of the circle were the renowned linguists Roman Jakobson, Nikolai Trubetskoi, Sergei Kartsevskii (1884–1955), and Nikolai Durnovo (1876–1937). The German linguists who participated in the circle's research were Eugen Rippl (1888–1945), who taught the Czech language at the German University in Prague; musicologist Gustav Becking (1895–1945); and Friedrich Slotty (1881–1963), an expert on comparative Indo-European languages.[37] The members from the Ukrainian scholarly spheres were Chyzhevs'kyi, Artymovych, and Simovych. Chyzhevs'kyi in particular was highly active in the circle; he delivered many lectures and published his works in the circle's organ, *Travaux du Cercle linguistique de Prague* (Works of the Prague Linguistic Circle, 1929–39).

In 1935, the circle established the scholarly journal *Slovo a slovesnost* (Word and Letters), which was long the most significant Czech linguistic journal and is still being published today. The participation of Ukrainian scholars in the circle was reportedly not extensive, and their names, except for Chyzhevs'kyi, were absent among the authors of *Travaux du Cercle linguistique de Prague*. However, they delivered several lectures at the circle's gatherings: Artymovych on the theory of language, and Simovych on the inflection of Ukrainian adjectives. Participation in the group was definitely important for them. Simovych recalled the following about the circle: "Every evening we had discussions, every evening one learned something new, every time we saw linguistic phenomen[a] in a new light. How much joy we have experienced." After moving to L'viv in 1933, Simovych organized another linguistic circle (Movoznavchyi hurtok) there. This circle's goal was to promote the phonological approach of the Prague Linguistic Circle. Whether successful or not, it shows that the legacy of the circle in Prague lived on.[38]

In 1930, Ukrainian engineers in different countries founded an organization that had as its goal to establish contacts with non-Ukrainian professional societies as well as Ukrainian scholarly societies. This umbrella organization was called the Union of Ukrainian Engineers' Organizations Abroad (Soiuz orhanizatsii inzheneriv ukraintsiv na emigratsii), and it was intended to unite various engineering societies and organizations in Czechoslovakia, Poland, France, and other countries where Ukrainian engineers resided. With its head office in Poděbrady, the union had 556 members by 1931. This idea of unification was not very popular; by 1932, the largest organization of Ukrainian engineers in Czechoslovakia, the Society of Ukrainian Engineers, had left the union to continue its activities separately. Sharp disagreements likely characterized many émigré groups, not only Ukrainian engineerss. The union managed to publish four issues of its journal *Ukrains'kyi inzhener* (The Ukrainian Engineer, 1931–32) and tried to help a number of Ukrainian engineers find employment. In 1937, as Ukrainian life in Czechoslovakia and other countries became less active and many engineers found – or failed to find – employment, the union ceased its activities.[39]

In May 1930, the Ukrainian Pedagogical Society (Ukrains'ke pedagogichne tovarystvo) was established, aiming to study pedagogical practice and theory. In its first year alone the society had thirty-four members. It held several meetings at which presenters discussed past and present education in the Ukrainian lands, as well as education reforms in Czechoslovakia. As well as Ukrainians, several Czech professors presented their research at some of these meetings. At this time, the society established contacts with pedagogical and cultural institutions in Galicia, Bukovyna, the Transcarpathian region, and Canada. These contacts helped the society become more aware of the situation in these lands. In 1932, it published the volume *Ukrains'ke shkil'nytstvo na Bukovyni, v Halychyni, na Zakarpatti ta v Kanadi* (Ukrainian Schooling in Bukovyna, Galicia, the Transcarpathian region, and Canada, 1932). It also negotiated on behalf of teachers for jobs in the Transcarpathian region. It was too late, however, for the society to actively develop. In 1933, the Ukrainian Higher Pedagogical Institute was closed; many individuals who taught there had been members of the society. The economic calamity in the 1930s and the waning hope of returning to Ukraine undoubtedly contributed to the cessation of the society's activities.[40]

The societies discussed above played an important role in Ukrainian émigré scholarly and professional life. The role of the Ukrainian Academic Committee as the umbrella organization was to unite various groups and represent Ukrainian scholarship. The Ukrainian Historical–Philological Society provided a forum where scholars conducted hundreds scholarly meetings, presented research, and debated issues. The Ukrainian Bibliophile Society was notable in the field of Ukrainian bibliography. Its periodical *Knyholiub* registered Ukrainian publications in Czechoslovakia and abroad and is still a very useful resource for studying Ukrainian intellectual life between the wars. The Ukrainian Law Society organized Ukrainian legal scholars so that they could continue presenting their research and getting their colleagues' feedback. The Union of Ukrainian Doctors in Czechoslovakia brought together Ukrainian émigré doctors. Its publications, including the medical scholarly periodical *Ukrains'kyi medychnyi vistnyk,* were also significant. In addition to the scholarly and professional societies discussed above, there were many other smaller and less active societies and organizations for Ukrainian émigrés in Czechoslovakia. All of these societies had important roles to play in the Ukrainian intellectual world in interwar Czechoslovakia.

Chapter Seven

Libraries, Archives, and Museums

The Slavonic Library

The Slavonic Library in Prague was one of the major collections created in Europe between the wars. Its primary goal was, and still is, to build collections pertaining to the cultures of Slavic peoples. The library was founded in 1924 as a research library of the Ministry of Foreign Affairs of the Czechoslovak Republic and was directly connected with the government assistance program. Girsa, in particular, played a prominent role in its founding. Until 1927, the library was known as the Russian Library of the Ministry of Foreign Affairs (Ruská knihovna ministerstva zahraničních věcí). Initially, its main holdings were Russian collections based on the rich collection of Russian books and periodicals of the founder of the library, the literary scholar and bibliographer Vladimir Tukalevskii.[1] Along with Russian materials, Ukrainian and Belarusian ones were collected from the inception of the library. In 1927, the library started to collect books and periodicals about all Slavic peoples, and the library's name was changed to the Slavonic Library of the Ministry of Foreign Affairs (Slovanská knihovna ministerstva zahraničních věcí). In 1928, the Ukrainian department was established. At that time, the library was divided into eleven departments – Czechoslovak, Russian, Ukrainian, Belarusian, Polish, Bulgarian, Serbo-Croatian, Slovene, Sorbian, general Slavic, and general non-Slavic.[2]

The library's mission included supporting the activities of the newly created Institute of Slavic Studies. At this early stage, the ministry generously supported the library financially, enabling it to buy materials from twelve countries. In 1925, for example, the library budget was 225,000 crowns, which was quite substantial. In 1928, for the purchase of its rich collections of Slavic periodicals alone, the ministry paid around 35,000 crowns. By 1929, the library housed five hundred periodical titles in a variety of Slavic languages. In addition, an international exchange program was established, and in 1928 the Slavonic Library had exchanges with 284 libraries, publishing houses, and scholars, as well as research institutions in 150 cities in twenty-six countries.[3]

Otto Křížek (1884–1971), the director of the library after 1928, contributed considerably to its development in the interwar years. He created a system based on scholars' needs, developed guidelines on collection development, divided the library into departments based on different nations, and hired librarians. The library also employed several staff of Russian and Ukrainian émigré background. Those staff were appointed to develop collections in Slavic languages as well as to support the Institute of Slavic Studies. The library also created a book committee to manage the library and develop its collections. In the late 1920s, the library was transferred to the Clementinum, a former Jesuit college in the centre of Prague, where it is still located today.[4] As noted, the library began collecting Ukrainian materials as soon as it was founded. From the end of 1920s, the curator of the Ukrainian department was Oleksander Haimanivs'kyi. During the revolution he had served in various military capacities. He studied law, first in the Russian empire, then in Prague, and then after his habilitation he taught law at the Ukrainian Free University. In 1945, he shared the tragic fate of those who did not leave Prague. He was arrested in 1945 and sent to the Gulag, from which he only returned to Prague in 1957; he died several years later. Other Ukrainians worked at the library – for instance, Mykola Mykhal'chuk (1896–1969), a graduate of the Ukrainian Free University and the State Library School (Státní knihovnická škola) in Prague. He started working there in 1925 and remained until 1958. Another person, who started working there much later, in 1937, was Mykhailo Bashmak (1892–1976), who had studied at the Ukrainian Higher Pedagogical Institute and was the author of a Ukrainian-language textbook for Czechs. He also worked in the library until 1958. Zlenko, a graduate of the Ukrainian Higher Pedagogical Institute as well as the State Library School, worked in the library after 1936 in the Department of Book Culture (Obor knižní kultury). He was also the editor of the newspaper *Ukrains'kyi tyzhden'* and published many articles in *Knyholiub*. In 1945, he was arrested by NKVD and sent to the Gulag, where he died in 1954.[5]

The Ukrainian department included publications issued before the revolution in Kyiv and other parts of the former Russian empire. Ukrainian books, periodicals, and brochures published in the former Austro-Hungarian lands, Galicia, Bukovyna, and the Transcarpathian region were also housed at the library. Materials published in the 1920s and 1930s in Kyiv, Kharkiv, and L'viv were collected as well. The library collected publications issued by the Shevchenko Scientific Society in L'viv, the Ukrainian Academy of Sciences, and other academic institutions in Soviet Ukraine. It also housed materials in economics, literature, and folklore and contained several sets of publications and textbooks, often lithographic, published by the Ukrainian Free University, the Ukrainian Economic Academy, and the Ukrainian Higher Pedagogical Institute. The collection of periodicals likewise was substantial and included journals published in Soviet-ruled Ukraine and by émigrés. The Ukrainian collection eventually grew to 14,000 books. The library was intended for individuals working on their dissertations and for independent researchers.[6]

Between the wars, the Slavonic Library played a vital role as a scholarly and cultural centre for Slavic peoples, particularly émigrés. Thanks to the government's support, extensive collections were built during this period, particularly in relation to Russia and Ukraine. The history of the library after the interwar period is beyond the scope of this study. It has been an (independent) department of the National Library of the Czech Republic since 1958. It continues to be an important intellectual centre for Slavic scholarship and culture. Scholars from around the world continue to use its rich collections.

The Ukrainian émigrés founded a number of libraries at the institutions of higher education they created. These were primarily for the use of the faculty and students. Collection development at these institutions depended heavily on government funding, as well as gifts and exchanges. When times were hard and funding was scarce, these libraries were unable to develop their collections as they had hoped. In difficult circumstances, scholars working as archivists and librarians managed to build remarkable archival and library collections.

The Ukrainian Free University Library

In April 1922, the Ukrainian Free University established a library on its premises. It opened with only 150 books, but by 1938 it housed more than 10,000. For seventeen years, the head of the library was Dmytro Antonovych. The library established a committee that included Dmytro Doroshenko from the Department of Philosophy and Starosol's'kyi from the Department of Law, who were responsible for collection development in their areas of expertise. Since the library had a very modest budget, it grew largely through donations and exchanges and only to a small extent from purchased acquisitions. In 1924 and 1925 scholars contributed 866 books to the library, with Dmytro Doroshenko donating 111 books and Antonovych 172; Shelukhin, Iakovliv, and Sliusarenko also contributed items. The library also received materials from Vienna, Warsaw, and Kyiv. The Carnegie Foundation included the library on its list of donation recipients, and it received forty-three publications in 1926. Student scholarly societies contributed their publications to the library. The following figures are available: in the 1925–26 academic year, the library's holdings included 4,261 volumes, of which 1,629 were in the humanities, 483 in the natural sciences, and 1,262 in the social sciences; a further 887 were reference materials and bibliographies. Since money was always tight, Antonovych worked without pay.[7]

In the 1928–29 academic year, the library received a subversion of 6,000 crowns from the government. This money allowed the development of a card catalogue and an inventory, likely for a portion of the collection. A year later, the library was able to buy books from antiquarian booksellers as well as from personal libraries with rare editions. In the 1920s, it received valuable publications from the Ukrainian Academy of Sciences in Kyiv; among them were several monographs by the Orientalist, linguist, and polyglot Ahatanhel Kryms'kyi (1871–1942). In the 1930s these connections with Soviet Ukraine were severed as a consequence of the extensive purges there.[8]

In late 1938, the curators of the Society of Friends of the Ukrainian Free University offered the post of head of the library to Haimanivs'kyi. He was only able to start his duties in May 1939, after a lawsuit regarding the ownership of the library. He inherited a library with 6,708 of its 10,380 books uninventoried. The director, Antonovych, had responsibilities in many other scholarly and cultural obligations; his pet project was the museum, to which he devoted himself fully. This may be why the university library was left neglected.[9]

The library was underfunded and was only built up thanks to the enthusiasm and devotion of scholars. It did not achieve the status of other Ukrainian libraries and archives in Prague. Scholars living in Prague had the opportunity to use the rapidly growing Ukrainian collections in the Slavonic Library. However, the library had some importance for the scholars and students of the university.

The Ukrainian Economic Academy Library

The Ukrainian Economic Academy Library was founded in August 1922. During the years of its existence it assembled a rich collection of materials on Ukraine in various fields, including for its especially important socio-economics section. By January 1931, the library held 28,845 books in various languages. Located in the main building of the academy, the historical castle of King George of Poděbrady (Zámek Poděbrady), the library had a reading room were readers could consult more than one hundred periodicals. It also had a processing room and, of course, stacks. The library was organized with alphabetical and subject catalogues using the international Dewey Decimal Classification

System, meaning that its books were classified according to the following categories: general, philosophy, religion, social sciences, languages and philology, mathematics and natural sciences, applied sciences, arts, literature, and history and geography. Books and periodicals were bought using the budget of the academy; also, institutions and individuals made gifts. By the time it closed, the inventory of the library was valued at 700,000 crowns.[10]

After the library's initial organizational difficulties, Isaak Mazepa, the former prime minister of the Ukrainian People's Republic, became its director. Under his leadership, acquisition was systematic and was supervised by a library committee, on which all departments were represented. At the peak of its activities, the library staff included the director, Mazepa; the assistant director, Modest Levyts'kyi and two assistants. After Mazepa's resignation, Levyts'kyi became director of the library. Table 14 shows the growth of the library's book holdings from 1923 to 1928.

Table 15 shows the book holdings by language. As shown in Table 15, while Ukrainian literature in technical fields was still developing, the majority of the books in the library were in Russian and German. These disciplines were well-developed in those languages, and most of the academy's faculty and students could read Russian or German.

The library's book holdings were grouped by subject, as shown in Table 16. Table 16 indicates that socio-economics books comprised as much as 50 per cent of the library's total holdings. Students at the academy studied these subjects extensively, and the library's holdings supported their work. Titles in agronomy, engineering, and exact sciences were also well-represented; the rest of the titles covered subjects that were less relevant to the academy but that were important for students' general knowledge of, for instance, history and geography.

The library created two additional sections for textbooks and theses. The first of these collected ten copies of each publication published

Table 14. Book titles in the Ukrainian Economic Academy Library, 1923–28[11]

Year	# of book titles	# of volumes
1923	1,258	1,991
1924	3,697	5,782
1925	6,920	10,368
1926	10,036	15,954
1927	11,884	19,954
1928	13,821	24,750

Table 15. Book titles in the Ukrainian Economic Academy Library by language (on 1 January 1927)[12]

Language	# of book titles	% of total
Ukrainian	2,376	20
Czech	1,188	10
German	2,736	23
French	832	7
English	1,069	9
Russian	3,564	30
Polish	60	0.5
Other	59	0.5
Total	11,884	100

Table 16. Book titles in the Ukrainian Economic Academy Library by subject (on 1 January 1927)[13]

Subject	# of book titles	% of total
Socio-economics	5,940	50
Agronomy	1,782	15
Engineering	1,663	14
Exact sciences	1,554	13
History and geography	475	4
Fiction	235	2
Philology	119	1
Other	116	1
Total	11,884	100

by the academy and its publishing house, as well as six copies of all works typed but not published, such as lectures. The second section collected theses by all of the academy's graduates.[14] The library also subscribed to 139 periodicals in fields relevant to the subjects taught in the academy.

As shown in Table 17, the periodical holdings were obviously geared toward the disciplines taught in the academy. The faculty and students read and consulted predominantly journals in the Czech and German languages, with the remainder in French, English, and Russian.

The library was very important to the life of the academy and well served the needs of the faculty and students. It was highly specialized, supporting the technical subjects studied at the academy, but also had smaller holdings of a more general nature. The library's periodical

Table 17. Periodicals that the library subscribed to by subject and language[15]

Subject Language	Ukrainian	Czech	German	French	English	Russian	Other	Total
General	16	0	3	1	2	7	1	30
Natural sciences	0	3	7	2	0	0	0	12
Economics and cooperatives	0	9	20	6	4	7	0	46
Agronomy and forestry	0	14	9	0	0	0	1	24
Engineering	1	10	11	4	0	0	1	27
Total	17	36	50	13	6	14	3	139

holdings, again, closely reflected the disciplines in which the academy trained its students. The importance of the library can be even better understood when we take into account its location in the small town Poděbrady. While in Prague, scholars and students could use the rich holdings of various libraries; in the small town, even in close proximity to Prague, they were largely confined to their library, which served them well.

The Ukrainian Higher Pedagogical Institute Library

The Ukrainian Higher Pedagogical Institute Library was another collection created by Ukrainian émigré scholars. For faculty and students of the institute, this library was important because in Prague's libraries it was difficult to find all the relevant materials for the subjects taught at the institution. This was not surprising, given that many of these disciplines still needed to be developed in the Ukrainian language. The founders wished to organize and preserve the library's collections for future researchers and saw them as "a source of Ukrainian cultural work," as Zlenko put it.[16] This was the case with all émigré institutions.

In its first estimate submitted to the foreign ministry, the Ukrainian Civic Committee requested 10,000 crowns for the creation of a library. The first librarian, who served until July 1925, was lawyer and political figure Stepan Ripets'kyi (1894–1986). After the institute was transformed into an institution of higher education, the library staff included the head of the library, Oleksander Shapoval (1888–1972), and his student assistant. After the head of the library departed in 1930, Zlenko took over his role. In the senate of the institution, advisers in library matters were designated. During the institute's existence, those advisers were Simovych, Steshko, Sliusarenko, Panas Fedenko (1893–1981), and, later, Myron Dol'nyts'kyi (1892–1968). Favouritism evidently played a role in the choice of personnel; for example, Oleksander Shapoval, was the brother of the all-powerful head of the Ukrainian Civic Committee, Mykyta Shapoval.[17]

The library adopted the international Dewey Decimal Classification System. It subscribed to a number of periodicals – at its peak in 1928, to forty-two such titles. A reading room was available at the library. The average annual circulation was 4,234 books, with a peak of 5,664 books in the 1927–28 academic year. The library primarily housed scholarly books on topics that were most relevant to the institute, namely history, literature, and natural and social sciences.[18] The institution's budget designated 2,000 crowns per month for collection development, which, for example, allowed it to obtain 2,000 books in its first year. The collection development sum was even increased in later years. Moreover, the library purchased several private collections, besides receiving many gifts. It also acquired books in exchange for publications issued by the institute's publishing society, Siiach (The Sower). When it closed, the library held 8,610 titles and 10,728 volumes, of which 7,982 had been purchased and 2,746 had been gifted or obtained from exchange.[19] Table 18 shows the library's acquisition of books by language.

In the final year of the institution's existence, the education ministry agreed to leave the library to it. The Czechoslovak Academy of Agriculture (Československá akademie zemědělská), for a very small fee, provided accommodation for the institution's office and library in its building on Slezská Street in Prague – a demonstration of support for

Table 18. Number of books in the Ukrainian Higher Pedagogical Institute Library by language (1933)[20]

Language	Quantity	% of total
Ukrainian	5,681	52.9
Russian	2,750	25.6
Czech	805	7.5
Other Slavic	216	2
German	879	8.2
French	319	3
English	26	0.3
Other	52	0.5
Total	10,728	100

Ukrainian institutions by the Czech academic community. When the institute finally closed, its collections were transferred to the Slavonic Library and the gymnasium.[21]

The Museum of the Struggle for the Liberation of Ukraine

The Museum of the Struggle for the Liberation of Ukraine played a seminal role in the cultural and scholarly life of Ukrainian émigrés. This museum was financially supported by Ukrainians worldwide. It thus became the only financially independent Ukrainian scholarly institution in Czechoslovakia, and over time it became the cultural and scholarly centre for Ukrainians both in Prague and abroad. The museum's position as the all-Ukrainian cultural and scholarly centre was, above all, the extraordinary achievement of its long-time director Dmytro Antonovych and his colleagues.[22]

Antonovych played various crucial roles in the Ukrainian émigré community in Prague. However, it was the museum to which he fully and uncompromisingly devoted himself. Earlier in his life, between 1906 and 1911, he had lived and studied art in Paris, London, Munich, and Berlin, as well as Florence, Milan, Rome, and other cities and towns in Italy. This experience, especially his time in Italy, had greatly increased his lifelong love of theatre and the arts, and these later also became his scholarly interests. His exploration of Italian cultural monuments had a significant impact on his life, and the arts became an integral part of him. During the revolutionary years, Antonovych had held a position at the Ministry of Arts besides heading the Department for Protection of Art and Culture in Kyiv. In the latter post, he had saved many galleries, museums, and private collections. So he understood very well the national role of museums. The idea of creating the Museum of the Struggle for the Liberation of Ukraine – indeed, its very name – was likely inspired by museums he had visited in Italy. In the first issue of *Visty Muzeiu vyzvol'noi borot'by* (News of the Museum of the Struggle for the Liberation of Ukraine), the museum's newsletter, he stated that in Italy "every city and sometimes towns have their local *Museo del Risorgimento*. These dozens of museums of Italian revival presented comprehensive material for the whole Italian revival movement as well as the local highlights of this movement."[23]

The Society of the Museum of the Struggle for the Liberation of Ukraine (Tovarystvo "Muzeiu vyzvol'noi borot'by Ukrainy") was initiated by the professors of the Ukrainian Free University, who set out to found and support the museum. Horbachevs'kyi became the society's head, and the Czechoslovak government approved the statute that would regulate it. The museum was founded in May 1925. Many Ukrainian émigrés, not only those in Czechoslovakia, had valuable archives they had taken with them when leaving Ukraine. Also, some Ukrainian diplomatic missions had retained their archives, and they donated their contents to the museum. The museum's primary mission was to collect and preserve historical documents, artefacts, and archives related to the struggle for the liberation of Ukraine. This included materials connected to the First World War, the revolution, and the war for independence. The archive intended to save these materials for future historians.[24]

Émigrés generally regarded Antonovych as an honest, talented, hard-working, self-sacrificing, and principled man. He was able to gather the best of the Ukrainian intellectual world in Prague around the museum, and many professors of Ukrainian institutions were members of the society. They supported the museum financially and by donating their archival materials, and they trusted it as an institution because it was led by respected scholars. Though it collected many materials related to political events, the museum was a purely scholarly and non-political institution.

The museum was initially divided into four sections that reflected the nature of donated materials. The first was the diplomatic section, which grew very quickly during the museum's early days. Antonovych himself donated documents from the diplomatic missions of the Ukrainian People's Republic. The second was the military section, which presented archives and artefacts from First World War POW camps in Germany and Austria, as well as from Ukrainian internment camps in Czechoslovakia. The third section was dedicated to Ukrainian emigration and collected materials on the cultural, political, and scholarly activities of Ukrainian émigrés around the world. This section included unpublished manuscripts and artistic artefacts such as sculptures, paintings, and engravings. The last, miscellaneous section contained everything that did not fit into the other three sections. Over time, additional sections were established, such as a special one devoted to Shevchenko in 1936. There were also smaller sections dedicated to topics such as the history of Ukrainian theatre and the arts; these particular examples reflected Antonovych's own scholarly interests.[25]

The museum's collection of periodicals was also very rich; in 1936, it consisted of 1,323 catalogued titles of Ukrainian periodicals and 279 periodicals devoted to Ukraine (*ukrainika*). Several of these periodicals were printed, lithographed, or even handwritten. The museum also catalogued forty-three personal libraries donated by individuals; these were left unaltered out of respect for their provenance. A special catalogue listed the collection in which each book was located. These personal libraries were often of very high value; for example, in 1938 Kolessa donated 1,162 volumes from his library.[26]

As noted, from its inception Antonovych insisted that the museum would be totally independent, that materials would only be donated, not bought, and that it would be funded only by contributions and donations. The collections were growing at a rapid pace, and the lack of space for them was always an issue. At first, the government paid the rent for the museum's building; however, after the museum refused to hand over its collections, the government cancelled the rental arrangement in 1926. In 1929, the Ukrainian American businessman and philanthropist Hryhorii Kalenyk-Lysiuk (1889–1980) visited the museum. He was astonished by museum's valuable collections and promised to subsidize it. Between 1929 and 1939 he sponsored the museum at a rate of 300–400 US dollars per month. Antonovych and the museum's deputy director Narizhnyi were both hard-working and dedicated. Overall, the working conditions in the museum were difficult. For example, the building was intentionally left unheated all year round to prevent damage to the collections.[27]

To address the ongoing shortage of space, in the early 1930s a campaign was launched to collect funds to build a Ukrainian national home (Ukrains'kyi dim) in Prague. This "home" would be not just for the museum but for other Ukrainian institutions as well. Many fundraising campaigns were undertaken, and Ukrainians donated funds for the future Ukrainian home and the museum. Support for these initiatives came from Ukrainians living in Galicia, Volhynia, Bukovyna, France, the United States, Canada, and other countries, as well as from Ukrainians in Czechoslovakia. The breadth of support was reflected in the long lists of donors regularly published in *Visty Muzeiu vyzvol'noi borot'by*. The donors, though they often only gave small amounts, nevertheless supported the ideas behind the project and understood their importance. Antonovych resorted to additional means to raise funds for the Ukrainian home and museum. For instance, in 1936, he appealed for assistance to Volodymyr Doroshenko (1879–1963), a librarian at the Shevchenko Scientific Society in L'viv. Antonovych asked him, as someone familiar with the museum and its goals, to help the museum by writing articles or shorter pieces on topics related to it and publish them in periodicals that regularly featured his writing or give them to the museum for publication. The necessary funds were finally collected, and the museum purchased a house in Prague's Nusle district on 16 March 1938, not long before the Munich Agreement. The fate of the museum was tragic; in February 1945, a bombing raid over Prague partly destroyed its building. After the Soviets took the city, the museum was closed, although it later reopened. In 1948, many of the museum's materials were taken to the Soviet Union and stored in the Soviet archives, where they were inaccessible. Only in recent decades have these previously unknown pages of Ukrainian history become available for researchers.[28]

The Ukrainian National Museum and Archive

In late 1923, the Ukrainian Civic Committee founded another institution in Prague, the Ukrainian National Museum and Archive. Its mission was to collect materials and relics related to Ukraine's revolution and independence movement and to Ukrainian émigré life. The core holdings of the museum/archive were materials from the archive of the Ukrainian People's Republic that writer and ethnologist Mykhailo Obidnyi (1889–1938) had brought from Tarnów, Poland. The museum/archive was supposedly open to all Ukrainians regardless of their political orientation as well as to any other scholar working in the field. In practice, however, it was closely associated with the Ukrainian Socialist-Revolutionary Party, given that it was the party committee that had founded it and now supported it. From the start, the activities of the museum/archive found few sympathizers among other Ukrainian émigré circles.[29]

In December 1923, the government approved the statute of the museum/archive; its principal tasks would be to collect and preserve Ukrainian cultural artefacts, to open them to other scholars, and to create conditions in which émigré Slavists could study Ukraine. In 1923–25, there were only two staff: the head, Obidnyi, and the director, Nykyfir Hryhoryiv. Obidnyi appealed to the Ukrainian community to work together to preserve the important historical materials scattered in different places. In that appeal, he explained the importance of preserving this material. He also recommended that witnesses to and participants in the revolution write their memoirs of that event for future research. Over the first five years of its existence, the museum/archive collected tens of thousands of documents.[30]

Arkadii Zhyvotko also worked in the museum/archive. He was a historian of the Ukrainian press as well as an educator, archivist, librarian, journalist, and civic and political figure. His major work, *Istoriia ukrains'koi presy* (A History of the Ukrainian Press), was researched in the 1930s and first published in Germany in 1946. It was reprinted several times and became a textbook for journalism students in present-day Ukraine. His other works were in library science, education, regional studies, politics, and archival science.[31]

The museum/archive had three departments: archives, periodicals and books, and museum. The archival department was evidently the richest, for it included documents from 1917–21 as well as the emigration period. It contained personal collections from many participants. The periodical department had, by 1928, acquired 874 runs of newspapers and 220 runs of journals from the late nineteenth century to the present. These periodicals were published in all the Ukrainian lands and in countries where Ukrainians lived. The book collection had around 1,000 items, including scholarly monographs, memoirs, and calendars. The museum department included artefacts from 1917 to 1920. Between 1927 and 1930 alone, the museum/archive received 3,232 items, including Rusova's memoirs and batches of correspondence from Chykalenko and other prominent Ukrainian figures.[32]

In 1925, the museum/archive became a separate entity of the Ukrainian Sociological Institute. Between 1924 and 1926, it received 100–200 crowns from the committee; this was evidently an internal decision of that committee since at the time, the Czechoslovak government was generously supporting the émigré community and providing the committee with large sums of money. In 1927, the government began providing the museum/archive with 5,000 crowns per month, which allowed it to expand its acquisition activities. That same year, a board was created for the selection of the material, headed by Shelukhin and his deputy. Bidnov, Antonovych, Shcherbakivs'kyi, and Shcherbyna were invited to participate in board activities, but they refused to do so. The museum/archive's collections were suffering due to the fact that many Ukrainian émigrés did not wish to donate their materials to it. Furthermore, the Museum of the Struggle for the Liberation of Ukraine had been founded in 1925, and was largely associated with respected scholars who did not want to interact with the museum/archive. There was a clear rivalry between the two Ukrainian museums in Prague, where, in the 1920s, antagonisms among the various Ukrainian political groups were still raw.[33]

The museum/archive also had a Belarusian section. Ukrainians had provided support to Belarusians in Prague before this, and there was no separate Belarusian archive in that city. In 1929, the Czechoslovakian foreign ministry cut funding to the museum/archive and insisted on placing it under its control. The museum/archive administration was forced to comply with this after considerable failed efforts to find a new home for the museum/archive. During this search, there was even an unsuccessful attempt to donate collections of the museum/archive to the Hoover Institution on War, Revolution, and Peace at Stanford University.[34]

The Ukrainian Historical Institute

After the government cancelled its funding of the museum/archive, Zhyvotko and Obidnyi tried to save it. To that end, they approached Czechoslovak officials in February 1930. Zhyvotko and Obidnyi were informed that the museum/archive could be preserved only if it was transferred to the foreign ministry. This led to the founding of the Ukrainian Historical Institute, which was based on the museum/archive's collections. The organizational phase began in 1929; the institute started its work in the fall of 1930, under the foreign ministry. Its goal was to systematically collect materials on Ukraine and to prepare them for scholarly research.[35]

The head of the institute was the Czech historian and archivist Jan Slavík (1885–1978), a representative of the foreign ministry. As a specialist in Czech, Russian, and Soviet history, Slavík also supervised the Russian Historical Archive Abroad in Prague (Russkii zagranichnyi istoricheskii arkhiv v Prage), which was the largest archive of the Russian emigration in interwar Europe. The Ukrainian Historical Institute's director was Mykhailo Obidnyi. The ministry, which on many occasions supported the idea of creating such an institution, provided financial assistance to the institute, which occupied seven rooms of the Tuscan Palace (Toskánský palác) in Prague: the largest of these was a reading room, and the rest were for storing and processing the materials. During its first eighteen months, the institute created a bibliographic index of Ukrainian periodicals from their inception; began to compile reviews based on periodicals covering contemporary aspects of Ukrainian life in all territories in which they lived; reviewed books and periodicals in Ukrainian studies from several libraries; and created an overview of Czech history, literature, and culture in Ukrainian periodicals. The institute also began to work on press reviews of contemporary life for Ukrainian people in all Ukrainian lands and in emigration; this included scholarly and cultural life, economics, and education, among other subjects. Around this time, about one hundred Ukrainians responded to the institute's appeal for donors. In addition, 137 editorial offices started sending their periodicals to the institute *gratis*. In early 1932, the institute widened its mission: in addition to the tasks outlined above, it began collecting Ukrainian historical archives. This process was launched with a donation of documents from the period of the Ukrainian People's Republic as well as collections from the defunct museum/archive. The archival collections of the defunct Ukrainian Sociological Institute were also donated to the institute in that year.[36]

The institute had three departments: archival, library, and newspaper. The archival collections spanned the following topics: pre-1914, the First World War, the Central Council period, the Hetmanate, the Directory of the Ukrainian People's Republic, and the post-independence period. The institute's collections also covered the later historical periods and other topics: military internment camps, the Ukrainian lands after 1921, the Ukrainian emigration, personal collections, correspondences, memoirs, manuscripts of scholarly and literary works, and collections of maps and photographs. Bochkovs'kyi was one of the first individuals to donate his library collection to the institute. His collection of earlier Ukrainian periodicals was a starting point for the institute's collection of these materials. In addition, a library belonging to Viacheslav Lypyns'kyi was given to the institute after his death. Materials from other notable Ukrainian figures such as Shelukhin and Shapoval were later given to the institute.[37]

The library held books, almanacs, brochures, collective volumes, and journals. The period covered by the collections spanned from the first half of the nineteenth century to the 1930s. The collections were strong in the fields of history, literature, law, statistics, ethnography, and bibliography. They included works by Volodymyr Antonovych and the historian Denys Zubryts'kyi (1777–1862), among many others. The journal collection was also rich and included L'viv journals from the nineteenth century, such as *Pchola* (Bee, 1849) *Zoria* (Star, 1880–97), *Zhytie i slovo* (Life and Word, 1894–97), and periodicals from the early twentieth century, such as *Iliustrovana Ukraina* (Illustrated Ukraine, 1913–14).

The institute's newspaper collections were particularly strong; of the 235 newspaper titles – covering 330 collections (*zbirky*) and 9,714 copies – received by the institute in 1931, 47 collections came from Soviet-ruled Ukraine; 105 from Galicia; 59 from the United States, Canada, and Brazil; 12 from Austria; 3 from Italy; and 2 from Switzerland. Titles varied, from Soviet periodicals such as *Bil'shovyk Poltavshchyny* (Bolshevik of Poltava) and *Komsomolets' Ukrainy* (Komsomolets of Ukraine), published in Poltava and Kharkiv, respectively, to the émigré newspapers *Vistnyk ukrains'koi hromady u Frantsii* (The Herald of the Ukrainian Society in France) and *Nezalezhnist'* (Independence), published in Paris. The institute also carried Ukrainian newspapers published by American Ukrainians, such as *Dnipro* (The Dnieper River) and *Svoboda* (Freedom), published in Philadelphia and New Jersey, respectively. Thus, the institute collected Ukrainian periodicals from all Ukrainian lands and published by Ukrainians in various countries. Similarly, books and journals were sent to the institute not only by

Ukrainian institutions in Czechoslovakia but also from those abroad. The Prosvita Society sent materials to the institute, as did the publishing house the Red Guelder Rose (Chervona kalyna) in L'viv. As a result, by January 1932 the institute had a small library of 850 book titles and its collection of periodicals consisted of 14,209 issues (2,663 journals and 11,546 newspapers).[38]

Ukrainian publishing houses, individuals, and organizations worldwide supported the institute by donating materials. By 1939, the institute's book collection consisted of 22,000 donated books, brochures, and journals. Its newspaper collection was created in a similar manner. Table 19 lists the institute's holdings.

To spread knowledge about the cultural and social life of Ukrainians as well as the past and present development of Ukrainian life, the institute organized several exhibitions. The first exhibit of periodicals from the Transcarpathian region, past and present, was held jointly with the Society of Ukrainian Writers and Journalists from 31 May to 2 June 1934. It was accompanied by lectures and other informational events and was attended by Ukrainians and non-Ukrainians alike. Two other exhibitions were held on the premises of the institute, devoted to earlier Ukrainian periodicals and contemporary Ukrainian journalism. The institute also loaned its materials to exhibitions organized by other institutions, including three exhibitions dedicated to Slavic illustrated journals. Two of these exhibitions were held in Prague, one in Brno. The first of the two Prague exhibitions was held in the Central City Bookstore from 22 April to 7 May 1933 and featured more than seventy illustrated journals from the institute. The second took place from 1 to 15 October of the same year on the premises of the Czechoslovak Academy of Agriculture. In this second exhibition, the institute exhibited 178 illustrated journals in the fields of literature, arts, history, cultural

Table 19. Collections of the Ukrainian Historical Institute[39]

Collections	Acquired in 1930	Acquired in 1939	Total 1930–39	% of materials purchased
Documents	43 leaves	79,098 leaves	211,415 leaves	3.6
Books, brochures, and collective volumes	210 volumes	3,183 volumes	19,947 volumes	9.9
Periodicals	694 issues	1,999 issues	17,591 issues (1,705 volumes)	1.4
Newspapers	1,832 issues	4,475 issues	156,676 issues (1,151 volumes)	18.07

and public life, husbandry, and technology, as well as periodicals for children and youth. The institute also took part in other exhibitions, including a pedagogical exhibition in 1934 and one devoted to Havlíček in 1936.[40]

The Ukrainian Historical Institute and the Museum of the Struggle for the Liberation of Ukraine were two Ukrainian institutions in interwar Prague with a common mission of collecting and preserving archival, library, and museum collections. But whereas the former was financially independent, the latter was government-funded. Oleksander Mytsiuk, in an article in the journal *Nasha kul'tura* (Our Culture), emphasized that these two institutions did not compete and indeed complemented each other by catering to different sections of Ukrainian émigré society.[41] Nevertheless, there was tension between the two, as Kateryna Antonovych recalled:

> Concerning the transfer of museum archives, which was called the Ukrainian museum, I know because I was then in Prague. It belonged to the Czechs and they had money and bought different materials, sometimes very interesting, and paid the staff; I remember how my husband was upset that these materials were acquired by the museum because for the Museum of the Struggle for the Liberation of Ukraine nothing was bought and everything was donated by the Ukrainian community ... this transfer of the museum to the Bolsheviks made a painful impression on all of us. And we were happy that the Museum of the Struggle for the Liberation of Ukraine did not take money from the Czechs and they had no right to it and had nothing to do with it.[42]

The fates of the two institutions, however, were similar. In September 1945, a document was signed between Czechoslovak and Soviet officials regarding the allegedly voluntary transfer of the institute's collections to the Soviet Union. The special Soviet archival search group – headed by Chief of the Main Archival Administration of the NKVD in Ukraine Pavlo I. Pavliuk – which had the special task of finding and gathering collections created by émigrés, located the institute's collections. The materials of the Museum of the Struggle for the Liberation of Ukraine were taken to the Soviet Union in 1948. The transfer of the archives, and of archives from other émigré institutions, was undeniably motivated by politics, as these collections had been created by the émigrés, who by definition were opponents of the Soviet regime. These collections were closed in the Soviet Union and were opened for researchers only in the 1990s. The collections transferred from the institute and the museum currently form the basis of the Prague Archive (Praz'kyi arkhiv) at the Central State Archive of Higher Organs of Government and Administration of Ukraine in Kyiv.[43]

The libraries, museums, and archives founded and supported by Ukrainian émigrés were an extremely important part of their efforts to preserve and develop their culture and heritage. The Slavonic Library's Ukrainian Department is a significant accomplishment. The libraries at the institutions were helpful for their respective faculties and students. The Czechoslovak government supported all of them, with one exception. The fates of all of them are similarly tragic.

Chapter Eight

Ukrainian-Language Scholarly Publishing in Czechoslovakia

Overview

Between the wars, Czechoslovakia became the major centre of Ukrainian-language publishing in Europe. Ukrainian materials were published in other countries, but it was in Czechoslovakia that the publishing industry most thrived, particularly in the 1920s. The Czechoslovak government played a major role in financially assisting that industry. Besides supporting émigré institutions, it financed the publication of many émigré books and periodicals. There were several stages in the development of Ukrainian-language publishing in Czechoslovakia. The first period began in the early 1920s, when Ukrainian institutions were founded, and lasted until the early 1930s, when subsidies from the Czechoslovak government were slashed and some institutions were dissolved. The second period began in the early 1930s and lasted until the end of the Second World War. Whereas the first period was characterized by the prevalence of scholarly publishing and was funded predominantly by the Czechoslovak government, the second was characterized by the appearance of private Ukrainian-language publishing houses that focused largely on political literature and fiction. According to Maruniak, in terms of numbers, from 1900 to 1945 there were fourteen large and around ten small Ukrainian publishing houses in Czechoslovakia. *Knyholiub* listed fifty-six Ukrainian publishing houses for the period 1918–27 in Europe; most of them were located in Czechoslovakia, with smaller numbers in Austria and Germany. (It should be noted that this list covered all Ukrainian publishing houses, not just scholarly ones.) As this study focuses on Ukrainian scholarly life, the period in which scholarly literature was foremost in Ukrainian-language publishing is the object of inquiry in this chapter; only brief attention will be paid to the years in which private publishing prevailed.[1]

Prior to the Ukrainian interwar emigration, there were already two small Ukrainian publishing houses in Prague: Chas (Time) and Vsesvit (Universe). The diplomatic mission of the Ukrainian People's Republic subsidized them until 1921. Time published thirty-six short books that included more than a dozen informative brochures in the Czech language about Ukraine, and Universe published nine short works. Without financial support, these publishing houses soon went bankrupt, as did similar Ukrainian publishing houses in Austria and Germany.[2]

The dominance of scholarly writing in Ukrainian-language publishing was directly related to the major Ukrainian scholarly institutions in Prague and Poděbrady. During that period, six major institutions and organizations published Ukrainian-language scholarly works, namely the Ukrainian Civic Publishing Fund, the Ukrainian Free University, the Ukrainian Economic Academy, the Ukrainian Higher Pedagogical Institute, the Ukrainian Historical–Philological Society, and the Ukrainian Sociological Institute. To carry out their publishing activities, some institutions created their own publishing houses; these were established on a voluntary basis, with shares offered to their faculty and students. The Publishing Society at the Ukrainian Economic Academy (Vydavnyche tovarystvo pry UHA) was founded at the academy, and the Ukrainian Publishing Society "Siiach" (Ukrains'ke vydavnyche tovarystvo "Siiach") was established at the institute. According to Maruniak, the university did not have such a society; it published its professors' works via other publishing houses, including the State Publishing House in Prague (Státní nakladatelství v Praze) and the Ukrainian Civic Publishing Fund prior to 1925.[3]

According to Maruniak, from 1920 to 1939, Ukrainians in Czechoslovakia published 1,164 scholarly or education-related works. Besides purely scholarly publications, these works included popular science literature, textbooks, and manuals for students. They were published in the form of books, brochures, and printouts. Between the wars, scholarly publications constituted more than 79 per cent of all Ukrainian publications produced in Czechoslovakia.[4] Table 20 depicts the variety of topics in Ukrainian-language scholarly literature published in Czechoslovakia between 1900 and 1945.

Around 80 per cent of all financing for Ukrainian publishing in Czechoslovakia was provided by the Czechoslovak government; this amounted to about 3 million crowns. The remaining money came from Ukrainian diplomatic missions, prior to 1921, and beginning in the early 1930s from Ukrainians' private funds. Financial support from the government was provided directly, as a one-time sum to start a publishing house. It was also delivered indirectly by being included in the

Table 20. Scholarly publications by institution and subject, 1900–45[5]

Subject	UEA	UFU	UHPI	УТТІ	UCPF	UHPS	Others	Other countries	Total
Collections	7	6	3	–	–	5	8	–	29
Information publications	15	43	1	2	–	18	23	–	102
Monographs, scripts, historical narratives	–	11	6	2	1	21	65	33	139
Linguistics	2	4	6	6	1	2	29	11	61
Literary criticism	1	6	3	1	2	10	27	5	55
Arts	1	9	7	–	5	4	43	18	87
Philosophy	–	9	7	–	2	4	22	3	47
National sociology [*sic*]	6	3	1	2	1	3	19	3	38
Law	12	26	–	5	–	–	7	7	57
Geography	–	2	2	2	–	–	6	3	15
Cooperation and trade	22	–	–	4	1	–	12	2	41
Political economy	26	4	1	3	2	–	26	16	78
Mathematical sciences	28	–	9	7	3	–	4	–	51
Technology and industry	28	1	–	8	3	–	3	–	43
Journalism	–	–	–	4	–	–	2	–	6
Schooling and pedagogy	–	–	9	–	1	–	16	7	33
Agricultural disciplines	19	–	–	9	1	–	12	7	48
Forestry	26	–	–	1	–	–	2	1	30
Zoology and physiology	11	–	3	–	1	–	–	3	18
Botany	7	–	–	2	–	–	2	–	11
Geodesy and construction	21	–	15	–	5	–	–	2	43
Medicine	–	–	–	–	4	–	7	–	11
Finance	20	–	–	3	–	–	–	–	23
Other fields	36	6	6	14	4	8	19	14	107
Total	288	130	79	75	37	75	354	135	1,173

Ukrainian institutions' budgets for publishing textbooks, lectures, and manuals for students.[6]

The Ukrainian Civic Publishing Fund

The Ukrainian Civic Committee created the Ukrainian Civic Publishing Fund in Prague on 24 April 1923. This was around the time the major Ukrainian institutions were founded, and the main goal of this fund was to publish scholarly works. The plan was to publish original works, translations into Ukrainian, textbooks for secondary and post-secondary schools, reference works, and fiction. The Publishing Council (Vydavnycha rada) was created along with its executive organ, the Office of the Fund (Biuro Ukrains'koho hromads'koho vydavnychoho fondu, BUHVF), under the leadership of Ievhen Vyrovyi. The council approved books for publication, set annual budgets, and decided on the order in which books would be published. The office, for its part, held meetings, signed contracts, and organized the editing and distribution of works. The editorial board, led by the biologist and founder of the Ukrainian anatomy school Arsen Starkov (1874–1927), made the decisions about future publications. The Czechoslovak government provided the initial 1.8 million crowns for the publishing fund – a considerable sum. Further funding was expected to come from membership fees, donations from community members, and loans from credit institutions. The membership fee was 1,000 crowns, and by 1925 the fund had 112 members, twenty-five of which were Ukrainian institutions and organizations. The fund published thirty-seven books in various fields, including Ukrainian literary criticism, philosophy, ethnography, anthropology, and art, as well as monographs in mathematics, statistics, agriculture, pedagogy, medicine, history, music, and political economy.[7]

The first director of the publishing house was the publisher, educator, and civic figure Ievhen Vyrovyi. He was born in 1889 in the city of Smila in the Cherkasy region and studied at a pedagogical institute in Hlukhiv. In 1917, he headed the Prosvita Society in Katerynoslav and helped found the Ukrainian publishing house there. At one point, he was secretary and adviser to Pavlo Skoropads'kyi. He continued to publish books in Kam'ianets'-Podil's'kyi – the next city to which he moved – and in 1922 founded a publishing house for Ukrainian youth in Berlin. In Czechoslovakia, he wrote many articles on bibliography that were published in *Knyholiub* and elsewhere. Vyrovyi was also a passionate philatelist who compiled several albums of Ukrainian postage stamps. His stamp collection was praised many times at international exhibits. Vyrovyi's end was tragic; in 1945, he was unable to leave Prague for health reasons, and when the NKVD came to arrest him he committed suicide by jumping out a window.[8]

Pavlo Bohats'kyi (1883–1962), a Ukrainian literary scholar, bibliographer, journalist, and civic figure, was the fund's next director. Born into a priest family in the Podolia region in 1883, he studied at the seminary in Kam'ianets'-Podil's'kyi before his interests turned to literature and the revolutionary movement. He was expelled from the seminary for his revolutionary activities. He moved to Vilnius, where he completed his studies at a military school, and then was sent to the Poltava region. For his involvement in revolutionary groups, he was arrested, imprisoned, and expelled from the military. Around 1906, he turned to literature, and his works were published in many Ukrainian periodicals in western Ukraine. Bohats'kyi wrote collections of short stories, a novel, and a bibliography, among other works. In 1909, with Shapoval, he founded the journal *Ukrains'ka khata* (The Ukrainian House) in Kyiv, which they edited until 1914, when Bohats'kyi was arrested and sent away by the Russian authorities. In 1917, he returned to Kyiv and became the city's militia chief. In emigration, he was active in his role as the head of the fund and after the Second World War, he emigrated to Australia, where he was active in Ukrainian public life and as a journalist. There he also worked on *Mala literaturna entsyklopediia* (The Concise Literary Encyclopaedia), which was not published until the beginning of the twenty-first century. Bohats'kyi died in 1962 in New South Wales, Australia. He was a man who explored different and often diametrically opposed paths. However, literature and journalism seemed to occupy a special place in his life.[9]

The Ukrainian Civic Publishing Fund published many works by the faculty of Ukrainian institutions of higher education in Czechoslovakia – for example, *Arkhitektura starokniazivs'koi doby. (X [i.e. desiate]-XIII [i.e. trynadtsiate] st.)* (Architecture of the Old Princely Era, Tenth to Thirteenth Centuries, 1926) by Sichyns'kyi, and *Providni idei fil'osofii Tomy Masaryka* (The Main Philosophic Ideas of Thomas Masaryk, 1925) by Iakym Iarema.[10] By 1926, the fund had published twenty-four titles in 52,000 copies. Only 17.8 per cent of its publications were sold in Czechoslovakia; 60 per cent were vended in Galicia, 11 per cent in Soviet Ukraine, 6.7 per cent in the United States and Canada, and 4.5 per cent elsewhere. As is evident from these figures, fewer than one fifth of all its Ukrainian books were read in Czechoslovakia; meanwhile, though, there was high demand for those books in Galicia, where Ukrainian-language scholarly publications could not be produced on a similar scale, and certainly not with government support. At this time, some members of the council wanted to expand its list of popular science literature, reference works, and fiction, while continuing to produce textbooks. It was also suggested that the fund print its books in Galicia, specifically in L'viv.[11]

The fund was especially active between 1923 and 1928, when it published its most important works. Its activities later tailed off, and in 1932, the fund ceased to exist. Its accomplishments in Ukrainian-language scholarly publishing were important, as were those of other publishing houses that published scholarly literature in the Ukrainian language in interwar Czechoslovakia.[12]

The Ukrainian Free University's Publishing Activities

The publishing activities of the Ukrainian Free University began at its founding. The institution's most successful years in this regard coincided with the first period of Ukrainian-language publishing in Czechoslovakia. During those years, the university published monographs, textbooks, and collective works. Among the monographs produced in lithographic form were *Skorochenyi kurs istorii ukrains'koho mystetstva* (A Short Course of the History of Ukrainian Art, 1923) by Dmytro Antonovych, *Richeve pravo* (Property Law, 1923) by Dnistrians'kyi, and *Osnovy zemleznannia Ukrainy* (Foundations of the Earth Science of Ukraine, 1923) by Stepan Rudnyts'kyi. Important printed works included the above-mentioned *Ohliad ukrains'koi istoriohrafii* by Dmytro Doroshenko and *Orhanichna khemiia* by Horbachevs'kyi. In terms of publishing, 1923 was a particularly active year; in that year alone, the university published around thirty scholarly works by its professors.[13]

Each year, the university published its curricula as they related to the various disciplines taught at the university. These curricula demonstrated the similarities between the subjects it taught and those on the curricula of other universities at that time. Additional subjects in Ukrainian studies that had been developed by the professors were included in the university's curricula. Among the university's publications during this period were two anniversary volumes devoted to Masaryk, published in 1925 and 1930. The first volume, around 430 pages in length, was published in 1925 for the occasion of the president's seventy-fifth birthday. This scholarly volume included works by twelve professors, including Dmytro Doroshenko's a hundred-page bibliography of Ukrainian-language works published in the Russian empire from 1798 to 1897. The second volume was published in 1930, in celebration of Masaryk's eightieth birthday. It was 265 pages long and contained articles written by thirteen professors, including an article on social law by Opanas Andriievs'kyi, Narizhnyi's work on the Treaty of Hadiach in the light of Ukrainian historiography, and an article by

Shul'hyn on the influence of Jean-Jacques Rousseau. Both volumes were of high quality; they presented Ukrainian professors' research results in various fields and expressed the appreciation for the president.[14]

In addition, in the period under discussion, the university published two volumes of its collective works (*zbirnyky*) in 1923 and 1930. In the first volume, Dnistrians'kyi discussed major ideas in the history and theory of international private law, Kolessa wrote about a settlement in southern Volhynia and manuscripts of the twelfth to sixteenth centuries, Lashchenko wrote about the Lithuanian Statute, and Shcherbakivs'kyi wrote on Neolithic ceramics in the Poltava region. The volume included other articles; all were heavily footnoted and were presumably based on research conducted before their authors came to Prague. The second volume was published much later and contained only four articles, devoted to topics in history, linguistics, ethnology, and law. The first volume was published at the dawn of Ukrainian scholarly life in Czechoslovakia; the second was released at a time when activities were starting to decrease; the change is evident when these two volumes are compared.[15]

The university's publishing activities were not as extensive as they could have been. In the 1925–26 academic year, for example, university professors in both faculties had various works prepared for publication, but they remained unpublished. In the 1930s, the university's publishing activities almost ceased. As noted, from 1932 until the war began it brought out only its curricula. It published only two works by its professors: one by Shelukhin in 1934 and one by Shcherbakivs'kyi in 1938. The fiscal situation was definitely an issue: all of the university's reports mentioned the difficult financial circumstances for both the university and its publishing arm. Politics played a role as well. Earlier, on 19 June 1925, the university had taken the advice of the Czechoslovak government and signed a contract with the Ukrainian Civic Publishing Fund to establish the Foundation of the University (Fundatsiia universytetu) within it for publishing monographs and textbooks. Apparently, the government was attempting to bring all Ukrainian-language publishing activities under one roof. Émigré misunderstandings and infighting, however, prevented this outcome, and very soon afterwards the university cancelled the agreement. Notwithstanding the lack of unity among Ukrainian publishers, the fund published important works by professors during this period, including *Trysta rokiv ukrains'koho teatru 1619–1919* (300 Years of the Ukrainian Theatre, *1619–1919*, 1925) by Antonovych and *Osnovy ukrains'koi literaturno-naukovoi krytyky: sproba literaturno-naukovoi metodolohii*, the work by Bilets'kyi mentioned earlier.[16] When opportunities arose for them to do so, scholars at the university published in other places and in different languages. Their works appeared in Berlin, Warsaw, Vienna, Winnipeg,

Geneva, Zagreb, Kyiv, Leipzig, London, Munich, Paris, Przemyśl, Rivne, Chernivtsi, Chicago, and elsewhere.[17] The most recent bibliography for this period, published by the Ukrainian Free University in 2011, indicates that 111 titles were published between 1921 and 1938. That number included monographs, programs, and printouts.[18]

The Ukrainian Economic Academy's Publishing Activities

Publishing was also an important task for the Ukrainian Economic Academy. As noted, professors and lecturers saw it as one of their missions to write textbooks for students in the Ukrainian language as well as Ukrainian-language works in their field. As discussed in chapter 3, when the academy was established, technical and economics textbooks in Ukrainian were very scarce. This is why, when professors were hired, it was a condition of their employment that they develop Ukrainian-language textbooks in the disciplines they were going to teach. The academy, as well as other Ukrainian émigré scholarly institutions, placed an emphasis on producing such materials to fill the gap.[19]

The academy published works in many disciplines, but mostly in economics, sociology, and law. Books and other materials in mathematics and the natural sciences were also produced, as well as works on construction, technology, chemistry, agronomy, and zootechnics. A small number of books were written on hydrotechnology and forestry. In general, most of these publications were produced by lithographic means in runs of 50 to 150 copies. A small number of publications for minor disciplines were published in loose-leaf form, with six to eight copies made of each using a typewriter.[20]

Publishing was initially concentrated within the Publishing Society at the Ukrainian Economic Academy, which had been founded in 1922 by students and professors at the academy. In this early period, works were published in the fields of geometry, chemistry, physics, statistics, mechanics, mineralogy, forestry, botany, and zoology, among many other subjects. The society issued *Kurs analitychnoi geometrii v prostoryni* (A Course of Analytical Geometry in Three Dimensions, 1923), the 404-page *Prykladna mekhanyka* (Applied Mechanics, 1925) by Oleksander Kovalenko (1875–1963), and *Narysna heometriia* (Geometry, 1923) and *Melioratsiia* (Melioration, 1925) by Ievhen Sokovych (1864–1946), among many other works. The Publishing Society was credited with the release of 75 per cent of the academy's published works. In the late 1920s, all functions were transferred to the academy itself, which continued the work. It primarily published textbooks written by the university's academic staff and, to a lesser degree, translations of professional textbooks and manuals from the Czech, German, and Russian languages. The academy designated 500,000 crowns in total for publishing activities and published 229 books: of these, 157 were published in lithographic format, 35 as looseleafs, and 37 as printed volumes.[21]

The academy also published several works in conjunction with the Ukrainian Civic Publishing Fund, the most notable being the extensive *Geodeziia* (Geodesy, 1928) by Hrabyna, published in two parts. Other books published with the fund included Borodaievs'kyi's vast *Istoriia kooperatsii* (History of Cooperation, 1925) and an economic survey of Kuban titled *Kuban'. Ekonomychnyi narys* by Ivan Ivasiuk (1879–1933), published in 1925.

The house also published *Zapysky Ukrains'koi hospodars'koi akademii v Chekhoslovats'kii Respublitsi* (The Annals of the Ukrainian Economic Academy in Czechoslovakia). Three volumes in seven parts were published in 1927, 1929, and 1931, with the first and second volumes published in 500 and 600 copies, respectively. These volumes included detailed articles by Ivanyts'kyi, Borodaievs'kyi, Shovheniv, and many other faculty members. The predominant subjects of these articles were economics, technology, sociology, forestry, and agriculture. The first volume was "part-less" and contained works of faculty members from all three departments; the articles in each of the other two volumes were divided into three parts, with members of the economics and cooperative, engineering, and agriculture and forestry faculties contributing articles to their respective parts. The publication of these volumes was a valuable contribution to Ukrainian-language scholarship in all of the above fields.[22]

Various materials were created using a typewriter – for example, *Derzhavnyi kredyt* (State Credit) by Mykola Dobrylovs'kyi (1888–1971), and *Kooperatyvna reviziia* (Cooperative Audit) by Martos. Some of these works were translations from the Czech, German, and English languages. In addition, a number of organizations and associations affiliated with the academy created their own publishing bodies. These included the Agronomy Society (Agronomichne tovarystvo pry U.H.A.), the Office of People's Economy (Kabinet narodn'oho hospodarstva), and the Society of Cooperators (Tovarystvo kooperatoriv). Many of their works were produced as lithographs, and many of these bodies were short-lived.[23]

In general, publishing endeavours held a prominent place at the academy. Over the ten years of its existence, the academy's scholars wrote and published many works in various fields. These included monographs and textbooks in technology, agriculture, economics, forestry, finance, chemistry, biology, political economy, algebra, and statistics, among other areas. Publications were produced with great enthusiasm and were often based on knowledge and research developed before the emigration. In circumstances that were not always favourable, the scholars did impressive work with regard to publishing technical literature.

The Ukrainian Publishing Society "Siiach"

The Ukrainian Publishing Society "Siiach" was established on 17 May 1924 at the Ukrainian Higher Pedagogical Institute for the purpose of publishing textbooks written by the institute's faculty. According to the statute of the society, it was created to satisfy the demand for scholarly monographs and textbooks. It also had a mandate to publish specialized books in pedagogy as well as broadly scholarly books on a variety of disciplines in the Ukrainian language. The heads of the society were Bilets'kyi in 1924, economist and lawyer Ivan Kabachkiv (1874–1962) in 1925 and 1926, then Chyzhevs'kyi until 1932, and, after his departure, Sichyns'kyi. At its inception, the publishing house received 104,000 crowns from the Czechoslovak government. It was also supported financially by subsidies from the institute as well as from dues.[24]

The publishing house played a significant role in Ukrainian-language publishing in Czechoslovakia and produced some impressive works. In addition to Chyzhevs'kyi's work on philosophy discussed earlier, it published *Hrets'ka fil'osofiia do Pliatona. Khrestomatiia* (Greek Philosophy until Plato: A Reader, 1926) by the same author, which was intended to be a collection of exercises for students at the institute. The publishing house's works in pedagogy included Rusova's *Teoriia pedagogiky na osnovi psykhol'ogii* (Theory of Pedagogy Based on Psychology, 1924) and *Dydaktyka* (Didactics, 1925). In the area of language studies, the 462-page handwritten *Pidruchnyk nimets'koi movy* (The German Textbook, 1925) by Kushnir came out, as well as *Praktychna hramatyka latyns'koi movy* (A Practical Grammar of the Latin Language, vols. 1 (1927) and 2 (1929 [1930]) by Artymovych. Its publications in art history included two editions of *Konspekt istorii vsesvitn'oho mystetstva. Ch. 1. Do Renesansa* (An Abstract of the History of World Art, Part 1: Before the Renaissance, 1st ed. 1925, 2nd ed. 1928) and *Styli* (Styles [1926]) by Sichyns'kyi. The latter was the companion album of pictures for *Konspekt istorii vsesvitn'oho mystetstva*, drawn by the author.[25]

Most of the publishing house's books were printed in runs of 100 to 150. During the ten years of its existence, it issued 5,506 copies of 44 books. It also published 35 printouts of its professors' works, as well as three volumes of the organ of the institute, *Pratsi Ukrains'koho vysokoho pedagogichnoho instytutu im. Mykhaila Drahomanova u Prazi* (Works of the Ukrainian Higher Pedagogical Institute, named after Mykhailo

Drahomanov in Prague), which were issued in 1929, 1930–32, and 1932–34, all under the editorship of Simovych. The first volume, of almost six hundred pages, contained scholarly articles by the institute's faculty members; the second consisted of fifteen works devoted to Drahomanov; the third contained many articles devoted to Czech–Ukrainian relations.[26]

Since the publishing house did not have adequate means to print books in large runs, the Ukrainian Civic Publishing Fund published some works by the institute's professors. The fund published eleven books by them, in runs of 1,000 to 3,000, which considerably exceeded Siiach's publishing capacity. Books published by the fund included *Teoriia i praktyka doshkil'noho vykhovannia* by Rusova, mentioned in chapter 4, and the extensive *Kurs analitychnoi heometrii [...] Osnovy analitychnoi heometrii na ploshchi* (A Course of Analytical Geometry [...] Foundations of Analytical Geometry of Two Dimensions, 1925) by Ivanenko, both of which were published in runs of 2,000.[27]

The publishing house exchanged its publications with other organizations and sent free copies to a variety of institutions and individuals. In Czechoslovakia, it sent its books not only to Ukrainian institutions but also to the library of Charles University and the National Museum (Národní muzeum), as well as to ministries that supported the institute. In the 1920s, it also sent its works to Soviet Ukraine – specifically, to the Book Chamber, an organization tasked with registering all current publications, to the Academy of Sciences in Kyiv, and to the Institutes of People's Education in Kyiv, Kharkiv, Katerynoslav, and Kam'ianets'-Podil's'kyi. The publishing house also sent its published books to the Shevchenko Scientific Society and the Ukrainian Pedagogical Society in L'viv and distributed its works in Paris, Berlin, and Lithuania.[28]

In the 1930s, due to funding cuts, there were fewer and fewer opportunities for Ukrainian-language publishing in Czechoslovakia. The same was true in Galicia. Kolessa, in a letter to Studyns'kyi, complained that the Shevchenko Scientific Society would not reply to his inquiry about publishing dramatic works by Fed'kovych, which he had initially been tasked to do. Kolessa added that he had prepared other works as well but did not know where to publish them. In general, works published by these houses were important for Ukrainian-language scholarly publishing. The value of many of these works endures today. For instance, Chyzhevs'kyi's and Mirchuk's works have recently been reissued by the Ukrainian Free University in Munich, and works by Antonovych, Rusova, and Simovych have been reprinted in independent Ukraine. The topics of the scholarly publications reflected the expertise of the Ukrainian émigré scholars. There were gaps as well, such as a dearth of in-depth works on foreign and political aspects of the struggle for Ukraine's independence and the small number of translations of Western European works of literature. However, this did not diminish the substantial accomplishment of the émigré academics in Ukrainian-language scholarly publishing.[29]

"The Czech–Ukrainian Book" Publishing House

As noted earlier, scholarly publishing produced by Ukrainian émigré scholars thrived until the early 1930s, when the number of scholarly publications gradually decreased in tandem with reduced government funding. At this time, small publishing houses privately owned by Ukrainians started to appear in Czechoslovakia. Their mission was different from that of the scholarly publishers: they focused largely on fiction and political literature. For the most part, these publishing houses and the people who launched them were not part of Ukrainian émigré academic circles, so they are not part of the discussion in this study. However, some of the individuals involved had links to the scholarly world and produced valuable works, including biographies of notable figures, so these texts merit discussion.

"The Czech–Ukrainian Book" Publishing House (Vydavnytstvo "Ches'ko-ukrains'ka knyha") was founded in the late 1920s by the feminist educator, publisher, and civic figure Marie Omelčenková (Mariia Omel'chenko) (1874–?) and her husband, the scholar and civic figure Hryhorii Omel'chenko. This publishing house was their creation and survived largely through their hard work. As its name suggests, its primary goal was to strengthen Czech–Ukrainian relations, and it focused on publishing literature about Czechs in the Ukrainian language. The press also published several books in the Czech and Russian languages. Omelčenková was a highly educated woman. She was born in the Voronezh region and completed the Higher Courses for Women in St Petersburg (Bestuzhevskie kursy), after which she lived in the Kuban region and worked in social care. She arrived in Prague in 1920, and between 1923 and 1929 she studied at Charles University in the Natural Sciences Department.[30]

As she explained in the introduction to her extensive and heavily footnoted biography of Masaryk, *T.G. Masaryk (1850–1930)*, published in 1931 in 1,000 copies, her interest in him was lifelong from the time she was a student – not so much from her studies as from direct interactions with Czechs. Omelčenková also wrote numerous articles for Czech and Ukrainian periodicals, as well as several for French, Bulgarian, and Slovenian ones. Her articles also appeared in the Czech-language periodical *Věstník* (Bulletin), published in Texas. Omelčenková was an advocate for women's equality, and much of her writing was devoted to various outstanding Czech and Ukrainian women. Her bibliography in 1931 contained ninety-four items, most of them on women-related subjects, and included biographies of renowned women. Omelčenková belonged to many Czech and Ukrainian societies; she also co-edited the periodical *La femme slave* (The Slavic Woman, 1933–[?]), which published materials about the lives of influential women. The press's publications showed her interest in and lifelong dedication to Czech and Ukrainian themes. The first book it published was dedicated to Czech–Ukrainian relations, and the second was a reprint of a translation of Havlíček by Franko. A list of the press's publications available today contains twelve works, with the last one published in 1936.[31]

The publishing house's second co-founder, Hryhorii Omel'chenko, was born in the Kuban region. Omel'chenko was a literary historian and an associate professor at the Department of Slavic Literature at the Ukrainian Higher Pedagogical Institute. He taught a variety of courses: an introduction to Slavic studies, the history of Polish literature, the history of Russian literature, and the history of South Slavic literature. From 1936 until 1940 he was a director of the Ukrainian gymnasium. At the publishing house he produced a translation into Ukrainian of Masaryk's 1898 work, *Jak pracovat?* (How to Work?), as well as a book about Beneš as a statesman. A current list of his publications contains more than ten works, including 3 volumes on satirical poetry by Havlíček titled *Dějiny textu Křest sv. Vladimíra: básně Karla Havlíčka Borovského*. Omel'chenko's end was heartbreaking. After his arrest by the NKVD, he was deported to the Soviet Union, condemned to ten years in the Gulag and soon died. The works produced by the "Czech–Ukrainian Book" Publishing House helped strengthen Czech–Ukrainian relations in interwar Czechoslovakia and belong to Czech as well as Ukrainian culture.[32]

The Tyshchenko Publishing House

A discussion of Ukrainian publishing would be incomplete without mentioning a publisher vital to the development of Ukrainian-language book publishing: Iurii Tyshchenko. His Tyshchenko Publishing House (Vydavnytstvo Iuriia Tyshchenka) does not fall strictly within the scope of this study, since he primarily published popular science books, but this publisher dedicated his life to Ukrainian-language publishing, and a brief discussion of his life and work will add to our understanding of the development of the Ukrainian-language publishing as a whole and in Czechoslovakia in particular.

Kateryna Antonovych recalled Tyshchenko as a talented publisher who often put books out with almost no money. He published Ukrainian books for a general readership, Ukrainian scholarly books, and children's books. At a time when Ukrainian publishing was banned in the

Russian empire, Tyshchenko was under constant threat of arrest. Every time he had to escape, he always returned to found a new publishing house. He also opened bookstores, specifically in Kyiv and Kharkiv as well as in Katerynodar (now Krasnodar) in the Kuban region. After the revolution of 1905, when it became possible to publish books in Ukrainian, Tyshchenko opened a library at the publishing house Dzvin (Bell) and launched large-scale publishing activities. From 1907 until 1913, he served as director of the bookstore of *Literary Scholarly Herald* (Knyharnia *"Literaturno-naukovoho vistnyka"*) of the Shevchenko Scientific Society in Kyiv. During the revolution, he again worked in publishing, after which he was sent to Germany and Austria to organize the publication of Ukrainian-language textbooks. He was a passionate publisher; Kateryna Antonovych recalled that he rejoiced with every new volume. He later found himself in Czechoslovakia, and in 1925, while in Prague, in a letter to Studyns'kyi, he asked for a document confirming that he had worked as the director of a bookstore of the Shevchenko Scientific Society. Tyshchenko claimed that this letter would help him launch and develop Ukrainian-language publishing in Czechoslovakia. After that, he worked as a publisher in the Transcarpathian region as well as in Prague. In 1945, he escaped from Prague with only a small bag; the books, manuscripts, and other materials he left in Germany were destroyed in the bombings. By 1946 he had begun publishing again in Germany on a not-for-profit basis. In 1950, when he immigrated to the United States, he established the George Tyshchenko Publishing House, which published twelve volumes of Lesia Ukrainka's work, among other publications. He died in 1953 in New York. His lifelong dedication to Ukrainian-language publishing makes him one of the most important Ukrainian publishers of the first half of the twentieth century.[33]

The émigré scholars in the field of Ukrainian-language scholarly publishing contributed greatly to the intellectual history of Ukraine. The scholarly publications of the Ukrainian Civic Publishing Fund, the Ukrainian Free University, the Ukrainian Economic Academy, the Ukrainian Publishing Society "Siiach," "The Czech–Ukrainian Book" Publishing House, and other scholarly and professional societies form a significant part of Ukrainian scholarly publishing history. These publishing houses succeeded in publishing important scholarly works in the Ukrainian language at a time when doing so was impossible in Soviet Ukraine and difficult in Galicia or Bukovyna. Moreover, Ukraine itself was little-known in the West, and the publication of scholarship in Ukrainian made a vital contribution to the Ukrainian émigré scholars' mission of promoting Ukraine in the West. Many of these publications still have value today and are of interest not only in the context of Ukrainian scholarly publishing history but also as contributions to Ukrainian scholarship in various fields.

Chapter Nine

The Ukrainian Scholarly Community and the Outside World

The émigré scholars did a great deal to promote Ukrainian scholarship in Europe's academic world. These outward-looking scholarly activities were imperative in spreading knowledge about Ukraine into diverse fields. The following chapter is devoted to the exploration of these activities.

Cooperation with the Committee on Intellectual Cooperation at the League of Nations

One goal of the Ukrainian Academic Committee (UAC) was to join the Committee on Intellectual Cooperation at the League of Nations in Geneva, and its executive branch, the Paris-based Institute of Intellectual Cooperation. The committee was founded in 1922 mainly to establish and develop intellectual and cultural relations among scientists, scholars, teachers, artists, and other intellectuals worldwide. The French essayist, philosopher, and poet Paul Valéry called this organization the "League of Minds." Among its members were renowned scientists and intellectuals like Marie Skłodowska Curie (1867–1934), Henri Bergson (1859–1941), Albert Einstein (1879–1955), and Thomas Mann (1875–1955). The committee aimed to improve the working conditions of intellectuals by organizing exchange programs, conferences, and art fairs, as well as by providing scholarships to academics and students. While it lasted (i.e., until 1946), the committee supported research, forged many connections among intellectuals, and established new contacts among organizations.[1]

In early 1926, the UAC applied to the Committee on Intellectual Cooperation for recognition. Several months later, on 29 July 1926, that committee discussed the matter during one of its sessions in Geneva. The following academics were present: the chairman, Dutch physicist Hendrik Antoon Lorentz (1853–1928), a former professor of theoretical physics at the University of Leiden, a member of the Amsterdam Academy of Sciences, and an honorary member of many other scientific academies; Gonzague de Reynold (1880–1970), a professor of French literature at the University of Bern; and Kristine Bonnevie (1872–1948), a Norwegian biologist and Norway's first female professor. At this meeting, Reynold informed the attendees that the subcommittee on university relations had received a request from the UAC to develop relations. He emphasized that the UAC was not asking to be included as a national committee but, rather, desired the same status as the Association of Russian Emigrants, which was considered a "B type" committee. Reynold stated that on the basis of documents the UAC had sent him, he considered it an important organization that did significant work. The UAC was not asking for financial assistance; it only wanted to be included so that it could join in international efforts at intellectual cooperation. Reynold said he was fascinated by the scholarly activities of the Ukrainian intellectuals, and he asked the committee to "regard its request with sympathy." A brief discussion followed, during which the members discussed several issues, including the need to stress that the relations would be purely intellectual. Eventually, a decision was made: "It was understood that the Director of the Institute and the Secretary of the Committee on Intellectual Cooperation should fulfil the request as long as they [the UAC] understood their unofficial character." That same year, the committee's bulletin published a short item on the Ukrainian Free University and its faculty. The same publication stated that the university, through the UAC, could collaborate with the Committee on Intellectual Cooperation.[2]

The committee's acceptance of the UAC was very important to the Ukrainians. The very fact that they had been recognized by the international body boosted their confidence and offered a much-needed opportunity to include themselves in the international scholarly and intellectual world. This had been accomplished thanks to the efforts of Kolessa and Shul'hyn. After the UAC had been accepted, Kolessa received communiqués, bulletins, and other materials from Paris or Geneva almost every week. In a letter to Studyns'kyi, Kolessa confided that before then no one had known them, whereas now they were asking him for information. In the same letter, Kolessa asked Studyns'kyi to send him information about the scholarly activities of the Shevchenko Scientific Society to pass on to Paris and Geneva.[3]

Ukrainians also obtained several scholarships from the International Committee on Intellectual Cooperation. For example, Sichyns'kyi received a scholarship to study the history of engraving in Eastern Europe. Thanks to this, he was able to visit L'viv, Lublin, Zamość, Warsaw, and Cracow and explore many collections of engravings.

Sichyns'kyi unearthed many valuable and previously unknown materials. In 1934, Dmytro Antonovych mentioned that Sichyns'kyi intended to write a book about Ukrainian engravers in the sixteenth to eighteenth centuries in order to promote Eastern European art in Western Europe. In 1937, Sichyns'kyi did publish a book in L'viv, titled *Istoriia ukrains'koho graverstva: XVI–XVIII stolittia* (A History of Ukrainian Engraving from the Sixteenth to Eighteenth Centuries), presumably based on the materials he had collected while funded by this grant.[4]

However, the UAC's acceptance had largely symbolic effects. Being accepted into this international organization certainly made Ukrainian scholars in Czechoslovakia feel more included, but it is doubtful whether this feeling lasted long or had many practical benefits. When, for example, the UAC appealed to the Committee on Intellectual Cooperation to protest the persecution of Ukrainian intellectuals in the Soviet Union, that body remained deaf to the requests. The UAC remained in the Committee on Intellectual Cooperation until 1934, when the Soviet Union was accepted into the League of Nations. Ukrainians protested in many ways against this, in vain. After the acceptance of the Soviet Union, the UAC and its Russian equivalent ceased being members of this international organization.[5]

Prague as the Centre of Slavic Scholarship and Cooperation between Czech and Ukrainian Scholars

When discussing Czech–Ukrainian scholarly relations in interwar Prague, it is important to emphasize the role played by this city in the Slavic scholarly and intellectual world at the time. Prague had a long tradition of Slavic scholarship. As Chyzhevs'kyi states, "Russian and Polish Slavic studies laid their foundation on accomplishments of Czech Slavic studies, [and] made their progress in ties with the Czech one." The romantic notion of the unity of Slavic peoples and their cultures had been very popular among the Czech enlighteners. In interwar Czechoslovakia, tracking the thinking of Masaryk and Beneš, the government made it official policy to place Prague at the centre of European Slavic studies, and concrete steps were taken to that end. Masaryk outlined his vision of the Slavic question in his work *Česká otázka: snahy a tužby národního obrození* (The Czech Question: The Efforts and Aspirations of the National Revival, 1895). In it he stated that love of other Slavic nations had to be conscious; "mistakes" made by Slavic nations should not be buried but instead critically studied. He underscored the need to study Slavs' present and to better understand their past. The prominent Czech scholar Adolf Černý (1864–1952), the founder and long-time editor of *Slovanský přehled* (Slavic

Review), stated in his editorial for the first issue of that journal: "Let us know ourselves ..." – which was the motto of Edvard Jelínek, who published *Slovanský sborník* (Slavic Yearbook) from 1881 to 1887. And to this he added – "... and always in accordance with the truth."[6]

In interwar Europe, Prague was the perfect place for seeking Slavic knowledge: it had a long tradition of Slavic studies, it was now building a democratic society, and its president was also a scholar who had studied Slavic nations during his academic career. At this time, Czechoslovakia was a new state and was having to build its own institutions, including new universities, besides developing policies. This socio-political situation contributed to the prestige of the field of Slavic philology at Charles University in the 1920s. It was a stimulating time for Slavists in Prague.[7]

After the early 1920s, in accordance with government policy, experts in Slavic studies from other countries were invited to Prague. New positions were being created for which scholars and pedagogues with international reputations would be required. The founding of a Slavic journal was part of this initiative; so was the Institute of Slavic Studies. Matyáš Murko, a Slovenian scholar who had taught in Graz and Leipzig before the First World War, was invited to teach at the university and was tasked with reorganizing the Slavic seminar at the Department of Philosophy at Charles University. Murko was a philologist, literary historian, and folklorist. He had been elected an honorary professor of Charles University in 1909.[8]

The Slavic seminar had to be completely restructured. It had long focused mainly on Bohemian studies; during the 1920s, however, it made considerable revisions to the subjects it taught. It would now include sections on the Czech language, Czech literature, new Czech literature, Polish language and literature, Slovak literature, Russian language and literature, new Slavic languages and literatures, South Slavic languages and literatures, and Ukrainian language and literature. The courses apparently changed over time. This seminar was the largest in the department, taking up the entire ground floor and part of the basement of the new department building. Between the wars, its library expanded from 3,500 volumes to more than 18,000.[9] A number of eminent Slavists taught at the Slavic seminar, including Russians Vladimir Andreevich Frantsev and Evgenii Aleksandrovich Liaskii, and lecturers of Bulgarian literature Josef Páta (1886–1942) and then Kiril Christov (1875–1944). Later, in 1933, Páta became associate professor of Sorb-Serbian philology. The head of Polish studies was Marian Szyjkowski (1883–1952); Murko, until his retirement in 1932, taught South Slavic languages and literatures; a section on comparative Slavic literatures was taught in various years by Jan Máchal (1855–1939), Jiří Horák (1884–1975), and Julius

Dolanský-Heidenreich (1903–1975). Old Church Slavonic and dialectology were taught by František Pastrnek and Miloš Weingart; Slovak literature was taught by Jaroslav Vlček (1860–1930), Flora Kleinschnitzová (1891–1946), and Albert Pražák (1880–1956). Emil Smetánka (1875–1948) taught Czech language and literature. In addition, a Polish linguist and Slavist, Jan Baudouin de Courtenay (1845–1929), taught in Prague in 1922 and 1923.[10]

As this list of scholars demonstrates, Slavic studies at the university in the 1920s were thriving. This development was highly beneficial to Ukrainians, and several prominent figures in the Ukrainian scholarly world taught at Charles University. In 1926, Kolessa was invited to teach Ukrainian language and literature as a contract professor at the Department of Philosophy at Charles University; later, he became a full professor. From the early 1930s, Kolessa also led a new Ukrainian section of the Slavic seminar. In 1929, he also became a member of the Institute of Slavic Studies in Prague. He, Smal'-Stots'kyi, and Bilets'kyi were elected members of this institute. In 1928, Dmytro Doroshenko began lecturing in Ukrainian history as a contract professor at Charles University. As mentioned, Dnistrians'kyi was a professor at the German University in Prague and Shovheniv taught at the Technical University.[11]

For their part, Czech scholars took some part in the teaching and scholarly life of the Ukrainian scholarly milieu. Of particular note were the collaborations between Ukrainians and the Czech professors at Charles University, including Bidlo, Pastrnek, Rypka, and Jiří Polívka (1858–1933), as well as a cohort of Czech professors who taught at the Ukrainian Economic Academy. Another notable example of cooperation between the Czechs and Ukrainians was Dmytro Doroshenko's collaboration with renowned Czech Orientalist Jan Rypka. Together, in 1936, they wrote a work titled *Polsko, Ukrajina, Krym a Vysoká Porta v první pol[ovině] XVII. stol[etí]* (Poland, Ukraine, Crimea, and the Sublime Porte in the First Half of the Seventeenth Century), based on rare Turkish archival materials. Rypka was also on the council of the Ukrainian Free University in the 1930s. He was a founding member of the Oriental Institute (Orientální ústav) in Prague and for many years was on the editorial board of its periodical *Archív Orientální* (Oriental Archive, 1929). Later, in 1956, under his editorialship, the elaborate work *Dějiny perské a tádžické literatury* (A History of Persian and Tadzik Literature) was published. This book was written with his colleagues and was translated into German, English, Polish, Russian, and Persian. Additionally, between 1934 and 1937 five volumes with an index of the influential work *Tvůrcové dějin. Čtyři tisíciletí světových dějin v obrazech dob a osobností* (The Creators of History: Four Millennia of World History in Images and Personalities) were published in Prague. In these volumes Dmytro Doroshenko penned five articles – one devoted to Danylo Romanovych, one to Petro Mohyla, one to Bohdan Khmel'nyts'kyi, one to Ivan Mazepa, and one to Taras Shevchenko. This edition was a translation of an earlier German-language edition published in Vienna; the Czech edition included new articles written by émigré scholars (mostly Russian).[12]

Hrushevs'kyi maintained some contact with Czech scholars even after he left for Soviet Ukraine. In a 1926 letter, Hrushevs'kyi thanked Bidlo for his positive review in *Prager Presse* (Prague Press), a German-language newspaper founded by Masaryk and published by the Czechoslovak government in an effort to integrate the country's German population. This publication ran hundreds of items about Ukraine. It also reviewed Ukrainian materials published by the Ukrainian Academy of Sciences and the Shevchenko Scientific Society. Bidlo also published a short book in 1935 titled *Michal Hruševs'kyj* through the Czechoslovak Academy of Science in Prague, to commemorate the life of that great historian.[13]

Ukrainian scholars belonged to various Czechoslovak institutions and societies. For example, Oleh Kandyba, a poet, archaeologist, and – later in life – a nationalist leader, worked in the Archaeology Department of the National Museum in Prague in addition to his work at the Ukrainian Free University.[14] Ukrainian academics also contributed some works in Czech and Slovak studies. Chyzhevs'kyi was the most prolific in this regard, exploring many Czech and Slovak topics. Ivan Borkovs'kyi, Prague Castle's archaeologist, published many works on the castle and on other themes in archaeology. Several faculty members at the Ukrainian Free University explored topics with Czech–Ukrainian contexts: Iakovliv produced a monograph on the influences of old Bohemian law on Ukrainian law in the fifteenth and sixteenth centuries; Dmytro Doroshenko, besides co-authoring works with Rypka, wrote an article on František Palacký for *Pratsi Ukrains'koho vysokoho pedagogichnoho instytutu*; Kostiantyn Chekhovych (1896–1987) wrote about literary relations; and Steshko explored topics in musicology.[15]

Ukrainian academics managed to build some connections with their Czech counterparts. While some of them were well-integrated and had contacts among Czech academics, this was not the case for others, who may have felt isolated. For those who had integrated themselves, the academic projects and positions they found in Czechoslovakia helped them forge good relations between Ukrainian and Czechoslovak intellectuals at various institutions. So through their efforts to make connections with other academies, Ukrainian scholars in Czechoslovakia promoted Ukrainian studies in the country. Integration also enabled Ukrainian scholars to make a living despite the challenges of emigration. The benefits, presumably, were mutual, in that some Czech scholars taught in Ukrainian institutions, participated in Ukrainian events, and took part in joint projects. These interactions benefited scholars and scholarship on both sides.[16]

Contact with the Ukrainian Scholarly Worlds in Galicia and Soviet Ukraine

Between the wars, Ukrainian émigré scholars in Czechoslovakia maintained strong ties with the Shevchenko Scientific Society in L'viv. There were obvious differences between the scholarly work in Polish-ruled Galicia and in the emigration. In L'viv, and elsewhere in Galicia, Ukrainian intellectuals were surrounded by Ukrainians and had access to archives and other vital sources; however, it was not possible to set up Ukrainian institutions of higher education there. By contrast, in Czechoslovakia the émigré scholars were able to establish Ukrainian institutions of higher learning and educate many young Ukrainians, and they were surrounded by European culture, but they lacked direct contact with their native land and its people.[17]

Correspondence between Ukrainian intellectuals in Czechoslovakia and L'viv reveals ongoing connections between them during this period. This cooperation between the scholarly world in Prague and, in particular, the Shevchenko Scientific Society in L'viv, was important, and personal connections played a significant role in this. Before the war, many of these scholars had been colleagues, friends, or rivals. They then found themselves in countries with different political climates and worked to promote their cause regardless of the circumstances. These groups of Ukrainian intellectuals collaborated and supported each other to a degree. The exchange of scholarly books between the Ukrainian Free University and the Shevchenko Scientific Society was quite intensive. Letters exchanged by Volodymyr Doroshenko, Antonovych, and Bidnov, for example, show that they cooperated closely and helped one another in many ways. They attended one another's conferences and congresses, they published, reviewed, and commented on one another's works in their respective countries, and they sent one another books and other materials. They also promoted one another's work in Ukrainian periodicals in Czechoslovakia and Galicia. For the most part, they maintained an official style of correspondence when discussing matters related to Ukrainian scholarly life in both countries, but they also sometimes wrote less formal, more personal letters.[18]

In the 1920s, Ukrainian physicians and the Union of Ukrainian Doctors in Czechoslovakia maintained contact with their colleagues in

Galicia, particularly with the Ukrainian Doctors' Society (Ukrains'ke likars'ke tovarystvo) in L'viv. Between the wars, Ukrainian émigré doctors attended, presented, or sent their papers to five out of the six congresses of physicians and natural scientists in L'viv. They also collected and donated more than 15,000 crowns for the People's Hospital (Narodna lichnytsia) in L'viv. Furthermore, some editorial offices in L'viv invited émigré doctors from Czechoslovakia to contribute to their publications.[19] Also, in the early 1920s, the members of the Union of Ukrainian Doctors in Czechoslovakia maintained contact with a number of physicians in Soviet Ukraine. In their correspondence, the union members often asked them to send books, dictionaries, and other materials they lacked. In the 1920s, physicians from Soviet Ukraine published their scholarly works in their union's periodical, *Ukrains'kyi medychnyi vistnyk;* eight articles published by doctors from Kyiv were included in the journal's last volume in 1925. In addition, in 1927 the union sent a large collection of medical literature in the German language to the Medical Section of the Ukrainian Academy of Sciences. The collection had been purchased in 1919 and stored in Berlin.[20]

Contacts between Ukrainian émigré scholars and other Slavists helped link the Ukrainian communities, as did their very presence in the scholarly world in Prague. Some journal and newspaper editors from Prague contacted the Shevchenko Scientific Society asking members to send them their materials. In July 1922, Murko, the founder of *Slavia* – the new Slavic studies journal – sent its first issue to the editorial office of the society and promised to send subsequent volumes to them regularly if the society in turn sent in their scholarly works in Slavic philology, so that the editorial office of *Slavia* could inform its readers about the publications. In May 1926, the editorial office of *Prager Presse* wrote a letter to the society thanking it for its new volumes and informing it that it would feature information about these volumes on its pages. The editorial office assured the society that information about all materials sent would be included in the newspaper. The *Prager Presse* editorial office also asked the society to send in all the materials the society published, including highly specialized ones. Also, in August 1929, the Prague journal *Střední Evropa* (Central Europe) sent a letter to the society requesting several volumes and a book by Filaret Kolessa for review. These contacts between Ukrainian scholars and other Slavists raised awareness of Ukrainians and their scholarhip, not only in Czechoslovakia but also abroad.[21]

Cooperation between Ukrainian émigré scholars and Ukrainian scholars in Soviet Ukraine faced many hurdles. The émigré scholars' uneasy attitude toward, and ideological non-acceptance of, the Soviet regime played a significant role in shaping these interactions. Moreover, the Soviet regime raised more and more obstacles to their communications over time. In the 1920s, there was still contact between some émigré scholars in Czechoslovakia and their colleagues in Soviet Ukraine; by the end of 1920s, due to the purges of scholarship in Soviet Ukraine, all contact had ceased.

In general, Ukrainian scholars in Czechoslovakia paid close attention to the work of their colleagues in Kyiv and Kharkiv. Some of them corresponded sporadically with scholars from the Ukrainian Academy of Sciences in Kyiv; notably, Kolessa occasionally corresponded with Hrushevs'kyi and with Serhii Iefremov (1876–1939), a literary scholar, literary historian, and vice-president of the Ukrainian Academy of Sciences, perished in the purges in the 1930s. Chykalenko also corresponded with Iefremov during the 1920s in order to foster good relations and sustain intellectual interest, and also because he was worried about his two sons, who lived in Soviet Ukraine. Bilets'kyi corresponded with his mentor, Perets, and Dnistrians'kyi with economist and geographer Kostiantyn Voblii (1876–1947) as well as legal scholar and historian Mykola Vasylenko (1866–1935). Dnistrians'kyi also actively corresponded with his brother-in-law, Stepan Rudnyts'kyi, after he left for Soviet Ukraine. When Rudnyts'kyi left Czechoslovakia, his letters were full of positive reflections on his surroundings. The tone of his letters changed greatly as time passed; more and more negative observations appeared in his letters.[22]

Most émigré scholars strongly rejected the idea of moving to the Soviet Union, while some, including Rudnyts'kyi after his arrival in Soviet Ukraine, were supportive of it. Interestingly, Dnistrians'kyi seriously considered moving to Soviet Ukraine, undoubtedly influenced by Rudnyts'kyi as well as the worsening conditions of émigré life. In 1926, Dnistrians'kyi received the offer of a professorship in private law at the Institute of People's Education in Kyiv, which he neither accepted nor rejected. As evident from their correspondence, Rudnyts'kyi and Dnistrians'kyi discussed the possibility of the Dnistrians'kyi family returning to Soviet Ukraine and obtaining positions at the academy. In 1926, Dnistrians'kyi had submitted his two substantial works, *Kul'tura, tsyvilizatsiia ta pravo* (Culture, Civilization, and Law) and *Potreba novoi systemy pryvatnoho prava* (The Need for a New System of Private Law), to Kharkiv University for publication. However, they were never published. In 1928, Dnistrians'kyi was elected to the Ukrainian Academy of Sciences and named the head of a department. Being a Polish citizen, Dnistrians'kyi submitted the required documents to the Soviet and Polish embassies; the latter raised obstacles to his obtaining a passport. After several attempts to acquire a passport, Dnistrians'kyi abandoned the idea of returning, which ultimately saved him and his wife from the repressions of the late 1920s and 1930s.[23]

Few works by Ukrainian émigrés were published in Soviet Ukraine. Rusova published her memoirs in a Kyiv journal edited by Hrushevs'kyi titled *Za sto lit* (In One Hundred Years, 1927–30). That journal was devoted to the history of literature and civic life in the Ukrainian lands in the nineteenth and early twentieth centuries. It also published archival materials, memoirs, and correspondence. In total, 66 authors – some of whom perished later in the purges – published 112 articles as well as smaller items in these volumes. Only six volumes were released, and all of them demonstrated high-quality scholarship. The journal ceased publishing with the wave of purges of scholars and intellectuals in Soviet Ukraine. In this periodical, Hrushevs'kyi had reportedly intended to publish the memoirs of Dmytro Antonovych of Prague, in connection with the twenty-fifth anniversary of the death of his father, the renowned historian Volodymyr Antonovych. Dmytro Antonovych, however, never sent his memoirs to Hrushevs'kyi. There are many possible reasons for this, the most likely being that the émigré scholars could not forgive Hrushevs'kyi for returning to Soviet Ukraine. Except for Rusova with her memoirs, émigré scholars did not participate in this publication.[24]

There were more contacts between Ukrainian émigré scholars and those in Soviet Ukraine. Simovych even attended the All-Ukrainian Orthographic Conference in Kharkiv (Vseukrains'ka pravopysna konferentsiia), held from 26 May to 6 June 1927. The aim of the conference was to systematize Ukrainian orthography, and it attracted Ukrainian linguists from all Ukrainian lands as well as émigré scholars. As a result, a new, standardized orthography was adopted a year later. Obviously, not all émigré scholars attended; Smal' Stots'kyi, for example, a staunch opponent of the Soviet regime, refused to do so.[25]

There were inevitable tensions between Ukrainian émigré scholars and those who lived in Galicia and Soviet Ukraine. For example, while preparing for the Prague First Ukrainian Scholarly Congress in 1926, its organizing committee invited Ukrainian scholars at the Ukrainian Academy of Sciences and the Shevchenko Scientific Society. The scholars from both these institutions, however, did not participate. The academy rejected the invitation; the society's refusal to participate was motivated by its politically neutral orientation. Despite these divisions, the émigré scholars in Czechoslovakia maintained ties with their colleagues in Polish-ruled Galicia and Soviet Ukraine. They exchanged books and periodicals, participated in one another's events, and promoted one another's works to the outside world. Cooperation with Ukrainian intellectuals in Galicia was extensive and endured throughout the period under discussion; émigré scholars' contacts with colleagues in Kyiv and Kharkiv were more sporadic and existed only in the 1920s.[26]

Participation in Conferences

Ukrainian émigré scholars participated in a variety of European scholarly congresses and conferences. They viewed this participation as important for promoting their scholarship about Ukraine to the outside world. They also regarded it as a bridge to building relations and reputations within scholarly circles in various countries at a time when information about Ukraine was very scarce. The Ukrainian émigré scholars took part in conferences and congresses in Prague, Warsaw, Brussels, Paris, Lund, Oslo, and Basel, among many other cities. Their participation was at its highest in the 1920s; in the 1930s, it declined sharply due to harsh cuts in financial support from the Czechoslovak government.[27]

The Ukrainian émigré scholars presented their research at scholarly gatherings in various disciplines. Artymovych and Simovych participated in linguistics conferences, Dmytro Antonovych in art congresses, Dmytro Doroshenko in historians' conferences, and Mirchuk and Chyzhevs'kyi in many philosophy conferences. Martos and Borodaievs'kyi took part in several conferences related to the cooperative movement, while Shelukhin and Los'kyi attended law conferences, and Horbachevs'kyi and Matiushenko medical ones.

Some scholars participated in more conferences and congresses than others. As mentioned earlier, Shcherbakivs'kyi was very active in this respect, taking part in many conferences around Europe. He presented papers at the Fifth International Congress of the History of Religion, held in Lund, Sweden, in August 1929; he also participated in the International Congress of Anthropology in Paris in 1931, in the Fifteenth Congress of Anthropology and Prehistorical Archaeology and in the First Congress of Prehistorical and Pro-Historical Studies in London in 1932, and in the Twentieth Prehistorical and Pro-Historical Studies Conference in Oslo in 1936. Chyzhevs'kyi was another prolific scholar who took part in a large number of conferences and congresses. At the Hegel Congress in The Hague, held in April 1930, he presented a paper about Hegel in Slavic thought ("Hegel bei den Slaven"); he also attended the above-mentioned congress in Lund with a paper about the plant as a religious symbol. Chyzhevs'kyi participated in many other scholarly gatherings as well, particularly in Germany. In the summer of 1927, he participated in two conferences in Halle: the Congress of Aesthetics and General Art Theory and the conference of the Kant Society (Kantgesellschaft). In his report, Chyzhevs'kyi noted that the congress included representatives from many disciplines and many nations, including the English, Germans, Japanese, Czechs, Poles, Russians, and Ukrainians. At the conference of the society, the participants were mostly from German universities, the Netherlands, Switzerland, and Japan. In May 1929, Chyzhevs'kyi attended the Kant Society conference and the Congress of Aesthetics and General Art Theory again.[28]

For obvious reasons, the Ukrainian scholars participated most often in conferences and congresses in Prague and other cities in Czechoslovakia. In 1924, a congress of anthropologists was held in Prague in which Petro Andriievs'kyi, Shcherbakivs'kyi, and Lev Chykalenko (1888–1965) participated. In 1925, Ukrainian scholars participated in a congress of Czech ethnographers in Brno and in the congress of Czech jurists in Prague. As noted, in the 1930s the participation of the scholars in congresses considerably diminished. They still, however, took part in some of them, including the Congress of Folk Art in Antwerp, in November 1930, and an international congress of technology and city hygiene in Milan, in 1931. Mirchuk also took part in the International Congress of Philosophy, held in Oxford from 1 to 6 September 1930.[29]

In the interwar period, two Slavic congresses in Czechoslovakia and Poland took place, in 1929 and 1934 respectively. The First Congress of Slavic Philologists was held from 6 to 13 October 1929 in Prague, and Ukrainian émigré scholars took an active part in it. This congress was very important to the further development of Slavic studies on a European scale. It was the first scholarly gathering of its kind that presented and summarized the state of research in various fields of Slavic studies. At the congress, the Ukrainian scholars delivered papers on the following subjects: Bilets'kyi talked about major directions in Ukrainian scholarly criticism over the preceding fifty years; Oleksander Kolessa spoke on the findings and publication of Slavic works of apocryphal literature; Simovych discussed the historical development of Ukrainian male baptismal names; Siropolko talked about Ukrainian bibliography and the bibliography of Ukrainica in philology; and Smal'-Stots'kyi highlighted the objectives of Slavic studies. The participation of Ukrainian scholars was noteworthy. However, as Simovych noted, from an organizational point of view the Ukrainian scholars did not fully achieve their objectives – they had wanted to play an even more active role.[30]

The Second International Congress of Slavists took place from 23 to 27 September 1934 in Warsaw and from 28 to 30 September 1934 in Cracow. More than three hundred scholars attended this congress, and a delegation from Czechoslovakia led by Murko was the largest group in attendance. The Ukrainian émigré scholars delivered the following papers: Borkovs'kyi presented in German on cord culture, while Smal'-Stots'kyi spoke on the Old Slavic (Eastern) language; Artymovych presented a paper in German on the potential of language. Other Ukrainian scholars participated as well.[31]

The First International Congress of Geographers and Ethnographers took place from 4 to 8 June 1924 in Prague. At the congress, several Ukrainian scholars presented papers: Stepan Rudnyts'kyi presented "Problems of Geology and Morphology of Subcarpathian Rus'" as well as "Natural Areas of Ukraine"; Volodymyr Tymoshenko, "Theory of the World Economy in the Economic Geography"; Bilets'kyi, "Prospects for Scholarly Experimentation of Ukrainian Folk Poetry"; Oleksander Kolessa, "Major Directions and Methods in Studying Ukrainian Folklore"; Sichyns'kyi, "Ukrainian Wooden Construction and Methods of Research"; and Shcherbakivs'kyi, "The Significance of the Ukrainian Painted Easter Egg in the Symbolism of the Sun Cult."[32]

In October 1927, Kolessa presented an address at the commemoration of the French scientist Pierre Eugène Marcellin Berthelot at the Sorbonne in Paris. During this visit, he stopped in at the Institute of Intellectual Cooperation with Iakovliv and Shul'hyn. Much later, on 25–26 June 1937, in the halls of the Sorbonne, Shul'hyn took part in the annual conference organized by the International Institute for Research on the French Revolution. His paper was devoted to the ideological debate surrounding Jean-Jacques Rousseau between 1762 and 1768 in Geneva. It was based on new documents, presented new facts, and received a positive review from University of Geneva professor Charles Borgeaud.[33]

While the scholars who participated in conferences were mainly from the Ukrainian Free University, academics from other Ukrainian institutions took part as well. For example, scholars from the Ukrainian Higher Pedagogical Institute took part in some above-mentioned international conferences: "By School to Peace" congress in Prague in 1927, in the Congress of Czechoslovak Teachers and the Congress of the Extracurricular Activities in 1928 in Brno, in the educational congress organized by the Prosvita Society in L'viv in 1929, and in international pedagogical congresses in Heidelberg and Geneva. Eikhel'man represented the institute at the Fifth Sociological congress in Vienna in the fall of 1926. In October 1928, Sichyns'kyi participated in the Congress of People's Art in Prague, organized by the Institute of Intellectual Cooperation.[34]

Contributions to Encyclopaedias

Ukrainian émigré scholars contributed to a variety of encyclopaedias published between the wars in Czechoslovakia and abroad. In the 1920s, in Czechoslovakia, several previously published encyclopaedias were reissued and new ones were created. Encyclopaedias were also published in other European countries. By writing about various aspects of Ukraine's history, culture, literature, and politics, Ukrainian academics promoted knowledge about the country.

Ukrainian émigré scholars in Czechoslovakia helped create the path-breaking three-volume encyclopaedia titled *Ukrains'ka zahal'na entsykl'opediia. Knyha znannia v 3-okh tomakh* (Ukrainian General Encyclopaedia: The Knowledge Book in Three Volumes), published in Galicia between 1930 and 1935. It was produced under the editorship of Ivan Rakovs'kyi (1874–1949), an anthropologist and zoologist as well as a public figure. The other editors of the encyclopaedia were Volodymyr Doroshenko, writer and literary critic Mykhailo Rudnyts'kyi (1889–1975), and Vasyl' Simovych. This was the first reference work of its kind in the Ukrainian language, and its development depended on public involvement and fundraising. It had around 34,000 entries and articles, to which 136 authors contributed. Ukrainian émigré professors wrote entries for the general part of the encyclopaedia: Artymovych on linguistics, Chyzhevs'kyi on philosophy, Bilets'kyi on the history of writing in the fifteenth to eighteenth centuries, and Starosol's'kyi on the social sciences.[35]

A long section of Volume III of the encyclopaedia titled *Ukrainica*, edited by Simovych, gave an overview of almost all areas of knowledge about Ukraine and Ukrainians. It included more than 320 doubled-columned, closely typeset pages, as well as illustrations and coloured foldout maps. Rakovs'kyi, the prime mover of the encyclopaedia project, had recruited Simovych to the *Ukrainica* section, and Simovych in turn recruited other Ukrainian émigré scholars in Czechoslovakia. Overall, sixty authors wrote forty-nine articles in various fields for the *Ukrainica*. The contributors to the encyclopaedia's technical section were faculty at the academy in Poděbrady; their rector, Ivanyts'kyi was that section's editor. Sichyns'kyi enriched the section of the encyclopaedia dedicated to art; he wrote articles about stone and wooden architecture, carving, paintings, graphics and engraving, applied art, ceramics (with archaeologist Iaroslav Pasternak (1892–1969)), glassware, and paperware.[36] Table 21 lists articles written by émigré scholars from Czechoslovakia in the *Ukrainica* section.

This encyclopaedia was not without its flaws and inconsistencies. The mere fact of its creation, however, by the members of a stateless nation in Polish-ruled Galicia with considerable contributions from Ukrainian émigré scholars, illustrates the dedication of the Ukrainians. In addition to above-mentioned input to *Ukrains'ka zahal'na entsykl'opediia*, the émigré scholars contributed to encyclopaedias published in their host country. Entries on Horbachevs'kyi and the physicist and

Table 21. Articles by the Ukrainian scholars in Czechoslovakia in *Ukrains'ka zahal'na entsykl'opediia*[37]

Name	Article
Antonovych, Dmytro	Theatre
Artymovych, Agenor	Schooling in the Transcarpathian region
Bidnov, Vasyl'	Orthodox Church; History of the Orthodox Church; History of schooling before the nineteenth century; History of money
Bilets'kyi, Leonid	Schooling in Dnieper Ukraine in the nineteenth and twentieth centuries; Political emigration from the 1870s to 1914; Ukrainian literature from the fifteenth to eighteenth centuries
Borodaievs'kyi, Serhii	Cooperative movement in Dnieper Ukraine
Chykalenko, Lev	Prehistory; Paleolithic era
Doroshenko, Dmytro	Education and culture of Dnieper Ukraine and Kuban in the nineteenth and twentieth centuries; Scholarly life
Fedenko, Panas	Ukrainian history from 1638 until the eighteenth century; Dnieper Ukraine from the nineteenth century until the 1930s; Emigration from Dnieper Ukraine after 1919–1920
Iakovliv, Andrii	Law in Kyivan Rus'; Law of the Lithuanian Commonwealth; Law in the Cossack State; Law of the Ukrainian People's Republic; Law of the Hetmanate
Mazepa, Isaak	Dnieper Ukraine under Soviet rule
Narizhnyi, Symon	Ukrainian history until 1638; Historiography
Pasternak, Iaroslav	Prehistory; Bronze era; Ceramics (seventh and eighth centuries)
Shcherbakivs'kyi, Vadym	Prehistory; Eneolithic period (Copper era)
Shul'hyn, Oleksander	Ukrainian government activities from 1917
Sichyns'kyi, Volodymyr	Art
Simovych, Vasyl'	Ukrainian language; Grammar [doslidy]; History of Ukrainian orthography; Bukovyna
Smal'-Stots'kyi, Stepan	History of the Ukrainian language
Steshko, Fedir	Music history
Vyrovyi, Ievhen	Philately
Zlenko, Petro	Bibliography; Bibliology; Publishing houses

electrotechnician Ivan Puliui (1845–1918) had appeared in the renowned *Ottův slovník naučný. Illustrovaná encyklopaedie obecných vědomostí* (Otto's Encyclopaedia, 1888–1909) as early as 1896 and 1903, respectively. This twenty-eight-volume encyclopaedia had been published at the turn of the twentieth century by Jan Otto's publishing house and was the largest encyclopaedia in the Czech language. In 1930, the same house began publishing a supplement to it titled *Ottův slovník naučný nové doby* (Otto's Encyclopaedia of the New Era). This very broad supplement reflected recent political and historical events. Most of the entries and articles in this encyclopaedia were new; only a small number of them were revisions of the earlier edition. Twelve volumes had been published by 1943, when the project was halted by the Nazis; the entries for the letters V to Z never appeared. Around forty Ukrainian and Russian scholars were invited to contribute to this new Czechoslovak encyclopaedia; among them were Antonovych, Kolessa, Horbachevs'kyi, Bilets'kyi, Haimanivs'kyi, Shcherbakivs'kyi, Sichyns'kyi, Siropolko, Borkovs'kyi, and Steshko. It is also telling that entries about émigré scholars – Dmytro Doroshenko, Antonovych, Bilets'kyi, Kolessa, and Siropolko – appeared in this encyclopaedia. In another encyclopaedia published between 1925 and 1933, *Masarykův slovník naučný: lidová encyklopedie všeobecných vědomostí* (Masaryk's Encyclopaedia: Popular Encyclopaedia of General Knowledge), several entries on Ukraine were written by émigré scholars; for example, Siropolko provided entries on Ukraine and Ukrainians.[38]

Several Ukrainian émigré scholars contributed articles and shorter entries on Ukraine to important encyclopaedias published between the wars in other European countries. In Germany, the fifteenth edition of *Der Große Brockhaus. Handbuch des Wissens in zwanzig Bänden* (The Great Brockhaus: Manual of Knowledge in 20 Volumes) was published between 1928 and 1935 by the renowned Brockhaus publishing house in Leipzig. This edition featured a general article on Ukraine that provided demographics as well as a brief history of the country, along with a description of the revolutionary events and Ukraine's division among four states. It also contained an entry on Ukrainian geography and traditions, followed by an entry on Ukrainian literature and the Ukrainian language. According to Narizhnyi, the author of these articles was Dmytro Doroshenko. The bibliographies to these entries included works by Doroshenko and one by Smal'-Stots'kyi, along with other works published by émigrés and other scholars.[39]

In 1928, an article on Ukraine by Hans Jensen appeared in the influential Danish encyclopaedia *Salmonsens Konversationsleksikon* (Salmon's Conversation Lexicon, 2nd ed.), published between 1915 and 1930. It was based on a source published in Prague. In addition, an article on Ukraine was published in the Swedish encyclopaedia *Bonniers konversationslexikon* (Bonnier's Conversation Lexicon, 1937–50). The author of this entry is unknown, but clearly, the work of Ukrainian scholars in Czechoslovakia influenced the decision to include this information in the encyclopaedia, particularly an article by Dmytro Doroshenko published in 1937 in the prestigious Swedish historical journal *Historisk tidskrift* (The Historical Journal, 1881–). Another important encyclopaedia,

Larousse du XXe siècle (Larousse of the Twentieth Century), was published in France between 1928 and 1933. It too included an article on Ukraine that detailed its geography, history, language, and literature. The article's author is not noted, but Shul'hyn was a likely candidate as he was living in Paris at that time and promoting the Ukrainian cause in his French circles.[40] Ukrainian émigré scholars' efforts to contribute information about Ukraine and its history, language, culture, and politics to European encyclopaedias were important, for by these means Ukraine became better known to readers in the respective countries.

Émigré Scholarly Publications Elsewhere

Ukrainian émigré scholars in Czechoslovakia published their works in various European scholarly journals in several languages. Their scholarship was published predominantly in Czech, German, French, Polish, and English, but also in Swedish, Turkish, and other languages. Ukrainian émigré scholars displayed their scholarship in many fields of expertise, including history, literature, linguistics, philosophy, and law. They published most widely in Czech- and German-language scholarly periodicals. Their scholarship appeared in the journals *Slovanský přehled, Slavia, Časopis Národního muzea v Praze* (Journal of the National Museum in Prague), and *Český časopis historický* (Czech Historical Journal), among others. It also appeared in *Prager Presse* and *Slavische Rundschau* (Slavic Review), published in Prague. Between the wars, *Slovanský přehled* evolved into a prestigious journal with a focus on history, culture, and social and economic issues in all the Slavic countries. This journal's content reflected the rich cultural and scholarly life not just in Prague but throughout the region. In the 1920s, its pages were full of articles, book reviews, obituaries, and announcements of cultural events. Many noteworthy scholars and political figures presented their scholarship or views in its pages and it covered the most important events in the Slavic world. In *Slovanský přehled,* Ukrainian scholarship featured most heavily in the 1920s. For instance, in 1925, Bochkovs'kyi published his article "Poznámky k otázce ukrajinské" (Notes on the Ukrainian Question). The same volume reviewed various Slavic periodicals, including Prague-based *Nova Ukraina* (New Ukraine, 1922–28), a Ukrainian journal that contained rich materials on Ukrainian scholars and their activities.[41]

Dmytro Doroshenko published his works in many languages. His comprehensive works on Ukrainian history informed scholarly audiences across Europe and in North America about many aspects of the unknown country and its people. In particular, his works appeared in periodicals issued in Czechoslovakia. For example, in 1935, in *Časopis Národního muzea v Praze,* he published a piece devoted to a translation of an article from *Národní listy* by Kostomarov.[42] Other scholars published their works as well: Siropolko's article dedicated to Ladislav Jan Živný (1872–1949), a renowned Czech bibliographer, appeared in *Časopis československých knihovníků;* Dnistrians'kyi wrote several articles for the journal *Právník* (Jurist) Pasternak published an article devoted to archaeological scholarship in eastern Galicia in the first volume of *Slavische Rundschau,* published in 1929; and Chyzhevs'kyi published many of his works in *Slovo a slovesnost* and *Slavische Rundschau,* and in many other venues.[43] During this period, Ukrainian émigré scholars also published books in various languages. In 1939, a thick English-language volume on the history of Ukraine by Dmytro Doroshenko was released in Canada. In 1930, a 220-page book on Ukraine and its struggle for independence by the civic and political figure Volodymyr Murs'kyi (1888–1935) appeared in Turkish in Istanbul. Many more such publications by the Ukrainian émigré scholars were published.[44]

To conclude, in order to promote their scholarship and the cause, Ukrainian émigré scholars in Czechoslovakia established ties with the Committee on Intellectual Cooperation at the League of Nations in Geneva. They cooperated with Czech and other Slavic scholars in Czechoslovakia participating in various conferences in their host country and abroad. Academics published their research in a number of scholarly journals and produced books in several languages. While all of these activities encountered obstacles, their input clearly contributed to the intellectual history of Ukraine.

Conclusion

In the interwar years, Czechoslovakia became the leading intellectual centre for Ukrainian émigrés in Europe. This was possible because of considerable support from the Czechoslovak government. In the early 1920s, favourable conditions caused many Ukrainian scholars to move to Czechoslovakia. Prior to their emigration, many of these individuals had taken part in the struggle for independence from 1917 to 1921 in Ukraine. In Czechoslovakia, however, most of them confined themselves to scholarly work.

In interwar Czechoslovakia, Ukrainian émigré scholars founded several institutions of higher learning that succeeded in developing a new generation of educated Ukrainians. Scholarly and professional societies and organizations were established. Hundreds of scholarly works were published. In addition, émigré scholars participated in numerous international congresses and conferences and contributed information on Ukraine to various encyclopaedias published across Europe. This was scholarship created in emigration by individuals who, while often experiencing hardships, considered it their duty. It is important to remember that some of these scholars, especially those from the former Austro-Hungarian empire, who had stronger connections and linguistic skills, could have explored other prospects in Czechoslovakia. They could have sought opportunities in other institutions to teach subjects not related to Ukraine. While some of the scholars, in addition to their jobs at Ukrainian institutions, found employment elsewhere in Czechoslovakia, they continued to work, sometimes without pecuniary reward, in the Ukrainian institutions. The result was a vibrant Ukrainian intellectual life in interwar Prague and in Poděbrady.

Moreover, these academics were able to create a new cohort of Ukrainian scholars and professionals. Many of the Ukrainian émigrés in Czechoslovakia were young – most of them had been soldiers in the Ukrainian armies. For many of them, the First World War and the subsequent revolutionary events had interrupted their education. These individuals were eager to start or continue their studies, and the Ukrainian institutions of higher learning in Czechoslovakia helped them do so. In general, it can be said that living, studying, and working in the democratic country proved a very positive experience for them, and most of them succeeded in their later professions.

Being a liberal democracy governed by the rule of law, Czechoslovakia provided an environment where people from various Slavic nations could develop. At that time, the Ukrainians and Russians established their own networks of educational and cultural institutions in the country, which itself was in the stage of state-building. Masaryk's vision played a crucial role in saving émigré scholars and cultural figures from dispersion and degradation; it provided them with opportunities to work as well as to develop themselves. The Czechoslovak government helped create a new generation of educated persons by turning soldiers into students.

The Czechoslovak government's policies towards Ukrainians differed strikingly from those of other governments in interwar Europe, notably the Polish and Romanian governments. Ukrainian schools were closing in those countries; in Czechoslovakia, they were being opening. As Rusova noted, the Ukrainian emigration "distinguished itself by its cultural work and earned respect for our own [Ukrainian] scholarship by participating in a various congresses in Berlin, Stockholm, Prague, Geneva, Heidelberg, Rome, and other cities ... The Czechoslovak Ministry of Foreign Affairs can be proud that it provided such an enormous help in those difficult times in 1920–1922, and it [the emigration], in my view, used this support primarily to enrich Ukrainian culture."[1]

Prague was seen by the political elite and by scholars generally as a centre of Slavic scholarship and culture, and the centre was built with the help of émigré intellectuals. Cooperation among Slavic peoples was a key plank of Czechoslovakian policy. To that end, the government provided considerable support to émigré scholars, invited renowned Slavic scholars to come to Prague, and founded the Institute of Slavic Studies and the Slavonic Library.

Indeed, for some time, it was mainly in interwar Czechoslovakia that Ukrainians could create and preserve a high intellectual culture in their own language. Antonovych, Kolessa, Dmytro Doroshenko, Horbachevs'kyi, Dnistrians'kyi, and Shcherbakivs'kyi in particular contributed to the development of a Ukrainian intellectual milieu in Prague. It was thanks to their exertions that scholarly societies and institutions of higher learning were founded there. As one would expect, their efforts did not always run smoothly. They had arrived in Czechoslovakia from different parts of the Ukrainian lands, and their experiences living and working in the former Austro-Hungarian and Russian empires influenced their attitudes and behaviours toward the outside world and to one another. They also came from various locations on the political spectrum. In Czechoslovakia they had to work together, so personal and political clashes were unavoidable. The émigrés found themselves living in a state that was succeeding in building a democracy, and this reminded them constantly of their failed efforts to forge a democratic Ukraine. All of this undoubtedly influenced their lives, their work, and their relations. Even though Ukrainian émigrés felt quite comfortable in Czechoslovakia, living abroad was still painful for them.

In the 1920s, some émigrés returned to Soviet Ukraine – a tragic mistake, as it turned out for them. Before long, most of them had been arrested and had vanished into the Gulag. Some émigrés remained in touch with those who had returned during the 1920s, and all of them paid close attention to the brief but impressive development of scholarship and science in various fields in Soviet Ukraine at that time. But in the 1930s, scholars in Czechoslovakia could only watch from a distance as their colleagues and friends in Soviet Ukraine were persecuted and killed, and their contributions to science and scholarship destroyed. Émigré scholars now felt all the more responsible for developing Ukrainian scholarship, given that they were its only surviving representatives.

In the interwar period, the Czechoslovak government created a unique environment for émigrés. The country generously supported Ukrainian, Russian, and Belarusian institutions, the initial hope being that the students would all return to their now-democratic countries with professions, skills, and knowledge obtained in Czechoslovakia. This support enabled these émigré institutions to develop and to create a new generation of professionals. The Czechoslovak government's welcoming of émigrés also raised the country's prestige on the world stage. Politics naturally played a crucial role, and the government's attitude toward the assistance program shifted as various political parties ascended to and fell from power. Regardless, this assistance from the young democratic state was noteworthy.

The Ukrainian Free University had significant value for Ukrainian scholarship and culture. It was founded by scholars who had already contributed to Ukrainian scholarship, and some of them had been involved in building scholarly and cultural institutions in Ukraine between 1917 and 1921. In emigration, these intellectuals tried to build the institutions they had been unable to establish at home. The Free

University was based on the Western model and offered various subjects for students to explore. It saw its mission as educating a young generation of Ukrainians while representing Ukrainian scholarship in Europe. The Free University's position as an émigré institution was often difficult to manage, and it was repeatedly threatened with closure. In the 1930s, it had to cut back its activities due to a lack of funding and reduced student numbers, as students moved to other countries or chose to study in other institutions in Czechoslovakia. When the Czechoslovak government drastically reduced its funding, the university failed to change its model. For example, it never offered correspondence teaching. It would have been able to continue teaching in that format, particularly its courses in Ukrainian history, literature, and other subjects. This would have been of particular interest to Ukrainians in Canada, the United States, and other countries with Ukrainian communities. But that did not happen. In spite of this, the continued significance of the university was real. The scholarship of its professors is now being reassessed and disseminated in Ukraine and beyond.

The Ukrainian Economic Academy was an example of how Ukrainian technical scholars created a generation of Ukrainian technical professionals. The Czechoslovak government provided substantial funding for this academy, which was especially productive during its early years. Its faculty wrote the first textbooks in the Ukrainian language in various technical disciplines. These scholars were also active at conferences, congresses, and other scholarly and professional gatherings. The entire cohort of students obtained technical knowledge and applied it – again, not in an independent Ukraine, as was intended at the outset, but in other countries. They included economists, engineers, foresters, and agronomists. Of course, the academy faced a number of challenges. As with other institutions, with each passing year financial challenges became more pressing. Also, the faculty and students gradually realized they would not be returning home, and this too became a factor. Various groups were formed in Poděbrady, including nationalist ones – a common development in the 1930s. The Czechoslovak government eventually closed the academy for various reasons, including the global economic depression and the changing international position of Czechoslovakia.

The Ukrainian Higher Pedagogical Institute was founded to train secondary school teachers for an independent Ukraine. It educated an entire generation of Ukrainian teachers and published dozens of textbooks and monographs. The founding of the Ukrainian gymnasium was of no less importance, and an entire generation of Ukrainian children received secondary education there. After the Second World War, those students found themselves in different countries and on different continents; however, they carried with them what they had learned at the gymnasium. Another institution, the Ukrainian School of Plastic Arts, for decades offered an artistic enclave for Ukrainian artists and for those of other nationalities. It was established by Antonovych in an attempt to realize his unfulfilled dream of an Academy of Arts in an independent Ukraine. Supporting various artistic styles, the school gathered talented and seasoned artists who, in turn, trained a young generation. Its many exhibitions were interesting and well-attended.

Scholarly and professional societies created by Ukrainian émigrés in Czechoslovakia had a notable impact on their lives. In these societies, Ukrainian émigrés could present, discuss, and debate their research, while the professional societies helped them develop networks of like-minded professionals and stay connected. The Ukrainian Historical–Philological Society, in particular, was a scholarly forum where research in various fields was tested before being published or presented at conferences. Many of these papers, delivered at scholarly meetings, still have value today. The Ukrainian Bibliophile Society aided Ukrainian bibliography. The impact the Ukrainian Law Society had on legal scholars was considerable. The Union of Ukrainian Doctors brought together physicians in various medical fields in Czechoslovakia. In addition to its other activities, it established a medical journal of high quality that became a forum for Ukrainian physicians in Czechoslovakia and abroad. Its work on a medical dictionary contributed to the development of Ukrainian medical terminology.

Except for Chyzhevs'kyi, Ukrainian linguists had only slight involvement in the Prague Linguistic Circle; however, that group had an impact on their own research. The Ukrainian Pedagogical Society also had some influence on the lives of Ukrainian pedagogues, as did the Society of Ukrainian Engineers on the lives of Ukrainian engineers. Some societies had short life spans, but others lasted as long as twenty years. The activities of all these groups were important to the entire Ukrainian émigré intellectual world. Libraries, archives, and museums also played a role. Libraries at the Ukrainian institutions of higher learning provided much-needed resources for scholars; several of them grew quickly and were vital for students as well. The Museum of the Struggle for the Liberation of Ukraine was especially valued as a scholarly centre. In addition, in the long run the Ukrainian-language publishing of scholarly works, particularly in the 1920s, had importance generally for scholars, their students, and Ukrainian scholarship everywhere.

Ukrainian émigré scholars in Czechoslovakia strived – indeed, successfully – to present their scholarship on Ukraine to the broader scholarly world. They viewed this task as fundamental. Their participation in international conferences and congresses brought more awareness about Ukrainian culture to various scholarly communities. Émigré scholars contributed to periodicals in a variety of European countries and published their findings in various fields and languages. They also contributed articles about many aspects of Ukrainian history, literature, language, and other fields to several important encyclopaedias.

The fates of Ukrainian émigré scholars varied greatly. In 1945, when Soviet troops arrived in Czechoslovakia, some of them were arrested and vanished into the Gulag; a few committed suicide; many managed to flee to the West. The destruction of what Ukrainian émigré scholars had built in Czechoslovakia between the wars left its mark on those who managed to escape. But until the fall of communism in Czechoslovakia, and of the Soviet regime in Ukraine, all information about Ukrainian émigrés and their deeds was banned; in the Soviet Union, even mentioning these people was impossible. Archival documents taken from Czechoslovakia were locked away, and no information was available to researchers or the public. Similarly, interwar Ukrainian émigrés were not studied in Communist Czechoslovakia. Although some scholarly monographs on Czech–Ukrainian relations were published and a few conferences were held, no exploration of the topic was possible under the communist regime. Archival collections were sealed, no books were written, individuals were forgotten, and artistic works were lost. Once the communists fell, however, scholars, bibliographers, and archivists promptly began exploring the hidden chapters of the history of émigrés in Czechoslovakia between the wars. After that, many conferences took place in the Czech Republic, Slovakia, and Ukraine; books and articles were written in those countries, and artworks created by Ukrainian émigrés was found, commented on, and published.

The activities of Ukrainian émigré scholars in Czechoslovakia in the interwar years are an important part of the intellectual history of Ukraine. The years 1921 to 1938 were a unique period in Ukrainian émigré history and should be viewed in the context of the intellectual and institutional history of Ukraine and in connection with other scholarly communities in Europe. The support of Czechoslovakia was crucial to the favourable environment for Ukrainian émigré scholarship. For their part, Ukrainian intellectuals made an enormous effort to educate the younger generation and promote Ukrainian scholarship worldwide. It was their specific goal to preserve and develop the intellectual resources of the nation.

In creating a high intellectual culture in their own language in a foreign country, they forged a legacy that would continue beyond the years in question and extend to various Ukrainian communities worldwide. Without their work, in the postwar era in the countries where many of them settled (particularly in Canada and the United States), the development of Ukrainian scholarship would not have flourished to the degree it has. The émigré scholars in Czechoslovakia provided continuity as well as a bridge for Ukrainian scholarship from its inception at the end of the nineteenth century to the development of Ukrainian studies in the twenty-first century. In spite of all the difficulties, Ukrainian émigré scholars in Czechoslovakia realized their objective of creating the first generation of young Ukrainian scholars and professionals who received their education in Ukrainian institutions of higher learning in their own language, even if it did not happen in their native land. They also succeeded in preserving and developing Ukrainian scholarship and promoting it in the outside world, most especially in democratic Czechoslovakia, but also in other countries.

Notes

Introduction

1 For a brief overview of the infrastructure, see Vidnians'kyi, "Ukrains'kyi vil'nyi universytet u Prazi," 95.
2 For many examples of such letters expressing gratitude, see Topinka, comp., *Tomash Masaryk i ukraintsi*, passim.
3 Citation: Stepan Smal'-Stots'kyi to Kyrylo Studyns'kyi, Prague, 7 November 1923, in Topinka, *Masaryk i ukraintsi*, 165.
4 For the numbers, see Topinka, Shebesta, Baiharova, and Sen'kiv, *Zbirnyk statei ta dokumentiv*, 18.
5 Subtelny, *Ukraine: A History*, 552.
6 For more, see Narizhnyi, *Ukrains'ka emigratsiia*, vol. 1, 209. Note: unless otherwise stated vol. 1 is cited below.
7 For the list of Shcherbyna's works, see Mytsiuk, *Naukova diial'nist' statystyka F.A. Shcherbyny*, 24–6; other scholars will be discussed in the following chapters.
8 More on the archives see, Grimsted, *Trophies of War and Empire*, 330–88; see also Boriak, *Dokumental'na spadshchyna ukrains'koi emihratsii*; Paliienko, *Arkhivni tsentry ukrains'koi emihratsii*.

1. Czechoslovak Émigré Policy and Characteristics of the Ukrainian Emigration

1 On the assistance program in English, see Chinyaeva, *Russians outside Russia*, 41–68; on émigrés from various countries, see Barvíková et al., *Exil v Praze a Československu 1918–1938*; on positions of the Czechoslovak government on the émigré issue, see Vidnians'kyi, "Polityka chekhoslovats'koho uriadu," 37.
2 On the Ministry of Foreign Affairs and the personal backing of Masaryk, see Chinyaeva, *Russians outside Russia*, 47; on the two directions of

the program and the Czech colonists, see Vidnians'kyi, "Polityka chekhoslovats'koho uriadu," 39.

3 On preservation of cultural potential, see Huntington, *The Homesick Million*, 109; on the primary schools and gymnasiums, see Sládek and Běloševská et al., comps., *Dokumenty k dějinám*, 8; on Bratislava and other places, see Vidnians'kyi, "Polityka chekhoslovats'koho uriadu," 42.

4 On the Czechoslovak government in the eyes of Europe, see V. Vidnians'kyi and S. Vidnians'kyi, "Ukraintsi v mizhvoiennii Chekhoslovachchyni," 202; for more on the composition of the émigré community, see Ministerstvo zahraničních věcí, *Československá pomoc ruské a ukrajinské emigraci*, 3–4; on Ukraine's place in the politics of the Czechoslovak government, see Vidnians'kyi, "Ukrains'ke pytannia v pohliadakh T.G. Masaryka," 20–1.

5 On the objectives, see Ministerstvo zahraničních věcí, *Československá pomoc*, 4–5; see also, Vidnians'kyi, "Polityka chekhoslovats'koho uriadu," 42.

6 On the groups of immigrants, see Ministerstvo zahraničních věcí, *Československá pomoc*, 6–7; on the motives of the government, see ibid., 3; see also, Chinyaeva, *Russians outside Russia*, 52–4.

7 On the prestige for Czechoslovakia, see Chinyaeva, *Russians outside Russia*, 54; for more on relations between Masaryk and Kramář and their stand on the assistance program, see ibid., 42–5.

8 On the Czechoslovak government's approach towards émigrés, see Vidnians'kyi, "Polityka chekhoslovats'koho uriadu," 37; on the efforts of some Czechoslovak officials to make the program international, see Chinyaeva, *Russians outside Russia*, 53.

9 On Masaryk's vision of Prague as the major centre of Slavic studies in Europe, see Chinyaeva, *Russians outside Russia*, 54; the the Slavonic library in chapter 7; for more on the popularization of Czechoslovak culture worldwide and on establishing the Institute of Slavic Studies in Paris, see Kudělka, et al., eds. *Československá slavistika v letech 1918–1939*, 37–8.

10 On support of the democratic forces among émigré circles Vidnians'kyi, *Kul'turno-osvitnia pratsia*, 8; on Alice Masaryk's and Beneš's support, see Sládek and Běloševská, et al., comps., *Dokumenty k dějinám*, 9.

11 Huntington, *The Homesick Million*, 109.

12 Sládek and Běloševská, et al., comps., *Dokumenty k dějinám*, 9.

13 Chinyaeva, *Russians outside Russia*, 64 (total recalculated). Note on the currency: the exchange rate was on around 52–88 crowns per dollar in 1921 and 31–52 per dollar in 1922, after which the currency stabilized at 33–34 crowns per dollar from 1923 until 1933 before fluctuating between 20 crowns and 29 crowns per dollar from 1934 to 1939; for more detailed information, see Bidwell, *Currency Conversion Tables*, 12–3.

14 The table is based on Maruniak, ed., *Ukrains'ka himnaziia*, 94.

15 For the numbers, see ibid., 94–5.
16 For the Ministry of Foreign Affairs' numbers, see Ministerstvo zahraničních věcí, *Československá pomoc*, 72; on the number of Ukrainians graduated from Czechoslovak institutions, see Andic, "The Economic Aspects of Aid," 182.
17 For more on the developments in the internal circles of the Czechoslovak political establishment regarding the Ukrainian question, see Vidnians'kyi, "Ukraina ta "ukrains'ke pytannia"," 177–81; see also Vidnians'kyi, "Ukrains'ke pytannia v zovnishn'opolitychnykh kontseptsiiakh Chekhoslovachchyny," 43–61.
18 On Prague as the most vibrant centre of Ukrainian emigration, see Vidnians'kyi, "Ukrains'ke pytannia v pohliadakh T.G. Masaryka," 31; on the mobilization of strong scholarly and educated individuals, see, for example, Vidnians'kyi, "Ukraina ta "ukrains'ke pytannia"," 186; on the Czechoslovak government saving Ukrainian scholars, see Doroshenko, "Organizatsiia ukrains'koi naukovoi pratsi na emigratsii ta ii vyslidy za ostannie desiatylittia," 23–4. Note: as there were two individuals with the same last name in this study, when it is not obvious, the first and last names will always be noted: Dmytro Doroshenko and Volodymyr Doroshenko.
19 For more, see Lukes, *Czechoslovakia between Stalin and Hitler*.
20 On the reasons for the change of the attitude, see, for example, Vidnians'kyi, "Ukraina ta "ukrains'ke pytannia"," 187–8.
21 For more on the letter to Nansen and on the affair in general, see *Informatsiinyi biuleten' Komisii v spravi t. zv. Nansenovs'kykh pasportiv*, 27 January 1930; see also *Komunikat vykonavchoi komisii ukrains'kykh emigrans'kykh organizatsii v Ch.S.R.*, 18 March 1930; on the positive result, see ibid., 18 June 1930.
22 Maruniak, ed., *Ukrains'ka himnaziia*, 33–4.
23 On Girsa's reputation, see, for example, *Ukrains'ka hospodars'ka akademiia v Ch.S.R. 1922–1935*, 105.
24 On Nečas's commitment to the Ukrainian cause, see Topinka, *Masaryk i ukraintsi*, 144n; on his translation of some of Shevchenko's poetry, see *Ukrains'ka hospodars'ka akademiia v Ch.S.R. 1922–1935*, 105.
25 For the story, see Maruniak, ed., *Ukrains'ka himnaziia*, 175–6.
26 For more, see also Aulická, Léblová, and Tomeš, eds., *Československý biografický slovník*, 484.
27 See letter from [?] Hrytsai and M. Shapoval to Tomáš Garrigue Masaryk, Prague, 25 October 1921, in Topinka, *Masaryk i ukraintsi*, 107–8 in Czech, 110 in Ukrainian.
28 For the the composition of the Ukrainian émigré population, see Vidnian'kyi, "Polityka chekhoslovats'koho uriadu," 36.

29 For the numbers, see Vidnians'kyi, "Ukraintsi v mizhvoiennii Chekhoslovachchyni," 200.

30 More on the composition of the Ukrainian emigration, see Ukrains'kyi hromads'kyi komitet, *Try roky pratsi*, 3–4; see also the Antonovych Collection, LAC, MG 31, H 50, Biographical Notes, vol. 2, f. 59; for the return as betrayal, see Rusova, *Memuary. Shchodennyk*, 9; for more on the Czechoslovak government's concerns about former military men, see a letter appendix, Presidium ministerstva vnitra, Prague, 3 May 1921, in Topinka, *Masaryk i ukraintsi*, 96–101; on seventy camps in 1921, see Vidnians'kyi, "Polityka chekhoslovats'koho uriadu," 43.

31 The role and functions of the Ukrainian Civic Committee are discussed throughout the text.

32 For the numbers on individuals by nationality, see Ukrains'kyi hromads'kyi komitet, *Try roky pratsi*, 12; note that Czechs refers to those Czechs who moved out of the country earlier and became citizens of other countries, that is, mainly Russian citizens.

33 For the numbers on individuals by place of origin, see ibid., 12. Note: The Green Wedge (*Zelenyi klyn*) refers to the area in the Far East (southwestern Siberia) where many Ukrainian immigrants settled; in 1926, according to official statistics, almost 599,000 of the total population of 1,256,292 were Ukrainians; see also M. Derev'ianko, "Zelenyi Klyn i Mandzhuriia," in Ivan Rakovs'kyi et al., eds., *Ukrains'ka zahal'na entsykl'opediia*, vol. 3, 988–90.

34 For the numbers on individuals by social background, see Ukrains'kyi hromads'kyi komitet, *Try roky pratsi*, 11.

35 For the numbers on individuals by age, see ibid., 11.

36 For the numbers on individuals by level of education, see ibid., 12.

2. The Ukrainian Free University in Prague

1 For the statement, see Wynar, "Ukrainian Scholarship in Postwar Germany," 313.

2 For more, see Patzke, Szafowal, and Yaremko, eds., *Universitas Libera Ucrainensis 1921–2011*, 8; see also Sydorčuk, "Kulturelles Leben," 61–92.

3 Starosol's'kyi most likely discussed the first constitution of Russia adopted on 10 July 1918, which governed the Russian Socialist Federative Soviet Republic.

4 For more, see Sydorchuk-Potul'nyts'ka, "Videns'kyi ta praz'kyi periody UVU," 9; for discussion, see Patzke, Szafowal, and Yaremko, eds., *Universitas Libera Ucrainensis 1921–2011*, 8–9; see also Polons'ka-Vasylenko, "Ukrains'kyi vil'nyi universytet," 17; citation: Rusova, *Memuary. Shchodennyk*, 227.

5 For more, see Sydorčuk, "Kulturelles Leben," 63–6; for more on the Union of Ukrainian Journalists and Writers, see Kubijovyč and Struk, eds., *Encyclopedia of Ukraine*, vol. 5, 505; for their statute, see Soiuz ukrains'kykh zhurnalistiv ta pys'mennykiv, *Statut Soiuza ukrains'kykh zhurnalistiv ta pys'mennykiv*.

6 For the story, see Vidnians'kyi, *Kul'turno-osvitnia pratsia*, 9–10; for another version of the story, see Mirchuk, "Ukrains'kyi vil'nyi universytet," vii–viii.

7 For more on Hrushevs'kyi's requirements, see Vidnians'kyi, *Kul'turno-osvitnia pratsia*, 10–11; see also Narizhnyi, *Ukrains'ka emigratsiia*, 119–20; for more on the first steps of the university establishment, see Patzke, Szafowal, and Yaremko, eds., *Universitas Libera Ucrainensis 1921–2011*, 9–13; on the scholars' previous work together and their disagreements, see Zaitseva, *Ukrains'kyi naukovyi rukh*, 77, 101; later on Hrushevs'kyi considered moving to Prague. Apparently, the Ukrainian Economic Academy and the Ukrainian Higher Pedagogical Institute invited him. However, the academy moved its schedule to the next year so it did not happen; for the story, see a letter from Hrushevs'kyi to Bidlo in "Vpershe drukom: dokumenty Masaryka," 23.

8 For more on financing, see Patzke, Szafowal, and Yaremko, eds., *Universitas Libera Ucrainensis: 1921–2011*, 14–16; on Oles' and his role, see Ukrains'kyi vil'nyi universytet, *Ukrains'kyi vil'nyi universytet v Prazi v rokakh 1921–1926*, 65; see also in Szafowal and Yaremko, eds., *Universitas Libera Ucrainensis: 1921–2006*, 18; on attempts to find other sources of income, see Patzke, Szafowal, and Yaremko, eds., *Universitas Libera Ucrainensis: 1921–2011*, 15–16.

9 For the faculty, see Patzke, Szafowal, and Yaremko, eds., *Universitas Libera Ucrainensis: 1921–2011*, 14, 159; see also Vidnians'kyi, *Kul'turno-osvitnia pratsia*, 13. In 2011, the year of ninetieth anniversary of the opening of the university, a plaque was installed on the building; see Patzke, Szafowal, and Yaremko, eds., *Universitas Libera Ucrainensis: 1921–2011*, 16n; for more, see Ukrains'kyi vil'nyi universytet, *Ukrains'kyi vil'nyi universytet v Prazi v rokakh 1921–1926*, 65.

10 For more, see Patzke, Szafowal, and Yaremko, eds., *Universitas Libera Ucrainensis: 1921–2011*, 20–2.

11 The table is based on Ukrains'kyi vil'nyi universytet, *Ukrains'kyi vil'nyi universytet v Prazi v rokakh 1921–1926*, 66–7.

12 For the numbers, see ibid., 67; for the only thesis and the first publication, see also Patzke, Szafowal, and Yaremko, eds., *Universitas Libera Ucrainensis: 1921–2011*, 23.

13 On the importance of Kolessa, see Patzke, Szafowal, and Yaremko, eds., *Universitas Libera Ucrainensis: 1921–2011*, 24–5; on the promise of a

Ukrainian university in the Austro-Hungarian empire, see the Kolessa Collection, PNP, folder *Avhustyn Voloshyn*, letter from Kolessa to Voloshyn, Prague, 4 April 1937, 1; see also Magocsi, *A History of Ukraine*, 631.

14 For more, see Ukrains'kyi vil'nyi universytet, *Ukrains'kyi vil'nyi universytet v Prazi v rokakh 1921–1926*, 68; on the composition of the Ukrainian émigré community, see also Vidnians'kyi, *Kul'turno-osvitnia pratsia*, 18–19.

15 See the letter in Vidnians'kyi, *Kul'turno-osvitnia pratsia*, 76–8; on the delegation, see Patzke, Szafowal, and Yaremko, eds., *Universitas Libera Ucrainensis: 1921–2011*, 24; on roles played by Masaryk and Beneš, see the Kolessa Collection, PNP, folder *Avhustyn Voloshyn*, letter from Kolessa to Voloshyn, Prague, 4 April 1937, 1; for an alternative story of the transfer of the university to Prague, see Mirchuk, "Ukrains'kyi vil'nyi universytet," vii.

16 On the decrees, see Patzke, Szafowal, and Yaremko, eds., *Universitas Libera Ucrainensis: 1921–2011*, 25; on the acceptance of émigrés, see V. Vidnians'kyi and S. Vidnians'kyi, "Ukraintsi v mizhvoiennii Chekhoslovachchyni," 202; on the change in perception of Ukrainians, see the Kolessa Collection, PNP, folder *Avhustyn Voloshyn*, letter from Kolessa to Voloshyn, Prague, 4 April 1937, 2–3.

17 On the law on the structure of universities, and professors' qualifications and programs, see Vidnians'kyi, *Kul'turno-osvitnia pratsia*, 25–7; for Dmytro Antonovych's letter to Kolessa informing him about sending the rector's election documentation to the ministry, see the Kolessa Collection, PNP, folder *Dmytro Antonovych*, letter from Antonovych to Kolessa, Prague, 5 July 1929[4]; on lectures and other university classes at Charles University, see Narizhnyi, *Ukrains'ka emigratsiia*, 122; on the lack of diploma recognition, see the Kolessa Collection, PNP, folder *Avhustyn Voloshyn*, letter from Kolessa to Voloshyn, Prague, 4 April 1937, 2.

18 On a subvention adopted by the Czechoslovak parliament, see the Kolessa Collection, PNP, folder *Avhustyn Voloshyn*, letter from Kolessa to Voloshyn, Prague, 4 April 1937, 2.

19 On the reduced assistance in 1922, see Ukrains'kyi vil'nyi universytet, *Ukrains'kyi vil'nyi universytet v Prazi v rokakh 1921–1926*, 78; on 60,000 crowns monthly, see ibid., 222; on professors on unpaid leave, see Ukrains'kyi vil'nyi universytet, *Ukrains'kyi vil'nyi universytet v Prazi v rokakh 1926–1931*, 14; on the equalization of the university with other Czechoslovak universities, see ibid., 26; on professors' salaries and not paying assistant professors *privat*, see ibid., 28–9; on support for students, see ibid., 56; on the Masaryk's Fund payments until 1938, see Narizhnyi, *Ukrains'ka emigratsiia*, 133. Note: as there were two individuals (brothers) with the same last name in this study, when it is not obvious, the first and last names will always be noted: Volodymyr Tymoshenko and Serhii Tymoshenko.

20 On various sources of help for students, see Narizhnyi, *Ukrains'ka emigratsiia*, 72; on the work of the Czech–Ukrainian Committee for Ukrainian, see Ukrains'kyi vil'nyi universytet, *Universytet v Prazi v rokakh 1926–1931*, 3; for more on the work of the committee, see Narizhnyi, *Ukrains'ka emigratsiia*, 73–5; on Masaryk's Fund, see *Ukrains'kyi vil'nyi universytet v Prazi v rokakh 1921–1926*, 118–19.

21 On the financial support provided to several postdoctoral students and conference travel funding for several scholars to Sweden, see Ukrains'kyi vil'nyi universytet, *Universytet v Prazi v rokakh 1926–1931*, 72; on the figure for 1932–33 and on the founding of the Society of Friends of the Ukrainian Free University in Prague, see Ukrains'kyi vil'nyi universytet, *Ukrains'kyi vil'nyi universytet v Prazi v rokakh 1931–1941*, 12.

22 On Rypka's involvement and the university's financial difficulties, see "1933 r. chervnia 13. – Z protokolu zahal'nykh zboriv Ukrains'koho vil'noho universytetu v Prazi pro finansove zabezpechennia ioho potreb," in *Z istorii mizhnarodnykh zv'iazkiv Ukrainy*, ed. Varvartsev et al., 167; on the change in government policies, see Patzke, Szafowal, and Yaremko, eds., *Universitas Libera Ucrainensis: 1921–2011*, 28.

23 For more, see Mirchuk, "Ukrains'kyi vil'nyi universytet," viii.

24 The table is based on Patzke, Szafowal, and Yaremko, eds., *Universitas Libera Ucrainensis: 1921–2011*, 163–77.

25 Hons'kyi, *Ivan Horbachevs'kyi*, 41, 43, 49; for more on Horbachevs'kyi, see Holovats'kyi, *Ivan Horbachevs'kyi*; Note: in 1882, the university was divided into two separate institutions, one Czech and one German.

26 On Horbachevs'kyi's mentorship of Czech doctors and chemists, see Hons'kyi, *Ivan Horbachevs'kyi*, 45, 50; see also Purchla et al., eds., *The Myth of Galicia*, 438; on Horbachevs'kyi's contribution to the sanitarian council in Prague, see Hons'kyi, *Ivan Horbachevs'kyi*, 85; for a list of his major publications, see Holovats'kyi, *Ivan Horbachevs'kyi*, 119–22.

27 For more on Kolessa, see Motornyi, "Oleksandr Kolessa i ukrains'ko-ches'ki vzaiemyny," 110–17; see also Vidnians'kyi, *Kul'turno-osvitnia pratsia*, 40.

28 All institutions will be discussed in detail later in this study; for more on Antonovych, see Miiakovs'kyi, *Dmytro Antonovych*; see also Petišková, ed. *Dmytro Antonovyč a ukrajinská umĕnovĕda*; see also Shapoval, *Dmytro Antonovych*.

29 For more on Dnistrians'kyi, see Mushynka, *Akademik Stanislav Dnistrians'kyi*; see also Mushynka, ed. *Lysty Stepana Rudnytskoho*.

30 For more on Smal'-Stots'kyi, see Botushans'kyi, *Stepan Smal'-Stots'kyi*; Danylenko and Dobrzhans'kyi, *Akademik Stepan Smal'-Stots'kyi*; on Franko's recollection of Smal'-Stots'kyi's European scholarly method, see a letter from Franko to Drahomanov, 7 December 1890, in Franko,

Zibrannia tvoriv u p'iatdesiaty tomakh, vol. 49, 264; on Kolessa and Simovych as students of Smal'-Stots'kyi, see Mel'nychuk, "Dorohoiu zavdovzhky sto dvadtsiat' lit," 70; for the story of Smal'-Stots'kyi's help to Shcherbakivs'kyi in Chernivtsi, see Shcherbakivs'kyi, "Memuary," 67–8.

31 For more on Doroshenko, see Prymak, "Dmytro Doroshenko," 31–56; see also Vynar, "Dmytro Ivanovych Doroshenko"; see also Wynar, *Dmytro Doroshenko, 1882–1951*; see also Bilets'kyi, *Dmytro Doroshenko*.

32 For more on Stepan Rudnyts'kyi, see Stebelsky, *Placing Ukraine on the Map*; Shtoiko, *Stepan Rudnyts'kyi*; see also Babak, Danylenko, and Plekan, *Praha – Kharkiv – Solovky*; for correspondence, see Mushynka, *Lysty Stepana Rudnytskoho*; see also Rudnyts'kyi, *Lystuvannia Stepana Rudnyts'koho*.

33 On the many conferences attended by Shcherbakivs'kyi, see Narizhnyi, *Ukrains'ka emigratsiia*, 257n; see also Shcherbakivs'kyi, "Pratsia v haluzi arkheologii," 53.

34 For more, see Vidnians'kyi, "Ukrains'kyi vil'nyi universytet u Prazi," 96.

35 For more, see Narizhnyi, *Ukrains'ka emigratsiia*, 127–8.

36 For the numbers, see Ukrains'kyi vil'nyi universytet v Prazi v rokakh 1921–1926, 78; see also Ukrains'kyi vil'nyi universytet, *Universytet v Prazi v rokakh 1926–1931*, 111; on Doroshenko's leave, see, for example, the Doroshenko Collection, PNP, folder *Bidnov Vasyl*, letter from Bidnov to Volodymyr Doroshenko, 31 July 1926; on Doroshenko in Warsaw, see Prymak, "Doroshenko," 36.

37 For Antonovych's letter to Kolessa, see the Kolessa Collection, PNP, folder *Dmytro Antonovych*, letter from Antonovych to Kolessa, Prague, 14 August 1929; for Jaroslav Rudnyts'kyi's recollections, see the Rudnyckyj Collection, LAC, MG 31 D 58, vol. 1, Autobiography, pt 1 (Prague 1941–1945), 228.

38 For more on the arrested and deported in 1945, see, for example, Zilynskyj, *Ukrajinci v Čechách a na Moravě*, 55–7.

39 For more, see Narizhnyi, *Ukrains'ka emigratsiia*, 71.

40 For more, see Troshchyns'kyi, "Persha konferentsiia ukrains'koi emihratsii," 81–2; more on students, see, for example, Vidnians'kyi, *Kul'turno-osvitnia pratsia*, 60–7; on the numbers of students who signed up for courses, see Ukrains'kyi vil'nyi universytet, *Universytet v Prazi v rokakh 1926–1931*, xi–xii; on the numbers of Ukrainians studying at Charles University, see *Ročenka Československé republiky*, vol. 2 (1923), p. 185; on the amounts received by students, see Andic, "The Economic Aspects of Aid," 183 (recalculated).

41 For more on students, see Vidnians'kyi, "Studenty i vypusknyky UVU v Prazi," 105–12.

42 For more on the committee, see Ministerstvo zahraničních věcí, *Československá pomoc*, 20–3; on the Belarusian students and on students' travel in 1923, see Narizhnyi, *Ukrains'ka emigratsiia*, 73–4.

43 Havránek and Pousta, eds., *A History of Charles University 1802–1990*, vol. 2, 195.

44 On 15 per cent of all students, see ibid., 187; on other international students in the late 1920s, see ibid., 217; on the fifty-two Ukrainian students who defended their dissertations in the Natural Sciences Department, see a table in Břetislav Fajkus, "Přírodovědecká fakulta 1920–1945," 163–80, in *Dějiny Univerzity Karlovy 1918–1990*, ed. Havránek and Pousta, vol. 4, 178; for the figures and the breakdown of students by the subjects and language of their dissertations, see Havránek and Pousta, eds., *A History of Charles University*, vol. 2, 239.

45 On Ukrainian students, see Ukrains'kyi vil'nyi universytet, *Ukrains'kyi vil'nyi universytet v Prazi v rokakh 1921–1926*, 85; citation: a letter from Fr. Pastrnek to K. Studyns'kyi, Prague, November 1923, in *U pivstolitnikh zmahanniakh*, comp. Haiova, Iedlins'ka, and Svarnyk, 404.

46 For more, see Ukrains'kyi vil'nyi universytet, *Universytet v Prazi v rokakh 1926–1931*, x–xi; for more on those who became members of the teaching staff, see Narizhnyi, *Ukrains'ka emigratsiia*, 132; on the number of scholars who received their doctorate, see ibid., 75n.

47 For more on women at the university, see Antonovych, *Rolia ukrains'koi zhinky v pratsi U.V.U.*, 11–15; see also her notes, the Antonovych Collection, LAC, MG 31, H 50, Ukrainian Technical Academy (Ukrains'ka hospodars'ka akademia) Prague, including references to the Free Ukrainian University, vol. 2, file 60; for help received from Czech women's organizations by Ukrainian women, see Bohachevsky-Chomiak, *Feminists Despite Themselves*, 249–50.

48 For more, see Ukrains'kyi akademichnyi komitet, *Ukrains'kyi naukovyi zizd u Prazi 3–7 zhovtnia 1926 r.*, 3–4, 10.

49 For more, see ibid., 8–9.

50 On the sections and subsections see ibid., 10; for more on papers delivered, see ibid., 11–71; for an abstract of Shul'hyn's paper, see ibid., 12; for an abstract of Bidnov's paper, see ibid., 16; for an abstract of Dnistrians'kyi's paper, see ibid., 33. Note: there is a discrepancy in the numbers of the papers delivered; see ibid., 10, which states that 134 applied and 198 papers were delivered; however, based on the following abstracts, a total of 154 papers were delivered and discussed by the university's professors in these sections and subsections (calculated by myself). It is possible that not all papers were included in the proceedings, which would explain the discrepancy.

51 Table: ibid., 72 (totals recalculated).

52 Calculation of 137 participants based on "Spysok chleniv 2. Ukrains'koho naukovoho zizdu," in Ukrains'kyi akademichnyi komitet 2. *Ukrains'kyi naukovyi zizd u Prazi*, 8–13; on the location of the congress, see ibid., 5; on the opening remarks see, ibid., 17.

53 On the book exhibition and visits to the museum, see ibid., 5–6; The Museum of the Struggle for the Liberation of Ukraine is discussed in chapter 7.
54 For Rudnyts'kyi's statement, see the Rudnyckyj Collection, LAC, MG 31, D 58, vol. 1, Autobiography, pt 1 (Prague 1941–1945), 231.

3. The Ukrainian Economic Academy in Poděbrady

1 For more, see Tovarystvo prykhyl'nykiv Ukrains'koi hospodars'koi akademii, *Ukrains'ka hospodars'ka akademiia* (1931), 8; these institutions will be discussed in the following chapters.
2 On the foundation of the academy, see *Ukrains'ka hospodars'ka akademiia v Ch.S.R. 1922–1935*, 14–17; see also Ukrains'kyi hromas'kyi komitet v Ch.S.R., *Ukrains'ka hospodars'ka akademiia v Ch.S.R.* (1923), 4–5; on the dedication of the committee, see Martos's recollections in *Ukrains'ka hospodars'ka akademiia v Ch.S.R. 1922–1935*, 107.
3 For more on the opposition to the academy, see *Ukrains'ka hospodars'ka akademiia v Ch.S.R.* (1923), 6, 8; on the preparation steps, see *Ukrains'ka hospodars'ka akademiia v Ch.S.R. 1922–1935*, 104–8; on Masaryk's reception of the delegation, see ibid., 105.
4 On the location of the academy, see *Ukrains'ka hospodars'ka akademiia v Ch.S.R. 1922–1935*, 15–16; see also *Ukrains'ka hospodars'ka akademiia v Ch. S. R.* (1923), 8–9.
5 On the approval, see Šyjaniv, *Ukrajinská hospodářská akademie v Č.S.R.*, 4; for the government decree, see *Ukrains'ka hospodars'ka akademiia v Ch.S.R. 1922–1935*, 15; on the first joint meeting and Shapoval's speech, see *Ukrains'ka hospodars'ka akademiia v Ch.S.R.* (1923), 9–11; on the independent status of the academy, see *Ukrains'ka hospodars'ka akademiia v Ch.S.R. 1922–1935*, 16; for the new statute, see Ukrains'ka hospodars'ka akademiia. *Statut Ukrains'koi hospodars'koi akademii v Ch. S. R.*; on the languages of instruction, see ibid., 4.
6 On the preparation of experts for the future Ukraine, see *Ukrains'ka hospodars'ka akademiia v Ch.S.R.* (1923), 40.
7 On the creation of new professional literature in Ukrainian, see M. Dobrylovs'kyi, *Fakhovo-literaturna chynnist' Ukrains'koi hospodars'koi akademii*, 3; on the terminological committee, see *Ukrains'ka hospodars'ka akademiia v Ch.S.R. 1922–1935*, 112.
8 On Masaryk's words, see the epigraph to this monograph; cited in Šyjaniv, *Ukrajinská hospodářská akademie v Č.S.R.*, 5; for two photographs of Masaryk's visit, see *Ukrains'ka hospodars'ka akademiia v Ch.S.R.* (1923), 7.
9 On the subordination of the academy to the ministries, see *Ukrains'ka hospodars'ka akademiia v Ch.S.R. 1922–1935*, 21; on the structure of the academy

and for the supervision of the ministries, see Tovarystvo prykhyl'nykiv Ukrains'koi hospodars'koi akademii, *Ukrains'ka hospodars'ka akademiia* (1931), 13–14; on the structure, see also Ukrains'ka hospodars'ka akademiia, *Statut*, 7–18; on the preparation of professionals for the Ukrainian lands, see Ukrajinská hospodářská akademie. *Ukrains'ka hospodars'ka akademiia v Chekhoslovats'kii Respublitsi*, 5.

10 The table is based on *Ukrains'ka hospodars'ka akademiia v Ch.S.R. 1922–1935*, 10, 73.

11 On the additional units, see ibid., 73; for a list of seminars, see ibid., 74; for a description of the program, see, for example, Tovarystvo prykhyl'nykiv Ukrains'koi hospodars'koi akademii, *Ukrains'ka hospodars'ka akademiia* (1931), 6.

12 On the assistance of the government, see Tovarystvo prykhyl'nykiv Ukrains'koi hospodars'koi akademii, *Ukrains'ka hospodars'ka akademiia* (1931), 10; on the increased subsidies, and the numbers, see Ukrajinská hospodářská akademie, *Ukrains'ka hospodars'ka akademiia v Chekhoslovats'kii Respublitsi*, 7.

13 For the numbers, see Tovarystvo prykhyl'nykiv Ukrains'koi hospodars'koi akademii, *Ukrains'ka hospodars'ka akademiia* (1931), 10, 12; on equipment for laboratories, see ibid., 12–13; on the gradual abolition of the academy, see ibid., 9–10.

14 For the numbers and on Bukovyna, see ibid., 28; for more on the student committee and its work, see *Ukrains'ka hospodars'ka akademiia v Ch.S.R. 1922–1935*, 86–7.

15 On the education of professors and other academy staff, see Šyjaniv, *Ukrajinská hospodářská akademie*, 7; on the teaching staff in 1928, see Ukrajinská hospodářská akademie, *Ukrains'ka hospodars'ka akademiia v Chekhoslovats'kii Respublitsi*, 12; on the numbers from 1922 to 1932, see Narizhnyi, *Ukrains'ka emigratsiia*, 159; for slightly different numbers, see *Ukrains'ka hospodars'ka akademiia v Ch.S.R. 1922–1935*, 38.

16 Rusova, *Memuary. Shchodennyk*, 232.

17 On staff members living on a limited income and on salaries and other figures, see *Ukrains'ka hospodars'ka akademiia v Ch.S.R. 1922–1935*, 109–10; for the figures in US dollars, see Tovarystvo prykhyl'nykiv Ukrains'koi hospodars'koi akademii, *Ukrains'ka hospodars'ka akademiia* (1931), 12.

18 For more on Shovheniv, see Bykovs'kyi, *Ivan Shovheniv (1874–1943)*.

19 For more on Ivanyts'kyi, see *Ukrains'ka hospodars'ka akademiia v Ch.S.R. 1922–1935*, 53–64; on Ivanyts'kyi's work at the forest department, see Rusova, *Memuary. Shchodennyk*, 232.

20 For more on Tymoshenko, see *Ukrains'ka hospodars'ka akademiia v Ch.S.R. 1922–1935*, 65–8.

21 For a list of Czech scholars who taught at the academy, see ibid., 46–8; see also Šyjaniv, *Ukrajinská hospodářská akademie*, 7–8; for another list, see

Ukrajinská hospodářská akademie, *Ukrains'ka hospodars'ka akademiia v Chekhoslovats'kii Respublitsi*, 15.

22 For one student's recollections on Kukač, Hrásky, and Ježdik, see Simiantsiv, *Students'ki chasy*, 120–4.

23 On the composition of the students, see Doroshenko, "Organizatsiia ukrains'koi naukovoi pratsi," 26; see also, Simiantsiv, *Students'ki chasy*, 60.

24 On the courses, see Tovarystvo prykhyl'nykiv Ukrains'koi hospodars'koi akademii, *Ukrains'ka hospodars'ka akademiia* (1931), 30, 32; on students' choice between the academy and Czechoslovak institutions, see Simiantsiv, *Students'ki chasy*, 69–70.

25 On students' place of origin, see Tovarystvo prykhyl'nykiv Ukrains'koi hospodars'koi akademii, *Ukrains'ka hospodars'ka akademiia* (1931), 26; statistics on students from Czechoslovakia are as follows: 16.5 per cent in 1922, 33.8 per cent in 1923, 24.3 per cent in 1924, 32 per cent in 1925, 56.2 per cent in 1926, 10.4 per cent in 1927, and the rest came from Poland and other countries; see ibid., 26; for a list of all graduates, see *Ukrains'ka hospodars'ka akademiia v Ch.S.R. 1922–1935*, 90–102; on Belarusians, see Tovarystvo prykhyl'nykiv Ukrains'koi hospodars'koi akademii, *Ukrains'ka hospodars'ka akademiia* (1931), 27; for the total number of graduates, see Narizhnyi, *Ukrains'ka emigratsiia*, 141.

26 All figures are taken from Shramchenko, "Ukrains'ke, bilorus'ke ta hruzyns'ke studentstvo," 248–80; for example, on students' marital status, see ibid., 253; on the students' choice of education, see, ibid. 257; on students' health problems, see ibid., 271–3.

27 On the requirement to work in the Ukrainian lands, see Dubrivnyi and Bykovs'kyi, eds., *Ukrain'ska hospodars'ka akademiia v Ch.S.R.*, 23; on Kateryna Antonovych's recollections, see the Antonovych Collection, LAC, MG 31, H 50, Autobiographical Notes, vol. 1, f. 48.

28 On the academy's laboratories and offices and on students in the apprenticeship, see Simiantsiv, *Students'ki chasy*, 83, 141; on the warm attitude towards students, see ibid., 7.

29 For Rusova's memoirs, see Rusova, *Memuary. Shchodennyk*, 238; on instances of suicide, see Simiantsiv, *Students'ki chasy*, 169; on get-togethers of Slavic students, see ibid., 72; on cases of non-assimilation, see ibid., 163.

30 On the twenty-four individuals who became staff members, see Tovarystvo prykhyl'nykiv Ukrains'koi hospodars'koi akademii, *Ukrains'ka hospodars'ka akademiia* (1931), 20, 22; on students who continued doing research after graduation, see Dobrylovs'kyi, *Fakhovo-literaturna chynnist'*, 10–11.

31 For more, see Tovarystvo prykhyl'nykiv Ukrains'koi hospodars'koi akademii, *Ukrains'ka hospodars'ka akademiia* (1931), 35–7; see also Ukrajinská hospodářská akademie, *Ukrains'ka hospodars'ka akademiia v Chekhoslovats'kii Respublitsi*, 53–4.

32 On young engineers improving the regional agriculture, see Dubrivnyi and Bykovs'kyi, eds. *Ukrain'ska hospodars'ka akademiia v Ch.S.R.*, 3; for the figures and on the good reputation of young professionals, see Tovarystvo prykhyl'nykiv Ukrains'koi hospodars'koi akademii, *Ukrains'ka hospodars'ka akademiia* (1931), 29–30.
33 On conferences and congresses, see Cherediiv, "Pratsi ukrains'koi emigratsii v diliantsi agronomichnii," 73; see also Hrabyna, "Ohliad pratsi na poli budivel'no-mezhovykh nauk," in ibid., 81; for more on participation, see Narizhnyi, *Ukrains'ka emigratsiia*, 258; on Borodaievs'kyi's participation, see *Naukovyi zbirnyk Ukrains'koho universytetu v Prazi* 3 (1942), 14; for more on participation in conferences and congresses, see chapter 9.
34 The calculation is based on Ukrains'kyi akademichnyi komitet, *Ukrains'kyi naukovyi zizd u Prazi 3–7 zhovtnia 1926 r.*, 72.
35 The table is based on ibid., 72.
36 For the papers, see Ukrains'kyi akademichnyi komitet, 2. *Ukrains'kyi naukovyi zizd u Prazi*; for Hrabyna's paper, see ibid., 76–81; for Ivanyts'kyi's paper, see ibid., 64–7; for Komarets'kyi's paper, see ibid., 82–7; for Martos' paper, see Ibid., 102–7; on Harmashiv's paper, see Ibid., 90–3; on Cherediiv's paper, see Ibid., 67–76.
37 On the numbers of research trips, see Dobrylovs'kyi, *Fakhovo-literaturna chynnist'*, 4; on research trips, see Cherediiv, "Pratsi ukrains'koi emigratsii v diliantsi agronomichnii," 73; Ivanyts'kyi, "Desiatylitnia chynnist' ukrains'koi emigratsii na poli lisovoi nauky," 66–7. As there were two individuals with the same last name in this study, the first and last names will always be noted: Petro Andriievs'kyi and Opanas Andriievs'kyi.
38 For more on research output and textbooks, see Dobrylovs'kyi, *Fakhovo-literaturna chynnist'*, 4–10.
39 See Dubrivnyi and Bykovs'kyi, eds., *Ukrain'ska hospodars'ka akademiia v Ch.S.R. i Ukrains'kyi technichno-hospodars'kyi instytut*, 22; For more on the participation in the Chicago World's Fair, see Nazystrich, 15 April 1934.
40 On outreach, see *Ukrains'ka hospodars'ka akademiia v Ch.S.R. 1922–1935*, 112–13; on the invitation of influential persons, see Simiantsiv, *Students'ki chasy*, 162. Note: presumably many Ukrainians did not know the Czech language well and that was also one of the reasons of not acclimatizing well.
41 For the numbers, see Narizhnyi, *Ukrains'ka emigratsiia*, 167; on Bochkovs'kyi's trip, see Kanevs'ka, "Ol'gerd Ipolyt Bochkovs'kyi – narys biohrafii," 70–85, in Bochkovs'kyi, *Vybrani pratsi ta dokumenty*, vol. 1; on support from the Ukrainian community there; see also O. Bochkovs'kyi, "Vidpovid' na odvertyi lyst," *Novyi chas*, 1 September 1936; for a sample of Bochkovs'kyi's speech, see "Radiozaklyk prof. I.O. Bochkovs'koho do Ukrains'koi molodi v Kanadi," *Dilo*, 11 November 1936.
42 For more, see Narizhnyi, *Ukrains'ka emigratsiia*, 167–71; for more on biographies of students, see Dubrivnyi and Bykovs'kyi, eds., *Ukrain'ska*

hospodars'ka akademiia v Ch.S.R.; after 1945, this institute was transferred to Munich and Regensburg in the American Zone of Occupation in Bavaria, and the professors who managed to get there tried their best to get back to classroom learning again; by June 1945, they had reopened the institute with three faculties: agronomy and forestry, economics, and engineering, in Regensburg, and two additional departments, pharmacy and veterinary, opened in Munich; in that form, it existed until 1952, when most professors and students moved to the United States and Canada. After that the institution was transformed into a research institute, which published scholarly works and organized conferences. It donated its archive to the National University of Kyiv–Mohyla Academy in Kyiv in 2007.

43 Rusova, *Memuary. Shchodennyk*, 232.

4. The Ukrainian Higher Pedagogical Institute

1 Citation: Čapek, *Hovory s T.G. Masarykem*, 16; there were some reservations on the government's side about the institute because an assumption has been made made that this institution was being formed in order to compete with the Ukrainian Free University. According to Mirnyi, a Czechoslovak official was present at the opening of the institute. But a day earlier, the suggestion had been made that only Nečas attend it in an unofficial capacity. Apparently, it was no easy task for the government to maintain a politically balanced position towards various émigré groups. For the suggestion that only Nečas be present at the opening, see a note to the letter, Kancelář prezidenta republiky to Ukrajinský hromadský komitét v Čsl. Republice, Prague, 6 July 1923, in Topinka, *Masaryk i ukraintsi*, 144–5. This source states that representatives of the government were present at the opening; see Mirnyi, *Ukrains'kyi vysokyi pedagogichnyi instytut*, 11.

2 On the intention to train administrators for Ukrainian schools and on other goals, see Mirnyi, *Ukrains'kyi vysokyi pedagogichnyi instytut*, 4; on the change of the mission, see ibid., 9; on graduates, see Narizhnyi, *Ukrains'ka emigratsiia*, 179–80.

3 On the founding of the institute, see Mirnyi, *Ukrains'kyi vysokyi pedagogichnyi instytut*, 3–11.

4 For more, see ibid., 4.

5 On the new independent status of the institute, see ibid., 18–20; on the three departments and the six sections, see ibid., 74–5; on the Department of Music and Pedagogy, see 14–15; on the mandatory courses, see 78–83.

6 For more on the subjects taught at the Department of History and Literature, see ibid., 74–6.

7 For more on the subjects taught at the Department of Mathematics and Natural Sciences, see ibid., 76–7.

8 For more on the curriculum, see Mirnyi, *Ukrains'kyi vysokyi pedagogichnyi instytut*, 73–90; for information on the full curriculum, see ibid., 78–90.
9 On the figures and scholarships, see ibid., 5 and passim; on the staff salaries, see ibid., 6n.
10 For more on the financial situation, see ibid., 38–9, 44–5.
11 On reduced student scholarships, see ibid., 24 and passim; on twenty-six stipends, see ibid., 109–10.
12 For an example of such reports, see Základní dokumenty, 1927, file 2, 3, Ukrajinský pedagogický institut Mychajla Drahomanova, SsSk; for an example of such lists, see ibid., 1930, file 5.
13 For the number of faculty, see Narizhnyi, *Ukrains'ka emigratsiia*, 174; for more on the faculty, see Mirnyi, *Ukrains'kyi vysokyi pedagogichnyi instytut*, 62–73.
14 For more on Bilets'kyi and his biography in the interwar period, see Mandryka, *Leonid Bilets'kyi*, 19–22; for *Kobzar*, see Shevchenko, *Kobzar*.
15 For more on Simovych, see Simovych, *Pratsi v dvokh tomakh*, vol. 1, 13–28; see also Bilous and Terlak, *Vasyl' Simovych*; see also Kovaliv, *Vasyl' Simovych*; on Simovych's letters to Řehoř, see the Řehoř Collection, PNP, letters dated 10 August 1897 and 1 October 1897; for Symovych's archive donated to Chernivtsi University by his wife at his request and now housed in the Rare Book Library at the University Library and on letters to Chyzhevs'kyi, see Pshenychnyi and Iantsen, "Lystuvannia Dmytra Chyzhevs'koho z Vasylem Simovychem," 251–330.
16 For more on Harmashiv, see Dziuba et al., eds., *Entsyklopediia suchasnoi Ukrainy*, vol. 5, 406.
17 For more on Artymovych, see "Agenor Artymovych: Hrudka zemli na ioho mohylu u Prazi," *Dilo*, 23 October 1935; on his scholarly work, see Ukrains'kyi vil'nyi universytet, *Universytet v Prazi v rokakh 1926–1931*, 137.
18 On Chyzhevs'kyi at home among Ukrainians, Russians, and Czechs, see Sherekh, *Ia – mene – meni*, vol. 2, 124; for more on Chyzhevs'kyi, see, for example, Pshenychnyi, Mnykh, and Iantsen, eds., *Dmytro Chyzhevs'kyi i ievropeis'ka kul'tura*; see also Valiavko, Chudnov, and Iantsen, comps., *Dmytro Ivanovych Chyzhevs'kyi i ioho suchasnyky*; see Blashkiv, *Ches'ka i slovats'ka kul'tura*, vol. 6; see also Rachůnková, Sokolová, and Šišková, eds., *Dmytro Čyževskyj, osobnost a dílo*.
19 For more on Rusova, see Bednářová, *Sofija Rusovová*; for her memoirs, see Rusova, *Memuary. Shchodennyk*; and Rusova, *Moi spomyny*.
20 For more on Sichyns'kyi, see Keivan, *Volodymyr Sichyns'kyi*; for his bibliography, see Kostiuk, comp., *Volodymyr Sichyns'kyi*.
21 On professors teaching for free, see Základní dokumenty, 1927, file 2, Ukrajinský pedagogický institut Mychajla Drahomanova, SsSk.
22 For more on students, see Narizhnyi, *Ukrains'ka emigratsiia*, 178–9.

23 For the figures, see Mirnyi, *Ukrains'kyi vysokyi pedagogichnyi instytut*, 107–8; for lists of graduates, see ibid., Appendixes, 142–3.
24 On students in general, see ibid., 101–8; the percentage of female students was calculated based on the table in ibid., 104; on poor employment of the students in Poland, see ibid., 31.
25 For more on the student societies, see ibid., 110–12.
26 For more on excursions, see ibid., 91–2.
27 On this recollection, see Rusova, *Memuary. Shchodennyk*, 240; for more on the institute, see also Kovalenko, "Ukrainskii vysshii pedagogicheskii institut," 97–104.
28 On the topics that scholars explored, see Siropolko, "Pratsia v haluzi pedagogiky," 62–3.
29 For more, see Mirnyi, *Ukrains'kyi vysokyi pedagogichnyi instytut*, 99–100; scholars' participation in conferences is discussed in more detail in chapter 9.
30 For more on lectures and other events, see ibid., 115–20.
31 For more on a school in Szczypiorno and on the arrival of the orphans, see Maruniak, ed., *Ukrains'ka himnaziia*, 9–10; for more on the Ukrainian Graduation course, see Mirnyi, *Ukrains'kyi vysokyi pedagogichnyi instytut*, ibid., 112–13.
32 For more on the committee, see Mirnyi, *Ukrains'kyi vysokyi pedagogichnyi instytut*, 22–3, 34.
33 For more on the gymnasium in general, see Maruniak, ed., *Ukrains'ka himnaziia*; on the gymnasium's curriculum, see ibid., 205–6; on how students saw their professors, see ibid.; for a list of gymnasium pupils, see ibid., 239–47.
34 On the directors, see ibid., 217–19; on gymnasium, see also Narizhnyi, *Ukrains'ka emigratsiia*, 182–9.

5. The Ukrainian School of Plastic Arts in Prague

1 On Prague as one of Europe's centres of modern art, see Mudrak, "The Ukrainian Studio," 36; on openness to Western artistic influences and the influence of Prague art on Ukrainian artists, see Pelens'ka, "Praz'ka znakhidka iak znakova podiia," 24.
2 On the founding of the the Ukrainian School of Plastic Arts, see Ukrains'kyi hromads'kyi komitet, *Try roky pratsi*, 79; citation: Antonovych, Introduction to *Les Artistes du Studio de Prague*, 10; on Dmytro Antonovych replicating the cultural institutions, see Miiakovs'kyi, *Dmytro Antonovych*, 30.
3 On the objection of the Prague Academy of Arts, see Pelens'ka, *Ukrains'kyi portret*, 25; citation: Mudrak, "The Ukrainian Studio," 39.

4 For more on the courses and professors, see Mudrak, *Ponad kordonamy*, 25–7; see also Ukrains'kyi hromads'kyi komitet, *Try roky pratsi*, 79; on the academy playing a formative role in the careers of students of other backgrounds, see Pelens'ka, *Ukrains'kyi portret*, 19; citation: Mudrak, *Ponad kordonamy*, 25.
5 Mudrak, "The Ukrainian Studio," 36.
6 Citation 1: *Les Artistes du Studio de Prague*, 10; citation 2: Pelens'ka, *Ukrains'kyi portret*, 18.
7 Mudrak, "The Ukrainian Studio," 37.
8 On the financial assistance, see Pelens'ka, *Ukrains'kyi portret*, 24–5; on Antonovych's statement that the academy had been without assistance for five years (i.e., since 1930), see D. Antonovych, "10-a vystava Ukrains'koi 'Studii' v Prazi," *Ukrains'kyi tyzhden'*, 14 October 1935; see also the letters Šámal to Říha, Prague, 1 October 1930, and Říha to Šámal, Prague, 30 October 1930, in Topinka, *Masaryk i ukraintsi*, 320–1; on the role of Kulets', see Pelens'ka, *Ukrains'kyi portret*, 25; for more on Kulets', see ibid., 153–5; on pawning his father's watch, see Mazurenko, *Skyt poetiv*, 6.
9 On the structure, see Narizhnyi, *Ukrains'ka emigratsiia*, 190; citation: *Les Artistes du Studio de Prague*, 14.
10 For more, see Mudrak, "The Ukrainian Studio," 36.
11 Mudrak, "The Ukrainian Studio," 37.
12 For more on Mako, see Pelens'ka, *Ukrains'kyi portret*, 160–1; for various sources listing different places of birth for Mako, see ibid.
13 On the importance of Mozalevs'kyi's Prague period for his artistic career, see Pelens'ka, *Ukrains'kyi portret*, 29, 165; on Masaryk's portrait, see Lahutenko, "Tvorchist' Ivana Mozalevs'koho," 248; for the book, see [Masaryk], *Dobirni dumky Prof. T. Harrik-Masaryka*; on Mozalevs'kyi's articles in *Ukrains'ki visti*, see Shmahalo, "Ukrains'ka studia plastychnykh mystetstv," 135.
14 For more on Lisovs'kyi, see Iatsiv, *Robert Lisovs'kyi*.
15 On Stakhovs'kyi's studies and participation in exhibitions in London and Paris, see Bednarzhova and Ianchyk, *Ukrains'ki mohyly v Chekhii*, 45; citation: Leontovych-Loshak, "Spohady pro roky navchannia," 311.
16 Citation: Mudrak, "The Ukrainian Studio," 39; for the book, see Mirchuk, *Zahal'na estetyka*.
17 For more, see Antonovych, "10-a vystava."
18 On the artistic atmosphere in Prague, see Hordyns'kyi, ed., *Viktor Tsymbal*, 8.
19 Mudrak, *Ponad kordonamy*, 25.
20 On the duration of study, the requirements, and the maximum number of students, see Pelens'ka, *Ukrains'kyi portret*, 24; for more on students, see Fedoruk, "Praha obitovana iak spokusa Zakhodom," 35–8.

21 On students of different nationalities and on the number of Czechs and Slovaks, see Pelens'ka, "Praz'ka znakhidka," 24; for a list of Czechs and Slovaks who studied at the academy, see Mushynka, "Ukrainistyka Chekho-Slovachchyny," *Duklia* 39 (1991), no. 2, 61n; on artists of other nationalities, see Mudrak, "The Ukrainian Studio," 43n; on Mako's many Ukrainian and Russian students, see Mazurenko, *Skyt poetiv*, 6; on Mako's pedagogical talent, see Ierzhabkova, "Zobrazhennia dytyny," 193; on Kulets's accepting many Czech students, see Mazurenko, *Skyt poetiv*, 6.

22 For more, see Pelens'ka, "Praz'ka znakhidka," 23–4.

23 On Ukrainian students who attended the Prague Academy of Arts, see Hordyns'kyi, ed., *Viktor Tsymbal*, 8; on Mazepa's studies under Zdeněk Kratochvíl, see Ierzhabkova, "Zobrazhennia dytyny," 192.

24 For more on Liaturyns'ka, see Iatsiv, *Ukrains'ke mystetstvo XX stolittia*, 180–2; see also the Antonovych Collection, LAC, MG 31, H 50, Biographical Notes. Oksana Liaturyns'ka, vol. 2, f. 4.

25 For more on Mazurenko, see Iatsiv, *Ukrains'ke mystetstvo*, 176–9; for more on Mazurenko and Liaturyns'ka, see Morávková, "Oksana Liaturyns'ka i Halia Mazurenko," 166–7; see also LAC, MG 31, H 50, Biographical Notes. Halyna Mazepa-Koval', vol. 2, f. 6.

26 For more on Tsymbal and his training, see Hordyns'kyi, ed., *Viktor Tsymbal*, 8–9; for the portrait of Palacký, see ibid., 69.

27 For more on Levyts'ka, see Keivan, *Ukrains'ki mysttsi poza bat'kivshchynoiu*, 172–4; see also Babka, "Pražská Slovanská knihovna," in Babka et al., *Příběhy exilu*, 170.

28 For more on Kateryna Antonovych, see the Antonovych Collection, LAC, MG 31, H 50, Autobiographical Notes, vol. 1, f. 23–52; see also Kateryna Antonovych, *Z moikh spomyniv*.

29 For this recollection, see Mazurenko, *Skyt poetiv*, 9.

30 On the role of the exhibitions in artists' lives and the positive perception in Czech art circles, see Pelens'ka, "Praz'ka znakhidka," 25–6; for the exhibition dates, see *Les Artistes du Studio de Prague*, 10.

31 On the American delegation that bought a student work, see Antonovych, "10-a vystava"; on praise for Mozalevs'kyi's pupils, see Mudrak, *Ponad kordonamy*, 25; on items on display, see Antonovych, "10-a vystava"; on thirteen exhibitions by 1939, see Narizhnyi, *Ukrains'ka emigratsiia*, 191.

32 For the numbers, see Z.K., "Ukrains'ka knyzhkova ta grafichna vystavka u Prazi," *Litopys polityky, pys'menstva i mystetstva* 2, nos. 19–20 (1924): 300–1; for more on the exhibition, see Ukrains'kyi hromads'kyi komitet, *Try roky pratsi*, 87–94.

33 On reviews of some exhibitions, see Pelens'ka, "Praz'ka znakhidka," 25–6; see also Ukrains'kyi hromads'kyi komitet, *Try roky pratsi*, 93–4.

34 For more, see Narizhnyi, *Ukrains'ka emigratsiia*, vol. 2, 50.

35 For more on the exhibition of Ukrainian graphics that took place in Brussels in 1927, see Dm. Andriievs'kyi, "Vystavka ukrains'koho hrafychnoho mystetstva v Briuseli," *Tryzub*, no. 20 (1927), 15–18; on the exhibition in L'viv, see *Ukrains'kyi tyzhden'*, 7 October 1935.
36 Citation: The Antonovych Collection, LAC, MG 31, H 50, Biographical Notes. Oksana Liaturyns'ka, vol. 2, f. 4; on Mazepa's tragedy, see ibid., Biographical Notes. Halyna Mazepa-Koval', vol. 2, f. 6.
37 Mudrak, "Czech Modernism," 53.

6. Ukrainian Scholarly and Professional Societies and Organizations

1 The inclusion of the Committee on Intellectual Co-operation is discussed in detail in chapter 9; on representing Ukrainian scholarship abroad, see the Kolessa Collection, PNP, folder *Oleksander Shul'hyn*, letter from Shul'hyn to Kolessa, 12 September 1926.
2 For more, see Kolessa and Shul'hyn, *Zapyska pro orhanizatsiiu Ukrains'koho akademichnoho komitetu*, Další, file 16, Ukrajinský akademický komitét, SsSk.
3 The table is based on Narizhnyi, *Ukrains'ka emigratsiia*, 193–4.
4 For more, see ibid., 194; see also Ukrains'kyi akademichnyi komitet, *Ukrains'kyi naukovyi zizd u Prazi 3–7 zhovtnia 1926 r.*, 6–7.
5 For many drafts of Kolessa's speech, see the Kolessa Collection, PNP, folder *Ol'ha Kobylians'ka*.
6 For more, see Narizhnyi, *Ukrains'ka emigratsiia*, 195.
7 For more on the reasons for the foundation of the society, see *Pratsi Ukrains'koho istorychno-filolohychnoho tovarystva v Prazi*, vol. 1 (1926), 1–2; see also *Spravozdannia "Ukrains'koho istorychno-filologychnoho tovarystva v Prazi" za pershyi rik ioho diial'nosty (od 30-ho travnia 1923 roku do 31-ho travnia 1924 roku)*, 1–2; on the experience gained in societies, see Trembits'kyi, "Rodyna Sitsins'kykh-Sichyns'kykh," 307–8; on Doroshenko's letter to Lypyns'kyi, see Lypyns'kyi, *Arkhiv*, vol. 6, 91.
8 On the first meetings and members, see *Spravozdannia [...] (od 30-ho travnia 1923 roku do 31-ho travnia 1924 roku)*, vol. 1, 2; see also, *Pratsi*, vol. 1, 2; on the membership, see Narizhnyi, *Ukrains'ka emigratsiia*, 198–9; for figures on the membership, meetings, and delivered papers, see the table in ibid., 201.
9 On the goal of the society, see *Pratsi*, vol. 1, 2; for a list of all papers delivered, see Narizhnyi, *15 lit diial'nosty Ukrains'koho istorychno-filologichnoho tovarystva v Prazi (1923–1938)*, 9–16.
10 The calculation on delivered papers is based on Narizhnyi, *15 lit diial'nosty*; on the attendance of meetings, see *Spravozdannia [...] od 31. V. 1930. do 30. V. 1931*, 12; on several renowned Czech scholars attending meetings, see *Pratsi*, vol. 1, 3.

11 For the letter, see the Kolessa Collection, PNP, folder *Vasyl Bidnov*, letter from Bidnov to Kolessa, 2 November 1930.

12 On the first volume of *Pratsi*, see *Spravozdannia [...]od 31 travnia 1925 roku do 31 travnia 1926 roku*, 8–9; on the fact that the volume put financial pressure on the society, see Narizhnyi, *Ukrains'ka emigratsiia*, 206; the remaining volumes were released during the Second World War.

13 For more on the foundation of the society, see *Biuleten' Ukrains'koho tovarystva prykhyl'nykiv knyhy v Prazi*, 20 February 1927; for more on the society in general, see Narizhnyi, *Ukrains'ka emigratsiia*, 230–2.

14 On the goals of the society, see *Biuleten' Ukrains'koho tovarystva*, 20 February 1927, 1; see also the statute of the society in *Knyholiub* 1 (1927): 66–7.

15 On the structure of the society, see *Biuleten' Ukrains'koho tovarystva*, 20 February 1927; on seventy-one members in 1927, see Narizhnyi, *Ukrains'ka emigratsiia*, 230; for a list of ninety-six members, see *Zvit Ukrains'koho tovarystva prykhyl'nykiv knyhy v Prazi*, 1934, 27; on Czech organizations among the members of the society, see the list in ibid.; for Bykovs'kyi's book, see Bykovs'kyi, *Bibliotechna sprava*; on cooperation with *Časopis československých knihovníků*, see Vatsek, "Biblioteki," 211.

16 On the papers delivered at the first meeting, see *Biuleten' Ukrains'koho tovarystva*, 20 February 1927; on thirty-nine scholarly meetings and sixty-seven papers delivered, see Narizhnyi, *Ukrains'ka emigratsiia*, 230.

17 For more on the society, see Siropolko, "Ukrains'ka bibliografiia na emigratsii," 93–5.

18 On the exhibitions, see Narizhnyi, *Ukrains'ka emigratsiia*, 230; on the review, see *Z istorii mizhnarodnykh zv'iazkiv Ukrainy*, ed. Varvartsev et al., 129–30; on the International Congress of Librarians and Bibliophiles and its participants, see Vatsek, "Biblioteki," 211; on the catalogue of Ukrainian publishing logos in the 1926 exhibition, see Sichyns'kyi, *Katal'og vystavky znakiv ukrains'kykh vydavnytstv*; for more on the exhibition, see Lotots'kyi, *Ukrains'ka knyha*, 9; see also *Katalog výstavy ukrajinské grafiky 12.–26. března 1933*; on positive feedback on the exhibition in 1933 in the press, see Narizhnyi, *Ukrains'ka emigratsiia*, 231.

19 For the plans to collect materials for the National Library in Kyiv, see Siropolko, "Ukrains'ka bibliografiia na emigratsii," 94–5.

20 For more, see Ukrains'ke pravnyche tovarystvo v Ch.S.R., *Ukrains'ke pravnyche tovarystvo v Ch. S. R.*, 3–4.

21 For more on Dnistrians'kyi, see Chapter 2 n29.

22 For more on Iakovliv, see Padokh, "Predmet istorii ukrains'koho prava," 1038–9; on his not being nominated and on the unwritten textbook, see ibid., 1036.

23 For more on Lashchenko, see ibid., 1035–6.

24 For the figures and on unpublished articles and monographs, see Narizhnyi, *Ukrains'ka emigratsiia*, 228–9; for more on the work of Ukrainian legal scholars, see Iakovliv, "Naukova pratsia ukrains'koi emigratsii," 107–12.
25 For more on the congress and the themes discussed, see Dnistrians'kyi, "Zvit z Ukrains'koho pravnychoho zizdu u Prazi," 1–22; the number of papers delivered was calculated based on ibid.
26 For the participation of Ukrainian legal scholars in Czechoslovak congresses, see Iakovliv, "Naukova pratsia ukrains'koi emigratsii," 112; for the events, see Narizhnyi, *Ukrains'ka emigratsiia*, 228–9.
27 For a bibliography of Ukrainian legal scholars in interwar Czechoslovakia, see Petriv, *Naukovi pratsi ukrains'kykh pravnykiv*.
28 For Dniastrians'kyi's book, see Dnistrjanský, *Základy moderního práva soukromého*; for Iakovliv's work, see Iakovliv, *Vplyvy staroches'koho prava*; for the figures of more than one hundred scholarly works, see Petriv, *Zhurnal "Zhyttia i pravo,"* 4.
29 For an example of this interest, see Petriv, *Naukovi pratsi*.
30 For more on the foundation of the society and its objectives, see *Ukrains'kyi medychnyi vistnyk* 1 (1923), 97–8; on the numbers of members, see Narizhnyi, *Ukrains'ka emigratsiia*, 224; for a list of members, see ibid., 225n.
31 For the figures and the role of Girsa, see Narizhnyi, *Ukrains'ka emigratsiia*, 220–1; more on the union, see Matiushenko, "Ohliad medychnoi pratsi emigratsii," 95–7.
32 For more, see *Ukrains'kyi medychnyi vistnyk* 1 (1923), 99.
33 For more on Halyn, see Pundii, Hanitkevych, and Boiko, eds., *Ukrains'ki likari*, vol. 1, 53–4; for the dictionaries, see Halyn, *Rosiis'ko-ukrains'kyi medychnyi slovnyk*; and idem, *Medychnyi latyns'ko-ukrains'kyi slovnyk*; the figures are calculated by myself; for more on the work of the dictionary, see Matiushenko, "Ohliad medychnoi pratsi emigratsii," 96–7.
34 For the periodical, see *Ukrains'kyi medychnyi vistnyk*, 1923–25; on the volume devoted to Horbachvs'kyi and for the works of contributors, see *Ukrains'kyi medychnyi vistnyk* 3–4 (1924); on the work on the journal, see Matiushenko, "Ohliad medychnoi pratsi emigratsii," 96.
35 On the attitude of doctors in Czechoslovakia to their Ukrainian colleagues, see Narizhnyi, *Ukrains'ka emigratsiia*, 223.
36 For more on the matter, see ibid.
37 Citation 1: *New World Encyclopedia*, entry "Prague Linguistic Circle," http://www.newworldencyclopedia.org/entry/Prague_Linguistic_Circle; citation 2: Vasyl' Simovych, "Velyka vtrata dlia movoznavstva. Smert' M. Trubets'koho," *Dilo*, 20 July 1938; for more on the Prague Linguistic Circle, see Toman, *The Magic of a Common Language*; on the Russian members, see ibid., 123; see also, Valiavko, Chudnov, and Iantsen, comps., *Dmytro*

Ivanovych Chyzhevs'kyi, 47; on German scholars, see Toman, *The Magic*, 118–19; for a collection of documents, see Čermák, Poeta, and Čermák, eds., *Pražský lingvistický kroužek v dokumentech*.

38 Citation: Mnykh and Pshenychnyi, *Dmytro Chyzhevs'kyi i svitova slavistyka*, 269n; on the promotion of the phonological approach to linguistics, see Kovaliv, *Vasyl' Simovych*, 9.

39 For the number of members of the union, see Kubijovyč and Struk, *Encyclopedia of Ukraine*, vol. 5, 505; on the union assisting with the employment of Ukrainian engineers, see *Ukrains'kyi inzhener*, no. 1 (1931): 73; on the disagreement and the work of the Society of Ukrainian Engineers, see Narizhnyi, *Ukrains'ka emigratsiia*, 240–2.

40 For more on the society, see ibid., 233–4; for the book produced by the society, see Ukrains'ke pedagogichne tovarystvo v Prazi, *Ukrains'ke shkil'nytstvo na Bukovyni*.

7. Libraries, Archives, and Museums

1 On the history of the library, see Strnadel, ed., *Padesát let Slovanské knihovny*, 73–122; see also Vacek, *Slovanská knihovna*; see Babka, "Pražská Slovanská knihovna a téma ruské, ukrajinské a běloruské emigrace," in Babka et al., *Příběhy exilu*, 151–78; see also Babka, "The Slavonic Library in Prague"; see Opleštilová, "Collection Development"; on Girsa, see Chinyaeva, *Russians outside Russia*, 226; see also *Ročenka Slovanského ústavu* 1 (1928), 55; on the establishment of the library, see Strnadel, ed., *Padesát let*, 75–8; see also Kneeley and Kasinec, "The Slovanská knihovna in Prague," 123; on Tukalevs'kii and the library, see a detailed account, Magidova, *Pod znakom katalogov i materialov*.

2 On the change of the name and on the collection materials related to all Slavic peoples, see Strnadel, ed., *Padesát let*, 76–7; for a list of the departments in 1929, see *Ročenka Slovanského ústavu* 1 (1928), 57.

3 On buying materials from twelve countries and the budget, see Strnadel, ed. *Padesát let*, 77; on 35,000 crowns for periodicals and 500 periodical titles in Slavic languages, see *Ročenka Slovanského ústavu* 1 (1928), 38; on exchanges, see Strnadel, ed., *Padesát let*, 77.

4 On Křížek and hiring librarians, see Rachůnková et al., eds., *Slavonic Library*, 8; on staff members from Russian and Ukrainian émigré communities, see in Babka, "Pražská Slovanská knihovna," in Babka et al., *Příběhy exilu*, 169–71; see also Kneeley and Kasinec, "The Slovanská knihovna," 123.

5 On Haimanivs'kyi being the curator of the Ukrainian department and his fate, see Vacek, *Slovanská knihovna*, 16; for more on Haimanivs'kyi, see

Dziuba et al., *Entsyklopediia suchasnoi Ukrainy*, vol. 5, 310; see Vidnians'kyi, "Slov'ians'ka biblioteka v Prazi," in Varvartsev et al., eds., *Ukraina v mizhnarodnykh vidnosynakh*, vol. 4, 197; see also Vidnians'kyi, "Ukrains'kyi vil'nyi universytet u Prazi," 97; for the textbook, see Bašmak, *Praktická učebnice ukrajinského jazyka*.

6 In general, on the Ukrainian collections in the library, see Strnadel, ed., *Ukrajinská literatura*; see also idem, *Padesát let*, 87–8; see Babka, "Ukrains'ki materialy"; see also *Ročenka Slovanského ústavu* 1 (1928), 71–3; for a list of periodicals, see ibid., 122–9; on 14,000 books, see Vidnians'kyi, "Ukrains'kyi vil'nyi universytet u Prazi," 97.

7 For the figures, see Vidnians'kyi, *Kul'turno-osvitnia pratsia*, 57; see also Narizhnyi, *Ukrains'ka emigratsiia*, 131; on publications from the Carnegie Foundation that the library received in 1926, see Vidnians'kyi, *Kul'turno-osvitnia pratsia*, 57; see also Dubrovina, "Bibliotechna diial'nist'," 4.

8 On the library's financial assistance of 6,000 crowns, see *Universytet v Prazi v rokakh 1926–1931*, 73; on valuable publications from Kyiv, see Vidnians'kyi, *Kul'turno-osvitnia pratsia*, 58.

9 For the figures and the change of the head of the library, see Ukrains'kyi vil'nyi universytet, *Ukrains'kyi vil'nyi universytet v Prazi v rokakh 1931–1941*, 47.

10 On the library in general, see Bykovs'kyi, *Biblioteka Ukrains'koi hospodars'koi akademii*; for the figures, see Narizhnyi, *Ukrains'ka emigratsiia*, 161; on the location and structure of the library, and the use of the Dewey Decimal Classification System, see *Ukrains'ka hospodars'ka akademiia v Ch.S.R. 1922–1935*, 75.

11 Table, *Ukrains'ka hospodars'ka akademiia v Ch.S.R. 1922–1935*, 75.

12 Table, see ibid; see also Ukrajinská hospodářská akademie. *Ukrains'ka hospodars'ka akademiia v Chekhoslovats'kii Respublitsi*, 44–5.

13 Table, see ibid., 76.

14 On the two additional sections, see ibid., 76; the publishing house at the academy is discussed in chapter 8.

15 Table, see ibid., 76.

16 Zlenko, "Biblioteka Ukrains'koho pedahohichnoho instytutu," 46; for more on this library, see ibid., 44–56.

17 On 10,000 crowns for the creation of a library, see Mirnyi, *Ukrains'kyi vysokyi pedagogichnyi instytut*, 59; on the library staff, see ibid., 61.

18 For the figures, see ibid., 61; on the topics of the books, see Zlenko, "Biblioteka Ukrains'koho pedahohichnoho instytutu," 46.

19 For the figures, see Mirnyi, *Ukrains'kyi vysokyi pedagogichnyi instytut*, 59–60; the publishing house is discussed in chapter 8.

20 The table is based on ibid., 60.

21 On the accommodation for the office and the library, see Mirnyi, *Ukrains'kyi vysokyi pedagogichnyi instytut*, 44; on transferring the materials, see Narizhnyi, *Ukrains'ka emigratsiia*, 178.
22 For more on the museum, see Mushynka, *Muzei vyzvol'noi borot'by Ukrainy*; Petišková, ed., *Muzeum osvobozeneckého boje Ukrajiny*; Pelenská, "Muzeum osvobozeneckého boje Ukrajiny v Praze," in Babka, et al., *Příběhy exilu*, 227–41.
23 On the arts becoming an integral part of Antonovych's life, see Miiakovs'kyi, *Dmytro Antonovych*, 26; on Antonovych living abroad, see Ierzhabkova, "Dyrektor Muzeiu," 252; on Antonovych's many roles during the revolutionary events, see Miiakovs'kyi, *Dmytro Antonovych*, 29–30; on Antonovych saving galleries and museums in Kyiv, see Mushynka, "Dmytro Antonovych," 122; citation: [Dmytro Antonovych], [Vid redaktora], *Visty Muzeiu vyzvol'noi borot'by*, no. 1, July (1925), 1.
24 On the founding and the mission of the museum, see [Dmytro Antonovych], [Vid redaktora], Visty Muzeiu vyzvol'noi borot'by, no. 1, July (1925), 1–2.
25 On the division of the museum into four sections, see, for example, "Zvidomlennia T-va 'Muzei vyzvol'noi borot'by Ukrainy,'" *Visty Muzeiu vyzvol'noi borot'by*, no. 3, June (1930), 4; for more on the sections, see Antonovych, "Shevchenkivs'kyi viddil v Muzei vyzvol'noi borot'by Ukrainy," *Visty Muzeiu vyzvol'noi borot'by*, no. 11, February (1936), 2; for the Shevchenko section, see ibid., 2–4.
26 For the figures, see "Zahal'ni Zbory T-va "Muzei VBU" v Prazi," *Visty Muzeiu vyzvol'noi borot'by*, nos. 12–13, October (1936), 8; on the donation by Kolessa in 1938, see the Kolessa Collection, PNP, folder *Spolek "Muzeum osvobozeneckého boje Ukrajiny,"* letter from Siropolko to Kolessa, 15 April 1938.
27 On the rapid growth, rent issues, and the refusal, see Mushynka, "Dmytro Antonovych," 125–6; on Kalenyk-Lysiuk's donation, see [Dmytro Antonovych], [Vid redaktora], *Visty Muzeiu vyzvol'noi borot'by*, no. 3, June (1930), 1–2; see also Mušinka, "Muzeum osvobozeneckého"; on Antonovych and Narizhnyi, see Mushynka, "Dmytro Antonovych," 128; on Antonovych and Narizhnyi performing all the work, see "Akt Reviziinoi Komisii dlia perevedennia revizii zbirok Muzeiu VBU," *Visty Muzeiu vyzvol'noi borot'by*, nos. 12–13, October (1936), 9–10.
28 For fundraising campaigns, see various issues of *Visty Muzeiu vyzvol'noi borot'by*; on the letter, see the Doroshenko Collection, PNP, folder *Antonovyč Dmytro*, letter from Antonovych to Volodymyr Doroshenko, 12 June 1936; for Kateryna Antonovych's recollection of the bombardment, see the Antonovych Collection, LAC, 31 H 50, Museum of Ukrainian National Struggle for Liberation, Prague, 1945, vol. 2, f. 59; for the transfer

of material of the museum and the efforts of Narizhnyi to save it, see Mushynka, *Muzei vyzvo'lnoi borot'by Ukrainy*, 46–51.

29 For more on the founding of the museum and archive, see "Ukrains'kyi natsional'nyi muzei-arkhiv," *Vistnyk Ukrains'koho natsional'noho muzeiu-arkhivu*, no. 1 (1928), 1–3; on its structure, see Bezruchkova, "Organy Muzeiu-arkhivu ta ikh pratsia," in ibid., 4–5; on the political orientation of the founders, see Paliienko, "Zasnuvannia ukrains'koho arkhivu v Prazi. Dokumental'na kolektsiia Ukrains'koho natsional'noho muzeiu-arkhivu," in Paliienko, *Arkhivni tsentry*, 107; for more on the archive and museum, see ibid., 103–36.

30 On the goals and the statute, see Paliienko, "Zasnuvannia ukrains'koho arkhivu," 108; on the two members of staff in 1923–25, see ibid., 110; for Obidnyi's appeal, see "Nashi zavdannia v okhoroni pamiatok," *Vistnyk Ukrains'koho natsional'noho muzeiu-arkhivu*, no. 1 (1928), 6–12; on tens of thousands of documents, see ibid., 7; on the recommendation to write memoirs, see ibid., 8–9; for the article reprint, see Obidnyi, "Nashi zavdannia v okhoroni pam'iatok," *Pam'iatky Ukrainy* 37, no. 2 (2005): 126–7.

31 For more on Zhyvotko, see Boriak, "Ukrains'kyi istorychnyi cabinet."

32 On the three departments of the museum and archive, see *Ročenka Slovanského ústavu*, no. 1 (1928), 144; for the figures, see Paliienko, "Zasnuvannia ukrains'koho arkhivu," 121; for the number of acquisitions between 1927 and 1930, see ibid., 118–19.

33 On the assistance of 100–200 crowns from the committee, see Paliienko, "Zasnuvannia ukrains'koho arkhivu," 109; on the support provided by the Ministry of Foreign Affairs, see *Ročenka Slovanského ústavu*, no. 1 (1928), 144; on the assistance of 5,000 crowns and on the refusal of Ukrainian scholars to participate in board activities, see Paliienko, "Zasnuvannia ukrains'koho arkhivu," 122–3; on respected scholars who did not want to interact with the museum and archive, see ibid., 111.

34 On the Belarusian section, see *Vistnyk Ukrains'koho natsional'noho muzeiu-arkhivu*, no. 1 (1928), 31; for more on the funding cuts, demands of the government, and the response of the leadership of the museum and archive, see Paliienko, "Zasnuvannia ukrains'koho arkhivu," 128–32; on the attempt to donate to the Hoover Institution on War, Revolution and Peace, see ibid., 133–4; for more about the museum and archive in general, see ibid., 103–36; see also *Vistnyk Ukrains'koho natsional'noho muzeiu-arkhivu*, no. 1 (1928).

35 On the foundation of the institute, see Zhyvotko, *Desiat' rokiv*, 3–4; see also Boriak, "Ukrains'kyi istorychnyi kabinet," 138; on the goal of the institute, see *Biuleten' Ukrains'koho istorychnoho kabinetu v Prazi*, no. 1 (1932), 15.

36 On Slavík as the head and Obidnyi as the director of the institute, see Zhyvotko, *Desiat' rokiv*, 4; on the location of the institute, see Grimsted,

Trophies of War and Empire, 335; see also Kopřivová, *Ruská, ukrajinská a běloruská emigrace*, 24; on the seven rooms, see Zhyvotko, *Desiat' rokiv*, 44; on the results of their work in first eighteen months, see ibid., 4; on donations and materials sent *gratis*, see *Biuleten' Ukrains'koho istorychnoho kabinetu v Prazi*, no. 1 (1932), 15; on the donation of the Ukrainian Sociological Institute, see Zhyvotko, *Desiat' rokiv*, 11.

37 On the archival collections, see Zhyvotko, *Desiat' rokiv*, 12–19; on Bochkovs'kyi's donation and Lypyns'kyi's library, see ibid., 11; on Shelukhin's and Shapoval's collections, see ibid., 16, 19.

38 For more on the collections, see ibid., 19–34; for the figures on newspapers and their provenance, see *Biuleten' Ukrains'koho istorychnoho kabinetu v Prazi*, no. 1 (1932), 6; for more examples of titles, see ibid., 9–11; on the institute housing 14,209 issues in 1932, see Zhyvotko, *Desiat' rokiv*, 4.

39 The table is based on Zhyvotko, *Desiat' rokiv*, 42–3.

40 For more on the exhibitions, see ibid., 7–10.

41 Oleksander Mytsiuk, "Ukrains'kyi istorychnyi kabinet u Prazi. Z nahody p'iaty lit isnuvannia," *Nasha kul'tura: naukovo-literaturnyi misiachnyk*, no. 1 (1937), 48.

42 The Antonovych Collection, LAC, MG 31, H 50, Biographical Notes: Antonovych D.V., vol. 1, f. 54.

43 For more on the fate of the institute, see Grimsted, *Trophies of War and Empire*, 344–51.

8. Ukrainian-Language Scholarly Publishing in Czechoslovakia

1 On the government funding the publications of émigré books and periodicals, see Sládek and Běloševská, *Dokumenty k dějinám*, 8; for the numbers of Ukrainian publishing houses in Czechoslovakia, see Maruniak, "Vydavnycha diial'nist' ukrains'koi emigratsii," 664; for the list, see "Ukrains'ki vydavnytstva na chuzhyni (1918–1927)," *Knyholiub* 1 (1927): 84–6.

2 For more, see Maruniak, "Vydavnycha diial'nist'," 661–2. Note: the brochures published by the publishing house *Čas* in the series *Poznejme Ukrajinu* (*Discover Ukraine*) that I found are included in the bibliography.

3 For more, see ibid., 659–60.

4 For the figures, see ibid., 665. Note: These numbers are based on Maruniak's calculations and were published in 1983. It is probable that more works appeared, and with current electronic resources available it will now be easier to find most of those that survived.

5 The table is based on ibid., 667 (recalculated). Note: The timeline in this table exceeds the period under discussion; however, because there were no scholarly Ukrainian-language publications produced before 1920 and only

ninety in the period 1940–45, with the rest published between the wars, this table still is representative of the Ukrainian-language publications in Czechoslovakia.

6 For more, see ibid., 658–9.

7 For more on the fund, see Hal'chuk, "Ukrains'kyi hromads'kyi vydavnychyi fond," 43–6; on the organization of the fund and the figures, see ibid., 43–4; on 1.8 million crowns, see Maruniak, "Vydavnycha diial'nist'," 658; on thirty-seven books and the topics of the fund's publications, see ibid., 660.

8 For biographical details of Vyrovyi, see Bednarzhova and Ianchyk, *Ukrains'ki mohyly*, 16; see also Dziuba et al., *Entsyklopediia suchasnoi Ukrainy*, vol. 4, 439–40.

9 On Bohats'kyi, see Smolii et al., eds. *Entsyklopediia istorii Ukrainy*, vol. 1, 310–1; for the encyclopaedia, see Bohats'kyi, *Mala literaturna entsyklopediia.*

10 Further examples of the institutions' publications are noted below.

11 For more, see Hal'chuk, "Ukrains'kyi hromads'kyi vydavnychyi fond," 45.

12 For lists of the fund's publications, see ibid., 45–6; see also Rachůnková, Řeháková, and Vacek, comps., *Práce ruské, ukrajinské a běloruské emigrace*, vol. 3, 1248–52; see also lists of books published by the fund in some Ukrainian periodicals, such as *Ukrains'kyi inzhener* 1 (1931): 85.

13 For a list of the university's publications in the period under discussion, see Patzke, Szafowal, and Yaremko, eds., *Universitas Libera Ucrainensis: 1921–2011*, 537–56; see also Rachůnková, Řeháková, and Vacek, comps. *Práce ruské, ukrajinské a běloruské emigrace*, vol. 3, 1237–48.

14 Curriculums are discussed in chapter 2; for the volumes devoted to Masaryk, see Ukrains'kyi vil'nyi universytet, *Naukovyi iuvyleinyi zbirnyk.*

15 For the collective works, see ibid., vols. 1 (1923) and 2 (1930).

16 For a list of publications in this period, see Patzke, Szafowal, and Yaremko, eds., *Universitas Libera Ucrainensis: 1921–2011*, 554–6; for more on the cancelled agreement, see Ukrains'kyi vil'nyi universytet, *Ukrains'kyi universytet v Prazi 1921–1926*, 228.

17 For their publications, see Zlenko, comp., *Bibliografichnyi pokazhchyk naukovykh prats'*; see also see various issues of *Knyholiub.*

18 For a list of all publications in this period, see Patzke, Szafowal, and Yaremko, eds., *Universitas Libera Ucrainensis: 1921–2011*, 537–56.

19 For more, see *Ukrains'ka hospodars'ka akademiia v Ch.S.R. 1922–1935*, 77–8.

20 For the coverage, see ibid., 78; for a partial list of published works, see ibid., 79–85. Note: A largely complete list was apparently compiled in 1942 by a secretary at the academy, O. Kozlovs'kyi. It did not receive permission to be published and can be considered lost; see ibid., 79n.

21 On 75 per cent of the whole volume being published by the society, see Tovarystvo prykhyl'nykiv Ukrains'koi hospodars'koi akademii, *Ukrains'ka*

hospodars'ka akademiia (1931), 33; for the figures, see ibid. Maruniak provides the number of publications as 312 in the table; see Maruniak, "Vydavnycha diial'nist'," 667.

22 For the collective works, see *Zapysky Ukrains'koi hospodars'koi akademii v Chekhoslovats'kii Respublitsi*, vols. 1 (1927), 2 (1929), and 3 (1931).

23 For a list of such works, see *Ukrains'ka hospodars'ka akademiia v Ch.S.R. 1922–1935*, 83–4; for a list of publications published by organizations and associations affiliated with the academy, see ibid., 84–5.

24 For the foundation and goals, see Mirnyi, *Ukrains'kyi vysokyi pedagogichnyi instytut*, 93; for the directors, see ibid., 96; on the initial fund, see Maruniak, "Vydavnycha diial'nist'," 658.

25 For more on the institute's publishing, see Mirnyi, *Ukrains'kyi vysokyi pedagogichnyi instytut*, 93–6; for a list of the institute's publications, see Rachůnková, Řeháková, and Vacek, comps., *Práce ruské, ukrajinské a běloruské emigrace*, vol. 3, 1233–6.

26 For the figures, see Mirnyi, *Ukrains'kyi vysokyi pedagogichnyi instytut*, 95; see also Maruniak, "Vydavnycha diial'nist'," 660; for the organ of the institute, see *Pratsi Ukrains'koho vysokoho pedagogichnoho instytutu*, vols. 1 (1929) and 2 (1932); *Pratsi Ukrains'koho vysokoho pedagogichnoho instytutu. Drahomanivs'kyi zbirnyk*, vol. 1 (1930). Note: the years on the second volume and *Drahomanivs'kyi zbirnyk* have discrepancies; on the cover page of the second volume, the date is stated as 1934, while on the title page it is 1932; similarly, the cover of the *Drahomanivs'kyi zbirnyk* gives the date as 1932 and the title page lists it as 1930.

27 For all books written by the institute's professors and published by the fond, see Mirnyi, *Ukrains'kyi vysokyi pedagogichnyi instytut*, 96.

28 For more on the materials sent and the exchanges, see ibid., 95.

29 For the letter, see Kolessa to Studyns'kyi, Prague, 18 June 1934, in *U pivstolitnikh zmahanniakh*, comp. Haiova, Iedlins'ka, and Svarnyk, 641–2. Note: An examination of the Kolessa archive in the Museum of Czech Literature in Prague reveals a number of folders with various works prepared for publication. There are materials on Kotliarevs'kyi, Drahomanov, and Shashkevych, as well as on Western Ukrainian lands, Kyrylo Ustyianovych, early Ukrainian poetry, and Ukrainian literature of the eighteenth century, among other topics; see the Kolessa Collection, PNP; for some examples of recently reprinted works, see Chyzhevs'kyi, *Hrets'ka filosofiia do Platona. Khrestomatiia I.*; Rusova, *Vybrani pedahohichni tvory*; Simovych, *Pratsi v dvokh tomakh*, 2 vols.; for more on the limitations of Ukrainian-language publishing, see Maruniak, "Vydavnycha diial'nist'," 672.

30 For a record of Omelčenková at Charles University see, Ústav dějin Univerzity Karlovy a Archiv Univerzity Karlovy, "Matrika doktorů

Univerzity Karlovy VII. (1928–1931)," https://is.cuni.cz/webapps/archiv/public/book/bo/1836656452491438/208/?lang=cs.

31 Note on the surname of Omelčenková: In most of her works published by the publishing house, Mariia Omel'chenkova wrote her name in Czech as "Marie Omelčenková," even in Ukrainian-language publications. When she published in Ukrainian periodicals, she used "Omel'chenko." Since this discussion focuses on the publishing house that published her major works under the name "Marie Omelčenková," her name here will be written in Czech. For more on Omelčenková's biographical details, interactions with Czechs, her admiration of Masaryk, her interest in daily life, and a general history of Czechoslovakia, see Mariia Omel'chenkova, Introduction to *T.G. Masaryk (1850–1930)*, ix–xiii; on the monograph about Masaryk, see Mnich, "Zabytaia monografiia Marii Omel'chenko"; for the article, see Marie Omelčenková, "Marie, Jugoslovanská královna, jako matka a hospodyně," *Věstník* 23, no. 32 (19 June 1935): 7; for some biographical details of Omelčenková, see also Bednarzhova and Ianchyk, *Ukrains'ki mohyly*, 38; for a list of publications by the Czech–Ukrainian Book Publishing House, see Rachůnková, Řeháková, and Vacek, eds., *Práce ruské, ukrajinské a běloruské emigrace*, vol. 3, 1291–2.

32 On the courses taught by Omel'chenko, see Mirnyi, *Ukrains'kyi vysokyi pedagogichnyi instytut*, 79, 81, 83; for some examples of his books, see Masaryk, *Iak pratsiuvaty?*; Omel'chenko, *Edvard Benesh*; idem, *Dějiny textu Křest sv. Vladimíra*; for some biographical details of Omel'chenko, see Bednarzhova and Ianchyk, *Ukrains'ki mohyly*, 37–8.

33 For general information on Tyshchenko, see his memoirs, Tyshchenko, *Z moikh zustrichei*; see also Iurkevych, "Iurii Tyshchenko"; for Kateryna Antonovych's recollections, see the Antonovych Collection, LAC, MG 31, H 50, Autobiographical Notes, Ukraine period, vol. 1, file 36; for the letter, see Iu. Tyshchenko to K. Studyns'kyi, Prague, 6 March 1925, in *U pivstolitnikh zmahanniakh*, comp. Haiova, Iedlins'ka, and Svarnyk, 452–3.

9. The Ukrainian Scholarly Community and the Outside World

1 On one of the goals of the committee to become a member of the Committee on Intellectual Cooperation, see Ukrains'kyi akademichnyi komitet, *Ukrains'kyi naukovyi zizd u Prazi 3–7 zhovtnia 1926 r.*, 6; on Valéry calling this organization a "League of Minds," see [League of Nations. Secretariat], *Intellectual Co-Operation*, 30; for more on the organization, see Renoliet, *L'Unesco oubliée*.

2 On the postponing of the decision, see League of Nations, International Committee, 14–18 January (1926), 22; citation: ibid. 26–29 July (1926), 40; for Reynold's speech, see ibid., 26–29 July (1926), 39–40; on Reynold's

words on important scholarly work performed by the committee and on the decision to accept it, see ibid., 40.

3 In Ukrainian publications, professors never mentioned the unofficial nature of the Committee on Intellectual Cooperation's recognition of the Ukrainian Academic Committee; on the importance of the recognition discussed by Kolessa and Shul'hyn, see the Kolessa Collection, PNP, folder *Oleksandr Shul'hyn*, letter from Shul'hyn to Kolessa, from Paris, 12 September 1926; for the letter, see Kolessa to Studyns'kyi, Prague, 22 November 1926, in *U pivstolitnikh zmahanniakh*, comp. Haiova, Iedlins'ka, and Svarnyk, 488.

4 For Antonovych's mention, see Antonovych, "Pratsia v haluzi mystetstva," 54–5.

5 On the appeal to protest the persecution of Ukrainian intellectuals in the Soviet Union, see Renoliet, *L'Unesco oubliée*, 121; for the text of the appeal, see the letter dated 16 January 1930, in Ukrainian and French, the Ukrainian Academic Committee to the Committee on Intellectual Co-operation, Prague, 16 January 1930, Korespondence odeslaná, Společnost národů, file 14, Ukrajinský akademický komitét, SsSk; for an example of an appeal to protest against the acceptance of the Soviet Union, see Oleksander Shul'hyn, "Pered pryniattiam SSSR do Ligy Natsii," *Dilo*, 1 August 1934; on the cessation of the membership, see Renoliet, *L'Unesco oubliée*, 284.

6 Citation 1: Chyzhevs'kyi, "Slov'ians'kyi romantyzm," 73; on steps to implement these policies, see Petráň, "Filozofická fakulta v letech 1918–1939 (1945)," 121–61, in *Dějiny Univerzity Karlovy*, ed. Havránek and Pousta, vol. 4, 140; on Masaryk's view on the need to study Slavs' present and past, Charvát, "Masaryk a Ukrajinci," 113; citation 2: Hladký, "Stý první ročník Slovanského přehledu," 11.

7 For more on the development of Slavic Studies, see Petráň, "Filozofická fakulta," 141–5.

8 On the government's policies to make Prague a centre of Slavic Studies, see ibid., 140; on Murko, see Petráň, *Nástin dějin Filozofické fakulty*, 308–9.

9 For subjects taught at the Slavic seminar, see ibid., 330; for more on the subjects taught, see Petráň, "Filozofická fakulta," 141–5; on the size and location of the seminar and for its library holdings, see Havránek and Pousta, eds., *A History of Charles University*, vol. 2, 224.

10 For more on the scholars, see Petráň, "Filozofická fakulta," 141–5; on Courtenay, see Hejret, "Slovanstvo," 205.

11 On Kolessa becoming a professor, see Ukrains'kyi vil'nyi universytet, *Universytet v Prazi v rokakh 1926–1931*, 159; on Kolessa's becoming the head of the Ukrainian section of the Slavic seminar, see ibid., 160; see also Petráň, "Filozofická fakulta," 142; for a list of Russian and Ukrainian

professors who worked in non-Ukrainian institutions, see Vacek, "Interakce ruské a ukrajinské emigrace," 10.

12 On cooperation with Czech scholars, see Vidnians'kyi, "Ukrains'kyi vil'nyi universytet u Prazi," 96; Czech professors who taught at the Ukrainian Economic Academy are discussed in chapter 3; for the book, see Dorošenko and Rypka, *Polsko, Ukrajina*; on Rypka, see Filipský et al., eds., *Čeští a slovenští orientalisté*, 424–5; Stloukal, ed., *Tvůrcové dějin*.

13 For the review, see Bidlo, "Michajlo Hruševskyj," *Prager Presse*, 29 September 1926; on the hundreds of items on Ukraine in *Prager Presse*, see *Prager Presse*, passim; see also "1926 r., travnia 12. – Lyst redaktsii praz'koi hazety 'Prager Presse' do Naukovoho tovarystva im. Shevchenka u L'vovi z povidomlenniam pro vmishcheni v nii vidhuky na pratsi NTSh," in *Z istorii mizhnarodnykh zv'iazkiv*, ed. Varvartsev et al., 143–4.

14 More on Kandyba, see Vynar, "Naukova diial'nist' d-ra Oleha Kandyby."

15 See Iakovliv, *Vplyvy staroches'koho prava*; see also Doroshenko, "Diial'nist' Frantishka Paliats'koho"; see Chekhovych, *Ches'ki vplyvy na Frankovoho "Moiseia"*; see also Steško, *Čeští hudebníci*.

16 For more on cooperation, see Vacek, "Vztahy pedagogů," 123–5; for more on the cooperation of Czechoslovak scholars with Ukrainian and Russian scholars, see Vacek, "Interakce ruské a ukrajinské emigrace," 1–40.

17 For more, see "Urochyste vidkryttia zizdu," in Ukrains'kyi akademichnyi komitet, 2. *Ukrains'kyi naukovyi zizd u Prazi*, 18.

18 For many examples of such correspondence, see, the Doroshenko Collection, PNP.

19 For more, see Narizhnyi, *Ukrains'ka emigratsiia*, 222–3.

20 For the last volume of the periodical, see *Ukrains'kyi medychnyi vistnyk*, nos. 5–6 (1925); on sending medical literature to Ukraine, see Narizhnyi, *Ukrains'ka emigratsiia*, 223.

21 *Slavia* is still being published by the Institute of Slavic Studies at the Czech Academy of Sciences; on Murko's offer, see "1922 r., lypnia 14. – Lyst redaktsii praz'koho zhurnalu 'Slavia' do Naukovoho tovarystva im. Shevchenka u L'vovi z propozytsiieiu pro obmin slavistychnymy publikatsiiamy," in *Z istorii mizhnarodnykh zv'iazkiv Ukrainy*, ed. Varvartsev et al., 113; on the request of the *Prager Presse* editorial office, see ibid., 143–4; on the request by the *Střední Evropa* editorial office, see ibid., 158–9.

22 On examples of Kolessa's correspondence with Hrushevs'kyi, see the Kolessa Collection, PNP, folder *Mykhailo Hrushevs'kyi*, letter from Hrushevs'kyi to Kolessa, to Prague, n.d. [1927]; on examples of Kolessa's correspondence with Iefremov, see the Kolessa Collection, PNP, folder *Serhii Iefremov*, letter from Iefremov to Kolessa, 19 January 1927; on Chykalenko's correspondence with Iefremov, see Chykalenko, *Lysty Ievhena Chykalenka*; Chykalenko and Iefremov, *Ievhen Chykalenko, Serhii*

Iefremov; on the fate of Chykalenko's sons, see Piskun, "Ievhen Chykalenko v emigratsii," 259; for Rudnyts'kyi's correspondence, see Mushynka, ed. *Lysty Stepana Rudnytskoho;* see also Vidnians'kyi, "Ukrains'kyi vil'nyi universytet u Prazi," 98.

23 On Dnistrians'kyi's possible return, see Mushynka, *Akademik Stanislav Dnistrians'kyi,* 37–9.

24 For more about the periodical, see Pan'kova and Shevchuk, "'Za sto lit': pokazhchyk zmistu,"; for Rusova's memoirs, see Rusova, "Moi spomyny. Rr. 1861–1879," *Za sto lit,* no. 2 (1928): 135–75; idem, "Moi spomyny 1879–1915," *Za sto lit,* no. 3 (1928): 147–205. Extended and corrected version of the memoirs also published in L'viv; see idem, *Moi spomyny;* see also idem, *Memuary. Shchodennyk;* on Antonovych not sending his memoirs to Hrushevs'kyi, see ibid., 245.

25 For more, see, for example, Chykalenko and Iefremov, *Lystuvannia,* 274–5n.

26 On the refusal to participate in the congress, see ibid., 296. Note the comment made by Chykalenko in his letter to Iefremov on the non-political nature of the congress. For another statement on the non-political nature of the congress, see the letter from Kolessa to Studyns'kyi, Prague, 22 November 1926, in *U pivstolitnikh zmahanniakh,* comp. Haiova, Iedlins'ka, and Svarnyk, 487.

27 For more information on selected conferences and papers presented, see Narizhnyi, *Ukrains'ka emigratsiia,* 130, 257–8; see also, Ukrains'kyi akademichnyi komitet, 2. *Ukrains'kyi naukovyi zizd u Prazi,* passim.

28 On Shcherbakivskyi's participation in conferences, see Shcherbakivs'kyi, "Pratsia u haluzi arkheolohii," in ibid., 53; see also Narizhnyi, *Ukrains'ka emigratsiia,* 257n; on some examples of Chyzhevs'kyi's participation in conferences, see Ukrains'kyi vil'nyi universytet, *Universytet v Prazi v rokakh 1926–1931,* 183; for Chyzhevs'kyi's report on the conference in Lund in the Czech language, see Personálie – lektori, zamestnanci – Cyževs'kyj Dmytro, 1926–1931, file 14, Ukrajinský pedagogický institut Mychajla Drahomanova, SsSk.

29 For the participation in a congress of anthropologists, see Ukrains'kyi vil'nyi universytet, *Universytet v Prazi v rokakh 1921–1926,* 147; on participation in other conferences, see Narizhnyi, *Ukrains'ka emigratsiia,* 130; on Mirchuk being listed among the conference participants, see Ryle, ed., *Proceedings,* xxv.

30 For more on Slavic congresses and conferences in interwar Europe, see Kudělka et al., eds., *Československá slavistika,* 121–36; on the First Congress and for all papers presented by participants, including Ukrainian scholars, see Horák et al., eds., *Sborník prací;* see also Rejnková, ed. *I. sjezd slovanských filologů;* see also Smal'-Stots'kyi, "Pratsi lingvistychnoi sektsii," *Ukraina: naukovyi zhurnal ukrainoznavstva* 39 (1930): 166–73; S-yi,

"Pershyi zizd slavians'kykh fil'ol'ogiv u Prazi," *Novi shliakhy* 4 (1929): 174–80; on the importance of the congress for Slavic Studies, see Kudělka et al., *Československá slavistika*, 123; on the intent of Ukrainians to participate more than they did, see Vasyl' Simovych, "Velyka vtrata dlia movoznavstva. Smert' M. Trubets'koho," *Dilo*, 20 July (1938).

31 For more on the congress, see II Międzynarodowy zjazd slawistów, *Księga referatow. Recueil des communications*, Warsaw, 1934; see also Velinská et al., comp., *II. mezinárodní sjezd slavistů*; fourteen papers presented (or prepared, but not presented) at this conference by the Ukrainian scholars who were members of the Shevchenko Scientific Society were published in *Zapysky naukovoho tovarystva imeny Shevchenka* 155 (1937), 1–230; the third congress was scheduled in Belgrade for 18–25 September 1939, but did not happen because the Second World War had begun. The proceedings of this cancelled conference were still published in Belgrade in 1939.

32 On the International Congress of Ethnographers and Geographers, see *Sborník I. sjezdu slovanských geografů a ethnografů v Praze 1924* (1926).

33 On Kolessa's address at the Sorbonne and his visit to the Institute of Intellectual Cooperation with Iakovliv and Shul'hyn, see Ukrains'kyi vil'nyi universytet, *Universytet v Prazi v rokakh 1926–1931*, 30; on Shul'hyn's paper in Paris, see "Na konferentsii istorykiv frantsuz'koi revoliutsii," *Svoboda*, 23 July 1937.

34 On participation by scholars from the Ukrainian Higher Pedagogical Institute, see, for example, Siropolko, "Pratsia v haluzi pedagogiky," 62; on Eikhel'man, see Personálie - lektori, zamestnanci - Ejchel'man Otton, 1926–1931, file 21, Ukrajinský pedagogický institut Mychajla Drahomanova, SsSk; on Sichyns'kyi, see Personálie - lektori, zamestnanci - Sicyns'kyj Volodymyr, 1925–1931, file 75, Ibid.

35 For the encyclopaedia, Rakovs'kyi et al., eds., *Ukrains'ka zahal'na entsykl'opediia*; on the encyclopaedia, see Borchuk, *Ukrains'ka entsyklopedychna tradytsiia XX st.*, 323–63; for the numbers see ibid., 339.

36 For the numbers, see Borchuk, *Ukrains'ka entsyklopedychna tradytsiia XX st.*, 342; on Ivanyts'kyi being the editor of the technical section, see Rakovs'kyi, "V spravi "Ukrains'koi zahal'noi entsykl'opedii,." *Dilo*, 8 December 1929; see also St. Siropolko, "Shche do pytannia: iakoi nam treba entsykl'opedii," *Dilo*, 12 January 1930.

37 The table is based on Rakovs'kyi, *Ukrains'ka zahal'na entsykl'opediia*, vol. 3 [361]–[1000].

38 For the entry on Horbachevs'kyi, see *Ottův slovník naučný. Illustrovaná encyklopaedie obecných vědomostí*, vol. 11 (1897), 567–8; for Puliui, see ibid., vol. 20 (1903), 983–4; see more on *Ottův slovník naučný nové doby* in Sayer, *The Coasts of Bohemia*, 96–7; on forty Ukrainian and Russian scholars being invited to contribute to the encyclopaedia, see Vacek, "Vztahy

pedagogů," 125; for entries on the Ukrainian scholars, see *Ottův slovník naučný nové doby*, under the corresponding letters; see also Dvořáček et al., eds, *Masarykův slovník naučný*; for the entries written by, for example, Siropolko, see ibid., vol. 7 (1933), 454–7.

39 For the entries on Ukrainian literature and the Ukrainian language, see *Der Große Brockhaus*, vol. 19 (1934), 248–51; on Doroshenko's contribution to the encyclopaedia, see Narizhnyi, *Ukrains'ka emigratsiia*, 253.

40 For the article on Ukraine, see Blangstrup, Brøndum-Nielsen, and Raunkjær, eds., *Salmonsens konversationsleksikon*, vol. 24 (1928), 204; for an entry on Ukraine in the Swedish encyclopaedia, see Lorents and Johansson, eds., *Bonniers konversations lexikon*, vol. 12 (1937), 40–3; for Doroshenko's article, see Doroschenko, "Svensk-ukrainska förbindelser"; for the entry on Ukraine in the French encycopedia, see Augé, ed., *Larousse du XXe siècle*, vol. 6 (1933), 860.

41 For more on the history of *Slovanský přehled* see Hladký, "Stý první ročník Slovanského přehledu," *Slovanský přehled* 101, no. 1 (2015), 9–21; in English, see ibid., 23–37; for Bochkovs'kyi's article, see H. Boczkowski, "Poznámky k otázce ukrajinské," *Slovanský přehled* 17 (1925), 604–8.

42 For Doroshenko's bibliography, see Doroshenko, *Bibliohrafiia*; see also Prymak, "Dmytro Doroshenko," 31; for the article, see "Článek 'Národních listů' z r. 1862 v ukrajinském překladě N. Kostomarova," *Časopis Národního muzea v Praze* 109, no. 2 (1935), 119–26.

43 On Siropolko's article, see Siropolko, "L.J. Živný v ukrajinské knihovědné literatuře: bibliografická poznámka," *Časopis československých knihovníků* 12 (1933), 122–4; for an example of Dnistrians'kyi's article, see St. Dnistrjanskyj, "Právní vznik československého státu," *Právník* 68 (1929), 353–65; for more examples of Dnistrians'kyi's articles in this periodical, see Mushynka, *Akademik Stanislav Dnistrians'kyi*, 64, 66; on Pasternak's article, see J. Pasternak, "Der Stand der ukrainischen archäologischen Forschung in Ostgalizien während der letzten 10 Jahre," *Slavische Rundschau* 1 (1929), 542–4; for more, see, for example, Vacek, "Interakce ruské a ukrajinské emigrace," 32–7.

44 For the book, see Doroshenko, *History of the Ukraine*; Mursky, *Ukrayna ve istiklâl mücahedeleri*.

Conclusion

1 Citation: Rusova, *Memuary. Shchodennyk*, 242.

Bibliography

Note: The bibliography includes all sources for this monograph and all works by the scholars under discussion for which titles are given in the study. Relevant works that were consulted are also listed in the bibliography, even those that are not mentioned in the notes. This is the most complete up-to-date bibliography on the subject.

Archival Collections

ARCCU Archives and Research Collections, Carleton University, Ottawa, Canada

The Evhen Batchinsky Fonds

LAC Library and Archives Canada, Ottawa

The Jaroslav Rudnyckyj Collection

The Kateryna Antonovych Collection

NA Národní archiv

The National Archives of the Czech Republic, Prague, Czech Republic

Fond Ukrajinské muzeum v Praze

The Ukrainian Museum in Prague Collection

PNP Památník národního písemnictví

Museum of Czech Literature, Prague, Czech Republic

Fond Doroshenko Volodymyr

The Volodymyr Doroshenko Collection

Fond Kolessa Oleksander

The Oleksander Kolessa Collection

Fond Řehoř František

The František Řehoř Collection

SsSk Speciální sbírky Slovanské knihovny

Special Collections, Slavonic Library, Prague, Czech Republic

Ukrajinský akademický komitét

The Ukrainian Academic Committee

Ukrajinský pedagogický institut Mychajla Drahomanova

The Mykhailo Drahomanov Ukrainian Pedagogical Institute Collection

TsDAVO Tsentral'nyi derzhavnyi arkhiv vyshchykh orhaniv vlady ta upravlinnia Ukrainy

Central State Archives of Higher Organs of Government and Administration of Ukraine, Kyiv, Ukraine

Ukrains'ka hospodars'ka akademiia v Chekhoslovachchyni, m. Podebrady

The Ukrainian Economic Academy Collection

Ukrains'kyi vil'nyi universytet v Prazi

The Ukrainian Free University in Prague Collection

Encyclopaedias, Bibliographies, Bibliographic Guides, Biographical and Subject Dictionaries, Archival Guides, Indexes, and Directories

Andreichyn, Mykhailo, Ivan Vakarchuk, Iaroslav Dashkevych, Ivan Dziuba, Mykola Zhelezniak, Mykola Zhulyns'kyi, and Oleh Kupchyns'kyi, eds. *Naukove tovarystvo imeni Shevchenka: entsyklopediia*. Kyiv, L'viv, and Ternopil': Naukove tovarystvo im. Shevchenka: Instytut entsyklopedychnykh doslidzhen' NAN Ukrainy, 2012–.

Auftrag des Collegium Carolinum. *Biographisches Lexikon zur Geschichte der böhmischen Länder*. München: R. Oldenbourg Verlag, 1979–.

Augé, Paul, ed. *Larousse du XXe siècle*. 6 vols. Paris: Librairie Larousse, 1928–33.

Aulická, Hana, Alena Léblová, and Josef Tomeš, eds. *Československý biografický slovník*. Praha: Encyklopedický institut ČSAV, 1992.

Blangstrup, Christian, Johannes Brøndum-Nielsen, and Palle Peder Raunkjær, eds. *Salmonsens konversationsleksikon*. 2nd ed. 26 vols. København: J. H. Schultz Forlagsboghandel, 1915–30.

Bohats'kyi, Pavlo. *Mala literaturna entsyklopediia*. Sydney: [Fundatsiia Ukrainoznavchykh Studii v Avstralii], 2002.

Bykovs'kyi, Lev. *Ivan Shovheniv (1874–1943): bio-bibliohrafychni materiialy*. Zheneva: Ukrains'kyi mors'kyi instytut, 1947.

Churaň, Milan, Pavel Augusta, Ladislav Niklíček, Tomáš Pasák, Jiří Peňás, Milan Polák, and Jan Pömerl, eds. *Kdo byl kdo v našich dějinách ve 20. století*. Praha: Nakladatelství Libri, 1998.

Dandová, Marta, Marta Zahradníková, and Rumjana Dačeva, comps. *Ruská a ukrajinská meziválečná emigrace ve fondech Literárního archivu Památníku národního písemnictví. Soupis výtvarných děl ruských a ukrajinských výtvarníků emigrantů ze sbírky Karáskovy galerie*. Praha: Literární archiv Památníku národního písemnictví, 1999.

Dejmek, Jindřich, with the assistance of Jan Němeček and Slavomír Michálek. *Diplomacie Československa. Biografický slovník československých diplomatů (1918-1992)*, vol. 2. Praha: Academia, 2013.

Dvořáček, Jan, Rudolf Polz, Emanuel Rádl, Emil Svoboda, Antonín Stefánek, Zdeněk V. Tobolka, and Jaroslav Veselý, eds. *Masarykův slovník naučný: lidová encyklopedie všeobecných vědomostí*. 7 vols. Praha: Nákladem "Československého kompasu," 1925–33.

Dziuba, I.M., A.I. Zhukovs'kyi, O.M. Romaniv, M.H. Zhelezniak, V.M. Baranets'kyi, V.P. Burkat, and I.D. Hamkalo, eds. *Entsyklopediia suchasnoi Ukrainy*. Kyiv: Natsional'na akademiia nauk Ukrainy / Naukove tovarystvo im. Shevchenka / Instytut entsyklopedychnykh doslidzhen' NAN Ukrainy, 2001–.

Filipský, Jan, Josef Kolmaš, Viktor Krupa, and Josef Opatrný, eds. *Čeští a slovenští orientalisté, afrikanisté a iberoamerikanisté*. Praha: Nakladatelství Libri, 1999.

Ginneken, Anique H.M. van. *Historical Dictionary of the League of Nations*. Lanham: Scarecrow Press, 2006.

Grimsted, Patricia Kennedy. *Archives and Manuscript Repositories in the USSR: Ukraine and Moldavia*. Princeton: Princeton University Press, 1988.

– *Trophies of War and Empire: The Archival Heritage of Ukraine, World War II, and the International Politics of Restitution*. Cambridge, MA: Harvard Ukrainian Research Institute, 2001. Chapter 9 translated into Ukrainian under the title *"Praz'ki arkhivy" u Kyievi ta Moskvi: povoienni rozshuky i vyvezennia emihratsiinoi arkhivnoi Ukrainiky*. Kyiv: Derzhavnyi komitet arkhiviv Ukrainy, 2005.

Der Grosse Brockhaus: Handbuch des Wissens in zwanzig Bänden. 15th ed. 21 vols. Leipzig: Brockhaus, 1928–35.

Halyn, Martyrii. *Medychnyi latyns'ko-ukrains'kyi slovnyk*. Edited by B. Matiushenko and V. Nalyvaiko. Praha: Spilka ukrains'kykh likariv v Chekhoslovachchyni, 1926. Reprint, Detroit: Ukrains'ke likars'ke tovarystvo Pivnichnoi Ameryky, 1969.

– *Rosiis'ko-ukrains'kyi medychnyi slovnyk: materiialy do ukrains'koi medychnoi terminolohii*. Edited by O. Korchak-Chepurkivs'kyi. Kyiv: Kyivs'kyi huberniial'nyi vydil okhorony narodn'oho zdorovlia; Pidviddil medychnoi ta sanitarnoi prosvity, 1920.

Havránek, Jan, and Zdeněk Pousta, eds. *Dějiny Univerzity Karlovy 1918–1990*, vol. 4. Praha: Univerzita Karlova, 1998. Abridged and translated into English under the title *A History of Charles University*, vol. 2. Prague: Charles University, Karolinum Press, 2001.

Jaworsky, John S., and Olga S.A. Szkabarnicki. *The Batchinsky Collection. Carleton University Library*. Edmonton: Canadian Institute of Ukrainian Studies Press, University of Alberta, 1995.

Katalog výstavy ukrajinské grafiky 12.-26. března 1933. Praha: [Ukrajinský spolek přátel knihy v Praze], 1933.

Kolář, František, et al., eds. *Politická elita meziválečného Československa, 1918-1938: kdo byl kdo*. Praha: Pražska edice, 1998.

Kononenko, M.P., and H.S. Sazonenko. *Ukrains'ki vcheni – naturalisty, matematyky, likari, pedahohy: posibnyk-dovidnyk*. Kyiv: Ukrains'kyi tsentr dukhovnoi kul'tury, 2001.

Kopřivová, Anastasia. *Ruská, ukrajinská a běloruská emigrace v Praze: adresář*. Praha: Národní knihovna České republiky, Slovanská knihovna, 1999.

Kostiuk, S.P., comp. *Volodymyr Sichyns'kyi: biobibliohrafichnyi pokazhchyk*. L'viv: Natsional'na akademiia nauk Ukrainy / L'vivs'ka naukova biblioteka im. V. Stefanyka, 1996.

Kryvets', N.V., and N.A. Iarko, comps. *Stepan Vasyl'ovych Vidnians'kyi: [biobibliohrafiia]*. Kyiv: Instytut istorii Ukrainy, 2011.

Kubiiovych, Volodymyr, and Zenon Kuzelia. *Entsyklopediia ukrainoznavstva: v dvokh tomakh*. 2 vols. Miunkhen, New York, and Paris: Vydavnytstvo "Molode zhyttia," 1949–84.

Kubijovyč, Volodymyr, and Danylo Husar Struk, eds. *Encyclopedia of Ukraine*. 5 vols. Toronto: University of Toronto Press, 1984–93.

Lorents, Yngve, and Gotthard Johansson, eds. *Bonniers konversations lexikon: nationalupplaga*. 2nd ed. 15 vols. Stockholm: Bonnier, 1937–50.

Machatková, Raisa, comp. *Ukrains'kyi muzei u Prazi (1659) 1925–1948: Opys fondu = Ukrajinské muzeum v Praze (1659) 1925–1948: Inventář*. Translated by Oleh Peschanyi. Kyiv: Natsional'na akademiia nauk Ukrainy / Instytut ukrains'koi arkheohrafii ta dzhereloznavstva im. M.S. Hrushevs'koho; Praha: Státní ústřední archiv v Praze / Archívní správa Ministerstva vnitra ČR, 1996.

Maikher, Vasyl', comp. *Bibliohrafiia zapysok Naukovoho tovarystva imeni Shevchenka: tomy I-CCXL: 1892–2000*. L'viv: Naukove t-vo im. Shevchenka u L'vovi, 2003.

Murashko, Pavlo, comp. *Bibliography of Ukrainian and Slavic Studies Serials Located in the Slavonic Library, Prague*. Edmonton: Kanads'kyi instytut ukrains'kykh studii, Al'berts'kyi universytet, 1990.

Ottův slovník naučný. Illustrovaná encyklopaedie obecných vědomostí. 27 vols. Plus 1 supp. Praha: Vydavatel a nakladatel J. Otto, 1888–1909.

Ottův slovník naučný nové doby: dodatky k velikému Ottovu slovníku naučnému. 12 vols. Praha: Nakladatelství J. Otto společnost, from 1936 "Novina," 1930–43.

Pánek, Jaroslav, ed. *Akademická encyklopedie českých dějin*. Praha: Historický ústav, 2009–.

Pan'kova, Svitlana, and Halyna Shevchuk. "'Za sto lit': pokazhchyk zmistu." *Ukrains'kyi arkheolohichnyi shchorichnyk* 10–11 (2006): 240–87.

Petriv, M.I. *Naukovi pratsi ukrains'kykh pravnykiv v haluzi prava v Chekho-Slovats'kii Respublitsi v 1921–1940 rr.: bibliohrafichnyi pokazhchyk*. Kyiv: [Ukrains'ka vydavnycha spilka]; L'viv: [Vydavnytstvo Ottsiv Vasyliian "Misioner"], 1998.

Petriv, Mykhailo. *Zhurnal "Zhyttia i pravo" (1928–1939): systematychnyi pokazhchyk zmistu*. Edited by Luiza Il'nyts'ka. L'viv: Naukove tovarystvo imeni Shevchenka, 1995.

Podaný, Václav, and Hana Barvíková. *Ruská a ukrajinská emigrace v Československé republice 1918–1938: přehled archivních fondů a sbírek uložených v České republice*. Praha: Archiv Akademie věd České republiky / Literární archiv Památníku národního písemnictví, 1995.

Polski słownik biograficzny. Kraków: Nakładem Polskiej Akademji Umiejętności, 1935–.

Prosalova, Vira. *Ukrains'ka diaspora: literaturni postati, tvory, biobibliohrafichni vidomosti*. Donets'k: Skhidnyi vydavnychyi dim, 2012.

Pundii, Pavlo, Iaroslav Hanitkevych, and Maksym Boiko, eds. *Ukrains'ki likari: biobibliohrafichnyi dovidnyk*. 2 vols. L'viv and Chykago: Naukove tovarystvo im. T. Shevchenka u L'vovi / Likars'ka komisiia: Ukrains'ke likars'ke tovarystvo Pivnichnoi Ameryky, 1994–96.

Rachůnková, Zdeňka, Michaela Řeháková, and Jiří Vacek, comps. *Práce ruské, ukrajinské a běloruské emigrace vydané v Československu 1918–1945: bibliografie s biografickými údaji o autorech*. 3 vols. Praha: Národní knihovna České republiky, 1996.

Rachůnková, Zdeňka, et al., eds. *Slavonic Library: A Guide*. Praha: National Library of the Czech Republic, Slavonic Library, 2002.

Rakovs'kyi, Ivan, Volodymyr Doroshenko, Vasyl' Simovych, and Mykhailo Rudnyts'kyi, eds. *Ukrains'ka zahal'na entsykl'opediia: knyha znannia v 3-okh tomakh*. 3 vols. L'viv, Stanyslaviv, and Kolomyia: Vydannia kooperatyvy "Ridna shkola," 1930–35.

Rejnková, Růžena, ed. *I. sjezd slovanských filologů v Praze, 1929. Bibliografie*. Praha: Státní knihovna ČSSR–Slovanská knihovna, 1968.

Romaniuk, M.M., M.V. Halushko, and L.V. Snitsrchuk, eds. *Ukrains'ka presa v Ukraini ta sviti XIX–XX st.: istoryko-bibliohrafichne doslidzhennia*. L'viv: L'vivs'ka naukova biblioteka im. V. Stefanyka. Naukovo-doslidnyi tsentr periodyky, 2007–.

Rovenský, Jozef, Peter Vítek, Ľubica Harbuľová, Július Vajó, Pavel Čech, and Marián Bernadič, eds. *Ruskí a ukrajinskí lekári v Česku a na Slovensku.* Bratislava: SAP – Slovak Academic Press, 2016

Savka, Mar'iana. *Ukrains'ka emihratsiina presa u Chekhoslovats'kii Respublitsi, 20–30-ti rr. XX st.: istoryko-bibliohrafichne doslidzhennia.* L'viv: L'vivs'ka naukova biblioteka im. V. Stefanyka NAN Ukrainy, Naukovo-doslidnyi tsentr periodyky, 2002.

Smolii, V.A., V.F. Verstiuk, S.V. Vidnians'kyi, V.O. Horbyk, V.M. Danylenko, M.F. Dmytriienko, and Ia.D. Isaievych, eds. *Entsyklopediia istorii Ukrainy.* 10 vols. Kyiv: Vydavnytstvo "Naukova dumka", 2003–13.

Sowtis, Dennis, and Myron Momryk. *The Kateryna Antonovych Collection.* Edmonton: Canadian Institute of Ukrainian Studies, 1985.

Tomeš, Josef, Hana Aulická, Blanka Calábková, Vladislav Dudák, Miloš Fikejz, and Josef Heřman, eds. *Český biografický slovník XX. století.* 3 vols. Praha: Paseka Petr Meissner, 1999.

Vacek, Jiří, comp. *Ruská, ukrajinská a běloruská emigrace v Praze: katalog výstavy.* Praha: Národní knihovna České republiky, Slovanská knihovna, 1995.

Varvartsev, M.M., S.V. Vidnians'kyi, O.A. Ivanenko, A.Iu. Martynov, and I.M. Mel'nykova, eds. *Ukraina v mizhnarodnykh vidnosynakh: entsyklopedychnyi slovnyk-dovidnyk.* Kyiv: Instytut istorii Ukrainy NANU, 2009–16.

Velinská, Eva, et al., eds. *II. mezinárodní sjezd slavistů, Warszawa, 1934: bibliografie.* Praha: Státní knihovna České socialistické republiky, Slovanská knihovna, 1972.

Vošahlíková, Pavla, Jana Brabencová, Marcella Husová, Marie Makariusová, and Gustav Novotný, eds. *Biografický slovník českých zemí.* Praha: Historický ústav AV ČR, 2004–.

Vykoupil, Libor. *Slovník českých dějin.* Brno: Julius Zirkus, 2000.

Zlenko, Petro, comp. *Bibliografichnyi pokazhchyk naukovykh prats' ukrains'koi emigratsii 1920–1931.* Praha: Tisk Ludvík Kaucký, 1932. Reprint, Edmonton: Vydavnytstvo Kanads'koho instytutu ukrains'kykh studii, Al'berts'kyi universytet, 1990.

Selected Periodicals, Works, and Bulletins

Biuleten' Ukrains'koho istorychnoho kabinetu v Prazi (1932–34)

Biuleten' Ukrains'koho tovarystva prykhyl'nykiv knyhy v Prazi (1927)

Informatsiinyi biuleten' Komisii v spravi t. zv. Nansenovs'kykh pasportiv (1930–?)

Knyholiub (1927–32)

Komunikat vykonavchoi komisii ukrains'kykh emigrans'kykh organizatsii v Chekhoslovats'kii Respublitsi v spravi mizhnarodnykh (Nansenivs'kykh) pasportiv (1930–?)

Naukovyi zbirnyk Ukrains'koho universytetu v Prazi (1923–42)

Nova Ukraina (1922–28)
Pratsi Ukrains'koho istorychno-filolohychnoho tovarystva v Prazi (1926–44)
Pratsi Ukrains'koho vysokoho pedagogichnoho instytutu im. Mykhaila Drahomanova u Prazi (1929–32)
Ročenka Československé republiky (1922–33)
Ročenka Slovanského ústavu (1928–48)
Spravozdannia "Ukrains'koho istorychno-filologychnoho tovarystva v Prazi" (1923–41)
Students'kyi vistnyk (1923–31)
Ukrains'kyi inzhener (1931–32)
Ukrains'kyi medychnyi vistnyk (1923–25)
Ukrains'kyi tyzhden' (1932–38)
Visty Muzeiu vyzvol'noi borot'by (1925–38)
Vistnyk Ukrains'koho natsional'noho muzeiu-arkhivu (1928)
Zapysky Ukrains'koi hospodars'koi akademii v Chekhoslovats'kii Respublitsi (1927–31)

Books and Articles

Andic, V.E. "The Economic Aspects of Aid to Russian and Ukrainian Refugee Scholars in Czechoslovakia." *Journal of Central European Affairs* 21, no. 2 (1961): 176–87.

Andreyev, Catherine, and Ivan Savický. *Russia Abroad: Prague and the Russian Diaspora, 1918–1938*. New Haven: Yale University Press, 2004.

Antonovych, Dm. "Pratsia v haluzi mystetstva." In Ukrains'kyi akademichnyi komitet. 2. *Ukrains'kyi naukovyi zizd u Prazi*, 54–7.

Antonovych, Dmytro. *Skorochenyi kurs istorii ukrains'koho mystetstva*. Praha: Vydavnytstvo Ukrains'koho universytetu, 1923.

– *Trysta rokiv ukrains'koho teatru 1619–1919*. Praha: Ukrains'kyi hromads'kyi vydavnychyi fond, 1925. Reprint, L'viv: L'vivs'kyi natsional'nyi universytet imeni Ivana Franka, 2001.

– *Ukrains'ka kul'tura: kurs lektsii*. Regensburg: UTHI, 1947. First published in Poděbrady: Ukrains'kyi Technichno-Hospodars'kyi Instytut, 1940. Reprint, Miunkhen: Ukrains'kyi tekhnichno-hospodars'kyi instytut, 1988. Reprint, *Ukrains'ka kul'tura: lektsii za redaktsiieiu Dmytra Antonovycha*. Edited by Vasyl I. Ul'ianovs'kyi and Svitlana Ul'ianovs'ka. Kyiv: "Lybid," 1993.

Antonovych, Kateryna. *Rolia ukrains'koi zhinky v pratsi U.V.U.: dopovid' na iuvileinii sesii UVAN u Vinnipegu z nahody 30-littia Ukrains'koho vil'noho universytetu*. Vinnipeg: Nakladom Ukrains'koi vil'noi akademii nauk, 1953.

– *Z moikh spomyniv*. 5 vols. Vinnipeg: Nakladom Ukrains'koi vil'noi akademii nauk, 1965–73.

Les Artistes du Studio de Prague = Hrupa prazhs'koi studii. Prague-Praha: [Ukrains'kyi hromads'kyi vydavnychyi fond], 1925.

Artymovych, Agenor. *Praktychna hramatyka latyns'koi movy*, vol. 1. Praha: Ukrains'ke vydavnyche tovarystvo "Siiach," 1927; *Syntaksys*, vol. 2. 1929[30].

Babak, O.I., V.M. Danylenko, and Iu.V. Plekan. *Praha–Kharkiv–Solovky: arkhivno-slidcha sprava akademika Stepana Rudnyts'koho*. Kyiv: Instytut ukrains'koi arkheohrafii ta dzhereloznavstva im. M.S. Hrushevs'koho, 2007.

Babka, Lukáš. "The Slavonic Library in Prague: Its History and Russian Émigré Collections." *Slavic and East European Information Resources* 17, no. 3 (2016): 174–87.

Babka, Lukáš, Sergei Iakovlevich Gagen, Ľubica Harbuľová, Dana Hašková, Jakub Hauser, Julie Jančárková, Daniela Kolenovská, Anastazie Kopřivová, Michaela Kuthanová, Oksana Pelenská, Miroslav Tomek, and Olga Uhrová. *Příběhy exilu: osudy exulantů z území bývalého Ruského impéria v meziválečném Československu = Stories of Exile: the Destinies of Exiles from the Territory of the Former Russian Empire in Interwar Czechoslovakia = Istorii izgnaniia: sud'by emigrantov s territorii byvshei Rossiiskoi imperii v mezhvoennoi Chekhoslovakii*. Translated by Moe Binarová, Iekaterina Bobrakova-Timoskina, Melvyn Clarke, Barbara Day, Graeme Dibble, Tereza Chlaňová, Michaela Lemeškinová, and Anna Rosová. Praha: Památník národního písemnictví, 2018.

Babka, Lukash [*see* Babka, Lukáš] and Igor' Zolotarev, eds. *Russkaia aktsiia pomoshchi v Chekhoslovakii: istoriia, znachenie, nasledie*. Praga: Natsional'naia biblioteka Cheshskoi Respubliki – Slavianskaia biblioteka / Grazhdanskoe ob'edinenie "Russkaia traditsiia," 2012.

Babka, Lukash [*see* Babka, Lukáš]. "Ukrains'ki materialy u Slov'ians'kii bibliotetsi." *Problemy slov'ianoznavstva* 59 (2010): 243–6.

Barvíková, Helena, Petr Bednařík, Kateřina Čapková, Michal Frankl, Eva Irmanová, Vladimír Kaiser, and Anastazie Kopřivová. *Exil v Praze a Československu 1918–1938 = Exile in Prague and Czechoslovakia 1918–1938*. Translated by Elizabeth Kindlová, Štěpánka Magstadtová, Alice Nováková, Linda Paukertová, Lucie Vidmarová, and Gita Zbavitelová. Praha: Pražská edice, 2005.

Bašmak, Mychajlo. *Praktická učebnice ukrajinského jazyka*. Edited by František Tichý. Praha: Odborné knihkupectví Ferd. Svoboda, 1939.

Bednářová, Tetjana. *Sofija Rusovová: významná veřejná činitelka, ukrajinská nositelka osvěty, pedagožka, literární vědkyně Ukrajinské vysoké školy pedagogické M. Drahomanova v Praze*. Praha: Spolek Ukrajinek v České republice, 2001.

Bednarzhova, Tetiana [*see* Bednářová, Tetjana], and Fedir Ianchyk. *Ukrains'ki mohyly v Chekhii*. Praha: Leonardo, 2002.

Běloševská, L., ed. *Duchovní proudy ruské a ukrajinské emigrace v Československé republice, 1919–1939: méně známé aspekty*. Praha: Slovanský ústav AV ČR, 1999.

Bidlo, Jaroslav. *Michal Hruševs'kyj*. Praha: Nákladem České akademie věd a umění, 1935.

Bidwell, Robin Leonard. *Currency Conversion Tables: A Hundred Years of Change*. London: Rex Collings, 1970.

Bilets'kyi, Leonid. *Dmytro Doroshenko*. Vinnipeg: Nakladom Iuvileinoho komitetu dlia vshanuvannia 50-littia naukovoi i hromads'koi pratsi Dmytra Doroshenka, 1949.

– *Osnovy ukrains'koi literaturno-naukovoi krytyky: sproba literaturno-naukovoi metodolohii*. Vol. 1. Praha: Ukrains'kyi hromads'kyi vydavnychyi fond, 1925. Reprint, Kyiv: "Lybid," 1998.

Bilous, Mariia, and Zenovii Terlak. *Vasyl' Simovych, 1880–1944: zhyttiepysno-bibliohrafichnyi narys*. L'viv: Naukove tovarystvovo im. Shevchenka y L'vovi, 1995.

Blashkiv, Oksana. *Ches'ka i slovats'ka kul'tura v zhytti ta naukovii spadshchyni Dmytra Chyzhevs'koho*. Siedlce: Instytut Filologii Polskiej Uniwersytetu Przyrodniczno-Humanistyczny w Siedlcach, Colloquia litteraria siedlcensia, 2010.

Bochkovs'kyi, Ol'gerd Ipolyt. *Vybrani pratsi ta dokumenty*. Vol. 1. Kyiv: Ukraina Moderna – Dukh i Litera, 2018–.

Boczkowski, H. [see Bochkovs'kyi, Ol'gerd Ipolyt]. *Z dějin Ukrajiny a ukrajinského obrození. Poznejme Ukrajinu*, vols. 4–5. Kyjiv and Praha: Nákladem ukrajinského vydavatelského družstva "Čas," 1919.

Bohachevsky-Chomiak, Marta. *Feminists Despite Themselves: Women in Ukrainian Community Life, 1884–1939*. Edmonton: Canadian Institute of Ukrainian Studies, University of Alberta, 1988.

Borchuk, Stepan. *Ukrains'ka entsyklopedychna tradytsiia XX st.: proekty, vykonavtsi, perspektyvy doslidzhennia*. Ivano-Frankivs'k: Lileia-NV, 2014.

Boriak, Tetiana. *Dokumental'na spadshchyna ukrains'koi emihratsii v Ievropi: praz'kyi arkhiv (1945–2010)*. Nizhyn: Vydavnytstvo Nizhyns'koho derzhavnoho universytetu imeni Mykoly Hoholia, 2011.

– "Ukrains'kyi istorychnyi kabinet i fenomen Praz'koho arkhivu." In *Ukraina na istoriohrafichnii mapi mizhvoiennoi Ievropy. Materialy mizhnarodnoi naukovoi konferentsii (Miunkhen, Nimechchyna, 1–3 lypnia 2012) = Ukraine on the Historiographic Map of Interwar Europe: Proceedings of the International Conference (Munich, Germany, 1–3 July 2012)*, ed. Iaroslava Mel'nyk, Serhii Plokhii, Frank E. Sysyn, Valerii Smolii, and Oksana Iurkova, 133–48. Kyiv: Instytut istorii Ukrainy NANU, 2014.

Borodaievs'kyi, Serhii. "Istoriia kooperatsii." Praha: Ukrains'kyi hromads'kyi vydavnychyi fond, 1925.

Botushans'kyi, Vasyl'. *Stepan Smal'-Stots'kyi – vydatnyi diiach Bukovyny: shtrykhy do portreta*. Chernivtsi: Iavors'kyi S.N., 2010.

Bykovs'kyi, Lev. *Bibliotechna sprava v Chekhoslovachchyni 1924–1927*. Podiebrady: Vydavnytstvo "Ukrains'ke knyhoznavstvo," 1928.

– *Biblioteka Ukrains'koi hospodars'koi akademii: 1922–1947*. Zheneva: Fundacja popierania bibliotekoznawstwa imienia Maurycji Goczałkowskiej, 1947.
– *U sluzhbakh ukrains'kii knyzhtsi*. Edited by Liubomyr R. Vynar and Iaroslav D. Isaievych. L'viv and N'iu Iork: Ukrains'ke istorychne tovarystvo / Instytut ukrainoznavstva im. I. Kryp'iakevycha NANU / Mizhnarodna asotsiatsiia ukrainistiv / Komisiia bibliohrafii i informatyky, 1997.
Čapek, Karel. *Hovory s T.G. Masarykem*. Edited by Jiří Opelík. Praha: Ústav T.G. Masaryka / Masarykův ústav a Archiv AV ČR, 2013.
Čermák, Petr, Claudio, Poeta, and Jan Čermák, eds. *Pražský lingvistický kroužek v dokumentech*. Praha: Academia, 2012.
Charvát, V. "Masaryk a Ukrajinci." *Slovanský přehled* 12, no. 2 (1930): 112–27.
Chekhovych, Konstantyn. *Ches'ki vplyvy na Frankovoho "Moiseia" ta "Ivana Vyshens'koho."* Praha: Ukrains'ke istorychno-filologichne tovarystvo, 1937[8].
Cherediiv, V. "Pratsi ukrains'koi emigratsii v diliantsi agronomichnii." In Ukrains'kyi akademichnyi komitet. 2. *Ukrains'kyi naukovyi zizd u Prazi*, 67–76.
Chinyaeva, Elena. *Russians outside Russia: The Émigré Community in Czechoslovakia 1918–1938*. München: R. Oldenbourg Verlag, 2001.
Chizhevskii, Dmitrii. [*see* Chyzhevs'kyi, Dmytro]. *History of Russian Literature: From the Eleventh Century to the End of the Baroque*. 'S-Gravenhage: Mouton, 1960.
– *Gegel' v' Rossii*. Parizh": "Dom" knigi" i "Sovremennyia zapiski," 1939. Reprint, Sankt-Peterburg: Nauka, 2007. Reprint, translated into Ukrainian, vol. 4. Kyiv: Smoloskyp, 2005.
Chykalenko, Ievhen. *Lysty Ievhena Chykalenka z emihratsii do Serhiia Iefremova: (1923–1928 rr.)*. Edited by Inna Starovoitenko. Kyiv: Instytut ukrains'koi arkheohrafii ta dzhereloznavstva im. M.S. Hrushevs'koho NAN Ukrainy, 2003.
Chykalenko, Ievhen and Serhii Iefremov. *Ievhen Chykalenko, Serhii Iefremov: lystuvannia 1903–1928 roky*. Edited by Inna Starovoitenko. Kyiv: "Tempora," 2010.
Chyzhevs'kyi, Dmytro. *Fil'osofiia H.S. Skovorody*. Varshava: Ukrains'kyi naukovyi instytut, 1934. Reprint, Kharkiv: "Akta," 2003. Reprint, Kharkiv: Prapor, 2004.
– *Fil'osofiia na Ukraini: sproba istoriografii*. Praha: Vydavnytstvo "Siiach," 1926. Reprint, under the title *Narysy z istorii filosofii na Ukraini*. Praha: Ukrains'kyi hromads'kyi vydavnychyi fond, 1931.
– *Hrets'ka fil'osofiia do Pliatona. Khrestomatiia*. Praha: Tovarystvo "Siiach," 1926. Reprint, Miunkhen: Ukrains'kyi vil'nyi universytet, 2015.
– *L'ogika*. Praha: Vydavnyche t-vo "Siiach" pry Ukrains'komu pedagogichnomu Instytuti im. M. Drahomanova, 1924.
– *Narysy z istorii filosofii na Ukraini*. Praha: Ukrains'kyi hromads'kyi vydavnychyi fond, 1931. [Reprinted several times in Ukraine and abroad].
– "Slov'ians'kyi romantyzm." *Slovo i chas*, no. 9 (2005): 65–78.

– *Štúrova filozofia života: kapitola z dejín slovenskej filozofie*. Bratislava: SUS, 1941. Reprint, translated into Ukrainian, vol. 3. Kyiv: Smoloskyp, 2005.
Cipko, Serge. "In Search of a New Home: Ukrainian Emigration Patterns between the Two World Wars." *Journal of Ukrainian Studies* 16, nos. 1–2 (1991): 3–28.
Danylenko, Viktor, and Oleksandr Dobrzhans'kyi. *Akademik Stepan Smal'-Stots'kyi. Zhyttia i diial'nist: 1859–1938*. Kyiv and Chernivtsi: [Instytut istorii Ukrainy NAN Ukrainy], 1996.
Dnistrians'kyi, Stanislav. *Richeve pravo*. Praha: Ukrains'kyi hromads'kyi vydavnychyi fond, 1923.
– *Zahal'na nauka prava i polityky*. Praha: Naklad Ukrains'koho universytetu v Prazi, 1923.
– "Zvit z Ukrains'koho pravnychoho zizdu u Prazi, vid 4. do 7. zhovtnia 1933." *Zhyttia i pravo* 7, no. 1 (1934): 1–22.
Dnistrianśkyj, S. [*see* Dnistrians'kyi, Stanislav]. *Ukrajinci čechům (překlad z rukopisu). Poznejme Ukrajinu*, vol. 1. Kyjiv and Praha: Nákladem ukrajinského vydavatelského družstva "Čas," 1919.
Dnistrjanský, Stanislav [*see* Dnistrians'kyi, Stanislav]. *Základy moderního práva soukromého* Praha: Nákladem České akademie věd a umění, 1928.
Dobrylovs'kyi, M. *Fakhovo-literaturna chynnist' Ukrains'koi hospodars'koi akademii: umovy, napriamky, pidsumky*. Podiebrady: Vydavnytstvo Tovarystva prykhyl'nykiv Ukrains'koi hospodars'koi akademii, 1932. Also published in *Ukrains'kyi inzhener*, 1932, no. 4.
Dobrylovs'kyi, Mykola. *Derzhavnyi kredyt*. Podiebrady: Vydannia Ukrains'koi hospodars'koi akademii v Ch.S.R., 1928.
Dorošenko, D. [*see* Doroshenko, Dmytro]. *Mezinárodní orientace ukrajinců za války a revoluce. Poznejme Ukrajinu*, vol. 9. Kyjiv and Praha: Nákladem ukrajinského vydavatelského družstva "Čas," 1919.
Dorošenko, D. [*see* Doroshenko, Dmytro], and J. Rypka. *Polsko, Ukrajina, Krym a Vysoká Porta v první pol. XVII. stol.*. Praha: Nákladem vlastním, 1936. Offprint from *Časopis Národního Musea* 1 (1936): 19–49.
Doroshenko, Dmytro. *Bibliohrafiia prats' prof. D. Doroshenka za 1899–1942 roky*. Praha: Vydavnytstvo Iuriia Tyshchenka, 1942.
– "Diial'nist' Frantishka Paliats'koho i ukrains'ka sprava." *Pratsi Ukrains'koho vysokoho pedagogichnoho instytutu im. Mykhaila Drahomanova u Prazi* 2 (1932): 118–27.
– *History of the Ukraine*. Translated and abridged by Hanna Chykalenko-Keller. Edited and with an introduction by G.W. Simpson. Edmonton: Institute Press, 1939.
– *Ohliad ukrains'koi istoriohrafii*. Praha: Naklad Ukrains'koho universytetu. Drukom derzhavnoi drukarni, 1923. Translation, New York: Ukrainian Academy of Arts and Sciences in the U.S., 1957. Reprint, Kyiv: Vydavnytstvo "Ukrainoznavstvo," 1996.

– "Organizatsiia ukrains'koi naukovoi pratsi na emigratsii ta ii vyslidy za ostannie desiatylittia." In Ukrains'kyi akademichnyi komitet. 2. *Ukrains'kyi naukovyi zizd u Prazi*, 22–31.

– "Svensk-ukrainska förbindelser under 1600-och 1700-talen i belysning av den nyaste ukrainska histories-krivningen." *Historisk Tidskrift* 57 (1937): 129–49.

Doubek, Vratislav, et al., eds. *Korespondence: T.G. Masaryk – Slované. Rusové a Ukrajinci*, vol. 2. Praha: Masarykův ústav a Archiv AV ČR, 2016.

Dubrivnyi, Pavlo, and Lev Bykovs'kyi, eds. *Ukrain'ska hospodars'ka akademiia v Ch.S.R. i Ukrains'kyi technichno-hospodars'kyi instytut: Podiebrady-Regensburg-Miunkhen, 1932–1972*. Niu Iork: Vydannia absol'ventiv Ukrains'koi hospodars'koi akademii i Ukrains'koho tekhnichno-hospodars'koho instytutu, 1973.

Dubrovina, Liubov. "Bibliotechna diial'nist' emihrants'kykh ukrainoznavchykh tsentriv u 20-30-kh rokakh XX st.." *Bibliotechnyi visnyk*, no. 2 (2009): 3–13.

Evseienko, I.V. "Stanovlennia ukrains'ko-chekhoslovats'kykh vidnosyn 1917–1922 rr." *Mizhnarodni zv'iazky Ukrainy: naukovi poshuky i znakhidky* 8 (1999): 33–48.

Federální statistický úřad. *Historická statistická ročenka ČSSR*. Praha: Československo. Statistický úřad, 1985.

Fedoruk, Oleksander. "Praha obitovana iak spokusa Zakhodom: vkhodzhennia v moderne mystetsvto ukraintsiv vyhnannykiv." In *Ukrajinské výtvarné umění v meziválečném Československu: k 80. výročí založení Ukrajinského studia výtvarných umění v Praze*, ed. Dagmar Petišková, 29–38. Praha: Národní knihovna České republiky, Slovanská knihovna, 2005.

Franc, Martin, and Vlasta Mádlová. *The History of the Czech Academy of Sciences in Pictures = Dějiny Akademie věd v obrazech*. Praha: Academia, 2014.

Franko, Ivan. *Zibrannia tvoriv u p'iatdesiaty tomakh*. Vol. 49. Kyiv: Vydavnytstvo "Naukova dumka," 1986.

Frinta, Antonín, and František Tichý, eds. *Slovanský přehled 1914–1924: K šedesátým narozeninám Adolfa Černého*. Praha: Nákladem orbis, 1925.

Gagen, Sergei, Dana Hašková, Jakub Hauser, Tereza Chlaňová, Julie Jančárková, Anastazie Kopřivová, Michaela Kuthanová, Oksana Pelenská, Vlasta Smoláková, Irina Ščeblygina, and Věra Velemanová. *Zkušenost exilu: katalog výstavy "Osudy exulantů z území bývalého Ruského impéria v meziválečném Československu": 16.6.-29.10.2017, Letohrádek Hvězda = The Experience of Exile: Catalogue of the Exhibition "The Destinies of Exiles from the Territory of the Former Russian Empire in Interwar Czechoslovakia": June 16 – October 29, 2017, Star Summer Palace = Opyt izgnaniia: katalog vystavki "Sud'by emigrantov s territorii byvshei Rossiiskoi imperii v mezhvoennoi Chechoslovakii": 16 iiunia – 29 oktiabria 2017, Letnij dvorec Zvezda*. Translated by Moe

Binarová, Jekaterina Bobrakova-Timoškina, Barbara Day, Graeme Dibble, Sergei Gagen, Tereza Chlaňová, Michaela Lemeškinová, and Andrew Oakland. Praha: Památník národního písemnictví, 2017.

Haiova, Oksana, Uliana Iedlins'ka, and Halyna Svarnyk, comps. *U pivstolitnikh zmahanniakh: vybrani lysty do Kyryla Studyns'koho 1891–1941*. Kyiv: Naukova dumka, 1993.

Hal'chuk, Liudmyla. "Ukrains'kyi hromads'kyi vydavnychyi fond u Prazi." *Bibliotechnyi vistnyk*, no. 1 (1998): 43–6.

Harmashiv, Vsevolod. *Shkil'na hihiiena. Korotkyi kurs dlia studentiv i uchyteliv*. Praha: Ukrains'kyi hromads'kyi vydavnychyi fond, 1926.

Havel, Ondřej. "Začátek ruské pomocné akce a činnost ukrajinského hromadského komitétu v československu v letech 1921–1925." *Historica. Acta Universitatis Palackianae Olomucensis – Facultas philosophica* 35 (2009): 73–87.

Hejret, Jan. "Slovanstvo a jeho vzájemné styky v letech 1914–1925." In *Slovanský přehled*, ed. Frinta and Tichý, 202–12.

Hladký, Ladislav. "Stý první ročník Slovanského přehledu. Ohlédnutí za dosavadní historií časopisu." *Slovanský přehled* 101, no. 1 (2015): 9–21.

Hlaváček, Petr, and Mykhailo Fesenko. *(Ne)šťastná Ukrajina: osobnosti Ukrajinské svobodné univerzity v Praze 1921–1945*. Praha: Filozofická fakulta Univerzity Karlovy v Praze, 2015.

Holenda, I. "Sofiia Rusova – vydatnyi ukrains'kyi pedahoh, literaturoznavets' ta hromads'kyi diiach." *Kronika 2000* 16, no. 72 (2007): 636–44.

Holiat, Roman S. "Short History of the Ukrainian Free University." *Ukrainian Quarterly* 19, no. 3 (1963): 204–26.

Holovats'kyi, Ivan. *Ivan Horbachevs'kyi, 1854–1942: zhyttiepysno-bibliohrafichnyi narys*. L'viv: Naukove tovarystvo imeni Shevchenka u L'vovi, 1995.

Hons'kyi, Iaroslav. *Ivan Horbachevs'kyi u spohadakh i lystuvanniakh*. Ternopil': Ternopil's'ka derzhavna medychna akademiia im. I. Horbachevs'koho, "Ukrmedknyha," 2004.

Horák, Jiří, Matyáš Murko, Miloš Weingart, and Stanislav Petíra, eds. *Sborník prací I. sjezdu slovanských filologů v Praze 1929*. Praha: Výbor I. sjezdu slovanských filologů, 1932.

Horbachevs'kyi, Ivan. *Orhanichna khemiia*. Praha: Naklad Ukrains'koho universytetu v Prazi, 1924.

– *Naukovi pratsi, dokumenty i materialy profesora Ivana Horbachevs'koho: (do 150-richchia vid ioho narodzhennia)*. Edited by Ivan Holovats'kyi. L'viv: Naukove tovarystvo im. Shevchenka, 2005.

Hordyns'kyi, Sviatoslav, ed. *Viktor Tsymbal: maliar i hrafik*. N'iu Iork: Ukrains'ka vil'na akademiia nauk u SShA, 1972.

Hrabyna, Leonid. *Geodeziia*. Praha: Ukrains'kyi hromads'kyi vydavnychyi fond, 1928.

Hrabyna, L. "Ohliad pratsi na poli budivel'no-mezhovykh nauk." In Ukrains'kyi akademichnyi komitet. 2. *Ukrains'kyi naukovyi zizd u Prazi*, 76–81.

Hruševśkyj, Mychajlo [*see* Hrushevs'kyi, Mykhailo]. *Ukrajina a Rusko. Poznejme Ukrajinu*, vols. 10–11. Kyjiv and Praha: Nákladem ukrajinského vydavatelského družstva "Čas," 1919.

Huntington, William Chapin. *The Homesick Million: Russia-out-of-Russia*. Boston: Stratford, 1933.

Iakovliv, Andrii. "Naukova pratsia ukrains'koi emigratsii v haluzi prava." In Ukrains'kyi akademichnyi komitet. 2. *Ukrains'kyi naukovyi zizd u Prazi*, 107–12.

– *Vplyvy staroches'koho prava na pravo ukrains'ke lytovs'koi doby XV–XVI v.* Praha: Nakladom Ukrains'koho Universitetu v Prazi, 1929.

Iarema, Iakym. *Providni idei fil'osofii Tomy Masaryka*. Praha: Ukrains'kyi hromads'kyi vydavnychyi fond, 1925.

Iatsiv, Roman. *Robert Lisovs'kyi (1893–1982): dukh linii*. L'viv: "Apriori," 2015.

– *Ukrains'ke mystetstvo XX stolittia: idei, iavyshcha, personalii: zbirnyk statei*. L'viv: Natsional'na akademiia nauk Ukrainy, Instytut narodoznavstva, 2013.

Ierzhabkova, Blanka. "Dyrektor Muzeiu Vyzvol'noi Borot'by Ukrainy v Prazi prof. Dmytro Antonovych iak pedahoh i prosvitians'kyi diiach." In *Muzeum osvobozeneckého boje Ukrajiny. K 80. výročí založení: sborník příspěvků z konference (Praha, 12.–14. října 2005)*, ed. Dagmar Petišková. Praha: Národní knihovna ČR, Slovanská knihovna, 2006, 251–62.

– "Zobrazhennia dytyny v mystetstvi Halyny Mazepy – pedahohichnyi aspekt." In Petišková, *Ukrajinské výtvarné umění*, 191–9.

Iurkevych, Oleksandra. "Iurii Tyshchenko – vydavets', knyhar, publitsyst: period stanovlennia (1905–1913)." *Zapysky L'vivs'koi naukovoi biblioteky im. V. Stefanyka* 1 (2008): 127–57.

Ivanenko, Ievhen. *Kurs analitychnoi heometrii [...] Osnovy analitychnoi heometrii na ploshchi*. Praha: Ukrains'kyi hromads'kyi vydavnychyi fond, 1925.

Ivanyts'kyi, B. "Desiatylitnia chynnist' ukrains'koi emigratsii na poli lisovoi nauky." In Ukrains'kyi akademichnyi komitet. 2. *Ukrains'kyi naukovyi zizd u Prazi*, 64–7.

Ivasiuk, Ivan. *Kuban': ekonomychnyi narys*. Praha: Ukrains'kyi hromads'kyi vydavnychyi fond, 1925.

Kachor, Andrii. *Borys Martos*. Vinnipeg: Nakladom Ukrains'koi vil'noi akademii nauk, 1977.

Keivan, Ivan. *Volodymyr Sichyns'kyi: arkhitekt, mystets'-hrafik, mystetstvoznavets', doslidnyk*. Toronto: Vydavnytstvo "Ievshan-zillia," 1957.

– *Ukrains'ki mysttsi poza bat'kivshchynoiu*. Edmonton and Montrel: Clio Editions, 1996.

Kneeley, Richard J., and Edward Kasinec. "The Slovanská knihovna in Prague and Its RZIA Collection." *Slavic Review* 51, no. 1 (1992): 122–30.

Korduba, [Myron]. *Bukovina*. Bound with O. Gozdawa, *Uherská Ukrajina. Poznejme Ukrajinu*, vols. 6–7. Kyjiv and Praha: Nákladem ukrajinského vydavatelského družstva "Čas," 1919.

Kovalenko, Oleksander. *Kurs analitychnoi geometrii v prostoryni*. Praha: Vydavnyche tovarystvo pry Ukrains'kii hospodars'kii akademii, 1923.

– *Prykladna mekhanyka*. Podebrady: Vyd[avnytstvo] tov[arystva] pry Ukrains'kii hospodars'kii akademii v Ch.S.R., 1925.

Kovalenko, S.N. "Ukrainskii vysshii pedagogicheskii institut imeni M.P. Dragomanova v Prage kak kul'turno-obrazovatel'nyi tsentr ukrainskoi diaspory v ChSR." In *Russkaia aktsiia pomoshchi v Chekhoslovakii: istoriia, znachenie, nasledie*, ed. Lukash Babka and Igor' Zolotarev, 97–104. Praga: Natsional'naia biblioteka Cheshskoi Respubliki – Slavianskaia biblioteka / Grazhdanskoe ob'edinenie "Russkaia traditsiia," 2012.

Kovaliv, Panteleimon. *Vasyl' Simovych*. Vinnipeg: Nakladom tovarystva prosvita u Fort Viliiami, 1953.

Kudělka, Milan, Zdeněk Šimeček, Vladislav Šťastný, and Radoslav Večerka, eds. *Československá slavistika v letech 1918–1939*. Praha: Academia, 1977.

Kushnir, V[olodymyr]. *Pidruchnyk nimets'koi movy*. Praha: Vydavnyche t-vo "Siiach," 1925.

Lahutenko, Ol'ha. "Tvorchist' Ivana Mozalevs'koho v 1920-ti roky." In Petišková, *Ukrajinské výtvarné umění*, 245–53.

[League of Nations. Secretariat.] *Intellectual Co-operation*. Geneva: Information Section, 1937.

League of Nations, International Committee on Intellectual Cooperation. *List of National Committees on Intellectual Co-Operation*. Geneva: League of Nations, 1926.

– *Minutes of the Seventh Session. Held at Paris from Thursday, January 14th, to Monday, January 18th*. Geneva: League of Nations, 1926.

– *Minutes of the Eighth Session. Held at Geneva from Monday, July 26th, to Thursday July 29th*. Geneva: League of Nations, 1926.

Leontovych-Loshak, Mariia. "Spohady pro roky navchannia v Ukrains'kii studii plastychnoho mystetstva v Prazi." In Petišková, *Ukrajinské výtvarné umění*, 311.

Levkun, Ia.I. "Epistoliarna spadshchyna Ivana Borkovs'koho, ches'koho arkheoloha, ukraintsia za pokhodzhenniam." *Intelihentsiia i vlada* 31 (2014): 300–19.

Los'kyi, Kost'. *Istoriia i systema ryms'koho pryvatnoho prava. Istoriia dzherel ryms'koho prava*, vol. 1. Kyiv and Viden': Z drukarni Val'dhaim-Eberlie, 1921.

Lotots'kyi, Oleksander. *Ukrains'ka knyha*. Praha: Nakladom Ukrains'koho vystavovoho komitetu, 1926.

Lukes, Igor. *Czechoslovakia between Stalin and Hitler: The Diplomacy of Edvard Beneš in the 1930s*. New York: Oxford University Press, 1996.

Lypyns'kyi, Viacheslav. *Arkhiv. Lysty Dmytra Doroshenka do Viacheslava Lypyns'koho*. Edited by Ivan Korovyts'kyi. Vol. 6. Filiadelfiia: Skhidn'o-Evropeis'kyi doslidnyi instytut im. V.K. Lypyns'koho, 1973.

II Międzynarodowy zjazd slawistów (filologów słowiańskich). *Księga referatow. Recueil des communications*. Warsaw, 1934.

Máchal, J. *Taras Ševčenko. Poznejme Ukrajinu*, vol. 8. Kyjiv and Praha: Nákladem ukrajinského vydavatelského družstva "Čas," 1919.

Magidova, Mariia. *Pod znakom katalogov i materialov k ... V.N. Tukalevskii i russkaia kniga za rubezhom 1918–1936 gg*. Praga: Natsional'naia biblioteka Cheshskoi Respubliki – Slavianskaia biblioteka; Sankt-Peterburg: Symposium, 2016.

Magocsi, Paul Robert. *A History of Ukraine: The Land and Its Peoples*. Toronto: University of Toronto Press, 2010.

Mandryka, Mykyta. *Leonid Bilets'kyi*. Vinnipeg: Nakladom tovarystva "Prosvita" v Kenori, Ont., 1957.

Martos, B. *Kooperatyvna reviziia*. L'viv: Vyd-vo s[pil]ky "Dilo," 1928.

Martos, Borys. "Zasnuvannia Ukrains'koi hospodars'koi akademii." *Khronika 2000* 8, nos. 29–30 (1999): 192–210.

Maruniak, Volodymyr. "Vydavnycha diial'nist' ukrains'koi emigratsii v ChSR/Protektorati v 1900–1945 rr." In *Zbirnyk na poshanu prof. d-ra. Volodymyra Ianeva – Symbolae in honorem Volodymyri Janiw*, ed. Oleksa Horbach, 658–75. Miunkhen: Ukrains'kyi vil'nyi universytet, 1983.

Maruniak, Volodymyr, ed. *Ukrains'ka himnaziia v Chekhii 1925–1945. Al'manakh Ukrains'koi himnazii v Prazi-Rzhevnytsiakh-Modrzhanakh*. Miunkhen: Vydannia kol[yshnikh] uchniv URRH-URH, 1975.

Masaryk, Tomáš Garrigue. *Česká otázka: snahy a tužby národního obrození*. Praha: Nákladem "Času," 1895.

[Masaryk, Tomáš Garrigue]. *Dobirni dumky Prof. T. Harrik-Masaryka: Z nahody 75 lit zhyttia 1850–1925*. Edited by M. Halahan, N. Hryhoriiv, M. Shapoval, and Ia. Iarema. Praha: Ukrains'kyi hromads'kyi komitet v Ch.S.R., 1925.

Masaryk, Tomáš Garrigue. *Iak pratsiuvaty?: vyklady z 1898 r*. Translated by Hryhorii Omel'chenko. Praha: Vydavnytstvo Ches'ko-ukrains'ka knyha, 1930.

Matiushenko, Borys. "Ohliad medychnoi pratsi emigratsii za 10 rokiv." In Ukrains'kyi akademichnyi komitet. 2. *Ukrains'kyi naukovyi zizd u Prazi*, 95–7.

Mazurenko, Halia. *Skyt poetiv: zbirka zvychainykh ta siurrealistychnykh poezii*. London: Z drukarni Ukrains'koi vydavnychoi spilky, 1971.

Mel'nychuk, Bohdan. "Dorohoiu zavdovzhky sto dvadtsiat' lit (pro kafedru ukrains'koi literatury Chernivets'koho universytetu)." *Slovo i chas*, nos. 9–10 (1995): 69–75.

Miiakovs'kyi, Volodymyr. *Dmytro Antonovych.* Vinnipeg: Nakladom Ukrains'koi vil'noi akademii nauk, 1967.

Ministerstvo zahraničních věcí. *Československá pomoc ruské a ukrajinské emigraci.* Praha: Ministerstvo zahraničních věcí, 1924.

Mirchuk, Ivan. "Ukrains'kyi vil'nyi universytet." *Naukovyi zbirnyk Ukrains'koho universytetu: iuvileine vydannia* 5 (1948): vii–xiii.

– *Zahal'na estetyka.* Praha: Vydannia Ukrains'koi studii plastychnoho mystetstva, 1926. Reprint, under the title *Estetyka,* Miunkhen: Ukrains'kyi vil'nyi universytet, 2003.

Mirnyi, Ivan. *Ukrains'kyi vysokyi pedagogichnyi instytut im. M. Drahomanova, 1923–1933.* Praha: Vydannia Ukrains'kogo vysokoho pedagogichnoho instytutu, 1934.

Mnich, Ludmiła. "Zabytaia monografiia Marii Omel'chenko, ili Slavisticheskie idei Tomasha Masarika i Ukraina." In *Nosné tradice české slavistiky,* ed. Ivo Pospíšil and Josef Šaur, 39–47. Brno: Masarykova univerzita, 2012.

Mnykh, Roman, and Ievhen Pshenychnyi, eds. *Dmytro Chyzhevs'kyi i svitova slavistyka: zbirnyk naukovykh prats'. Materialy naukovoho seminaru Drohobych, 17–18 travnia 2003 roku.* Drohobych: Kolo, 2003.

Morávková, Alena. "Oksana Liaturyns'ka i Halia Mazurenko – studentky Ukrains'koi studii plastychnoho mystetstva." In Petišková, *Ukrajinské výtvarné umění,* 163–7.

Motornyi, Volodymyr. "Oleksandr Kolessa i ukrains'ko-ches'ki vzaiemyny mizhvoiennoho dvadtsiatylittia." *Problemy slov'ianoznavstva* 52 (2002): 110–17.

Mudrak, Myroslava. "Czech Modernism and the Ukrainian Studio of Plastic Arts: Parallel Strategies." In Petišková, *Ukrajinské výtvarné umění,* 53–63.

Mudrak, Myroslava M. "On the Liminality of Being and Belonging: The Ukrainian Studio of Plastic Arts (1923–1952) – a National Culture on Foreign Territory." *Centropa* 13, no. 3 (2013): 258–68.

– *Ponad kordonamy: Moderna ukrains'ka knyzhkova hrafika 1914–1945 = Beyond Borders: Modern Ukrainian Book Design 1914–1945.* Kyiv: Krytyka, 2008.

– "The Ukrainian Studio of Plastic Arts in Prague and the Art of Jan Kulec." *Art Journal* 49, no. 1 (1990): 36–43. Translated into Ukrainian by Natalia Vysots'ka. "Ukrains'ka studiia plastychnoho mystetstva u prazi ta tvorchist' Ivana Kuletsia." *Khronika 2000* 8, nos. 29–30 (1999): 253–69.

Mursky, Volodimir. *Ukrayna ve istiklâl mücahedeleri.* İstanbul: Cümhuriyet Matbaası, 1930.

Mushynka, Mykola. *Akademik Stanislav Dnistrians'kyi, 1870–1935: biobibliohrafiia.* Kyiv: Akademiia nauk Ukrainy, Arkheohrafichna komisiia / Instytut derzhavy i prava im. V.M. Korets'koho / Naukovo-doslidnyi viddil Kafedry ukrainistyky Filosofs'koho fakul'tetu universytetu im. P.-I. Shafaryka u Priashevi, 1992.

– "Arkhivy ukrains'koi emigratsii z Chekho-Slovachchyny (1917–1945): suchasnyi stan i mistsia zberihannia." In *Na sluzhbi Klio: zbirnyk naukovykh prats' na poshanu Liubomyra Romana Vynara, z nahody 50-littia ioho naukovoi diial'nosty*, ed. Mykhailo Braichevs'kyi, Oleksander Dombrovs'kyi, and Ihor Hyrych, 532–45. Kyiv and New York: Ukrains'ke istorychne tovarystvo u SShA, 2000.

– "Dmytro Antonovych i Muzei vyzvol'noi borot'by Ukrainy v Prazi." In *Dmytro Antonovyč a ukrajinská uměnověda. Vychází ke 130. výročí narození D. Antonovyče*, ed. Dagmar Petišková, 121–36. Praha: Národní knihovna České republiky, Slovanská knihovna, 2009.

– *Muzei vyzvol'noi borot'by Ukrainy ta dolia ioho fondiv*. Mel'burn: Universytet im. Monasha, Viddil slavistyky, 1996.

– "Ukrainistyka Chekho-Slovachchyny mizhvoiennoho periodu (1919–1945)." *Duklia* 39, no. 1 (1991): 67–70; no. 2 (1991): 61–6; nos. 3–4 (1991): 27–36; nos. 5–6 (1991): 28–34.

Mushynka, Mykola, ed. *Lysty Stepana Rudnytskoho do Sofii ta Stanislava Dnistrians'kykh (1926–1932)*. Edmonton: Vydavnytstvo Kanads'koho instytutu ukrains'kykh studii, Al'berts'kyi universytet, 1991.

– *Vid Naukovoho tovarystva im. Shevchenka do Ukrains'koho vil'noho universytetu: mizhnarodna naukova konferentsiia (Priashiv-Svydnyk, 12–15 chervnia 1991 r.): materialy*. Kyiv: Instytut ukrains'koi arkheohrafii AN Ukrainy, 1992.

Mušinka, Mykola [*see* Mushynka, Mykola]. "Muzeum osvobozeneckého boje Ukrajiny v Praze (1925–1948). Dějiny a současné rozmístění jeho fondů." In Petišková, *Muzeum osvobozeneckého boje Ukrajiny*, 25–51.

Mytsiuk, O. *Naukova diial'nist' statystyka F.A. Shcherbyny*. Podiebrady: Vydannia Ukrains'koi Hospodars'koi Akademii v Ch.S.R., 1931.

Ňachajová, Mária, ed. *Ukrajinská svobodná univerzita (1921–1996): vědecký sborník z konference, věnované 75. výročí založení university Praha, 29–30. listopadu 1996*. Praha: Národní knihovna České republiky, Slovanská knihovna / Ukrajinská svobodná univerzita v Mnichově, 1998.

Narizhna, Natalia. *Dytiachymy ochyma: spomyn*. Praha: Vydalo Sdružení Ukrajinek v České republice, 2010.

Narizhnyi, Symon. *15 lit diial'nosty Ukrains'koho istorychno-filologichnoho tovarystva v Prazi (1923–1938)*. Praha: 1940.

– *Ukrains'ka emigratsiia: kul'turna pratsia ukrains'koi emigratsii mizh dvoma svitovymy viinamy*, vol. 1. Praha: Muzei vyzvol'noi borot'by Ukrainy, 1942. Reprint: L'viv, Kent, and Ostroh: Naukove tovarystvo im. Shevchenka / Ukrains'ke istorychne tovarystvo / Natsional'nyi universytet "Ostroz'ka Akademiia", Instytut doslidzhennia ukrains'koi diaspory / Ukrains'ka amerykans'ka asotsiatsiia universytets'kykh profesoriv, 2008.

– *Ukrains'ka emigratsiia: kul'turna pratsia ukrains'koi emigratsii 1919–1939. Materialy, zibrani S. Narizhnym do chastyny druhoi*, vol. 2. Compiled by L.

Iakovlieva, H. Mykhailichenko, and A. Ohins'ka. Kyiv: Vydavnytstvo im. Oleny Telihy, 1999.

Národní knihovna České republiky. *Russkaia, ukrainskaia i belorusskaia emigratsiia v Chekhoslovakii mezhdu dvumia mirovymi voinami: rezul'taty i perspektivy issledovanii: fondy Slavianskoi biblioteki i prazhskikh arkhivov. Praga: 14–15 avgusta 1995 g.* 2 vols. Praha: Národní knihovna České republiky, 1995.

Nečas, Jaromír. *Prosím za jeden slovanský národ. (Našim delegátům na mírovém kongresu).* Brno: Tiskem Rolnické tiskárny. Nákladem vlastním, 1918.

– *Ukrajinská otázka.* Brno: Tiskem Rolnické tiskárny. Nákladem vlastním, 1918.

– *Upřímné slovo o stycích česko-ukrajinských. Poznejme Ukrajinu,* vol. 3. Kyjiv and Praha: Nákladem ukrajinského vydavatelského družstva "Čas," 1919.

Nevrlyi, Mykola. "UVU v ches'komu i ievropeis'komu konteksti." In Ňachajová, *Ukrajinská svobodná univerzita,* 56–63.

Omelčenková, Marie. *Česko-ukrajinské styky.* Praha: Nákladem "Vydavatelství česko-ukrajinská knihovná," 1928.

Omel'chenko, Hryhorii. *Dějiny textu Křest sv. Vladimíra: básně Karla Havlíčka Borovského.* 3 vols. in 1. Praha: Nákladem vlastním, 1933.

– *Edvard Benesh: Edvard Benesh, iak zhurnalist. Edvard Benesh, iak budivnychyi Chekhoslovats'koi derzhavy.* Praha: Vydavnytstvo "Ches'ko-ukrains'ka knyha," 1934.

Omel'chenkova, Mariia [*see* Omelčenková, Marie]. *T.G. Masaryk (1850–1930).* Praha: Vydavnytstvo "Ches'ko-ukrains'ka knyha," 1931.

Opleštilová, Hana. "Collection Development at the Slavonic Library, Prague." In *Libraries in Open Societies: Proceedings of the Fifth International Slavic Librarians' Conference,* ed. Harold M. Leich, 45–53. Binghamton: Haworth Information Press, 2002. Simultaneously published Opleštilová, Hana. "Collection Development at the Slavonic Library, Prague." *Slavic and East European Information Resources* 3, nos. 2–3 (2002): 45–53.

Padokh, Iaroslav. "Predmet istorii ukrains'koho prava v UVU i ioho vykladachi (1921–1981)." In *Zbirnyk na poshanu prof. d-ra. Volodymyra Ianeva = Symbolae in honorem Volodymyri Janiw,* ed. Oleksa Horbach, 1029–49. Miunkhen: Ukrains'kyi vil'nyi universytet, 1983.

Paliienko, Maryna. *Arkhivni tsentry ukrains'koi emihratsii: stvorennia, funktsionuvannia, dolia dokumental'nykh kolektsii.* Kyiv: Vydavnytstvo "Tempora," 2008.

– "Ukrains'ki pam'iatkookhoronni oseredky u mizhvoiennii Chekhoslovachchyni: vid sprob porozuminnia do protystoiannia." *Pam'iatky Ukrainy* 38, no. 4 (2006): 80–95.

Patzke, Una, Mykola Szafowal, and Roman Yaremko, eds. *Universitas Libera Ucrainensis: 1921–2011.* München: Ukrainische Freie Universität, 2011.

Pelens'ka, Oksana. "Praz'ka znakhidka iak znakova podiia v ievropeis'komu mystets'komu prostori." In Petišková, *Ukrajinské výtvarné umění,* 15–27.

– *Ukrains'kyi portret na tli Prahy: ukrains'ke mystets'ke seredovyshche v mizhvoiennii Chekho-Slovachchyni.* N'iu-Iork and Praha: Naukove Tovarystvo im. Shevchenka v Amerytsi / Natsional'na biblioteka Ches'koi Respubliky, Slov'ians'ka biblioteka, 2005.

Petišková, Dagmar, ed. *Dmytro Antonovyč a ukrajinská uměnověda. Vychází ke 130. výročí narození D. Antonovyče.* Praha: Národní knihovna České republiky, Slovanská knihovna, 2009.

– *Muzeum osvobozeneckého boje Ukrajiny. K 80. výročí založení: sborník příspěvků z konference (Praha, 12.–14. října 2005).* Praha: Národní knihovna ČR, Slovanská knihovna, 2006.

– *Ukrajinské výtvarné umění v meziválečném Československu. K 80. výročí založení Ukrajinského studia výtvarných umění v Praze.* Praha: Národní knihovna České republiky, Slovanská knihovna, 2005.

Petráň, Josef. *Nástin dějin Filozofické fakulty Univerzity Karlovy v Praze: do roku 1948.* Praha: Univerzita Karlova, 1983.

Petrohradská akademie věd o ukrajinském jazyku. Poznejme Ukrajinu, vols. 14–15. Kyjiv and Praha: Nákladem ukrajinského vydavatelského družstva "Čas," 1920.

Piskun, Valentyna. "Ievhen Chykalenko v emigratsii: politychnyi i osobystisno-pobutovyi vymir stosunkiv iz ukrains'kym seredovyshchem." In *Ievhen Chykalenko – budytel' ukrains'koi natsii (Do 150-richchia vid dnia narodzhennia),* ed. N.I. Myronets', V.M. Piskun, and I.M. Starovoitenko. Kyiv: Instytut ukrains'koi arkheohrafii ta dzhereloznavstva im. M.S. Hrushevs'koho NANU, 2014.

Plachý, Jiří. "Mezi Haličí, Vídní a Prahou. Prof. MUDr. Ivan Horbaczewski (1854–1942)." *Slovanský přehled* 91, no. 1 (2005): 147–52.

Polons'ka-Vasylenko, N. "Ukrains'kyi vil'nyi universytet (1921–1971)." *Ukrains'kyi istoryk* 8–9, nos. 1–2 (1971–72): 17–27.

Prokopchuk, V.S. "I.I. Ohiienko, S.O. Siropolko, L.U. Bykovs'kyi: liubov do knyhy – kriz' use zhyttia." *Vistnyk Kam'ianets'-Podil's'koho universytetu. Istorychni nauky* 4 (2011): 391–406.

Prosalova, Vira, comp. *Praz'ka literaturna shkola: lirychni ta epichni tvory.* Donets'k: "Skhidnyi vydavnychyi dim," 2008.

Prymak, Thomas M. "Dmytro Doroshenko: A Ukrainian Émigré Historian of the Interwar Period." *Harvard Ukrainian Studies* 25, nos. 1–2 (2001): 31–56.

Pshenychnyi, Ievhen, Roman Mnykh, and Volodymyr Iantsen, eds. *Dmytro Chyzhevs'kyi i ievropeis'ka kul'tura: zbirnyk naukovykh prats'. Materialy naukovoho seminaru Drohobych, 24–25 chervnia 2005 roku.* Drohobych: Kolo, 2011.

Pshenychnyi, Ievhen, and Volodymyr Iantsen. "Lystuvannia Dmytra Chyzhevs'koho z Vasylem Simovychem." In Mnykh and Pshenychnyi, *Dmytro Chyzhevs'kyi i svitova slavistyka,* 251–330.

Purchla, Jacek, and Wolfgang Kos, with the assistance of Żanna Komar, Monika Rydiger, and Werner Michael Schwarz, eds. *The Myth of Galicia*. Translated by Barbara Andrunik et al. Kraków: Międzynarodowe Centrum Kultury; Vienna: Wien Museum, 2014.

Rachůnková, Zdeňka, Františka Sokolová, and Růžena Šišková, eds. *Dmytro Čyževskyj, osobnost a dílo: sborník příspěvků z mezinárodní konference pořádané Slovanskou knihovnou při Národní knihovně ČR, Filozofickým ústavem AV ČR, Slovanským ústavem AV ČR a Ústavem pro českou literaturu AV ČR, 13.–15. června 2002 v Praze*. Praha: Národní knihovna České Republiky, Slovanská knihovna, 2004.

Renoliet, Jean-Jacques. *L'Unesco oubliée: la société des nations et la coopération intellectuelle, 1919–1946*. Paris: Publications de la Sorbonne, 1999.

Rudnyts'kyi, Stepan. *Lystuvannia Stepana Rudnyts'koho*. Compiled by Pavlo Shtoiko. Edited by Oleh Kupchyns'kyi. L'viv: Naukove tovarystvo im. Shevchenka, 2006.

– *Osnovy zemleznannia Ukrainy*. Praha: Vydavnytstvo Ukrains'koho universytetu v Prazi, 1923.

Rusanivs'kyi, V.M., et al., eds. *Slavistychni naukovo-osvitni tsentry v Ukraini: vchora, s'ohodni, zavtra: materialy Vseukrains'koi naukovo-praktychnoi konferentsii (m. Kyiv, 25–26 travnia 1994 r.)*. Kyiv: Natsional'na akademiia nauk Ukrainy, 1995.

Rusova, Sofiia. *Doshkil'ne vykhovannia*. Katerynoslav: Ukrains'ke vydavnytstvo, 1918.

– *Dydaktyka*. Praha: Vydavnyche t-vo "Siiach" pry Ukrains'komu pedahohichnomu instytuti im. M. Drahomanova, 1925.

– *Memuary. Shchodennyk*. Edited by Volodymyr Serhiichuk et al. Kyiv: Polihrafknyha, 2004.

– *Moi spomyny*. L'viv: Vydavnycha kooperatyva "Khortytsia," 1937.

– *Novi metody doshkil'noho vykhovannia*. Praha: "Siiach," 1927.

– *Teoriia i praktyka doshkil'noho vykhovannia*. Praha: Ukrains'kyi hromads'kyi vydavnychyi fond, 1924. Reprint, L'viv: Prosvita, 1993.

– *Teoriia pedagogiky na osnovi psykhol'ogii*. Praha: Vydavnyche t-vo "Siiach" pry Ukrains'komu pedagogichnomu instytuti im. M. Drahomanova, 1924.

– *Vybrani pedahohichni tvory*. Edited by O.V. Proskura. Kyiv: Osvita, 1996.

Ryle, Gilbert, ed. *Proceedings of the Seventh International Congress of Philosophy, Held at Oxford, England, September 1–6, 1930*. London: Humphrey Milford, 1931.

Rypka, Jan, Otakar Klíma, Věra Kubíčková, Jiří Cejpek, and Ivan Hrbek. *Dějiny perské a tádžické literatury*. Praha: Nakladatelství Československé akademie věd, 1956. Translation into German, Leipzig: Otto Harrassowitz, 1959; into English, Dordrecht: D. Reidel, 1968; into Polish (abridged), Warszawa: Państwowe Wydawnictwo Naukowe, 1970; into Russian, Moskva: Izdatel'stvo "Progress"; into Persian, [Tehran]: Markaz-i Mutala`at va Tahqiqat-i Farhangi-i Bayn al-Milali, 1993.

Sayer, Derek. *The Coasts of Bohemia: A Czech History*. Translated by Alena Sayer. Princeton: Princeton University Press, 1998.

Sborník I. sjezdu slovanských geografů a ethnografů v Praze 1924. Praha: Geografický ústav Karlovy university, 1926.

Shapoval, Andrii. *Dmytro Antonovych: zhyttia ta diial'nist'*. Myronivka: "Myronivs'ka drukarnia," 2012.

Shapoval, Mykyta. *Shchodennyk*. Edited by Sava Zerkal'. 2 vols. Novyi Iork: Ukrains'ka hromada im. M. Shapovala, 1958.

Shcherbakivs'kyi, Vadym. "Memuary." *Pam'iatky Ukrainy* 39, no. 4 (2007): 22–292.

Shcherbakivs'kyi, V. "Pratsia v haluzi arkheologii," in Ukrains'kyi akademichnyi komitet. 2. *Ukrains'kyi naukovyi zizd u Prazi*, 52–3.

Shcherbyna, Fedir ["Oleksander Kolessa"]. In *Ukrains'kyi universytet u Prazi v rokakh 1921–1926*, 177–81.

Sherekh, Iurii. *Ia – mene – meni. . . (i dovkruhy): spohady*. 2 vols. Kharkiv: "Folio," 2012.

Shevchenko, Taras. *Kobzar*. Edited by Leonid Bilets'kyi. 2nd ed., 4 vols. Vinnipeg: Vydavnycha Spilka "Tryzub," 1952–54.

Shmahalo, Rostyslav. "Ukrains'ka studia plastychnykh mystetstv u Prazi i mystets'ko-osvitnii rukh ukrains'koi emihratsii." In Petišková, *Ukrajinské výtvarné umění*, 125–53.

Shovheniv, Ivan. *Analitychna heometriia na ploshchi*. Podiebrady: Vydannia "Vydavnychoho tovarystva pry Ukrains'kii hospodars'kii akademii," 1923.

– *Hidravlika pidzemnykh vod: pidruchnyk dlia hidrotekhnikiv i meliorateriv*. Praha: Ukrains'kyi hromads'kyi vydavnychyi fond, 1929.

– *Hydravlyka. Ch. 1. Hydrostatyka*. Podiebrady: Vydannia "Vydavnychoho tovarystva pry Ukrains'kii hospodars'kii Akademii," 1923.

Shramchenko, L. "Ukrains'ke, bilorus'ke ta hruzyns'ke studentstvo na vysokych shkolach v Chekhoslovats'kii Respublitsi: statystychnyi narys." *Zapysky Ukrains'koi hospodars'koi akademii v Chekhoslovats'kii Respublitsi* 1 (1927): 248–80.

Shtoiko, Pavlo. *Stepan Rudnyts'kyi, 1877–1937: zhyttiepysno-bibliohrafichnyi narys*. L'viv: Naukove tovarystvo im. Shevchenka, 1997.

Sichyns'kyi, Volodymyr. *Arkhitektura starokniazivs'koi doby. (X [i.e. desiate]–XIII [i.e. trynadtsiate] st.)*. Praha: Ukrains'kyi hromads'kyi vydavnychyi fond, 1926.

– *Istoriia ukrains'koho graverstva: XVI–XVIII stolittia*. L'viv: Nakladom redaktsii "Zapysok ChSVV," 1937.

– *Katal'og vystavky znakiv ukrains'kykh vydavnytstv: vystavka knyzhnoi kul'tury pry Mizhnarodnomu z'izdi bibliotekariv i pryiateliv knyhy v Prazi, r. 1926*. Praha: "Siiach," 1926.

– *Konspekt istorii vsesvitn'oho* mystetstva. Praha: Vydavnytstvo "Siiach," 1925. Second edition in 1928.

– *Styli*. Praha: Vydavnytstvo "Siiach," [1926].

Šimeček, Zdeněk. "Ruští a ukrajinští slavisté v meziválečném Československu." *Slovanský přehled* 79, no. 1 (1993): 25–37.

Simiantsev, Valentyn [*see* Simiantsiv, Valentyn]. *Inzhener emihrant v Chekho-Slovachchyni: roky 1929–1945 = [An] Emigrant Engineer in Czechoslovakia 1929–1945*. Buenos-Aires: Vydavnytstvo Iuliiana Serediaka, 1978.

Simiantsiv, Valentyn. *Students'ki chasy (spohad): Chekho-Slovachchyna, roky 1923–1929*. Vashington: Svoboda Press, 1973.

Simovych, Vasyl'. *Praktychna hramatyka ukrains'koi movy*. Rashtat: Ukrains'kyi rukh, 1918. *Hramatyka ukrains'koi movy: dlia samonavchannia ta v dopomohu shkil'nii nautsi*. Kyiv and Liaiptsig: Ukrains'ka nakladnia, 1919.

– *Pratsi v dvokh tomakh*. Edited by Liudmyla Tkach and Oksana Ivasiuk, with the assistance of Rostyslav Pylypchuk and Iaroslava Pohrebennyk. 2 vols. Chernivtsi: Knyhy-XXI, 2005.

Siropolko, Stepan. *Istoriia osvity na Ukraini*. L'viv: Nakladom tovarystva "Vzaimna Pomich Ukrains'koho Vchytel'stva," 1937. Reprint, Kyiv: Naukova dumka, 2001.

– "L.J. Živný v ukrajinské knihovědné literatuře: bibliografická poznámka." *Časopis československých knihovníků* 12 (1933): 122–4.

– "Pratsia v haluzi pedagogiky." In Ukrains'kyi akademichnyi komitet. 2. *Ukrains'kyi naukovyi zizd u Prazi*, 62–4.

– "Ukrains'ka bibliografiia na emigratsii za ostanni desiat' rokiv." In Ukrains'kyi akademichnyi komitet. 2. *Ukrains'kyi naukovyi zizd u Prazi*, 93–5.

Sládek, Zdeněk, and Ljubov Běloševská, comps. *Dokumenty k dějinám ruské a ukrajinské emigrace v Československé republice (1918–1939)*. Praha: Slovanský ústav AV ČR, Euroslavica, 1998.

Smal-Stoćkyj, Š. [*see* Smal'-Stots'kyi, Stepan]. *Vyhlídky pravé vzájemnosti Československa a Ukrajiny*. *Poznejme Ukrajinu*, vols. 12–13. Kyjiv and Praha: Nákladem ukrajinského vydavatelského družstva "Čas," 1919.

Smal-Stoćkyj, Štěpán. [*see* Smal'-Stots'kyi, Stepan]. *Lvov, srdce západní Ukrajiny*. *Poznejme Ukrajinu*, vol. 2. Kyjiv and Praha: Nákladem ukrajinského vydavatelského družstva "Čas," 1919.

Smal'-Stots'kyi, Stepan. "Pratsi lingvistychnoi sektsii pershoho zizdu u slovians'kykh filolohiv u Prazi." *Ukraina: naukovyi zhurnal ukrainoznavstva* 39 (1930): 166–73.

– *Rozvytok pohliadiv pro semiu slovians'kykh mov i ikh vzaimne sporidnennia*. 2nd ed. Praha: Ukrains'kyi hromads'kyi vydavnychyi fond, 1927. First edition published in 1925 by the Shevchenko Scientific Society.

Smal'-Stots'kyi, Stepan, and Theodor Fedir Gartner. *Rus'ka hramatyka*. Reprint under the title *Ukrains'ka hramatyka*. Winnipeg: Rus'ka knyharnia, 1919.

Soiuz ukrains'kykh zhurnalistiv ta pys'mennykiv. *Statut Soiuza ukrains'kykh zhurnalistiv ta pys'mennykiv, ukhvalenyi na zahal'nykh zborakh dnia 10. i 12. veresnia 1919 u Vidni*. Kyiv and Viden': Soiuz ukrains'kykh zhurnalistiv ta pys'mennykiv, 1919.

Sokovych, Ie.O. *Melioratsiia*. Vol. 1. Podiebrady: Vydannia "Vydavnychoho T-va pry Ukr[ains'kii] hosp[odars'kii] akademii v Ch.S.R., 1925.

Sokovych, Ievhen. *Narysna heometriia*. Podiebrady: Vydannia "Vydavnychoho tovarystva pry Ukrains'kii hospodars'kii akademii," 1923.

Stebelsky, Ihor. *Placing Ukraine on the Map: Stepan Rudnytsky's Nation-Building Geography*. Kingston: Kashtan Press, 2014.

Steško, Fedir. *Čeští hudebníci v ukrajinské církevní hudbě: (z dějin haličsko-ukrajinské církevní hudby)*. Praha: Česká akademie věd a umění, 1935.

Štípek, Stanislav, ed. *Jan Horbaczewski (15.5.1854–24.5.1942): sborník přednášek na semináři ke 150. výročí narození zakladatele české lékařské chemie*. Praha: Nakladatelství Galén, 2005.

Stloukal, Karel, ed. *Tvůrcové dějin. Čtyři tisíciletí světových dějin v obrazech dob a osobností*. 5 vols. Praha: L. Mazáč, 1934–37. Translation from German with additions. *Menschen die Geschichte machten: viertausend Jahre Weltgeschichte in Zeit- und Lebensbildern*. Edited by Peter Richard Rohden. 2 vols. Wien: Seidel & Sohn, 1933.

Strnadel, Josef, ed. *Padesát let Slovanské knihovny v Praze*. Praha: Státní knihovna ČSR, Slovanská knihovna, 1976.

– *Ukrajinská literatura ve Slovanské knihovně*. Praha: Státní knihovna ČSSR, Slovanská knihovna, 1964.

Studyns'kyi, Kyrylo. "Pavlo Iosyp Shafaryk i ukraintsi. Do istorii ukrains'ko-ches'kykh zv'iazkiv." *Nasha kultura*, no. 7 (1935): 401–12.

Subtelny, Orest. *Ukraine: A History*. Toronto: University of Toronto Press, 2009.

Sydorčuk, Taisa. [*see* Sydorchuk, Taisiia M.] "Kulturelles Leben der Ukrainischen Emigration in Osterreich zwischen de Weltkriege." *Studien zu Deutsch-Ukrainischen Beziehungen* 2 (1996): 61–92.

Sydorchuk, Taisiia M. "Soiuz ukrains'kykh zhurnalistiv i pys'mennykiv. Videns'kyi period 1919–1923." *Ukrains'kyi arkheohrafichnyi shchorichnyk* 8–9 (2001): 134–51.

Sydorchuk-Potul'nyts'ka Taisiia. [*see* Sydorchuk, Taisiia M.] "Videns'kyi ta praz'kyi periody UVU: umovy i spetsyfika naukovo-pedahohichnoi diial'nosti." In Ňachajová, *Ukrajinská svobodná univerzita*, 6–17.

S-yi [*see* Smal'-Stots'kyi, Stepan]. "Pershyi zizd slavians'kykh fil'ol'ogiv u Prazi." *Novi shliakhy* 4 (1929): 174–80.

Šyjaniv, H. *Ukrajinská hospodářská akademie v Č.S.R.: soukromý ústav s vysokoškolskou organisací: 1922–1926*. Translated by O. Kozlovskyj. Lázně Poděbrady, 1926.

Szafowal, Mykola, and Roman Yaremko, eds. *Universitas Libera Ucrainensis: 1921–2006*. München: Ukrainische Freie Universität, 2006.

Szporluk, Roman. *The Political Thought of Thomas G. Masaryk*. Boulder: East European Monographs; New York: Distributed by Columbia University Press, 1981.

Tejchmanová, Světlana. "Dokumenty o ukrajinské emigraci v meziválečném Československu." *Slovanský přehled* 78, no. 2 (1992): 184–95.

Toman, Jindřich. *The Magic of a Common Language: Jakobson, Mathesius, Trubetzkoy, and the Prague Linguistic Circle*. Cambridge, MA: MIT Press, 1995.

Topinka, Ievhen, comp. *Tomash Masaryk i ukraintsi: arkhivni dokumenty = Tomáš Masaryk a Ukrajinci: (archiválie)*. L'viv: Vydavnytstvo "Tsentr Ievropy," 2010.

Topinka, Ievhen, Iosef Shebesta, Itka Baiharova, and Mar'iana Sen'kiv, eds. *Zbirnyk statei ta dokumentiv do istorii ches'ko-halyts'kykh stosunkiv. Do 140-richchia utvorennia tovarystva "Cheska beseda" u L'vovi (1867–2007)*. L'viv: Vydavnytstvo "Tsentr Ievropy," 2007.

Tovarystvo prykhyl'nykiv Ukrains'koi hospodars'koi akademii. *Ukrains'ka hospodars'ka akademiia*. Praha-Podiebrady: Nakladom Ukrains'koi hospodars'koi akademii, 1931. Reprint, *Ukrain'ska hospodars'ka akademiia*, Praha-Podiebrady: U.H.A., 1932.

Trembits'kyi, Anatolii. "Rodyna Sitsins'kykh-Sichyns'kykh ta Ukrains'ke istorychno-filolohichne tovarystvo v Prazi (1923–1945 pp.)." *Naukovi zapysky. Istorychni nauky* 11 (2008): 301–26.

Troshchyns'kyi, Volodymyr. "Mizhvoienna politychna emihratsiia: rezul'taty i aktual'ni napriamy vyvchennia problemy." *Ukrains'ka diaspora* 6, no. 10 (1997): 132–6.

– *Mizhvoienna ukrains'ka emihratsiia v Evropi, iak istorychne i sotsial'no-politychne iavyshche*. Kyiv: Intel, 1994.

– "Persha konferentsiia ukrains'koi emihratsii v Prazi i stvorennia Ukrains'koi Holovnoi Emihratsiinoi Rady (cherven' 1929 roku)." *Ukrains'ka diaspora* 1, no. 1 (1992): 77–85.

– "Vytoky ta istorychna dolia mizhvoiennoi ukrains'koi politychnoi emihratsii v Ievropi." *Ukrains'ka diaspora* 3, no. 5 (1994): 7–44; 3, no. 6 (1994): 5–31.

Tschižewskij, Dmitrij [*see* Chyzhevs'kyi, Dmytro]. *Vergleichende Geschichte der slavischen Literaturen*. Berlin: De Gruyter, 1968. Translated by Richard Noel Porter and Martin P. Rice. Edited and with a foreword by Serge A. Zenkovsky. Nashville: Vanderbilt University Press, 1971.

Tyshchenko, Iurii. *Z moikh zustrichei: spohady*. Kyiv: Doslidnyts'kyi tsentr istorii ukrains'koi presy, 1997.

Ukrains'ka hospodars'ka akademiia. *Statut Ukrains'koi hospodars'koi akademii v Ch S.R. zatverdzhenyi postanovoiu profesors'koi Rady akademii 23-ho travnia 1925 roku*. [Podiebrady: Ukraiins'ka hospodars'ka akademiia], 1925.

Ukrains'ka hospodars'ka akademiia. Ukrains'kyi tekhnichno-hospodarsikyi instytut pozaochnoho navchannia. *Ukrains'kyi tekhnichno-hospodars'kyi instytut pozaochnoho navchannia pry Ukrains'kii hospodars'kii akademii.* Podiebrady: Nakladom T-va prykhylnykiv UHA, 1934.

Ukrajinská hospodářská akademie. *Ukrains'ka hospodars'ka akademiia v Chekhoslovats'kii Respublitsi.* Lázně Poděbrady: Ukrajinská hospodářská akademie, 1928.

Ukrains'ka Hospodars'ka Akademiia v Ch.S.R. 1922–1935. Niu Iork: Vydano absol'ventamy Ukrains'koi hospodars'koi akademii ta Ukrains'koho tekhnichno-hospodars'koho instytutu, 1959.

Ukrains'ke pedagogichne tovarystvo v Prazi. *Ukrains'ke shkil'nytstvo na Bukovyni, v Halychyni, na Zakarpatti ta v Kanadi.* Praha: Ukrains'ke pedagogichne tovarystvo v Prazi, 1932.

Ukrains'ke pravnyche tovarystvo v Ch.S.R. *Ukrains'ke pravnyche tovarystvo v Ch.S.R. (17. bereznia 1923 – 17. bereznia 1928).* Praha: Vydannia "Ukrains'koho pravnychoho tovarystva v Ch.S.R.," 1928.

Ukrains'ke tovarystvo prykhyl'nykiv knyhy. *Zvit Ukrains'koho tovarystva prykhyl'nykiv knyhy v Prazi.* [Praha: Ukrains'ke tovarystvo prykhyl'nykiv knyhy], 1934.

Ukrains'kyi akademichnyi komitet. 2. *Ukrains'kyi naukovyi zizd u Prazi.* Praha: Ukrains'kyi akademichnyi komitet dlia mizhnarodn'oi inteliektual'noi spivpratsi pry Lizi Natsii, 1934.

– *Ukrains'kyi naukovyi zizd u Prazi 3–7 zhovtnia 1926 r. Zvidomlennia Prezidii organizatsiinoi komisii zizdu.* Praha: Ukrains'kyi akademichnyi komitet, 1928.

Ukrains'kyi hromads'kyi komitet. *Rik pratsi Ukrains'koho hromads'koho komitetu v ChSR.* Praha: [Ukrains'kyi hromads'kyi komitet], 1922.

– *Try roky pratsi Ukrain'skoho hromads'koho komitetu v Ch.S.R.* Praha: [Ukrains'kyi hromads'kyi komitet], 1924.

– *Ukrains'ka hospodars'ka akademiia v Ch.S.R.* Praha: Ukrains'kyi hromads'kyi komitet v *Ch.S.R.*, 1923.

Ukrains'kyi vil'nyi universytet. *Naukovyi iuvyleinyi zbirnyk Ukrains'koho universytetu v Prazi prysviachenyi Panovi Prezidentovi Ches'koslovens'koi Respubliky Prof. Dr. T.G. Masarykovi.* 2 vols. Praha: Ukrains'kyi vil'nyi universytet, 1925–30.

– *Ukrains'kyi v[il'nyi] universytet v Prazi v rokakh 1921–1926.* Praha: Derzhavna drukarnia, 1927.

– *Ukrains'kyi v[il'nyi] universytet v Prazi v rokakh 1926–1931.* Praha: Derzhavna drukarnia, 1931.

– *Ukrains'kyi vil'nyi universytet v Prazi v rokakh 1931–1941.* Praha: Nakladom Ukrains'koho vil'noho universytetu, 1942.

Universitas ucrainensis Pragensis. *1898–1923. Iuvileinyi zbirnyk v chest' profesora doktora Stanyslava Dnistrians'koho, pidnesenyi iuviliarovi z pryvodu

Ioho 25-litn'oho Iuvileiu naukovoi dial'nosty profesoramy fakul'teta prava i suspil'nykh nauk Ukrains'koho vil'noho universytetu v Prazi. Praha: Derzhavna drukarnia, 1923.

Ústav dějin Univerzity Karlovy a Archiv Univerzity Karlovy. "Matrika doktorů Univerzity Karlovy VII. (1928–1931)." https://is.cuni.cz/webapps/archiv/public/book/bo/1836656452491438/208/?lang=cs

Vacek, Jiří. "Interakce ruské a ukrajinské emigrace s českou a slovenskou vědou a kulturou v letech 1919–1945." In *Ruská a ukrajinská emigrace v ČSR v letech 1918–1945*, ed. Václav Veber et al. Vol. 2, 1–40.

– *Slovanská knihovna – můj osud: mozaika vzpomínek*. Praha: Národní knihovna České republiky, Slovanská knihovna, 2016.

– "Vztahy pedagogů Ukrajinské svobodné university v Praze k české a slovenské vědecké a kulturní sféře." In Ňachajová, *Ukrajinská svobodná univerzita*, 119–26.

Valiavko, Iryna, Oleksandr Chudnov, and Volodymyr Iantsen, comps. *Dmytro Ivanovych Chyzhevs'kyi i ioho suchasnyky. Lysty, spohady*. Kirovohrad: Imeks-LTD, 2013.

Varvartsev, M.M., S.V. Vidnians'kyi, I.V. Ievseienko, N.V. Kryvets', and V.V. Pavlenko, eds. *Z istorii mizhnarodnykh zv'iazkiv Ukrainy: nauka, osvita (XIX – 30-ti roky XX st. Dokumenty i materialy)*. Kyiv: Natsional'na akademiia nauk Ukrainy, Instytut istorii Ukrainy, 1999.

Vatsek, Iirzhi [*see* Vacek, Jiří]. "Biblioteki, knigovedcheskaia i bibliograficheskaia deiatel'nost' russkoi i ukrainskoi emigratsii v mezhvoennoi Chekhoslovakii." In Babka and Zolotarev, *Russkaia aktsiia pomoshchi v Chekhoslovakii: istoriia, znachenie, nasledie*, 207–16.

Veber, Václav, et al., eds. *Ruská a ukrajinská emigrace v ČSR v letech 1918–1945*. 4 vols. Praha: Seminář pro dějiny východní Evropy při Ústavu světových dějin FF UK, 1993–96.

Vidňanskyj, Stepan [*see* Vidnians'kyi, Stepan]. "Ukrajinská emigrácia v medzivojnovom Česko-Slovensku." *Historický časopis* 40, no. 3 (1992): 370–85.

Vidnians'kyi, Stepan. *Kul'turno-osvitnia pratsia i naukova diial'nist ukrains'koi emihratsii v Checho-Slovachchyni: Ukrains'kyi vil'nyi universytet (1921–1945)*. Kyiv: Natsional'na akademiia nauk Ukrainy, Instytut istorii Ukrainy, 1994.

– "Polityka chekhoslovats'koho uriadu shchodo ukrains'koi emihratsii v mizhvoiennyi period." *Mizhnarodni zv'iazky Ukrainy: naukovi poshuky i znakhidky* 3 (1993): 36–56.

– "Studenty i vypusknyky UVU v Prazi na sluzhbi ridnoho narodu." In Ňachajová, Ukrajinská svobodná univerzita, 105–12.

– "Ukraina ta "ukrains'ke pytannia" v polityts Chekhoslovachchyny." In *Ukrains'ka derzhavnist' u XX stolitti: istoryko-politolohichnyi analiz*, Oleksandr Derhachov et al., eds., 177–96. Kyiv: Politychna dumka, 1996.

– "Ukrains'ka emihratsiia v mizhvoiennii Chekhoslovachchyni ta znachennia ii diial'nosti dlia aktualizatsii "ukrains'koho pytannia" v Ievropi." *Mizhnarodni zv'iazky Ukrainy: naukovi poshuky i znakhidky* 17 (2008): 94–116.

– "Ukrains'ke pytannia v pohliadakh T.G. Masaryka ta politytsi pershoi Chekhoslovats'koi respubliky." In Vidnians'kyi, *T.G. Masaryk i nova Ievropa*, 20–33.

– "Ukrains'ke pytannia v zovnishn'opolitychnykh kontseptsiiakh Chekhoslovachchyny (1918–1989)." *Ukrains'kyi istorychnyi zhurnal*, no. 1 (1997): 43–61.

Vidnians'kyi, S[tepan].V. "Ukrains'kyi vil'nyi universytet u Prazi – mizhslov'ians'kyi oseredok naukovo-osvitnikh vzaiemyn." In Rusanivs'kyi, *Slavistychni naukovo-osvitni tsentry*, 94–8.

Vidnians'kyi, Stepan, ed. *T.G. Masaryk i nova Ievropa. Materialy Pershoi ukrains'ko-ches'koi naukovo-teoretychnoi konferentsii "Masarykivs'ki chytannia" (m. Kyiv, 7–8 kvitnia 1998 r.)*. Kyiv: Mizhnarosnyi naukovo-tekhnichnyi universytet / Posol'stvo Ches'koi Respubliky v Ukraini / Doslidnyts'ko-informatsiinyi tsentr "Mizhslov'ians'ka initsiatyva", 1998.

Vidnians'kyi, V., and S. Vidnians'kyi. "Ukraintsi v mizhvoiennii Chekhoslovachchyni: z dosvidu intehratsii kul'turnoho zhyttia slov'ians'kykh narodiv." *Mizhnarodni zv'iazky Ukrainy: naukovi poshuky i znakhidky* 7 (1998): 200–3.

Vidnians'kyi, S.V., and A.Iu. Martynov. *Ob'iednana Ievropa: vid mrii do real'nosti: Istorychni narysy pro bat'kiv-zasnovnykiv Ievropeis'koho Soiuzu*. Kyiv: Natsional'na akademiia nauk Ukrainy, Instytut istorii Ukrainy, 2009.

"Vpershe drukom: dokumenty Masaryka. (Z materialiv, peredanykh Prezydentom Ches'koi Respubliky Vatslavom Havelom pid chas vizytu v Kyiv dlia publikatsii na Ukraini)." *Khronika 2000* 8, nos. 29–30 (1999): 17–25.

Vynar, Liubomyr. "Dmytro Ivanovych Doroshenko: zhyttia i diial'nist' (u 50-littia smerty)." *Ukrains'kyi istoryk* 38, nos. 1–4 (2001): 9–67.

– "Dva lysty Mykhaila Hrushevs'koho do Dmytra Doroshenka z 1923 roku." *Ukrains'kyi istoryk* 43–4, nos. 4–1–2 (2006–7): 108–12.

– "Naukova diial'nist' d-ra Oleha Kandyby," *Ukrains'kyi istoryk* 22, nos. 1–4 (1985): 49–71.

Weingart, Miloš, Josef Dobiáš, and Milada Paulová, eds. *Z dějin východní Evropy a Slovanstva. Sborník věnovaný Jaroslavu Bidlovi profesoru Karlovy university k šedesátým narozeninám*. Praha: A. Bečková, 1928.

Wynar, Lubomyr R. [*see* Vynar, Liubomyr]. *Dmytro Doroshenko, 1882–1951*. Miunkhen, N'iu-Iork and Toronto: Ukrains'ke istorychne tovarystvo, 1983.

– "Ukrainian Scholarship in Postwar Germany, 1945–52." In *The Refugee Experience: Ukrainian Displaced Persons after World War II*, ed. Wsevolod W. Isajiw, Yury Boshyk, and Roman Senkus, 311–37. Edmonton: Canadian Institute of Ukrainian Studies, University of Alberta, 1992.

Zaitseva, Zinaida. *Ukrains'kyi naukovyi rukh: instytutsional'ni aspekty rozvytku (kinets' XIX – pochatok XX st.): monohrafiia*. Kyiv: Kyivs'kyi natsional'nyi ekonomichnyi universytet, 2006.

Zhuk, Andrii. "Avtobiohrafiia Dmytra Antonovycha." *Suchasnist'*, no. 1 (1961): 103–14.

Zhyvotko, Arkadii. *Desiat' rokiv Ukrains'koho istorychnoho kabinetu (1930–1940)*. Edited by Iaroslav Prokesh. Praha: Ministerstvo Vnutr[ishnikh] Sprav, 1940.

– *Istoriia ukrains'koi presy*. Regensburg: Ukrains'kyi tekhnichno-hospodars'kyi instytut, 1946. Reprint, Miunkhen: Ukrains'kyi tekhnichno-hospodars'kyi instytut, 1989–90. Reprint, Kyiv: Naukovo-vydavnychyi tsentr "Nasha kul'tura i nauka," 1999.

Zilynskyj, Bohdan. *Ukrajinci v Čechách a na Moravě: (1894) 1917–1945 (1994)*. Praha: Nakladatelství X-Egem, 1995.

Zlenko, Petro. "Biblioteka Ukrains'koho pedahohichnoho instytutu im. M. Drahomanova v Prazi." *Knyholiub*, nos. 3–4 (1928): 44–56.

Index

www.ingramcontent.com/pod-product-compliance
Lightning Source LLC
LaVergne TN
LVHW090154080826
844660LV00013B/809/J